AF262769

OBSTINATE DAUGHTERS

ALSO BY DENISE KIERNAN

We Gather Together
Giving Thanks
The Last Castle
The Girls of Atomic City
Signing Their Lives Away
Signing Their Rights Away
Stuff Every American Should Know

OBSTINATE DAUGHTERS

The Rebels, Writers, and Renegade Women

Who Ignited the American Revolution

DENISE KIERNAN

DUTTON

DUTTON

An imprint of Penguin Random House LLC
1745 Broadway, New York, NY 10019
penguinrandomhouse.com

Book design by Nancy Resnick

LIBRARY OF CONGRESS CATALOGING-IN-PUBLICATION DATA

has been applied for.

ISBN 9780593183434 (hardcover)
ISBN 9780593183458 (ebook)

Printed in the United States of America
1st Printing

The authorized representative in the EU for product safety and compliance is
Penguin Random House Ireland, Morrison Chambers, 32 Nassau Street,
Dublin D02 YH68, Ireland, https://eu-contact.penguin.ie.

For Joe

CONTENTS

OBSTINATE DAUGHTERS

Set in Stone

Pinpointing the exact moment I fell in love with history would prove challenging, but I know with certainty that it had something to do with a fire hydrant. And ancient Egypt.

I was standing in a crowd, peeking around flags and through grown-up legs and arms, contorting my small self as I tried to get a better look at things. This was Lexington, Missouri, population somewhere around 4,000. The year was 1976, and the country, not of my birth but the one I had always called home, was celebrating its two hundredth birthday.

Parades, fireworks, reenactments, and the like dominated that summer, with bunting and banners in every direction, red, white, and blue adorning every surface (fire hydrants included). I looked around the costumed crowds, seeking clues about what life might have been like two hundred years earlier. What people ate and wore, what musical instruments they played, which tunes they danced to—it all fascinated me. There were certainly girls and women in these patriotic pageants, and looking more closely at them I detected a backdrop of and devotion to duty. They were sewing flags, cooking, performing the tedious but vitally necessary act of laundering clothes. Girls around my age, when present, assisted grown women in these chores. I stood in a sea of Holly Hobbie–esque skirts and umpteen yards of gingham. To my young eyes, every woman and girl looked like an extra on *Little House on the Prairie*. At least some of the boys got to play fifes and drums. In colonial times, my elementary school mind thought, there must have been more for girls to do. There had to be more. But I didn't see more.

At that age, my own incarnation of youthful obstinacy was barely perceptible. This unspeakable and to most eyes nigh unnoticeable rebellion was perhaps best represented by my Brownie uniform.

It was picture day at Immaculate Conception School, and I was expected to wear a dress and put my lengthy black hair up in a bow. The last time I had attired myself in such fashion, I had served as a page at the Wentworth Military Academy ball, curtsying alongside one of the young ladies of the "court." I was not a big fan of skirts and dresses. I was a fan of trees and mud and sports. But I also wasn't one to disobey very often.

However, as photo day approached, I dug in and protested. My mother and I eventually reached a compromise: I could have my photo taken in my Brownie uniform. It was a jumper, yes, and did not feature pants, but to me it represented a step in my evolution away from that which was tacitly (or not) expected of me.

In the years that followed, finding girls and women from the past to inspire me, those who had done unexpected and wondrous things, would continue to prove difficult. Often, when I did uncover an inspirational woman in history, she was presented as an ornamental aside to the more lauded and heroic acts of men, as though female contributions were secondary and mere mentions of them were a gift for which all women should be grateful.

As I later discovered as a journalist and as an author, while many women and their contributions are not included, or merely glossed over, in the annals of history, others have been flat-out erased. I made it my mission to dig up as many of their stories as I could.

And so, many years later, as I meandered through mazes of sunbaked stone in Luxor, Egypt, the story of Hatshepsut rightly enthralled me.

Hatshepsut was never meant to be a ruler. The daughter of Thutmose I, she became queen of Egypt at around the age of twelve when she married her half brother Thutmose II, who died young. Normally the pharaonic line passed from father to son—no matter who happened to be the mother. Thutmose III, Hatshepsut's young stepson (and nephew), was destined to take up his father's crook. Hatshepsut was to serve as regent until Thutmose III was old enough to rule.

Ascend to the throne of Egypt she did. Several years into her role as regent, Hatshepsut ordered that she herself be crowned pharaoh—the sixth pharaoh of the Eighteenth Dynasty—and presided over a remarkable, prosperous reign that spanned about twenty-one years (1479–1458 BCE). Perhaps she proclaimed herself pharaoh in order to better protect her stepson's eventual kingdom. Perhaps she did it because she thought it would be best for Egypt. Perhaps she did it for the simple reason that it was what she wanted.

She carried herself as a man and chose to be portrayed as such, desiring to be seen in trousers and the de rigueur pharaonic fake beard long worn by those rulers who had preceded her. Art of the time depicted her with a buff, muscular, bare-chested, male physique, sporting the ceremonial trappings of previous Egyptian pharaohs. She took a new name for herself as well: Maatkare, which is interpreted as "Maat [the goddess of truth] is the life force of Re [the sun god]."

She flourished as a leader. Her reign saw trade expansion, the construction of remarkable temples and obelisks, and a fair amount of prosperity and peace. Her stepson, Thutmose III, became a fine commander of the army and succeeded Hatshepsut upon her death, at about fifty years of age, in 1458 BCE. The cause of her death remains a mystery, with theories ranging from the tantalizing to the trite, from a vengeful murder at the hands of Thutmose III to a fatal abscess after the removal of a tooth.

No matter the reason for her death, some twenty years after her passing, the evidence of her life and her reign was systematically erased, as though the line from Thutmose II passed directly to Thutmose III—and not through Hatshepsut. In the thousands of years that followed, various scholars speculated that Thutmose III's resentment led him to excise Hatshepsut from the Egyptian ruling record. Historians still debate this.

Near the tomb Hatshepsut built for herself and her father, archaeologists found a pit teeming with destroyed, defaced, almost unrecognizable statues of her. Images of Thutmose III replaced some of those of his stepmother. Much of the evidence of her time atop the throne—the statuaries, cartouches, and artistic representations that formed the historical record of her reign—was reduced to rubble, a desecration of memory as well as stone. To the ancient Egyptians, to erase the memory of someone's time on earth meant endangering their afterlife; their eternal journey after death could no longer be possible.

The mortuary temple Hatshepsut built remained, however, as did many other temples and projects of her reign. Only the architectural achievements of Ramses II—Ramses the Great—whose rule commenced roughly two hundred years after Hatshepsut became pharaoh, rivaled Hatshepsut's.

Her face had been chiseled away, but not her memory.

On a recent visit to the site, I navigated a shaded gauntlet of vendors selling Mohamed Salah soccer jerseys, miniature Nefertiti heads, countless ankhs, and pyramid paperweights to emerge into the Saharan sun. I climbed the stairs of the memorial complex, which sits at the base of limestone cliffs. As I studied what remained, I learned that Hatshepsut herself pondered the tenuous nature of her legacy. Across the Nile, in the Temple of Karnak, an inscription on two obelisks erected toward the end of Hatshepsut's tenure as pharaoh reads: "Now my heart turns this way and that, as I think what the people will say—those who shall see my monuments in years to come, and who shall speak of what I have done."

What is legacy? What brings someone's memory back into the collective consciousness and, more importantly, to what end and for whose purpose?

To remember is first to acknowledge and to value. We keep and catalogue the letters and ephemera of those who we think matter. We commit stories, analyses, and lore to those who dominated the landscape of history. For many events—the Revolutionary War among them—there exists a pyramid of remembrance: At the top reside the "important" people about whom countless stories have been and continue to be told—those who have been memorialized in myriad ways. The decision-makers. The people with perceived power. The revered and select few who "made" history. Yet there is no capstone without a foundation. There is no summit without a base. There is no crowning achievement of the few without the contributions of the often nameless masses who support them.

No matter the difficulty or how sparse the evidence of their existence, it is crucial these individuals somehow be included in the archives of our time here. If storytellers now, in the present day, continue to exclude these lives, experiences, and contributions from our ongoing historical record, we do ourselves and future generations a disservice. An already incomplete record only grows more opaque with passing time. To remember is first to see, to recognize, and then to value.

This sometimes means providing compelling information with frustratingly little elaboration. Yet, if an attempt to share what we have of these records is not made, the continued silencing of these marginalized yet vital voices further cements the belief that only *some* people matter. It increases the possibility that generations to come will fall prey to this same tendency to devalue and overlook, to ignore the illuminating yet muffled cries of the past.

The eradication of legacies requires no chisel. All we need to do is to deem a person's contributions somehow "less than." To discount and overlook them from the outset.

The people in the pages that follow are by no means perfect. Their deeds and beliefs do not necessarily represent mine; nor do they need to. These are mothers and lovers and fighters and artists and writers and workers. Some of these people eschewed staying in their prescribed societal boxes, while countless others thrived within those limitations to the benefit of many. Sock-darning, stew-stirring, farm-tending, gun-wielding people of all walks of life. So while they and their actions are certainly not without fault, they are also not by any stretch of the imagination insignificant.

Flaws and foibles remain as legacies evolve. May it be for the best when times are worst. May their deeds, if not their visages, endure, carved into memory, indelible and undeniable.

How It Begins

When does a revolution begin? What marks its start? Historians are often separated from the moments they study by decades, even centuries, and their perspectives benefit as a result. There is the luxury of time elapsed, the advantage of a long-range view. It is easier to analyze the outcome of a battle than it is to break down every messy, human confrontation that comprised it. It is simpler to characterize the needs and wants of an entire nation than to acknowledge the myriad wishes and struggles of its citizens. From the relative comfort of far, far away, we can look back and say, *There. That's where it all began.*

The American Revolution is not so much a unique event as it is an ensuing episode in a series of ongoing conflicts that raged on this continent long before any colonies declared for independence.

There is no day one. There is only that which came before.

At what is considered the start of the American Revolution in 1775, the Native Americans east of the Mississippi numbered roughly a quarter of a million people, representing more than eighty different tribal nations. By comparison, there were an estimated 2 million white people and nearly half a million individuals enslaved by them. Decades before tea was spilled in any harbor, Nanye'hi had already known years of conflict. From the moment a European foot trod upon North American ground, Native nations had been fighting to keep and protect their land, making choices and forging alliances that they hoped would help preserve and protect their rapidly eroding homeland and the way of life it supported.

Nanye'hi lived in Chota, capital of the eastern Cherokee settlements, in what is now eastern Tennessee. At the time of the European arrivals to the Southeast, Cherokee of that region lived in areas called Overhill Towns, Middle Towns, Valley Towns, and Lower Towns, all cradled by the Blue Ridge Mountains. When Nanye'hi was born, in the late 1730s, the Cherokee were already trading with the British and the French. Those relations would forever impact the Cherokee and the course of the burgeoning American colonies.

Over the years, clashes between Native American nations, and between those nations and European settlers, grew. These sorts of strained relationships impacted not only Nanye'hi and her people, the Cherokee, but all Indigenous nations throughout America. The newcomers increasingly imperiled all these people had ever known, and everything they cherished.

Between 10,000 and 14,500 years ago, the Paleo-Indians, living alongside mastodons, were the first known people to inhabit the untouched carpet of green and rock, of river and forest, lying in the shadow of the Appalachians, that mountainous eruption created by repeated Ordovician collisions. In the Archaic Period that followed, from around 8,500 BCE up through the first century or two of the Common Era, inhabitants developed their hunting and fishing methods. The Indigenous peoples of the Woodland Period brought the bow and arrow, pottery, and the cultivation of corn to the region. Trade routes extended farther and etched deeper into this land. More permanent villages began to take shape, rising on the landscape. During the Mississippian Period, between around 800 and 1600 CE, squash and beans joined a new cultivar of corn as Indigenous peoples brought the "Three Sisters," a staple of sustenance, into being.

To their delight, the early peoples found that this land was home to countless medicinal plants that had sprouted after the Ice Age in the southern Appalachians. Later writers and scholars would dub it the "seed cradle of the continent." Cherokee land covered nearly 140,000 square miles, extending throughout the Southeast, including lands in what is now Tennessee, Alabama, North and South Carolina, and Kentucky. Those lands were bordered to the south and east by the Muscogee ("Creek"), Choctaw, and Chickasaw.

Though Indigenous peoples had been here long before Spanish conquistador Hernando de Soto and his entourage of hundreds came through Cherokee lands in Southern Appalachia in 1540, the increasing influx of Europeans dramatically impacted those native to North America.

Their arrival in the Cherokee lands brought horses and metal goods, which were welcome, and also more trade, now primarily with the British. Both sides agreed upon prices for the exchange of materials and supplies. According to an agreement made between the Cherokee Lower Towns and the royal province of South Carolina in the early 1700s, a pistol was worth 20 deerskins or 120 bushels of corn; a hatchet, 3 deerskins or 18 bushels; and for a pair of scissors, the Cherokee would offer 1 deerskin or 6 bushels of corn as trade.

Beyond goods that the Cherokee and other Native Americans across North America could use, the European arrivals also brought something unwelcome to these shores: diseases to which the Indigenous peoples had no immunity. By 1650, the population of Native peoples throughout the Americas had dropped 90 percent from its high point in the late fifteenth century. The relationship between the Cherokee and the British soon began to deteriorate, as well as the Cherokee's relationship with the neighboring Creek.

Nanye'hi was in her teens when she married a man called Tsu-La (Kingfisher) in the 1750s. By then the Cherokee had been warring with the Creek for more than a decade—almost Nanye'hi's entire life. But one battle among many altered the course of her life and both her role within the Cherokee people of her time and Cherokee history, even through to the present day.

The Cherokee—like many Indigenous peoples—are a matrilineal society, with clan membership passing down generation to generation from mother to children, whether those children are male or female.

There were seven clans: A-ni-go-te-ge-wi (Wild Potato), A-ni-wo-di (Paint), A-ni-gi-lo-hi (Long Hair), A-ni-sa-ho-ni (Blue), A-ni-a-wi (Deer), A-ni-wa-ya (Wolf), and A-ni-tsi-s-qua (Bird). Kingfisher was a member of the Deer Clan, and Nanye'hi was Wolf Clan, like her mother, Tame Doe.

In 1755, early in her marriage, the Battle of Taliwa took place in what is now the city of Ball Ground in northern Georgia. Though the Cherokee and Creek had been fighting for years, Taliwa proved to be the site of perhaps the bloodiest and most brutal conflict. There Oconostota, the Cherokee war chief, fought with roughly five hundred Cherokee, but the Creek outnumbered them. Among those five hundred men was Kingfisher. Alongside Kingfisher on the field of combat stood Nanye'hi.

Nanye'hi was already a mother to a daughter—Ka-ti, or Catharine, born around 1752—and a son, Hiskyteehee—"Fivekiller"—born around the time of the Battle of Taliwa. As that battle raged, Nanye'hi crouched behind a log, preparing Kingfisher's ammunition. According to lore, she bit down hard and gnawed on the soft lead bullets destined for the barrel of Kingfisher's rifle. This was not an isolated practice, and reference to chewing (and/or poisoning) bullets goes back to at least 1670. The resulting tooth-pocked and jagged surfaces of the bullets were believed to inflict more damage on their fleshy targets.

As Nanye'hi prepared the deadly projectiles, a Creek bullet tore its way into Kingfisher's flesh and bone. Nanye'hi's husband fell dead beside her. She then picked up Kingfisher's rifle, loaded it with the ammunition she herself had prepared, and rose to fight.

When the battle ended, the Cherokee emerged victorious. Nanye'hi's actions did not go unnoticed. As a sign of their appreciation for her bravery in the bloody conflict, the Cherokee presented her with the "gift" of an enslaved person who had been left behind on the field of battle by the retreating Creek.

Nanye'hi returned to Chota and found that news of her fighting had preceded her arrival and made an impression on her people. They bestowed upon her the title of "Ghigau" ("Beloved Woman"), a position not only of respect but also of influence. Nanye'hi now had a more powerful voice in the community. She not only led the Women's Council; she had a vote on the Council of Chiefs. She used her voice on behalf of her people and also occasionally in defense of the increasing number of Europeans who kept settling on Cherokee lands.

Nanye'hi had watched as the presence of the English grew on Cherokee territories, further strengthened by Fort Loudon, the establishment northwest of Chota that the English built in 1756 on the banks of the Little Tennessee River. The English wanted to protect their trade with the Cherokee and prevent the French from making any inroads there. The French and Indian War was taking its toll. Still more traders arrived, enticed by routes already long traveled by Indigenous peoples.

One of these traders was Bryant Ward, whose business brought him to Nanye'hi's home of Chota. Though Ward had another (European) wife he had left behind at his home in South Carolina, he married Nanye'hi in 1759. From that point forward, her English name was Nancy Ward. The pair soon had a daughter whom they named Elizabeth. But Bryant Ward's sojourn on Cherokee land with his new family was brief: By 1760 he was gone.

The French and Indian War was a part of a larger, global conflict involving key European countries, the Seven Years' War. Those power struggles now reached across the Atlantic and had embroiled the kingdom of Great Britain, the French, the colonists, and Indigenous peoples in a costly war over control of territories on the North American continent.

England and France battled for control of land and trade with Indigenous people, as Cherokee-British relations continued to deteriorate. Treaties came and went, were agreed to and later broken. The first land treaty, in 1721, had ceded a portion of Cherokee land to the British colony of South Carolina, and a second ceded still more in 1755. These would not be the last treaties that drastically shrank Cherokee lands, no matter the pact or pledge. In 1759, a fresh war erupted with the British, which the Cherokee called the "War with the Red Coats." The onset of that bloody struggle brought with it a smallpox epidemic as well—the second the Cherokee had suffered in twenty years.

Raids. Retaliations. Prisoner exchanges. Negotiations. Both sides shouldered great losses. In 1760, officials in South Carolina captured and imprisoned thirty-two Cherokee during a battle and eventually killed twenty-two of them. That same year, Overhill Cherokee attacked the British outpost of Fort Loudon on the Little Tennessee River. A British colonial force made its way to the besieged fort, traveling along the Savannah River and setting fire to the Cherokee Lower Towns they came upon along the way. The attempt to relieve those at Fort Loudon failed, and another agreement between the Cherokee and the British imploded.

The Cherokee promised to leave the departing British garrison enough ammunition for the journey back to South Carolina. But before departing, the British laid waste to the rest of the Cherokee munitions and, in the process, to their lingering and tenuous agreement with the Cherokee. After this, in the aftermath of what was called the Battle of Echoee, the Cherokee attacked the garrison and killed in the neighborhood of twenty-two soldiers—about the same number of Cherokee prisoners that the British had killed in South Carolina.

In reprisal, refortified British colonial forces, along with allied Catawba, Chickasaw, Stockbridge, and Mohawk warriors and scouts, returned to the area near Echoee and attacked the Cherokee. Again, both sides suffered tremendous loss of life, supplies, crops, and more, leaving thousands of Cherokee with no homes or food. The Cherokee now numbered fewer than 2,500—less than half the 5,000 members counted in 1739.

In the summer of 1761, South Carolina sent a Lieutenant Colonel James Grant and more than 2,000 troops into Cherokee territory, eradicating fifteen towns and roughly 15,000 acres of crops. The Cherokee, under the leadership of Attakullakulla, Nanye'hi's uncle and the first Beloved Man of the tribe, had little choice: They signed peace treaties with both the colony of Virginia, in what is now the state of Tennessee, and the colony of South Carolina at Charles Town. Attakullakulla was the lead figure in Cherokee diplomatic efforts and traveled extensively, often to meet with colonial leadership in efforts to stem the flow of

European settlers onto Cherokee lands. The relief that the treaties of 1761 brought would not long endure.

The following year, in 1762, members of the Cherokee tribe traveled to London with Lieutenant Henry Timberlake, a journalist and cartographer, who had been living among the Cherokee in the Overhill Towns. He compiled his observations into writings about Cherokee life and culture that future generations would reference. Timberlake's cartographic skills resulted in comprehensive maps of Cherokee lands and communities, one of which was entitled *A Draught of the Cherokee Country.* Timberlake described Cherokee homes, weapons, lands, and more in a document that would be consulted by European friends and foes in years to come.

Native American diplomatic travels were not unusual during the eighteenth century. The Mohawk of the Six Nations had visited the court of Queen Anne in 1710. This 1762 voyage was not the first time that Cherokee had crossed the Atlantic to meet with a monarch. Attakullakulla had done so in 1730. The result of that voyage had been an alliance: The Cherokee would trade with the English. But agreements of this sort often had a short shelf life. Other nations—namely the French—made their *own* pacts with tribes as the presence of Europeans continued to spread throughout Indigenous lands, leading to ongoing conflicts among the various factions now inhabiting North America. This latest visit might help improve relations between the Cherokee and the British.

During the 1762 visit, one of the three Cherokee emissaries traveling with Timberlake was Ostenaco, a noted warrior and chief and a familiar face in places like Williamsburg, in colonial Virginia. In fact, during a dinner at the College of William & Mary, Ostenaco expressed the desire to meet King George III of England. And so it would be. Ostenaco and two other Cherokee, Cunne Shote (Stalking Turkey) and Woyi (the Pigeon), captivated residents of London, where the presence of the Cherokee fed the seemingly insatiable imaginations of the bustling city's residents.

"They are tall, well-made Men, near six feet high, dressed in their own Country Fashion, with only a Shirt, Trowsers and Mantle round them," *The St. James's Chronicle* wrote of the visitors. "Their Faces are painted of a Copper Colour, and their Heads adorned with Shells, Feathers, and Earrings, and other trifling Ornaments."

The group's translator, William Shorey, became ill and died during that sea voyage, and Timberlake was forced to try to interpret as best he could without Shorey's more adept linguistic skills. The language barrier did little to quell the excitement ignited by the visitors, and the Cherokee were feted to no end with dinners, trips to the theater, and song.

"When the Cherokee Chief and his attendants were at Vauxhall Gardens last week," *The Leeds Intelligencer and Yorkshire General Advertiser* reported, "they had a very sumptuous entertainment. The wines first set before them, were Burgundy and Claret, which however they did not seem greatly to relish. Others were placed on the table, when they fixed upon Frontiniac, the sweetness of which hit their palates, and they drank of it very freely."

The Haymarket Theatre advertised an added performance at its venue, citing:

> *By Desire of the CHEROKEE Kings And CHIEFS. The LAST Night but ONE . . . TUESDAY next Mr. FOOTE's ORATORICAL COURSE will be continued in the Evening, Previous to which, in order to compleat the Evening's Entertainments, will be given The MINOR.*

Both sides of the Atlantic made note of the Cherokee visit to England. Back in the colonies, *The South-Carolina Gazette* shared news that "the Cherokee Chiefs went to the Tower to see the curiosities there."

The Gloucester Journal wrote that the "Indian King and Two Chiefs" would be staying in a house on Suffolk Street. "Cloaths are also making after the English Fashion, in which they are to make their Appearance. They are to be clothed in Scarlet."

One newspaper writer, Henry Howard, penned a seven-verse satirical tune about the reactions of the English to the Cherokee titled "A

New Humorous Song On the Cherokee Chiefs. Inscribed to the Ladies of Great Britain."

> *. . . The Ladies, dear Creatures, so squeamish and dainty,*
> *Surround the great* Canada *Warriors in plenty.*
> Wives, Widows *and* Matrons, *and pert little* Misses,
> *Are pressing and squeezing for* Cherokee *Kisses.*
> *Each grave looking Prude, and each smart looking Belle, Sir,*
> *Declaring, no* Englishman *e'er kiss'd so well, Sir.*

The Cherokee visitors also sat for "pictures" with an artist named Mr. Reynolds. This became the most famous—though questionable—image of them. The resulting newspaper illustration included the image of a hunched, tricorne-clad, elderly British chap—this figure has at times been identified as "their interpreter that was poisoned"—eyeing the three Cherokee. All three individuals are wearing earrings, tunics, and thick half moon–shaped collar necklaces. The caption, which lists a number of early stereotypes of Native Americans, reads as follows:

> *The Three Cherokees, came over from the head of the River Sa*
> *vanna to London, 1762. 1: Their Interpreter that was Poisoned. 2:*
> *Outacite or Man-killer; who Sets up the War Whoop, as, (Woach*
> *Woach ha ha hoch Woach) with his Wampum. 3: Austenaco or*
> *King, a great Warrior who has his Calumet or Pipe, by taking a*
> *Whiff of which, is their most sacred emblem of Peace. 4: Uschesees*
> *[a] Great Hunter, or Scalpper, as the Character of a Warrior de-*
> *pends on the Number of Scalps, he has them without Number.*

The following year, King George III issued a royal proclamation that promised that there would be no more movement farther into Cherokee land, banning European settlement west of the Appalachians. This move sought to ease, at least somewhat, tensions with the Indigenous inhabitants: Wars were expensive and the Crown was already in debt. Moreover, it was intended to establish a clear line on the

Eastern Seaboard of those lands under the control of Britain. King George didn't want settlers moving farther west and gaining land—and therefore power and influence. Only the Crown could negotiate with Indigenous communities. Only King George or his representatives could purchase lands to the west. The so-called Proclamation Line of 1763 was promptly ignored by white settlers and the ceaseless encroachment onto Cherokee land continued.

"The number of Familys that have come from North Carolina & Virginia, & settled upon a great Part of our best lands, & the bold inroads of a few that are within an easy days march from our Towns, are circumstances very alarming to us," Cherokee chief Kittagusta protested in 1766—just three years later—to representatives of the British Indian Department at Fort Prince George in South Carolina. He referred to the "great Kings proclamation Relative to his Red Children," which, Kittagusta insisted, promised the Cherokee "quiet Possession of our Lands, & redress of our Grievances . . ."

Strings of beads were given. Belts of wampum and pipes were exchanged. Troubles continued.

A lease agreement between the Cherokee and the white pioneers living on their land eased the situation slightly, but trouble soon erupted again. Nanye'hi's role in her community began to evolve in unexpected ways, and with monumental consequences. Soon she would find herself in the midst of a battle with these settlers and a revolution that engulfed the entire Eastern Seaboard.

Regardless of any titles or honorifics that may or may not have been bestowed on them, the women in Cherokee society possessed influence and independence. Their fertility was considered a part of their power; when menstruating, their "medicine" was the strongest, and menstruating women were even encouraged to stay away from men who were preparing to compete in stickball for fear of diminishing the players' power. Anetsa, as the Cherokee refer to North American Indigenous stickball, was a serious activity often played between towns. It was physically demanding, competitive, and in times past sometimes resulted in serious injury or even death. Players needed their strength. Women also enjoyed as much sexual freedom as their male counterparts.

Cherokee women farmed and hunted. Cherokee women owned property. They held positions of power and influence within the tribe. They were at times sent to negotiate or trade with the European newcomers, should the men be away hunting. The independence and decision-making roles enjoyed by the Cherokee women within their community—and it was not unique to the Cherokee people alone—caught many settlers from places like England and France off guard. Most European women had no such ability to treat or trade.

Nanye'hi's position as Ghigau and a respected leader within her tribe was not viewed as unusual among the Cherokee, though it was still of great import and would prove consequential for her people. As a woman with power and influence, she was no outlier.

Nanye'hi was not the exception. She was the rule.

CHAPTER 2

A Bloody Time in Boston

The troops marched through Boston in an almost gallant fashion. Uniformed and organized, they disembarked at Long Wharf and strode through the streets, fifing and drumming along the way. Their arrival in 1768 was noted by all, was greeted with trepidation by some, and angered many.

"This was indeed a painful era," Mercy wrote when reflecting upon the show of force in the New England city. "The American War may be dated from the hostile parade of this day; a day which marks with infamy the councils of Britain."

This was no parade. This was a show of force, and the Crown intended to stay. The hostility would soon come, and Mercy Otis Warren would have much to say about it.

A petite woman with dark hair and eyes, Mercy's flourish with a pen was growing out of its infancy, evolving from the domestic prose and bucolic musings of the wife and mother she was into a more astute and at times acerbic take on what she saw going on around her. This talent for the written word had been hard won. Born on Cape Cod, Massachusetts, in the town of Barnstable, her father, James Otis, was a successful lawyer. Her mother, Mary (née Allyne), was descended of *Mayflower* passenger Edward Doty. Life on the Otis farm was comfortable, tended to by indentured servants, Indigenous people, and at least one enslaved worker.

Yet, despite her privilege, Mercy received no formal education, though her natural curiosity and insatiable appetite for reading were encouraged. She received, as many women of the day did, a hand-me-down education from her brother. James Otis Jr. had attended Harvard, and when "Jemmy" was home, his books became Mercy's, his lessons seeped into the substance of her being, and over time her mind sharpened and her pen sprang to life.

Married to James Warren, local merchant and sheriff, Mercy lived in Plymouth, the original seat of the Massachusetts government. Mercy and James had five children, and Mercy long exercised her love of the written word privately in letters and poems. But by the 1760s, the times and Mercy's tone began to change. Her brother, Jemmy, was already attracting attention from Massachusetts patriots. He and James Warren were soon in the Massachusetts legislature, and the Warren home was often the site of political discussions. Mercy heard the patriot outcries against the Crown's ever-tightening grasp on the economy and livelihoods of the colonists for years. Many of those cries emanated from her brother.

Seven years earlier, in 1761, James had stood in Boston's Old State House and delivered a fiery four-hour speech railing against Crown rule, stating, "Taxation without representation is tyranny." The colonists had no formal representation in the British Parliament. For their part, the Crown claimed that, naturally, the well-being of *all* their subjects was of the utmost concern. But more and more colonists did not want the British government making decisions regarding what was taxed and for how much without having any say in things whatsoever. James Otis just put the sentiment into words, and his inflammatory rhetoric caught the ear of a young barrister by the name of John Adams and that man's patriot cousin, Samuel. John and his wife, Abigail, soon befriended Mercy and her husband, James Warren. John called James Otis a "flame of fire," and indeed his words had ignited a spark of revolution in many Massachusetts citizens, including his sister and Adams, whom Mercy impressed with her keen mind. Now the situation in 1768 had worsened, providing much fodder for her pen as she observed her colony's capital overrun by redcoats.

How did it ever come to this?

The British victory in the French and Indian War may have cemented, if temporarily, the Crown's control over these lands, but it also incurred an extensive debt for the realm. Britain already had more than £70 million of debt at the start of the Seven Years' War, and although the Crown had done its best to pay it down, the total monies owed nearly doubled by the time the war ended in early 1763. (According to the National Archives of the United Kingdom and the Bank of England, that would put the debt at between £17 billion and £23 billion in 2025.)

The resulting hunger for revenue sent the Crown feasting on duties and taxes imposed upon its American colonists. True, many of the king's subjects had traversed the Atlantic seeking a better life, one theoretically characterized by political independence and religious freedom. But they also wanted comfort, if not economic prosperity, and they did not expect to render unto Caesar—George, rather—more than his just due. And for too long they had been singled out for a specious form of taxation—or so they believed.

Even before the French and Indian War in North America had ended, taxes such as those on molasses—first imposed in 1733—were being enforced with a new vigor, with British troops entering and searching homes and businesses without warning. This new enforcement was felt keenly by key centers of trade such as Boston, and the colonial outcry grew as a result.

The Sugar Act of 1764 ensued, and increased regulation of trade and imposed taxes on sugar and molasses. This was just the beginning of Britain's attempt to raise money from the colonies: "Whereas it is expedient that new provisions and regulations should be established for improving the revenue of this kingdom . . ." the act stated. (Despite the name, the act also levied taxes on wines, coffee, indigo, and various textiles.) This included:

> *For every hundred weight avoirdupois of such foreign white or clayed sugars, one pound two shillings, over and above all other duties imposed by any former act of parliament.*

> *For every pound weight avoirdupois of such foreign indigo, six pence.*
>
> *For every hundred weight avoirdupois of such foreign coffee, which shall be imported from any place, except Great Britain, two pounds, nineteen shillings, and nine pence.*

Mercy's brother, Jemmy, was publishing pamphlets decrying this and other measures that followed. In one, titled "The Rights of the British Colonies Asserted and Proved," he shared his fervent belief in what was the central tenet of the Enlightenment: "Nature has placed all in a state of equality and perfect freedom." Ahead of his time, James asserted that "the Colonists are by the law of nature free born, as indeed all men are, white or black." He additionally—and outrageously, for the times—declared that women and girls were as free as their male counterparts.

The Stamp Act of 1765 that followed was a costly and infuriating piece of legislation. While some citizens may have chosen to forgo unnecessary taxed goods such as playing cards, other purchases were more challenging for the colonists to boycott due to their role in day-to-day affairs, such as legal documents and newspapers.

Each new tax, every new duty on imported goods, stung like an insult and disrupted lives and pocketbooks. In many households, women held the purse strings, making the kinds of purchases that sustained not only their families but businesses in their communities. In this vital role, women wielded economic power and influence that could immediately impact commerce, especially if they chose to organize.

In 1766, *The Pennsylvania Gazette* reported that a group of "Eighteen DAUGHTERS OF LIBERTY, young Ladies of good Reputation," met at the home of a local doctor. That doctor had "discovered a laudable Zeal for introducing Home Manufactures. There they exhibited a fine Example of Industry, by spinning from Sunrise until Dark, and displayed a Spirit for saving their sinking Country rarely to be found among Persons of more Age and Experience."

The newspaper noted that these women had chosen to boycott tea as well.

> *Besides this Instance of Patriotism, before they separated, they unanimously resolved that the Stamp-Act was unconstitutional, that they would purchase no more British Manufactures unless it be repealed, and that they would not admit the Address of any Gentlemen, should they have Opportunity, without they were determined to oppose its Execution to the last Extremity, if Occasion required . . .*

Throughout the 1760s, other women in other colonies followed suit.

"Our accounts from every Province in America, contain the strongest Manifestations of the Union of the People, and their irreversible Purpose of defending their Liberties, at the Hazard of their Lives and Fortunes," opined an editorial.

The Virginia Gazette reported the actions of female residents of Charlestown, not three miles north of Boston on the other side of the Charles River. In one such case, a woman with a bevy of goods to purchase asked the shopkeeper whether he sold tea. The proprietor said that, yes, of course he did sell tea. Suddenly incensed, the woman instructed the purveyor of the oh-so-popular beverage to return all of her items to the shelves from whence she plucked them, "being determined," the newspaper reported, "as the inhabitants of that town had universally left off drinking tea, she would purchase nothing where that was sold." She turned on her heels and departed the premises, empty of hand yet full of conviction.

That same month, in the same town, forty or so women visited the homes of Reverend Mr. Abbot and, later that week, a Reverend Mr. Prentice. The group offered to spin an entire day for each, generating linen for about half a dozen shirts.

The process of hand-spinning wool or flax fibers to transform them into thread or yarn was a tedious one. For this reason, the American colonies habitually imported much of the fabric used in their daily lives from England. These spinning sit-ins were part of the burgeoning homespun movement, yet another way to boycott British goods and protest taxes levied against the residents of America.

Actions such as these continued to ripple throughout the colonies. They appeared simple when viewed as individual deeds, yet they struck with tsunamic power when coalescing as a unified movement of defiance. This act of rebellion required no weapons save the tenacity and fortitude of those who agreed to sacrifice daily staples and their precious time in order to protect a fast-eroding freedom of governance.

Boycotts by Daughters of Liberty and others drove the repeal of the Stamp Act in 1766. However, on June 29, 1767, Parliament unfurled the Townshend Revenue Act, which would go into effect November of that year: The proclamation began, "WHEREAS it is expedient that a revenue should be raised, in your Majesty's dominions in America, for making a more certain and adequate provision for defraying the charge of the administration of justice, and the support of civil government, in such provinces as it shall be found necessary . . ." and then rationalized the need for additional taxation. This language had become far too familiar to those living in the colonies.

The new act listed all the taxed items and the corresponding costs in shillings for every hundredweight of each: crown, plate, flint, and white glass; red lead, white lead, green glass, painters' colors. Every ream of Atlas fine paper would also be taxed, as well as, yes, every pound of tea. These duties may have increased revenue for the British government, but they added no further representation for colonists in Parliament.

The unrest that had resulted from the now defunct Stamp Act had been rekindled once again, and the collection of these fresh duties and taxes in turn necessitated enforcement. That continued thirst for control and order on the part of a government an ocean away was now seeking to be slaked by posting British troops in the seaport of Boston, Massachusetts. The "hostile parade" of 1768 was just the beginning.

Not everyone was opposed to the Crown's presence. Boston resident and stalwart loyalist Ann Hulton wrote to a friend still residing in

England, the country of Ann's birth, deploring the increased and often violent protests against the British rule, which she wholeheartedly supported. Her brother, Henry, was a customs officer—a public post that represented to many the tightening economic grasp of Britain's taxing fist. Ann watched with growing concern as the world around her grew ever more antagonistic, especially to those who supported the king. "We soon found that the Mobs here are very different from those in O[ld] England," she wrote in 1768, "where a few lights put into the Windows will pacify, or the interposition of a Magistrate restrain them, but here they act from principle & under Countenance, no person daring or willing to suppress their Outrages, or to punish the most notorious Offenders for any Crimes whatever. These Sons of Voilence after attacking Houses, break[in]g Window[s], beating, Stoning & bruizing several Gentlemen belong[in]g to the Customs, the Collector mortally, & burning his boat, They consult[e]d what was to be done next, & it was agreed to retire for the night. All was ended with a Speech from one of the Leaders, conclude[in]g thus, 'We will defend our Liberties & property, by the Strength of our Arm & the help of our God, to you Tents O Israel.' This is a Specimen of the Sons of Liberty, of whom no doubt you have heard & will hear more."

No matter one's loyalty, the sense everywhere in Boston was that more suffering was to come, with fiery tensions stoked by the quartering of British troops in the city. No one was safe from the "mob": Suffering could strike indiscriminately and mercilessly. And so it did in February of 1770.

Theophilus Lillie was a merchant and importer who openly broadcasted his intent to continue business as usual and ignore any boycotts of British goods that his neighbors called for. His stance and its patriot counterargument played out in the press, with local newspapers printing opinions and letters representing both sides of the nonimportation debate. On February 22, a mob descended upon Lillie's house, where protesters had hung a sign reading, "IMPORTER." A young boy named Christopher Seider, the son of German immigrants, was among those in the unruly crowd.

British customs officer Ebenezer Richardson arrived on the scene and attempted to quell the tension, but the crowd would have none of it. The mob pursued Richardson to his home, where the officer took to a window with his musket, determined to defend himself and disperse the horde. Richardson fired. Though his shots were small of caliber, they were more than enough to pierce eleven-year-old Seider's chest and take his life. Today, Seider is considered by some to be the first casualty of the American Revolution. Thousands turned out to attend his funeral on February 26, 1770. The loss of someone so young at the hands of an officer of the Crown enraged the populace.

"Government is extirpated, & it is quite a State of Anarchy," Ann wrote to her friend. "There are some sensible & good people that are greatly alarmed at their impending fate,—The infant Colonies have been advancing toward a State of Independancy. Many things have concurred to bring on the Crisis sooner than expected . . ."

Late on a day in March 1770, that crisis erupted, one that would live on in infamy, forever associated with the city of Boston.

British sentries stood guard at their post in front of the Custom House on King Street, a familiar if unwelcome sight. The building's location, near the wharf and shoreline, gave it an easy position from which to monitor imports and enforce the duties to be paid upon them. Gaiters, haversacks, spatterdashes, garters—the distinct and easily recognizable livery of the British soldier, from his stockings up to his wool cocked hat, popped out of the streetscape like a crimson scourge. The troops were there to "inforce oppressive Measures," *The Boston-Gazette* wrote, "to awe and controul the legislative as well as executive Power of the Province, and to quell a Spirit of Liberty, which however it may have been basely oppos'd and even ridicul'd by some, would do Honor to any Age or Country."

Boston now teemed with nearly 4,000 British troops, making up roughly one-quarter of the population of the colonial seaport. Altercation seemed mathematically probable, if not entirely unavoidable. What transpired that day was in part the culmination of two years' worth of resistance to the British occupation of this city, a hub of trade. Skirmishes were breaking out in most corners of the town. During the first days of March, workers of an Atkinson Street ropewalk had their own tussle with British troops.

The ropemaking industry was a thriving one in the coastal colony. In the 1760s and 1770s, a single wooden sailing vessel might require twenty-five to forty miles of rope. Every day, numerous laborers laid, twisted, tarred, and coiled strands of hemp into this seafaring staple. It was tough, exhausting, and often dangerous work, with hot tar and dry hemp making for a perpetual threat of fire. It did not take much for tempers to flare and raw materials to combust.

Precisely how the events of that first Friday of March 1770 unfolded would vary, depending upon who recounted the incident and where their loyalties lay. What seemed beyond question was that an altercation between ropewalk workers and soldiers escalated into a melee between the groups, necessitating medical attention for some. But it didn't stop there. Throughout the weekend, the rope workers and British soldiers taunted and harassed each other, itching for another fight.

On the following Monday, March 5, a woman named Jane Whitehouse could hear raised voices outside, their volume increasing to such an extent that she left her home on Royal Exchange Lane off of King Street to see what was causing the growing ruckus.

Boston sat icy and cold, the remnants of recent snow still on the ground. Passersby, troops, merchants, residents, and others dashed across the frigid streets, each perhaps unaware how their actions, even if negligible enough on their own, might merge and mingle, culminating in mayhem.

Thirty-year-old Private Hugh White, a soldier in His Majesty's Service for some eleven years now, stood at his post in front of a mansion turned British outpost, the office of the Customs Service, where Ann Hulton's brother was a noted official.

An argument erupted between a barber's apprentice named Edward Garrick and a captain of the 14th Regiment, John Goldfinch.

Elsewhere Edward Archbald, William Merchant, John Leech Jr., and Francis Archbald were just parting ways after having passed the corner where a Dr. Loring kept his office. Edward Archbald and Merchant walked down the alley. Up ahead, they spied what appeared to be sparks as a British soldier repeatedly glanced his sword across the brick wall in front of him. He was not alone. A cudgel-wielding man stood with him. Tensions escalated, and soon the soldier began shoving Archbald. The blade went wide and pierced Merchant's clothes under his arm, steel skewering skin.

The man with the cudgel ran off in the direction of a former distillery now being rented to British troops by a man named Murray. More soldiers arrived, their weapons of choice (or accessibility) being a shovel and a pair of iron tongs.

A colonist named John Hicks managed to knock a soldier to the ground. Despite pleas of passersby for folks to go home, the butt of Private White's musket found the barber's apprentice Garrick's head.

Perhaps feeling strength in numbers, the young men forced the soldiers back down toward their barracks. Then, perhaps foolishly, they waited. It wasn't long before a dozen or so soldiers emerged from "Murray's barracks," clubs and cutlasses in hand, and came for the unarmed boys, who ran. The soldiers headed toward Dock Square. A bystander named Samuel Atwood encountered them on their way there.

Do you mean to murder people? The *Boston-Gazette* later reported Samuel as saying.

Yes, by God, root and branch! came the answer.

Those comments were followed by a strike from a club, and then another. Samuel's shoulder was reduced to a pulpy mess.

A crowd continued to grow. Jane Whitehouse approached a sentry of the 29th Regiment posted outside the Custom House.

What is the noise? she asked. More townspeople emerged, coming from the direction of the Town House.

There is the Centry! There is the bloody-backed Son of a Bitch, Jane heard them shout.

The numbers of men grew, nearing forty. Oyster shells, snowballs, and slabs of wood flew through the night air. Jane saw them chase and pummel the sentry to the Custom House steps.

The men of the 29th Regiment made their way by Mr. Silsby's and up an alley to King Street, reportedly attacking anyone in their path. Crowds grew on King Street near the Custom House and Butcher's Hall.

Jane heard bells ring out. The peals caused many fearful inhabitants to assume there was a fire. As a result, some soon arrived on the scene toting buckets of water. The commotion carried over the night air, drawing attention all the way down to Griffin's Wharf. Residents and passersby heard a woman's voice above others screaming in panic, "It is no fire, good God, there will be murder committed this Night!"

Friend warned friend; strangers alerted fellow Bostonians. An unidentified woman stormed into a neighbor's house yelling, "Pray, sir, come out! There will be murder, the soldiers and people are fighting."

Sounds, screams, rose on the night air, prompting some to take cover and spurring others to join in the unrest that would soon boil over on King. Elizabeth Avery, a maid for the Green family working in the Custom House, ascended to the second floor of that building and watched the clash from the upstairs window.

Catherine Field and her husband begged their friend Patrick Carr not to join the growing crowd, but he would not listen. Another woman in the neighborhood had more success at persuading Carr to at least leave his sword behind, arguably thinking the lack of a weapon might keep him out of trouble. He dashed off in the direction of the rioting. Unarmed.

Jane continued to watch as Captain Thomas Preston of the 29th Regiment now appeared with a force of British soldiers bearing rifles fitted with bayonets. Jane stepped forward, eyeing the captain intently. She was yards away from the man when another bystander asked the officer if they would fire.

A sentry shoved Jane, strongly urging her to go home. If she did not, he warned, she would be killed.

Jane started to leave but had only taken a few nerve-wracked steps when she heard the shots. In the uproar, Jane did not hear Captain Preston give orders to fire. Others would later claim that he had. But fire the gathered soldiers did, right into the crowd.

Again and again, with at least eleven guns going off.

Bodies littered the street, some mangled, others barely clinging to life, the most unfortunate dead where they fell. Those who attempted to move the wounded found themselves being shoved along by the pointy ends of British bayonets. Elizabeth, the maid, waited upstairs inside the Custom House until the firing ceased and the soldiers fled. She walked out the door afterward and into the wintry, snow-dusted night.

The Boston-Gazette spared no hyperbole in reporting the events:

On the Evening of Monday, being the 5th Current, several Soldiers of the 29th Regiment were seen parading the Streets with their drawn Cutlasses and Bayonets, abusing and wounding Numbers of the Inhabitants.

We have known a Party of Soldiers in the face of Day fire off a loaded Musket upon the Inhabitants, others have been prick'd with Bayonets, and even our Magistrates assaulted and put in Danger of their Lives . . .

A detailed and grisly account of the dead and wounded followed.

"The dead are," the *Gazette* wrote, "Mr. Samuel Gray, killed on the spot, the ball entering his head and beating off a large portion of his skull.

"A mulatto man, named Crispus Attucks, who was born in Framingham, but lately belonged to New Providence and was here in order to go for North Carolina, also killed instantly; two balls entering his breast, one of them in special goring the right lobe of the lungs, and a great part of the liver most horribly."

Attucks, of African American and Wampanoag descent, worked at the seaport where the scuffle had erupted days earlier. The newspaper waxed on, paying homage to the dead and wounded, and the manner of their injury.

"Mr. James Caldwell, mate of Capt. Morton's vessel, . . . killed by two balls entering his back."

"Mr. Samuel Maverick, a promising youth of 17 years . . . [A] ball went through his belly, and was cut out at his back: He died the next morning."

"A lad named Christopher Monk . . . Mr. Edward Payne . . . standing at his entry door, received a ball in his arm, which shattered some of the bones . . ."

The newspaper spared few details, enumerating how and where musket balls had entered bodies, how they exited, or by whose hand. Merchants, shipwrights, seafarers, apprentices, breeches makers—all dead. Their organs skewered, their bodies rent to skeletal splinters, their blood spilled.

People soon gathered at the site. Some sought to care for the wounded and carry off the dead. In the end, eleven citizens of Boston had been shot. Three died in the streets. Two more would soon join them. Six of the wounded survived. Catherine Field's friend Patrick Carr was not so lucky: He lingered for several days with a wound from a musket ball that had ripped through his right hip and blasted through his backbone before he finally died.

The British rather quaintly referred to the event as "the incident on King Street." For Bostonians, for those who witnessed the bloodshed that night, it would forever be a massacre, no matter the tally of the dead and injured.

Morning shed light on the gruesome aftermath.

"Tuesday Morning presented a most chocking Scene," the newspaper reported, "the Blood of our Fellow Citizens running like Water thro' King-Street, and the Merchants Exchange the principal Spot of the Military Parade for about 18 Months past. Our Blood might also be track'd up to the Head of Long-Lane, and through divers other Streets and Passages."

By eleven o'clock that morning, a crowd had gathered at Faneuil Hall and a committee chosen to meet with acting governor Thomas Hutchinson. The message was delivered succinctly: "[It] is the unanimous opinion of this meeting that the inhabitants and soldiery can no longer live together in safety; that nothing can rationally be expected to restore the peace of the town and prevent further blood and carnage, but the immediate removal of the Troops . . ."

A replay of this scene followed nearby at the Old South Meeting House, where more townspeople had gathered. The report they heard was that His Honor was "extremely sorry for the unhappy differences" but the officers were under military orders and not his. They would be confined to their barracks and word sent to their commanding general.

The troops were later moved to barracks at Castle William, atop Castle Island in Boston Harbor, where a fort had stood since the early 1600s. The fort's duties had shifted over time with changing politics; it now served as a stronghold for the British presence in the colonies. "We expect the Town will soon be clear of all the Troops," the *Gazette* reported. Wrongly, it turned out.

The bodies of Samuel Gray, Samuel Maverick, James Caldwell, and Crispus Attucks—"the unhappy Victims who fell in the bloody Massacre"—were carried to their common grave in the Granary Burying Ground and buried on March 8. Nine days later, the body of Patrick Carr, Catherine Field's friend, joined the other victims. Ships paused in their duties. Bells tolled in Charlestown and Roxbury. People followed hearses on foot and in carriages as the procession moved through the Main-Street. The bodies were placed in one large vault. "The aggravated Circumstances of their Death, the Distress and Sorrow visible in every Countenance, together with the peculiar Solemnity with which the whole Funeral was conducted, surpass Description."

Later that year saw the trials of those men of the Crown, Captain Thomas Preston among them. Though he detested the violent incident, a thirty-four-year-old lawyer named John Adams felt compelled in his duty to defend the British. Among his tactics, he described Attucks as an outsider, using this characterization and the man's race to curry favor with the predominantly white Boston populace and call Attucks's motives into question. Despite the efforts of the prosecutors, who included Massachusetts representative Robert Treat Paine, Adams proved persuasive. In the end, the murder trial of those British soldiers involved in the shooting resulted in six soldiers found not guilty and two guilty only of manslaughter. The trial proceedings marked the inaugural utterance of the phrase "reasonable doubt" by a judge.

Ann Hulton and others who shared her antipatriot sentiments were pleased with the outcome. "The impartial trial and honorable acquital of Capt: Preston and the soldiers, has the most happy effect, it has exposed the conduct of the Faction and opened the eyes of the people, in general convinced them that they had been deceived by the false opinions and false representations of Facts . . ."

Ann Hulton could not have been more wrong.

For those living far beyond the land and waters of Boston, life carried on. That spring, a fourteen-year-old girl named Marie Antoinette married the heir apparent of France. She would become the last queen of that nation before it was consumed by its own revolution—a nation that would yet play a part in the disquiet simmering in the colonies. And not long after after the "incident on King Street," farther south in Manhattan, in the colony of New York, a crowd gathered to witness the unveiling of a gilded-lead statue of King George III of Great Britain. The statue portrayed His Royal Highness in gallant form atop a steed, in the likeness of a Caesar, toga clad and olive wreathed. The entire sculpture sat upon a marble column overlooking the small park of Bowling Green.

Shortly after what we now call the Boston Massacre, the Crown abolished the Townsend duties—all of them but the tax on tea. This beverage was consumed several times a day, to the tune of more than 1 million pounds by weight of the leafy drink per year. Abstaining from tea as a form of protest vexed a people who preferred it to coffee, which had to be roasted and ground before it could be brewed and imbibed. Boycotting the East India Company meant smuggling in tea from the Dutch in an effort to keep colonial palates happy. This did not please the Crown. As time passed, talk of independence—and tea—grew and remained steeped in an increasingly potent brew of unrest in the Northeast and beyond.

Though residents throughout the colonies had varying ideas of what it meant to be free, the ideals of freedom fell upon all ears. The cherished values of liberty and autonomy do not discriminate. The very thought of freedom—the hope of it—sprang up in unexpected places, erupting onto a landscape and time of perpetual change.

CHAPTER 3

Freedom's Many Trails

In heaven's eternal court it was decreed
How the first martyr for the cause should bleed
To clear the country of the hated brood
He whet his courage for the common good
Long hid before, a vile infernal here
Prevents Achilles in his mid career
Where'er this fury darts his Pois'nous breath
All are endanger'd to the Shafts of death . . .

So began a poem titled "On the Death of Mr. Snider Murder'd by Richardson," written by a young Boston poet and published in February of 1770, after the death of young Christopher Seider.

That poet had been abducted from her family in West Africa when she was just seven or eight years old and transported to North America aboard the slave ship *Phillis*, which docked at Long Wharf in Boston on July 11, 1761.

Two days later, on July 13, Susanna Wheatley went aboard the *Phillis* and saw the young girl who would take that ship's name as her own. Enslaved individuals accounted for roughly 10 percent of Boston's population by the mid-1750s, and now Phillis would be counted among them. Susanna, who was in her early fifties, was seeking a servant. Her husband, John, was a successful merchant and purveyor of whaling supplies who owned real estate, a ship, and a well-appointed home on King Street in Boston that was often frequented by some of that city's more well-to-do and influential residents. Susanna noticed Phillis, small and meek. She was looking for a "domestic," yes, but also a companion, someone who could care for her when she got older. Spying young Phillis, Susanna struck a bargain—"owing to the frailty of the child"—and took the girl home.

Only two of the Wheatleys' five children had survived past their youth. Their twins, Nathaniel and Mary, were about eighteen years old when Phillis arrived at the house on King Street. There were a handful of other enslaved individuals, but they were considerably older than Phillis. The Wheatley family quickly noticed that what Phillis may have lacked in strength, she more than made up for with intellect.

She quickly learned to read and write, instructed by Mary and Susanna, consuming Bible verses and more. By the time she was about seventeen years old, Phillis was not only writing letters but poetry as well, increasingly for a growing audience. The first *known* publication of one of Phillis's poems is "On Messrs Hussey and Coffin," which appeared in Rhode Island's *Newport Mercury* on December 21, 1767.

Though enslaved, Phillis's literacy and love of the written word somewhat opened the world to her, and what news reached her ears occasionally shaped her early work.

Later, in 1770, roughly six months after the Boston Massacre, a beloved local clergyman, Reverend George Whitefield, died. On the occasion of his death, Phillis penned a poem that was published along with the sermon commemorating the reverend's passing.

"An ELEGIAC POEM on his Death," the publication's title page read, "By PHILLIS, A NEGRO GIRL, of Seventeen Years of Age, Belonging to Mr J. Wheatley of Boston: She has been but Nine Years in this Country from Africa."

The final section of the poem also paid tribute to an individual who would impact Phillis's future.

> *Great COUNTESS! we Americans revere*
> *Thy Name, and thus console thy Grief sincere:*
> *We mourn with thee, that TOMB obscurely plac'd,*
> *In which thy Chaplain undisturb'd doth rest.*

New-England, sure, doth feel; the ORPHAN's Smart
Reveals the true Sensations of his Heart:
Since this fair Sun withdraws his golden Rays,
No more to brighten these distressful Days

The "Great Countess" in question was Selina Hastings, the Countess of Huntingdon, a dear friend of Reverend Whitefield. Whitefield had served as the countess's long-distance chaplain and confidant. Phillis wrote the countess in London directly to share her words, establishing a pattern she would repeat with other citizens of note.

To the Rt. Hon'ble the Countess of Huntingdon

Most noble Lady,

The Occasion of my addressing your Ladiship will, I hope,
Apologize for this my boldness in doing it: it is to enclose a few
lines on the decease of your worthy Chaplain, the Rev'd Mr.
Whitefield, in the loss of whom I Sincerely sympathize with your
Ladiship: but your great loss which is his Greater gain, will, I
hope, meet with infinite reparation, in the presence of God, the
Divine Benefactor whose image you bear by filial imitation.
The Tongues of the Learned are insufficient, much less the pen
of an untutor'd African, to paint in lively character, the
excellencies of this Citizen of Zion! I beg an Interest in your
Ladiship's Prayer and Am,

With great humility,
your Ladiship's most
Obedient Humble Servant
Phillis Wheatley

Intrigued and impressed by her new correspondent, the countess resolved to help the young writer. So commenced a correspondence between the Wheatley household and Selina Hastings.

Phillis Wheatley had already begun to make a name for herself as a poet. During this time, many in that city questioned Phillis's talents, arguing that the poems and letters credited to her could not possibly have been written by an uneducated enslaved young woman.

Prominent citizens leapt to defend her. Bostonian and Continental Congress member John Hancock, along with sixteen other figureheads in the city, publicly attested to Phillis's growing body of work, hoping to bring most—if not all—doubts about her authorship to an end.

One of Phillis's most frequent correspondents was her friend Obour Tanner, an enslaved woman of Newport, Rhode Island. The two shared feelings about religion, their relationship, and their home life. Phillis spoke often of her delicate physical condition, which most often manifested as a respiratory ailment. In July of 1772, Phillis wrote her friend:

> *I have been in a very poor state of health all the past winter and spring, and now reside in the country for the benefit of its more wholesome air. I came to town this morning to spend the Sabbath with my master and mistress. Let me be interested in your prayers that God would please to bless to me the means us'd for my recovery, if agreeable to his holy will . . . your affectionate friend, & humble serv't,*

> *Phillis Wheatley*

In 1773, perhaps to help boost her delicate health, the Wheatleys decided to send Phillis to London with their son Nathaniel. He was traveling to England on business, and the thinking was that Phillis might also be able to capitalize on her growing popularity and find a publisher for her poems while in that capital city. The sea air and changed climate might also be a balm for Phillis's condition. Susanna Wheatley alerted Countess Huntingdon of Phillis's impending arrival.

Well before the voyage, the Wheatleys had begun to contemplate how they might manumit Phillis in such a way that she would be able to support herself. Were Phillis not financially independent, her situation could potentially blow back on the Wheatley family, as laws in

Boston dictated that anyone manumitting an enslaved person would be responsible for that person's financial care should they become a "burden" to the city.

The most obvious means by which Phillis might support herself was through the publication of her works. Through the intercession of people in the Wheatleys' employ, the family sought the help of a London printer, who in turn visited the countess at her home and read her Phillis's poems aloud. The countess liked what she heard and agreed to promote the book. From that moment forward, Phillis and the Wheatleys began approaching friends and contacts to raise subscriptions for the coming work. All they needed was to get Phillis and her book to London.

In May of 1773, Phillis penned "A Farewell to America," perhaps as an optimistic ode to her voyage abroad.

I.
Adieu, New-England's smiling meads,
Adieu, th' flow'ry plain:
I leave thine op'ning charms, O spring,
And tempt the roaring main.

II.
In vain for me the flow'rets rise,
And boast their gaudy pride,
While here beneath the northern skies
I mourn for health deny'd . . .

While staying with Nathaniel in London, Phillis encountered influential members of London society, abolitionists, as well as noted inventor, printer, colonial ambassador, and electricity pioneer Benjamin Franklin, who was living in London at the time and serving as the representative of the Pennsylvania Assembly to the Crown.

Franklin called on Phillis as a favor to a relation who was a friend of the Wheatley family.

"Upon your Recommendation I went to see the black Poetess and offer'd her any Services I could do her," Franklin wrote his nephew Jonathan Williams Sr. on July 7, 1773. "Before I left the House, I understood her Master was there and had sent her to me but did not come into the Room himself, and I thought was not pleased with the Visit."

Williams had been "prevailed upon" by Phillis's "master and mistress" to contact his uncle in London on Phillis's behalf. After hearing of Franklin's reception, Williams wrote that he was "sorry he did."

During her stay, Phillis was unable to visit her supporter and literary benefactress Countess Huntingdon, who had taken ill and been advised by her own physician to recuperate in Wales. As she had long planned, Phillis dedicated what would become her first published book of poems to the countess. The collection was entitled *Poems on Various Subjects, Religious and Moral, by Phillis Wheatley, Negro Servant to Mr. John Wheatley, of Boston, in New England.*

Phillis had taken the precious manuscript with her to London. There, the book was printed by Archibald Bell, a bookseller in Aldgate. It was sold by Messrs. Cox and Berry, King-Street, Boston, in September of 1773.

Phillis did not stay in England to see the publication of her book but wrote Obour upon her return about the effects the journey had on her body and spirit.

"I can't say but my voyage to England has conduced to the recovery (in a great measure) of my health," she wrote. "The friends I found there among the nobility and gentry, their benevolent conduct towards me, the unexpected and unmerited civility and complaisance with which I was treated by all, fills me with astonishment. I can scarcely realize it."

The publishing of the book brought attention to Phillis's status within the Wheatley household. Some in England assumed she must be free, as she possessed such talent, and was now a published author. Some newspapers in London commented disparagingly about Phillis's continued enslavement.

Before departing England, Phillis met William Legge, 2nd Earl of Dartmouth, who served as secretary of state for the American colonies beginning in 1772 and to whom she addressed one of the poems in her book. She deftly and directly entwined her own bondage with notions of liberty and the underlying causes of the coming revolution:

No more, America, in mournful strain
Of wrongs, and grievance unredress'd complain,
No longer shalt thou dread the iron chain,
Which wanton Tyranny with lawless hand
Had made, and with it meant t' enslave the land.
. . . .
I, young in life, by seeming cruel fate
Was snatch'd from Afric's fancy'd happy seat:
What pangs excruciating must molest,
What sorrows labor in my parents' breast?
Steel'd was that soul, and by no misery mov'd
That from a father seiz'd his babe belov'd:
Such, such my case. And can I then but pray
Others may never feel tyrannic sway?

Elizabeth had certainly seen some of the men gathered at the Ashley home before. The house was a frequent site of meetings among the leading figures of Sheffield, Massachusetts. Colonel John Ashley, her enslaver, served as a representative in the colonial legislature and was also a judge. He owned substantial parcels of land and enjoyed hosting the most influential gentlemen of the community at his home: doctors, military men, lawyers, and clergy. Western Massachusetts didn't boast the same economy as the bustling seaport of Boston to its east. It was predominantly an agrarian society, with wealthy landowners living alongside impoverished farmers. Nevertheless, as unrest grew in the colonies, the men in and around Sheffield found their evenings of food and drink increasingly dominated by conversation and debates that took a more urgent tone. For some of these discussions in January 1773, Colonel Ashley served as moderator.

Elizabeth had had plenty of opportunities to hear the topics of the day as discussed within these walls for years now. She had been born into slavery some thirty years earlier, in the colony of New York. Her enslaver at the time had been Peter Hogeboom, who had a daughter named Hannah. When Hannah married Colonel Ashley, Hogeboom "gifted" Elizabeth and another enslaved person, believed to be named Lizzie, to his daughter to work in the Ashley home in Western Massachusetts. On a map, Elizabeth's new home in Sheffield was a little more than thirty miles away. But to these women, this was an entirely new world that demanded their constant caretaking—the home, the garden, the children—day in and day out.

Elizabeth had given birth to her own female child, also named Elizabeth. She never spoke of the child's father. (This may have been "Lizzie" or "Betsy.") Now about thirty years old, Elizabeth sought to protect those dear to her so long as they were enslaved by the Ashley family. The exhausting work was made worse by Hannah's frequent outbursts and abuse. "No doubt there were hard masters and cruel mistresses . . ." a writer named Catharine Sedgwick would later write of slavery as it was practiced in her home state of Massachusetts, "unrestrained power is not a fit human trust."

For Elizabeth, a "cruel mistress" was a daily reality. Early on in her tenure at the Ashley home, the power exerted by her enslavers was more than unrestrained; it had become unbearable, violent.

As she went about her duties in January 1773, Elizabeth likely heard the discussions of the men gathered in Colonel Ashley's parlor. As she moved to and fro, in and around the guests, carrying plates, preparing food, and toting laundry, she did so with the arm that still bore a scar savaged upon her by Hannah Ashley during one of her fits of anger.

On that day, Hannah had been berating Lizzie when Elizabeth stepped between them, seeking to protect the young girl. Enraged, Hannah grabbed a coal shovel from the nearby hearth and struck Elizabeth's arm. The searing-hot metal cut through flesh, down to the bone. The scar remained, and Elizabeth refused to cover it. Brandishing this incontrovertible proof of Hannah's abuse served as its own rebuke to Hannah. When visitors to the Ashley home asked Elizabeth what on earth had happened to her arm, she replied, simply, "Ask missus."

Her suffering contrasted sharply with the talk of liberty and independence in the house. She had grown accustomed to hearing the rarefied language of freedom bandied about within earshot. In early January 1773, discussions in the Ashley parlor most likely turned to a topic that would have a life-changing impact on Elizabeth's life.

Ashley was among a small group of men who played a role in the crafting and adoption of the Sheffield Resolves. Theodore Sedgwick, a noted lawyer, put ink to paper and massaged the language that would, shortly thereafter, appear in *The Massachusetts Spy, Or, Thomas's Boston Journal*, for all to read.

> Resolved, *that Mankind in a State of Nature are equal, free and independent of each other, and have a right to the undisturbed Enjoyment of their lives, their Liberty and Property.* Resolved *that the great end of political Society is to secure in a more effectual manner those rights and privileges wherewith God and Nature have made us free.* Resolved *that it hath a tendency to subvert the good end for which Society was instituted, to have in any part of the legislative body an Interest separate from and independent of the Interest of the people in general.*

"Equal, free and independent."
The very things lacking in Elizabeth's life in the Ashley home.

Sarah's brother Nathaniel and her husband, John, were not looking at all like themselves that Boston evening, and Sarah was to thank for their physical transformations. Her work was not over, however. Reversing their metamorphosis would be as important as creating it in the first place, if not more so.

It was December 1773, and Sarah Bradlee Fulton had been married to John Fulton just over ten years. The British had been a permanent and increasingly disruptive presence in Boston for nearly as long. On the night she worked her magic, Sarah had traveled from her home in nearby Medford, Massachusetts, to her brother's abode at the south corner of Hollis and Tremont Streets in Boston. Sarah had been there many times to visit with her brother. His home was attached to a carpentry shop and was a popular meeting place in that port city.

But this night, the motive for the meeting was different.

Protests had continued in Boston and elsewhere: the spinning sit-ins, the boycotts, or the burning of tea as residents of Lexington, Massachusetts, had done. But this particular evening attention turned to the soul of Boston: Griffin's Wharf. Sarah Fulton and her sister-in-law may not have ventured out with the men who gathered at Nathaniel's house that night, but their contribution was regarded as crucial. Repercussions from the British might well befall those whose faces could be easily recognized.

Sarah likely had only a few basic tools at her disposal. Whites and reds, blancs et rouges, were the facial enhancers of the day. Vinegar and lead chemically combined to create a pasty white yet desirable dermal canvas, with colorants such as red carmine used to accent cheeks and lips. With these few hues, combined with the readily accessible soot and mud, Sarah could apply the men's much-needed camouflage. Or she may have simply used soot and ash from the fireplace—a handy option for many to conceal their identities that night. One by one, she disguised the patriots before they set out for the wharf. The idea was to use makeup to give her brother, her husband, and the other men the appearance of Native Americans, hoping to shift the blame for the coming vandalism. Once Sarah's work was done, the group set off, stepping onto the streets of Boston and joining dozens more cloaked—or otherwise disguised—individuals headed for the harbor.

The ship *Dartmouth* had entered Boston's waters on November 28. The *Eleanor* made land on December 3, and finally the *Beaver* docked on December 7. Patriots of Boston had stood guard, preventing the ships' cargos of tea from being unloaded—they were tired of paying the tax on it—and wanted the ships turned back to England. Finally, on December 14, Samuel Adams convinced Francis Rotch, the owner of the *Dartmouth*, to ask permission of Massachusetts governor

Thomas Hutchinson to return to England without unloading his goods—and therefore forfeiting the duties owed on them. The governor denied his request. This denial had been anticipated by the Sons of Liberty and other patriots, and a response had already been planned.

"Hurrah for Griffin's Wharf! The Mohawks are coming!" Crowds cheered on the organized mob of between 130 and 150 men and boys—some as young as thirteen—who divided up and boarded the three ships laden with precious cargo.

Between the three ships, there were some 342 chests of tea, most weighing about 400 pounds. The protesters were organized and disciplined, promising the ships' captains that no other goods would be damaged. They hoisted the crates with block and tackle and threw them overboard, leaving the waters of Boston harbor blackened, leaf-strewn, and steeped in rebellion. Before they sank into the darkness at the end of the night, an estimated 92,600 pounds of tea with an estimated value of £9,659 at the time (about $2.5 million today) bobbed on the shallow waters.

Some of the individuals pocketed and stole a few handfuls of the precious leaves intentionally. Others did so quite by accident. A patriot named Thomas Melville, a banker, later found some tea lodged inside his shoe. He stuffed it in a bottle as a keepsake of that night. It would pass down for many generations in his family, which one day included his grandson, Herman Melville, the celebrated author of *Moby-Dick*.

The men in Sarah's circle of friends returned safely to Nathaniel's house. Sarah's artistry that evening had done the trick, but she was not finished. As soon as she could, Sarah set to reversing her cosmetic process, returning the men to their natural selves, thus preventing any loyalists or suspicious British soldiers from identifying them as participants in the night's rebellious pageant.

Just four days later, the hoopla in Boston's harbor inspired a similar destructive tea protest a little more than three hundred miles to the south, in the city of Philadelphia.

It would not be the last.

Boston Un-Common

The only place you can drink a cold Sam Adams while lookin' at a cold Sam Adams . . ." So proclaims the sandwich board outside the Beantown Pub, which is situated directly across the street from the more than 350-year-old Granary Burying Ground, final resting place of Declaration signer, rabble-rouser, and brewer Samuel Adams. So, yes, one can imbibe a pint of Boston's most famous lager while gazing at the headstones of some of the colonial seaport's most notable residents.

In addition to Sam Adams, the burial ground is the permanent home of Declaration signers John Hancock and Robert Treat Paine, Paul Revere, a host of governors, eleven-year-old Christopher Seider, and the victims of the Boston Massacre. The cemetery is *also* the resting place of one Mary Goose, aged forty-two, who died in 1690. Some guides (and many websites) love to spin a tale for tourists that this was the nursery rhyme goddess, Mother Goose. It's not. Scholars don't believe there ever lived a person with that moniker who penned tales for children. The rhymes originated in Europe, and can be traced to 1697, when a Frenchman named Charles Perrault published *Histoires ou contes du temps passé* (*Stories or Tales of the Past*). That book included stories we know today as *Cinderella* ("Cendrillon"), *Sleeping Beauty* ("La belle au bois dormant"), and *Little Red Riding Hood* ("Le petit chaperon rouge"). The rest is oft-obfuscated history. Nevertheless, there is a sirloin steak sandwich on the Beantown menu devoted to the good Mother. Only she, Sam Adams (Cajun chicken), and Paul Revere (Romanian pastrami and corned beef) are honored with a namesake repast.

———

I have visited Boston often, sometimes for research, always for a bit of history nerd fun. I've attended a reading of the Declaration of Independence on July 4 at the Old State House. Strolled many times past the larger-than-life statue of Samuel Adams outside Faneuil Hall. Stopped by the Old North Church (which offers an after-hours crypt tour). The Long Wharf, once the seafaring hub of this center of trade, now serves as a departure point for ferries to the Boston Harbor Islands or Salem, and sunset cruises. In Boston, rest assured, there's a bar on every corner and a chowder on every menu.

The city is exceedingly walkable. Leaving Beantown Pub and meandering through the Boston Common (if you need a rest, you can sit on the park bench on which Robin Williams perched in *Good Will Hunting*), you arrive at the Commonwealth Avenue Mall. Strolling this thirty-two-acre greenway, the shaded spine of Boston's tony Back Bay neighborhood, takes you past nine historic sculptures honoring everyone from Leif Erikson to the women I have come to see: Phillis Wheatley, Abigail Adams, and Lucy Stone. Dedicated in 2003, the Boston Women's Memorial is the newest of the mall's statuary tributes. Artist Meredith Bergmann sculpted these three women—the enslaved poet, the nation's second first lady and colonial letter writer, and the nineteenth-century suffragist and abolitionist—in bronze, each accompanied by a granite pedestal. However, none of the three stand atop the stone; rather, they interact with it, encouraging visitors to do the same.

Abigail Adams leans against her granite slab, arms crossed, defiant. Lucy Stone rests one hip on the stone, looking off into the distance with pen in hand. Phillis Wheatley is using her pedestal as a desk; her chin rests on one hand, while the other holds a quill. Stand over her shoulder and you can read her words etched in the surface. Her pose—the contemplative look on her face, the placement of her index finger—recalls the way she appears in a well-known engraving from the colonial era. This Phillis

Wheatley is a far cry from the terrified enslaved child who arrived in Boston, one of three very different women enslaved in Massachusetts whose own revolutions would coincide with that of the colonies.

———

I head out to nearby Medford, which lies only about five and a half miles northwest of Boston off I-93, which means it might be a thirty-minute drive or more in traffic. The Medford walking tour winds through the historic square bearing the town's name, and to the Salem Street Burying Ground, which dates to the late 1600s. Here, Boston Tea Party makeup artist Sarah Bradlee Fulton is buried, and a stone memorial dedicated by the Daughters of the American Revolution commemorates her as "Heroine of the Revolution." I cross the Cradock Bridge to get to the other side of the Mystic River. Originally built in 1637, it was dubbed the Mystic Bridge by residents, and it has long been associated with Paul Revere's visit to the town on the night of his famous ride, April 18, 1775. From there, it's a short jaunt down Main Street past Fulton's house, and, continuing just a bit farther, at the corner of George Street, you arrive at another historic home, the Royall House and Slave Quarters.

The property features a three-story brick home with a sage-green clapboard facade. Adjacent to the main house is the two-story brick-and-clapboard slave quarters. The surrounding gardens feature the remnants of what would have been the formal "summerhouse," which was a small octagonal structure with a cupola that once housed a statue of Mercury. Colonel Isaac Royall Sr. moved into the home in the 1730s, but the original part of the structure is likely one hundred years older. He took the colonial farmhouse and transformed it into a three-story Georgian mansion and added another structure, an "out kitchen," to the property. His son Isaac Royall Jr. moved in in 1739 and around 1760 had the out kitchen enclosed and more than doubled the size of the structure with a clapboard addition. This became what is called today the slave quarters, one of the only such freestanding homes that housed enslaved people in this part of the nation.

The house served a variety of purposes during the Revolutionary War—which I will share later in the book—and changed hands several times during the nineteenth century. At one point it came again to the heirs of the

Royall family, who sold it and used part of the profit to establish Harvard Law School. Near the turn of the century, the Sarah Bradlee Fulton chapter of the Daughters of the American Revolution decided to raise money to preserve the home, enlisted others in their cause, and eventually formed the Royall House Association. They helped to raise money for the Royall House Association to purchase the home and they still run the site today. It has been a National Historic Landmark since 1962.

Like many historic homes in New England, the house stands as a kind of snapshot of colonial life as it was lived by a certain class of citizens in the eighteenth century. There are gracious furnishings, oil paintings depicting the well-to-do Royall family, and many of the trappings associated with a number of sites of this sort on the East Coast. Sitting rooms, fine linens, elaborately tiled mantelpieces, decanters, and leather chairs. Archaeological excavations—which have recovered more than 65,000 objects on the grounds—have unearthed everything from a lice comb to port wine bottles bearing the Royall family seal.

Some of what has been uncovered—marbles, stone beads, pipes, amulets, and more—helps fill in the lesser-known stories of those who lived on these grounds. A placard over one of the house's fireplaces reads, "The colonists are by the law of nature freeborn, as indeed all men are, white or black." This quote, from Boston lawyer and Mercy's brother James "Jemmy" Otis's "Rights of the British Colonies," is one of the many reminders in the house that the focus here today is not the life and leisure of the Royall family as much as it is the experiences of those who were enslaved by them.

And among those enslaved by the Royall family during the American Revolution was a woman named Belinda Sutton. Unlike many enslaved men and women of the era, she did not go anonymously to her grave. She would leave behind a written testimony—albeit short—of her time on this earth and the role the Royall family played in it.

Once uncovered, silent strokes of pen and ink echo across the centuries.

CHAPTER 4

The Dismal and the Determined

1773

Dec 24.

An account from Boston, of 342 Chests of Tea, being thrown into the Sea.

Sitting in her home on Front Street in Philadelphia, Elizabeth Drinker jotted down this, the latest news out of Boston. More than a week had passed since the harbor uproar had left the waters around Griffin's Wharf brimming with tea leaves. Another such protest was soon to take place much closer to home, both literally and figuratively.

Nearing her thirty-ninth birthday, Elizabeth Sandwith Drinker had long been a dedicated diarist, penning volume upon volume of the goings-on in her daily life and, in some cases, life farther afield. Elizabeth was a Quaker and the wife of a merchant, Henry, and her religion and its impact on her and her family's lives often cropped up in her writings.

Many of her entries are plain and straightforward, with few of them assigned any more weight than others, despite the content or emotional consequences. Drinker's bloodlettings, visitors, dinner menus, and afternoon teas are treated with the same level of attention and concern as deaths, births, marriages, disappointments, successes, intentions to marry, and the occasional account of an acquaintance succumbing to smallpox. Joy and tragedy. All found themselves side by side in the tapestry of the daily life of a wife and mother during times of great upheaval.

1769 August. The Great Comet

E. D. was let Blood Febry. 22 1770.

Sally Stretch Dye'd March 29 1770.

Snow'd all Day the 2 April 1770.

ED was let Blood June 3. 1770.

October 30 Henry Sandwith Drinker born

Boiled Mutton and Kidney Beans . . .

1772 March 11 and 13 very Snowy days—the Snow very deep for the Season, we have had very frequent Snows, this Winter past.

April blood lettings for both ED and HD

Henry very ill. Worms . . . Billy with measles. Billy with Bloody flux

Pet Parrott of 21 years died

HD began to Chatter in the Spring 1772.

In her diaries, Drinker dutifully recorded household accounts and ledgers, knitting patterns, and weather observations. She kept lists of shifts, gowns, stockings, clouts, and frocks. She enumerated the acquisition, making, or mending of day caps and night caps. She noted her rides on horseback, her travels to the popular baths at Bristol, Pennsylvania, trips to the Quaker Meeting House, and yet more tea with friends.

She elaborated when she felt it necessary, but those more in-depth descriptions were not necessarily in direct proportion to their importance.

She did not wax poetic, for example, regarding the events that transpired in Philadelphia on and after Christmas 1773—just days after Boston's tea "party"—though she could not deny their impact on her personal life and the lives of her family members.

Philadelphia was the largest city in the colonies, with a population between 30,000 and 40,000. Only three other cities boasted populations larger than 10,000 inhabitants: Boston, New York, and Charles Town. All were major ports. All were buzzing hubs of commerce and trade. Philadelphia was all this and more, also serving as a cultural center and magnet for political discourse and revolutionary thought.

Elizabeth's husband, Henry, was a part of that booming Philadelphia trade. He was a partner in the firm of James & Drinker, which was under great pressure not to accept any arriving shipments containing tea from the global and omnipresent East India Company.

The East India Company (EIC) was a British enterprise that had long dominated trade, trafficking in spices, gold, silk, opium, and more. But in the 1770s an increasing share of the outfit's wealth came from tea, now representing nearly 50 percent of the EIC's income. The Crown reaped a benefit as well, in the form of duties collected. Colonists in America had been drinking tea for more than one hundred years, in a variety of manners, including, at times, eating the used tea leaves as a kind of side dish, serving the bitter brew remnants with butter and salt. The role of tea in daily life—as evidenced by Elizabeth's own detailed cataloguing of her schedule—is difficult to exaggerate. And as taxes took their toll, smuggling of tea into the colonies exploded. But the EIC and England still sought to deliver—and tax—tea destined for the colonies.

In early October, Philadelphia residents learned of a large shipment of tea bound for their city—698 chests' worth—aboard the ship *Polly*. It was one of the largest—if not the absolute largest—consignment of East India Company tea ever destined for the colonies.

A group of city leaders and influential residents met and came up with the Philadelphia Resolutions: eight pointed statements regarding not only the unjust taxation of the colonies and the detrimental effect it had on Americans but also how residents of Philadelphia should conduct themselves going forward. Soon after, the resolutions were presented to the citizens of Philadelphia, thousands of whom turned up at a town meeting on October 16 to overwhelmingly approve them.

The resolutions outlined the injustice of the intent and execution of these taxes levied and what citizens resolved to do about it. They stated that the tax "has a direct tendency to render assemblies useless and to introduce arbitrary government and slavery" and cited the necessity of "a virtuous and steady opposition to this ministerial plan of governing America . . . to preserve even the shadow of liberty."

The resolutions added that "it is the duty of every American to oppose" attempts to collect these taxes and that "whoever shall, directly or indirectly, countenance this attempt or in any wise aid or abet in unloading, receiving, or vending the tea sent or to be sent out by the East India Company while it remains subject to the payment of a duty here, is an enemy to his country."

Finally, resolution eight stated that a committee should be chosen "to wait on those gentlemen who, it is reported, are appointed by the East India Company to receive and sell said tea and request them, from a regard to their own characters and the peace and good order of the city and province, immediately to resign their appointment."

That last resolution affected Elizabeth and her family most directly. Henry and his business partner, Abel James, were consignees of the incoming shipment, and stood to profit greatly from its sale. This meant among the gentlemen who would receive a visit from this committee was Henry, and that visit would take place at the Drinker home.

Pressure on Henry's firm also appeared in print. One newspaper article referred to the firm's reluctance to take a stand against the tea tax and the East India Company, suggesting not so subtly that perhaps the merchants' storage facilities should be constructed of stone—as a stone structure was much more difficult to burn down than one made of wood.

Local patriots also inked pamphlets to distribute to pilots sailing the Delaware River to make sure that none of them considered escorting the *Polly* into Philadelphia via a more indirect waterway. The words of such a pamphlet, dated December 7, were none too subtle.

Referring to the man at the helm of the *Polly*, Captain Ayres, the leaflet read in part:

> Captain Ayres *was here in the time of the Stamp-Act, and ought to have known our People better, than to have expected we would be so mean as to suffer his* rotten TEA *to be funnel'd down our Throats, with the* Parliament's Duty *mixed with it.*
>
> *We know him well, and have calculated to a Gill and a Feather, how much it will require to fit him for an* American Exhibition. *And we hope, not one of your Body will behave so ill, as to oblige us to clap him in the Cart along Side of the* Captain.
>
> *We must repeat, that the SHIP POLLY is an* old black Ship, *of about Two Hundred and Fifty Tons burthen,* without a Head, *and* without Ornaments,—*and, that CAPTAIN AYRES is a* thick chunky Fellow—*As such, TAKE CARE to AVOID THEM.*
>
> *YOUR OLD FRIENDS,*
> *THE COMMITTEE FOR TARRING AND FEATHERING.*

On Christmas Day—just one day after Elizabeth and others became aware of the events at Griffin's Wharf in Boston—Philadelphia residents learned that the *Polly* was moored downriver in Chester.

Henry Drinker's decision whether to accept or refuse the wealth of goods aboard the *Polly* was rendered moot that same day. Patriots traveled to the *Polly* and escorted Captain Ayres from his ship to Philadelphia. There, on December 27, roughly 8,000 citizens of that city convened at the Philadelphia State House, necessitating that the gathering move outside. The message delivered was clear: Captain Ayres's crew would unload nothing from the ship. The next day, Captain Ayres set sail back across the Atlantic, the same goods weighing down his ship's cargo hold.

As conflicts with loyalists increased, and confrontations with the British grew more often and more deadly, the pressure that one had to pick a side, so to speak, was felt more keenly by those who wished to steer clear of any and all confrontation and those whose beliefs prevented them from supporting violent conflicts. However, to do so meant being viewed and often targeted as a loyalist to the Crown.

The Drinker family were Quakers. The Society of Friends, or Quakers, grew out of England in the 1600s and found themselves persecuted for beliefs that did not align with the Church of England. On March 4, 1681, King Charles II signed the charter of Pennsylvania and the noted writer and thinker William Penn brought the religion—and a refreshing brand of religious tolerance—to what became the colony of *Penn*sylvania, named for Penn's father, Admiral William Penn.

Many Quakers followed, as did Anglicans, Catholics, Jews, Lutherans, Presbyterians, Methodists, Moravians, Amish, and Mennonites. They all found a home in Philadelphia by the mid-eighteenth century. Muslims had been in North America since the 1500s, though many of them were enslaved and forced to convert to Christianity.

The early eighteenth century also saw the first of what would become four Great Awakenings in America's religious history, often characterized by a more evangelical approach to worship, a renewed focus on the importance of religion in general, and the appearance of new denominations.

Beginning in the 1730s and '40s, the Awakening had a strong impact on Protestant religious groups, and Baptist and Methodist faiths attracted many converts. The New Light Baptists were a part of this new wave of religious thought and practices that embraced a more fervent way of worshipping God. Prayer meetings and services were more ardently attended. The New Light Baptists exhibited a zealous approach to their relationship with God, an invoking of their spirituality. The Great Awakening came with expanded roles for women as well. It was not unusual for women to preach as well as attend services. Piety, evangelism, and impassioned displays of devotion enraptured those in North America, where freedom of religion felt akin to freedom, period.

Quakers did not believe in religious rituals. And they rejected war on principle, though with every passing day it felt to inhabitants of the colony as if war was coming and nothing could stand in its way.

Though the Society of Friends was populous and strong in Philadelphia, its members nevertheless encountered persecution in the burgeoning metropolis as trouble continued erupting up and down the East Coast of North America.

Quakers believed that an Inner Light, as opposed to the literal translation or interpretation of religious texts by a religious intermediary, could guide them to a direct connection to God. This was a time for questioning in America—questioning one's way of life, questioning the government, questioning the motives of one's friends and associates—and asserting one's relationship to whomever they envisioned and believed their God to be.

Stand fast therefore in the liberty wherewith Christ has made us free, and be not entangled again with the yoke of bondage.
—Galatians 5:1

The walk through the night was perilous and exhausting, but it was one Mary was determined to make as many times as she needed to. She trekked onward for ten miles, her infant child strapped to her back. The only shadows were cast by moonlight and the ever-present specter of capture. Though still enslaved, every time Mary wandered off into the backwoods, she preached to others of the gospel, liberation, and independence. The latter word was used frequently in the early 1770s but rarely applied across the entire spectrum of humanity.

Religion—whether Quaker, New Light Baptist, or other—was a driving force for individuals, no matter their race, gender, age, or size of their pocketbook. In the face of ongoing abuse, some people like Mary sought solace in spirituality, and others sought freedom in the wild. Those largely undiscovered corners of North America could feel at once hidden and foreboding and yet welcoming. The murky mire of the Great Dismal Swamp offered all of this to those who dared populate it.

Lying outside of Norfolk, and straddling the colonies of Virginia and neighboring North Carolina, the Great Dismal Swamp's name belied the sanctuary it had provided refugees since long before the establishment of any royal government. Humans had dwelled in the swamp and surrounding area for at least 6,000 years. The region had been the precolonial lands of the Nansemond. Other Indigenous communities looked upon the overall region as a destination for trade. People of the Iroquois, Muscogee, and Algonquin tribes, members of the Powhatan Confederacy, and others all converged there to share goods and information.

In time, of course, colonists encroached and settlers spread around areas outside the swamp. The landed gentry of Virginia and North Carolina craved even more territory. Many of those who sought liberty from these newcomers, or had been driven from their lands, turned inward to the Dismal Swamp in search of freedom and independence.

Native Americans, self-emancipated slaves, and free Black individuals seeking to evade a life of bondage burrowed deep into the Dismal Swamp to carve out a life. This land, entwined with thorns and briars growing over a floor of peat and beneath a ceiling of sky obscured by the overgrowth of time, became a sanctuary. The swamp provided the opportunity for *petit marronage*, an important form of resistance by means of escape. The Dismal Swamp represented a haven for those who did not want to be found. Individuals in the swamp formed their own communities and economies. In the swamp they self-emancipated. In the swamp they evaded enslavement. In the swamp they sought to regain an autonomy of life that had been wrested from them. In the swamp they were free.

In these days, the Dismal Swamp was vast, estimated to have sprawled some 20,000 acres. Swamp "islands"—land that was suitable to live upon, farm, and erect small abodes—dotted its interior. Some islands were as large as twenty acres, resting amid the mire. Here these "maroons"—free, enslaved, Indigenous, and indentured people—carved out their own way of life. They cleared their own trees and brush; they grew their own food and resources; they constructed their own homes. Of course, a place so oddly idyllic, a refuge, could never remain completely untouched by white settlers with money. And the swamp eventually attracted the attention of a thirty-one-year-old Virginia planter, surveyor, and Seven Years' War veteran by the name of George Washington.

In 1763, this land speculator and investor, along with Fielding Lewis, Burwell Bassett, and other associates, formed the "Adventurers for Draining the Dismal Swamp." This, the company's original moniker—and perhaps the least enticing business appellation ever conceived—described the company's objectives. The name was later shortened to the equally unappealing "Dismal Swamp Land Company." The General Assembly of Virginia sanctioned the endeavor. Each shareholder agreed to provide at least five enslaved individuals to clear the land. Newly created canals would transport felled trees destined for lumber, and the newly razed land would be slated for eventual farming. Those forced to work at the swamp were transported to an encampment called "Dismal Town" and began digging what became known as the "Washington Ditch." And so what was once a haven for the evicted, dejected, enslaved, threatened, and independent now became a labor camp.

But where colonists, plantation owners, and investors saw a business opportunity, Mary saw a congregation in need of spiritual uplifting.

In 1768, roughly five years after the plan to drain and clear the swamp had begun, Mary was enslaved to a man named John Willoughby of Norfolk. The Willoughby family had resided in the area and been amply landed since the 1600s. They had participated in civic and religious organizations, served as members of the Virginia House of Burgesses, and in the 1750s helped George Washington recruit a local militia. Mary became one of dozens of enslaved people on the Willoughby property. In her late twenties to early thirties, when she began what would become an on-again, off-again ministry, she was already a mother to Patience, who would soon have two younger sisters, Hannah and Zilpha, all of whom entered this world in bondage.

Willoughby's wife gifted Mary with a copy of the New Testament. As Mary learned to read that Bible, she felt the spiritual movement known as the First Great Awakening taking hold in the colonies—and beginning to awaken something in her as well. The presence of traveling preachers increased. But the kind of traveling and preaching Mary eventually practiced was driven by more than piety alone.

The Great Awakening had brought the Methodist faith into Mary's life, and she sought to share it with others. Those residing in the Dismal Swamp may have been called "maroons," but they were not alone. Now, in the early 1770s, when Mary was a mother of three, she routinely hiked ten miles to the swamp to deliver her sermons and ten miles back to the Willoughby property, her infant daughter Zilpha strapped to her back the entire time. Patience and Hannah remained in the Willoughby house during Mary's preaching sojourns into the Dismal.

The freedom the Lord promised in Galatians, amplified by Mary's voice, was embraced by the inhabitants of the *marronage*. It might someday be theirs—and hers as well.

In 1774, Mary Katharine Goddard was yet again taking over the reins of an established newspaper. This was not the first time she found herself running a print shop and bearing the myriad responsibilities that went along with it. And with each venture into print media, she was inserting herself ever more predominantly into what was already a lengthy history of women in publishing in America.

In 1762, after the death of Mary Katharine's father, Giles, her mother, Sarah Updike Goddard, relocated the family from New London, Connecticut, to Providence, Rhode Island. There, Sarah funded Mary Katharine's younger brother, William, to establish and run a print shop and newspaper. Twenty-four-year-old Mary Katharine worked for the newspaper alongside her younger brother and mother. Just three years later, in 1765, William ceased publication of the newspaper due to lackluster subscriptions and headed to Philadelphia to start another enterprise. After his departure, Mary Katharine and her mother, Sarah, took over the remaining operations at the print shop in Providence.

A woman running a print shop or newspaper was not an isolated incident in the colonies. As with many trades, one's participation in a particular business was often a result of familial connections, and sometimes—as in Sarah Goddard's case—a result of a spouse's death.

Elizabeth Timothy became the first female publisher of a newspaper in America when she took over publication of Charles Town's *South-Carolina Gazette* in 1739 after the death of her husband, Lewis. She continued working with Timothy's publishing partner, Benjamin Franklin, who thought Elizabeth ran the press better than Lewis had. Hallmarks of her performance were "regularity and exactitude." Franklin later wrote that she "managed the business with such success that she not only brought up reputably a family of children but at the expiration of her term was able to purchase of me the printing house and establish her son to it." She also did not abide past due accounts—before or after her husband's passing—once warning that "Persons will be employ'd" to collect monies from those subscribers who owed "from three to eight years."

But she was not the first woman to oversee a press. In the early 1640s, Elizabeth Harris Glover established the first printing press in the colonies after her husband, Joseph, died during the crossing from England. She remarried to Henry Dunster, first president of Harvard, and upon her death the press went to the school, and the Harvard University Press was born.

After the death of her husband, James, in 1735, Ann Smith Franklin took over his press—the first in Rhode Island—and became the official printer of the General Assembly of that colony, among other jobs. She printed novels, currency, broadsides, and more. She expanded the business's collection of type ornaments and ran the press alongside her daughters for more than ten years. Her son, James Jr., apprenticed with his uncle Benjamin Franklin in Philadelphia before returning to Rhode Island.

In the 1760s, Anne Catharine Hoof Green of Annapolis took up her husband Jonas's press upon his death. Jonas's business partner, William Rind, moved on to Williamsburg. And after his death, his wife, Clementina, took over publication of the *Virginia Gazette*. She published her own thoughts on the day, as well as those of others.

And these are but a few of the women who made their mark—literally, in ink—in the American press.

One year after her son William's departure, in 1766, "Sarah Goddard & Co." rebooted *The Providence Gazette and Country Journal*—"containing the Freshest Advices, both Foreign and Domestic"—with Mary Katharine at her side. In addition to the newspaper, the pair published leaflets, broadsides, and almanacs. That first year the *Journal* also printed the letters of poet and writer Lady Mary Wortley Montagu. It was the first known American edition of that collection.

The Goddard women also added a bindery and a bookstore to their growing media business. They remained in Providence until 1768, when they moved to Philadelphia to help William, who had launched a fresh endeavor, *The Pennsylvania Chronicle, and Universal Advertiser*.

Though William's name was emblazoned on the newspaper's masthead, Mary Katharine and Sarah took on the bulk of responsibilities during William's frequent absences. Two years after moving to Philadelphia, in 1770, Sarah Goddard died, and Mary Katharine's responsibilities—and abilities—as a publisher continued to grow. She was in charge whenever William was gone, which was often, and she remained in Philadelphia at the helm of the *Chronicle* when William departed for Baltimore, Maryland, to launch yet another publication.

In November 1772, William Goddard announced *The Maryland Journal, and the Baltimore Advertiser*,

> *to be printed in four large Folio Pages, equal in size to any of the Pennsylvania papers, at the moderate Price of TEN SHILLINGS, current Money, per Annum . . . Subscriptions are taken in at the Coffee Houses in Baltimore-Town and Annapolis . . .*

Goddard's printing office sat at the corner of South and Market Streets, "nearly opposite to Mrs. Chilton's in Baltimore-town," Chilton being one of countless female innkeepers who helped keep the colonies running. Baltimore was a port city and, though not as populous as Philadelphia, enjoyed access to nearby farmland as well as the Atlantic. As such, it became a boomtown for flour, with mills popping up in surrounding areas and warehouses sprouting near the wharves.

Now, less than two years after the debut of *The Maryland Journal, and the Baltimore Advertiser*, Mary Katharine was again taking over the day-to-day publication reins from her brother.

Her name was not yet on the masthead of *The Maryland Journal*, but that would soon change. And Mary Katharine's move to Baltimore would prove to be an auspicious one for the gifted printer and businesswoman. Though probably underappreciated by William, Mary Katharine Goddard's talents and reliability would not go unnoticed by others in the colonies, and she would soon be tasked with the greatest printing job of her career.

Hostilities continued to escalate everywhere, and there was much news to print. In March of 1774, the Coercive (or "Intolerable") Acts effectively closed the port of Boston. Troops were quartered in the homes of residents. The Crown was now completely in charge, Boston held hostage. The move alarmed residents up and down the coast.

Williamsburg, Virginia, printer Clementina Rind took to her *Virginia Gazette* and wrote that this "illegal and unwarrantable act of parliament . . . principally aimed against the Bostonians, whose patriotic conduct on so interesting an occasion deserves the highest applause, will not, it is hoped, quell their free spiring, now the storm is beginning, and more especially as there are so many united colonies to protect her at so critical a juncture."

From her home in Plymouth, Massachusetts, Mercy Otis Warren's writings continued to evolve along with the times. Her lines about domesticity and love had morphed into satirical missives and patriotic diatribes, though usually anonymously. Mercy's fluid and muscular prose led many to assume her work was written by a man. In 1772, her play *The Adulateur*, which ridiculed the governor, appeared in *The Massachusetts Spy*. A play titled *The Defeat* followed in 1773. Her pen attacked women as well, especially those who wore "fripperies" and other fashions that had clearly arrived from English shores.

Colonists were deciding how they were going to respond to this latest aggressive act of His Majesty's government. That summer, twelve of the thirteen colonies (all but Georgia) chose representatives to send to the First Continental Congress, convening in Philadelphia, where flags adorning the masts of ships in the harbor flew at half-mast and church bells were muffled. Among those heading to Philadelphia were John and Samuel Adams, the latter of whom encouraged Mercy to continue to let the politically charged venom spill from her pen. She clearly had his ear.

"Though you have condescended to ask my sentiments . . . to advise at this important crisis," she wrote before the pair set off for the inaugural congressional gathering in September, "I shall not be so presumptuous as to offer anything but my fervent wishes that the enemies of America may hereafter for ever tremble at the wisdom and firmness, the prudence and justice of the delegates . . ."

As Congress convened, tea protests continued up and down the East Coast, in New York, Maine, Annapolis, Charleston, and elsewhere.

In New York, the ship *London* sailed to Sandy Hook, in New Jersey, helmed by one Captain James Chambers. Claiming there was no tea on board, the crew of the *London* was allowed to make its way up to Murray's Wharf at the tail end of Wall Street. When Captain Chambers eventually revealed he did in fact did have tea, mobs boarded the *London*, pouncing upon and dumping its tea in the harbor.

Shortly after, near the shore of the bay in Annapolis, a man named Anthony Stewart, owner of the brig *Peggy Stewart*, burned his ship to the waterline, vainly hoping to appease citizens incensed by the seventeen boxes of tea he sought to import and by the requisite duties associated with them.

As Boston's harbor continued to float at a standstill thanks to the

Intolerable Acts, other colonies did what they could to help. North Carolina answered the need by shipping their own supplies of food to the beleaguered city. But protest came in other forms as well.

In Edenton, North Carolina, women took action of an entirely different kind. They dared to put their intentions, their resolves, and their names in print for all to read—including those on the other side of the Atlantic.

Penelope Barker, it is believed, approached her friend Elizabeth King with an idea: bring together fifty-one members of the Edenton Ladies' Patriotic Guild at Elizabeth's home to put their frustration with the Crown in writing.

The daughter of a prominent Edenton doctor, Penelope had married her sister's widower, John Hodgson, at seventeen and helped raise their three children. She was preparing to have a second child of her own when John, too, died. At twenty-one, Penelope was now a widow with five children, and money was tight. But her second marriage (to planter James Craven) and subsequent second widowhood made her one of the wealthiest women in North Carolina. At twenty-eight, the twice-widowed Penelope married Thomas Barker. He was often away, serving as a representative of the colony's Assembly in London. Penelope did not sit idly by.

The document the women of Edenton ultimately signed may have been written and circulated by Barker, or may have been signed at the gathering that some say Penelope organized.

In any case, a document was indeed produced and the fifty-one women who signed the resolution, dated October 27, 1774, saw their names in print, first in *The Virginia Gazette* on November 3:

> *As we cannot be indifferent on any occasion that appears nearly to affect the peace and happiness of our country, and as it has been thought necessary, for the public good, to enter into several particular resolves by a meeting of Members deputed from the whole Province, it is a duty which we owe, not only to our near and dear connections who have concurred in them, but to ourselves who are essentially interested in their welfare, to do everything as far as lies*

*in our power to testify our sincere adherence to the same; and we
do therefore accordingly subscribe this paper, as a witness of our
fixed intention and solemn determination to do so.*

England's *Morning Chronicle and London Advertiser* printed the document in its January 1775 edition, along with an excerpt from an introductory letter, the author of which is unknown:

*The provincial deputies of North Carolina, having resolved not to
drink any more tea, nor wear any British cloth &c., many ladies of
this province have determined give a memorable proof of their patriotism, and have, accordingly, entered into the following honourable and spirited association. I send it to you to show our fair
countrywomen how zealously and faithfully American ladies follow the laudable example of their husbands and what opposition
your matchless ministers may expect to receive from a people thus
firmly united against them.*

The daring women eventually saw their actions ridiculed across the pond. Two months after, in March 1775, a cartoon skewering the tea party titled "A Society of Patriotic Ladies, at Edenton in North Carolina" appeared in London and featured its own version of the re-solves:

*We the Ladys of Edenton do hereby solemnly Engage not to
Conform to that Pernicious Custom of Drinking Tea, or
that we the aforesaid Ladies, will not promote ye wear of
any Manufacture from England, untill such time that all
Acts which tend to Enslave this our Native Country shall be
Repealed . . .*

The satirical print depicted women signing documents, one such individual laid out on the signing table appearing to canoodle with a man, while others gulp out of enormous bowls and an enslaved person carries ink and quill on a tray. As for Penelope, she presides over the gathering, seated with a gavel in hand, depicted as a North Carolinian female King George. A dog lifts its leg near her feet.

A protest of a different sort came from Hartford, Connecticut, where the "Ladies of Hartford" published a list of resolves of their own, taking aim at the fashion industry, discussing everything from gewgaws to muslin—but not tea.

The style of their declaration starts with some measure of sarcasm and wit but grows increasingly angry. By the end, you know that they mean business. In many households, women continued to wield the enormous power of the purse. And they knew it.

RESOLUTIONS OF THE LADIES OF HARTFORD.

The Ladies in this City, attentive to the impoverished state of their Country, and to the well-founded charge of extravagance in our manner of living, offer to their sisters in this State the following considerations:—

1. *We consider it as a general truth, that the manners and fashions of every country should be adapted to its particular situation and circumstances.*

2. *We believe that the English and French fashions, which require the manufacture of an infinite variety of gewgaws and frippery, may be highly beneficial and even necessary in the countries where those articles are made; as they furnish employment and subsistence for poor people.*

3. *We believe, also, that it is very politic in foreign nations to introduce their fashions into this country, as they thus make a market for their useless manufactures, and enrich themselves at our expense.*

4. *But we are of the opinion, at the same time, that our implicit submission to the fashions of other countries is highly derogatory to the reputation of Americans, as it renders us dependent*

on the interest, or caprice, of foreigners, both for taste and manners; it prevents the exercise of our own ingenuity, and makes us the slaves of the milliners and mantua-makers in London or Paris.

5. *We consider, also, that this servile imitation of foreign fashions is one of the circumstances which operate to embarrass and distress this country.*

6. *We also consider many of the fashions which now prevail among us as in many respects extremely inconvenient, and consequently as proceeding from a false taste in dress, or a total want of taste.*

7. *We are of opinion that an attention to industry and economy, among all ages and ranks of people, is an infinitely better way to promote the prosperity, and to relieve the distresses, of this country, than quarreling with laws, debts, and courts of justice.*

Convinced of these truths, and desirous of silencing all complaints of extravagance, and of contributing all in our power to deliver the country from this slavery of fashions, and the consequent expenses and embarrassments, we subscribe to the following Articles:

ART. 1. *That after the signing of these articles, we will not purchase, or wear, any superfluous articles of dress, such as gauze, ribbons, flowers, feathers, lace, and other timings and frippery, designed merely as ornaments.*

ART. 2. *That we will not purchase the richer kinds of articles which are used as necessary dress; such as silks, muslins, expensive hats, &c., except a single suit for a wedding, or for mourning; but that for the future we will eat on visits, and in public places, such articles only as we have on hand, or newly purchased calicoes and other cheap articles, without ornaments or trimmings.*

ART. 3. *That we will endeavor to retrench the expenses of visits and entertainments, by not suffering them to interrupt*

> *our attention to industry, by reducing the number and*
> *price of the articles which furnish our tables, and partic-*
> *ularly by giving the preference to such articles of provision*
> *as our own country supplies.*
>
> ART. 4 *That we will not attend a public or private Assembly of-*
> *tener than once in three weeks.*
>
> ART. 5. *That we will use our influence to diffuse an attention to*
> *industry and frugality, and to render these virtues repu-*
> *table and permanent.*
>
> *Conscious to ourselves that our intentions are laudable, and*
> *calculated to secure the reputations, the morals, the prosperity, and*
> *the social happiness of our Country, we shall pay no regard to any*
> *reflections, or ridicule, that may be cast upon our conduct; but now*
> *pledge ourselves to each other and to the world, that we will carry*
> *these resolutions into practice.*

As the year 1774 drew to an end, tea and frippery would be eschewed by patriots seeking to ensure their idea of freedom. For her part, Mercy Otis Warren wrote, "When I took up my pen I determined to leave the field of politicks to those whose proper busines it is to speculate and to act at this important crisis; but the occurrences that have lately taken place are so alarming and the subject so interwoven with the enjoyments of social and domestic life as to command the attention of the mother and the wife . . ." She desired America to have an "equitable base," and wrote: "Though such an happy state, such an equal government, may be considered by some as an Utopian dream; yet you and I can easily conceive of nations and states rising to the highest consequence under more liberal plans than are pointed out by the marble-hearted despots of ancient or modern times."

The year 1775 would put these and all other patriotic sentiments to the bloodiest of tests.

CHAPTER 5

War Comes to All

A black Boston night saw two young lovers on a clandestine journey, fleeing their home, their business, and their families. Their destination was the patriot encampment just across the Charles River in Cambridge, but that made the trek no less perilous.

Lucy had sewn Henry's sword into his cloak in preparation for their escape. It was spring 1775, and a conflict that some still hoped might be avoided had erupted and lit the Massachusetts Bay Colony afire. Lucy was determined to stand by her husband, their destiny precarious.

The Flucker family had not envisioned this future for their daughter, and Lucy probably hadn't either. The shapely, dark-eyed eighteen-year-old was the daughter of Thomas Flucker, whom King George had appointed secretary of the province of Massachusetts. Her mother, Hannah, stood to inherit large swaths of land in the wilds of an area of the continent called Maine. The family lived in a town house on Summer Street in Boston, and Lucy's was a life of servants, fine clothing, and well-appointed parlors with imported European furnishings. Growing up in this staunchly loyalist Boston family, Lucy had been destined to marry someone at or above her station—certainly not a bookstore owner. But the bold and independent Lucy had other ideas and had set her sights on a very different sort of man.

The 1771 announcement had read, "This day is opened a new London Bookstore by Henry Knox, opposite Williams' Court in Cornhill, Boston, who has just imported in the last ships from London a large and very elegant assortment of the most modern books in all branches of Literature, Arts, and Sciences (catalogues of which will be published soon), and to be sold as cheap as can be bought at any place in town. Also a complete assortment of stationery."

Henry Knox was just twenty-one years old when he opened his bookstore, which boasted eclectic offerings for every kind of reader. He was the son of Scots immigrants, and Henry's shipwright father had left the family when Henry was just nine years old. This forced Henry's hasty departure from his studies at Boston Latin School. He took an apprenticeship with bookbinders Wharton & Bowes, which pleased the bright and bookish young man. The apprenticeship led to a job, and Henry eventually went into business for himself.

What Henry lacked in traditional schooling he would more than make up for with his voracious appetite for the written word and the countless publications in which he buried himself every day. The well-read bookshop owner had a particular fondness for volumes on artillery and engineering, but as the ad announcing the opening of his store claimed, his shop carried pamphlets, manuals, stationery, and literary diversions for all flavors of readers: *A Catalogue of Books, Imported and to be Sold by Henry Knox, at the London Book-Store, a little Southward of the Town-House, in Cornell, Boston, MDCCLXXIII*, featured everything from *Ambrose's War with the Devil* and *Art of Cookery Made Plain and Easy* to *Letter to the Ladies on the Preservation of Health and Beauty*.

There were works full of poems and Plutarch, philosophy and physics. Books such as *Sharpe's Military Guide*, 1767's *The History and Present State of Electricity*, astronomy texts, and Bibles for the penitent. His catalogue boasted "a large Assortment of Books for the Amusement and Instruction of Children, Seamen's Books of all Kinds, A Variety of Charts, Mapps, &c."

Scanning the catalogue lends credence to some historical evidence that literacy rates in colonial America were quite high. Henry imported—and fully expected to sell—books such as the ever popular *A Dissertation on the Gout, and All Chronic Diseases, Jointly Considered, As proceeding from the same Causes; What those Causes are; AND A rational and natural Method of Cure proposed. Addressed to all Inva-*

lids, by William Cadogan, College of Physicians (offered in England for one shilling and six pence), and the curiously titled *A New Lecture on Heads* by George Alexander Stevens, a comic actor, playwright, and more, which satirized the popular face-reading fad. Both publications had been reprinted for Henry for sale in the colonies.

Knox's catalogue offered items for those who wanted to fill pages as well as peruse them: "Makes and Binds Waste Books, Journals, Ledgers, and all other sorts of Blank Books at the shortest notice. Also Sells Books in all Languages, Arts, and Sciences, Stationary, &c. &c."

Indeed, if one sought slates, pencils, Dutch quills, gold leaf for bookbinders, sealing wax and wafers, Knox's bookstore was the place to go.

British soldiers posted in Boston and ladies of the Tory persuasion frequented Henry's shop as well. Soon, too, so did young Lucy Flucker, whose love of books led her to the newish bookstore in Boston's Cornhill neighborhood.

Henry's fascination with and appreciation of military matters extended beyond the door of his shop. A year after opening his business, in 1772, Henry enlisted in the local militia—as was expected of men his age. Militias were a common and necessary part of life in the colonies. Originally a part of a militia called the Train, he then helped found the Boston Grenadier Corps, soon rising to the unit's second-in-command. Militias trained regularly, sometimes on Boston Common, and exercises might involve mock battles, perhaps against the imaginary French. In 1773, Henry and the other Grenadiers paraded the streets of Boston, and Lucy took note of the bracing, stocky man, who stood well over six feet tall.

Soon, bookstore visits led to clandestine coffeeshop encounters and letters laced with professions of love and longing.

Correspondence at the time was ferried back and forth by post, by friends, and often, in Lucy's case, by someone in her family's employ.

"To the Coffee house tomorrow evening?" Henry wrote Lucy. "Or is it only like the banter affixed at the head of your letter? N-N-N-No . . . Let me hear from or see you. I could write a volume to you, but I write so much in a hurry as your woman is waiting, that you could not read. God have you in his kind protection is the desire of your Harry Knox . . ."

The pair had to keep their burgeoning love under wraps. Lucy hailed from a family with an inflexible loyalty to the Crown. Her father, Thomas Flucker, Esq., was against the match. Her brother, Thomas, with whom she was quite close, was a captain in the British Army. Lucy's sister Hannah, on the other hand, supported the pair. Marrying Henry Knox, one of ten children, the son of Scotch-Irish immigrants, would mean marrying below Lucy's class. A union with another wealthy family was Lucy's presumed lot in life. But the whip-smart, vivacious young lady was smitten by the industrious Henry, and he was beside himself wondering what might become of their seemingly doomed devotion.

Many more of Henry's letters survive than Lucy's, but he wrote so frequently that we can often surmise the context of her letters from his responses. Sometimes, it seems, he simply lost himself to passion:

"Every particle of heat seems to be eradicated from the head, or else entirely absorbed in the widely raging fire emitted from the heart . . . [T]o tell you how much I long to see you would be impossible . . ." Henry wrote in March of 1774. "What news? Have you spoken to your father, or he to you on the subject?" The subject, of course, was the pair's desire to marry.

". . . My love is, as it were, in its infancy," Henry wrote. "It will increase to youth, it will arrive at the most perfect manhood, it will grow with such a steady brightness that if the youth of both sexes do not esteem it their chiefest glory to come and light their tapers at it, want of discernment must be the reason."

But later that year, true love conquered (almost) all. An announcement spelled out the details:

"Last Thursday (the 16th), was married, by the Rev. Dr. Caner, Mr. Henry Knox of this town, to Miss Lucy Flucker, second daughter to the Hon. Thomas Flucker, Esq., Secretary of the Province." Lucy's parents declined to attend.

And so Lucy, a privileged daughter of Boston, eschewed the comforts of her upper-echelon life, abandoned her family and social circles, all for a working-class bookseller who decided to enlist in the very rebellion against the Crown that her family hoped would be quashed.

She paid a price for her choice. What Lucy knew of wealth, privilege, and family were gone. The couple lived in Henry's rented town house. Henry was her family, her life, now. And she, his.

As Henry grew more committed to the patriot cause, he did not shy away from offering what might have rubbed some of his military clientele the wrong way. In early 1775, his bookstore advertised the sale of a controversial pamphlet in *The Boston-Gazette* that sought to defend Congress's stance against British policies. Titled *The Farmer Refuted... Intended as a Further Vindication of the Congress*, it was the second publication penned by a recently arrived immigrant from the Caribbean. Thanks to the generosity of others, this young man with a mysterious past was able to attend King's College in New York (now Columbia University), where his fervor for independence grew. He wrote of Boston being a victim of vengeance. He applauded the colonies banding together as a result.

"Had the rest of America passively looked on, while a sister colony was subjugated," he wrote, "the same fate would gradually have overtaken all. The safety of the whole depends upon the mutual protection of every part. If the sword of oppression be permitted to lop off one limb without opposition, reiterated strokes will soon dismember the whole body."

The young man relished sharing his sentiments with whoever would listen, and Henry Knox gladly distributed them. The young man was becoming a force in work and action in the burgeoning revolt, and before long many would know his name: Alexander Hamilton.

"Is there no hope that the Dread Calamity of Civil Convulsions may yet be Averted, or must the Blood of the Best Citizens be poured out to Glut the Vengeance of the most Worthless and Wicked men Ever Nursed in the Lap of America," Mercy wrote to John Adams on April 4, 1775, from her home in Plymouth. "You Cannot Wonder sir at my perticuler anxiety and solicitude to know the sentiments of the judicious as Mr. Warren is Absent and in such a Remote quarter that I have not heard from him ..."

Within days, James, embroiled in patriot business, wrote her from Lexington. He missed her. He missed the children. He longed "to sit with you under our Vines etc and have none to make us afraid." He promised to "fly" home "as Prudence Duty and Honour will permitt."

Within weeks, events intervened that upended the lives of everyone across the colonies, and Mercy's question about the shedding of the "blood of the best citizens" was violently answered.

For many residents of Massachusetts and beyond, the events of April 19, though disheartening and foreboding, were hardly surprising. By then the possibility of reconciliation between the colonies and the Crown seemed a dim and distant one. Though the April incident felt a long time coming, no one could have anticipated just how those events unfolded, nor the repercussions they would have up and down the coast and across the Atlantic. Indeed, few were prepared for the fallout.

Massachusetts was considered by the Crown to be in a state of open rebellion. Commander in chief of the British North American forces, General Thomas Gage, was under orders to quell it.

On April 18, roughly seven hundred British soldiers ferried across the Charles River Basin from Back Bay Boston to Cambridge and marched toward the town of Concord, twenty miles or so northwest of Boston. The patriot colonists had a stash of supplies and ammunition there, and the British aimed to seize it.

"The People in the Country (who are all furnished with Arms & have what they call Minute Companys in every Town ready to march on any alarm), had a signal it's supposed by a light from one of the Steeples in Town, Upon the Troops embarkg," loyalist Ann Hulton would write after the event. "The alarm spread thro' the Country, so that before daybreak the people in general were in Arms & on their March to Concord."

That signal, two lanterns in the steeple of Christ Church, were indeed lit that evening of April 18. Alarm riders set out, tearing through the areas surrounding Boston to warn all of the British march toward Concord.

Paul Revere, William Dawes, and Samuel Prescott were among those riders. Revere, a silver- and goldsmith, engraver of copper plates, and fashioner of the occasional set of dentures from walrus ivory, crossed over the Mystic River via the bridge bearing that name and galloped through the town of Medford. His route took him down Main Street and High Street, passing Sarah and David Fulton's home. He stopped to alert Isaac Hall, captain of the Medford minutemen. His ride also took him past the home of Isaac Royall. The loyalist—and many others like him—had fled three days earlier. Revere called upon militia and warned houses along the way. Legend would later virtually cement the idea that Revere alone raised the alarm. But, though key, he was not the only one. As the alert spread, riders joined, warning neighbors of the impending arrival of British forces.

It appears that the patriots had had more than just an evening's notice of British intent. As for the desired munitions stash at Concord, Massachusetts, most of the supplies had already been moved. Some believed that an early warning came from General Gage's own American-born wife, Margaret, who had previously said she "hoped her husband would never be the instrument of sacrificing the lives of her countrymen." Whether or not she leaked the intelligence, a chain reaction of impassioned riders did the rest, tapping on windows, rapping on doors.

On the way to Concord, as the nineteenth of April dawned, the British found themselves confronted in the nearby town of Lexington, surrounded by more than seventy members of the militia.

Among them were a number of Indigenous and Black patriots, enslaved, indentured, and free, answering the call. Among them was Caesar Ferrit, an immigrant of African, Indigenous, French, and Dutch descent; Peter Salem of the Framingham minutemen had grown up enslaved, and was freed in order to fight; and Massachusetts's "Stockbridge Indian Company" stood alongside those white militiamen and against the British. (The Mohicans had formally aligned with the Continental Congress a year earlier.)

Fighting men of Britain and Massachusetts faced each other. Though the leaders of both sides ordered their men not to fire, someone somewhere in that stewing tension did just that. What eventually became known as the Revolutionary War had begun. After this history-changing confrontation, eight Americans were dead and one

British wounded. Standing on that green was Prince Estabrook, an enslaved man of Lexington, who took a musket ball to the shoulder.

The fighting at Lexington did not stop the British, and the troops marched on to their ultimate destination: Concord. There, more than four hundred colonists greeted His Majesty's troops, among them Private Sampson Yearney, a free Black man of Medford.

Experiencing more resistance than they likely anticipated, the British turned back to Boston, musket fire chasing them down along a sixteen-mile route that became known as Battle Road. From the junction of Bedford and Lexington Roads and then east toward Boston, they were beset on all sides at places like the Bloody Angle.

"In the road indeed in our rear, they were most numerous, and came on pretty close, frequently calling out, 'King Hancock forever,'" said Lieutenant Frederick Mackenzie of the Royal Welch Fusiliers.

The towns of Woburn. Reading. Hartwell. Shots came from inside homes, through windows, from among trees, and from behind stone walls as the colonials—organized militia, women, and more—appeared at every turn and descended upon the British. The Hartwell Tavern, an inn frequented by many along Bay Road, saw the British come and go, passing by the popular stopover.

"Even Weamin had firelocks," a British officer would later write. "One was seen to fire a Blunder bus between her Father, and Husband from their Windows . . ."

The militia pursued the British back to Boston, where they arrived at a well-defended position on Bunker Hill. By that time, more than 1,500 British soldiers and nearly 4,000 colonial militia had become embroiled in the fighting. But more were on their way.

Colonials streamed in from throughout Massachusetts and New Hampshire. From within Boston, British general Gage now watched as campfire after campfire was lit on the surrounding hills. The rebels were digging in.

Residents watched with growing dread of what might come next.

Loyalist Ann Hulton remained in Massachusetts, where she had lived roughly eight years since arriving from England. Her hopes of starting her own business or buying land seemed increasingly dashed as unrest and violence grew in the city around her. She wrote a friend describing the beginnings of the Siege of Boston that she saw unfolding around her:

> *At this time from the entrance of Boston Neck at Roxbury round by Cambridge to Charlestown is surrounded by at least 20,000 Men, who are raising batteries on three or four different Hills. We are now cut off from all communication with the Country & many people must soon perish with famine in this place . . .*
>
> *For several nights past, I have expected to be roused by the firing of Cannon.*

Individuals on both sides of the Atlantic had sought to avoid this. A gout-ridden William Pitt, "the Elder," Right Honourable Earl of Chatham and former prime minister, had traveled to England to speak to the House of Lords. A popular statesman and Whig, Pitt's address was a passionate and lengthy one, which when printed was titled "The speech, of the Right Honourable the Earl of Chatham, in the House of Lords, January 20th, 1775. On a motion for an address to His Majesty, to give immediate order for removing his troops from Boston forthwith, in order to quiet the minds and take away the apprehensions of his good subjects in America." Present that day was American Josiah Quincy Jr., whose papers recounted the fervent discourse:

> *My Lords there is no time to be lost: every moment is big with dangers. Nay, while I am now speaking the decisive blow may be struck, and millions are involved in the consequence. The very first drop of blood will make a wound, that will not easily be skinned over. Years, perhaps ages, may not heal it. It will be irritabile vulnus: A wound of that rancorous, malignant, corroding, festering nature, that in all probability it will mortify the whole body.*

Yet, while members of the militia throughout the area left to take up arms, the ones who stayed behind were left to fight their own battles.

Women and enslaved individuals toiled and tended to farms, businesses, homes, and children. So they mustered, in their own way, as well. Tending meant protecting lives and family from a war that knew no boundaries, that spared no soul.

The story that I have to tell
Is one that cannot vex;
It happened in old Pepperell,
In county Middlesex.

It was in Revolution days
The incident occurred;
Of those old times and stirring ways
You oftentimes have heard.

The women of that other time
Were brave as brave can be;
And one, the subject of this rhyme,
A heroine was she. . . .

Once the alarm rider passed through Pepperell, Massachusetts, on April 19, thirty-five-year-old Prudence Wright knew that her husband, David, five years her senior, would soon leave. He and the other men of Pepperell, nearby Groton, and elsewhere had begun training earlier that year for battles they thought might soon land at the doorstep of their communities, their homes, and their families.

Prudence had married David in 1761 and left her hometown of Hollis, just six miles to the north, over the border in New Hampshire. Pepperell sat just under forty miles northwest of Boston and twenty from Concord. Prudence and David lived in a house not far from the meandering Sucker Brook. Though the town was removed from the immediate hubbub and tensions surrounding Boston, the revolution was never far from anyone's mind.

Like many women of the time, ebony-eyed Prudence knew her way around a knitting needle and a spinning wheel and was a noted limner. If you needed a clothing pattern drawn, Prudence was the individual whose talents you sought out. The woods in and around Pepperell provided her with much in the way of foraging, including the wild sarsaparilla, which covered the ground, and sassafras trees rising overhead. Aromas emanating from sarsaparilla rhizomes and sassafras tree roots wafted throughout many a kitchen, where those simple ingredients, both long valued by the Indigenous peoples of the Northeast and much further afield, could be transformed by brewing and fermenting into root beers, which tempted the palate yet offered less alcohol than ale and less chance of the illness that might occur from drinking potentially contaminated groundwater.

Prudence was also handy with a mold—for utensils, yes, but also bullets. She and other women and children in town readied for war along with the men, molding bullets, preparing cartridges, and filling powder horns.

Pepperell was a strongly Whig-leaning area, but there were certainly Tories to be found as well. Residents had nicknamed one local watering hole "Tory Tavern" for its reputation as a drinking spot for loyalists. Prudence's hometown of Hollis, New Hampshire, had its share of Crown supporters, Prudence's own brothers among them.

Though the details of all that had transpired in Lexington and Concord had not yet arrived in town, David Wright and other members of the local militia mustered at Groton, their next destination as yet unknown. In the meantime, the women of Pepperell, Groton, Hollis, and other nearby rural communities vowed to resist anyone who might attempt to take their town while their husbands, fathers, and brothers were away. They chose to form their own militia, one that protected what they held most dear. They would stand guard as best they could. The woman they chose to command them was Prudence Wright.

This fresh responsibility came just over a month after Prudence lost her baby, Liberty, who had joined his sister Mary, the child Prudence had lost not quite a year earlier. But accept the charge she did, choosing Sarah Shattuck as her second-in-command. A number of other women, young and not so much so, would join them, including Susanna Quailes, wife of Groton's baker, and seventeen-year-old Elizabeth Hobart.

The men departed. More news arrived, this time whispers of a British messenger said to be on his way through the area, possibly carrying dispatches. Such a courier would have to cross the Nashua River. And Prudence and her guard knew just where.

> *They guarded bridge and forest wood—*
> *These women fair and slight;*
> *And for the right they ever stood,*
> *At morning, noon and night.*
>
> *. . . . .*
>
> *At Jewett's bridge they took their stand,*
> *And waited for the foe;*
> *They were a patriotic band,*
> *As any one might know . . .*

Prudence and the others grabbed their husbands' clothing and any muskets they had—pitchforks and the like if muskets were scarce—and made for the bridge. Darkness helped their cause. The curves of the road provided geographical camouflage: Any approaching riders would not see the bridge—or anyone guarding it—until they were upon it. Captain Leonard Whiting was one of those riders. He crossed, unaware of the troops awaiting him. Prudence and her guard surrounded Whiting, forced him to dismount, seized his horse, and searched him until they found papers in his boots.

From there the women escorted Whiting to a nearby tavern for safekeeping that night until local authorities could transport him to the Committee of Safety in Groton the next day. In 1899, Susan H. Wixon memorialized Wright's activities in *American Monthly Magazine*:

> *Their country's honor, in an hour*
> *Most serious and grave,*
> *Was thus upheld with grace and power,*
> *By women true and brave.*

And on the scroll where heroes' names
Appear in shining light;
With names our country proudly
claims,
Gleams that PRUDENCE WRIGHT.

Those who fought as minutemen or as British regulars, or formed their own ad hoc women's guards, inspired songs and poems and left vivid remembrances of their own. Among those was Lemuel Haynes, a Black man who had joined the minutemen of Granville, Massachusetts, in 1774. Shortly after the end of the war, Haynes became the first Black ordained minister in the United States.

Haynes wrote a lengthy poem in the weeks after his service at Lexington. It reads in part:

14

For Liberty each Freeman Strives
As its a Gift of God
And for it willing yield their Lives
And Seal it with their Blood

15

Thrice happy they who thus resign
Into the peacefull Grave
Much better there, in Death Confin'd
Than a Surviving Slave

16

This Motto may adorn their Tombs,
(Let tyrants come and view)
"We Rather Seek these silent Rooms
Than live as Slaves to You"

Whether by word of mouth, hoof, or post, news of the fighting spread well beyond Massachusetts. It had reached Bedford, New Hampshire, as soon as April 20. Expresses flew up and down the coast relating news of the bloodshed in Lexington and Concord.

On April 29, 1775, the Williamsburg, Virginia, Committee of Correspondence reported news arriving via express: "The blow . . . is now struck, a great deal of blood spilt, and much more, it is likely, that the present advices communicate . . ."

Mary Katharine Goddard unwittingly echoed the poem of Lemuel Haynes when addressing the events in *The Maryland Journal, and the Baltimore Advertiser*: "The ever memorable 19th of April gave a conclusive answer to the questions of American freedom. What think ye of Congress now? That day . . . evidenced that Americans would rather die than live slaves!"

In the aftermath of Lexington and Concord, Lucy and Henry made their cloaked escape from Boston. The British had already asked the military-minded Henry to join their ranks. When he refused, he became a wanted man under threat of arrest. Still, the pair could have stayed. Family, the comforts of home, wealth, Boston, and the role her relations played in it would likely have ensured their safety. But the couple would have none of it.

Lucy's new husband was concerned about her well-being and brought her to stay in Worcester, which he considered safer than his ultimate destination of Cambridge. Lucy had made her choice, and it was one for both love and country, one that would rend the fabric of her loyalist family and now separate her from her Henry.

Henry had made his choice as well. He was a bookseller no longer. At Cambridge he would present himself to Major General Artemas Ward and assume a post in the fast-growing military. His role in this new, upstart fighting force would expand more than he or Lucy could have imagined, impacting their lives forever.

CHAPTER 6

Of Loss and Loyalty

Events took on greater import and urgency after those April days. In May, patriots Benedict Arnold and Ethan Allen—along with his "Green Mountain Boys"—captured Fort Ticonderoga in New York, a significant early win for the burgeoning colonial forces. That same month, on May 10, the Continental Congress again convened in Philadelphia, and delegates streamed into that city in search of a place to stay. Throughout the colonies—and especially in hubs of commerce like Philadelphia—tavern keepers kept towns and cities running. On these congenial premises, ales were downed, plots were hatched, political discussions brewed. On the west side of Second Street, just north of Walnut, stood City Tavern, a frequent meeting place of delegates, whether conducting official business or tending to the business of libations. There was also the delightfully named A Man Full of Trouble Tavern and the Indian Queen Tavern. The Tun Tavern had stood in Philadelphia since 1693 and hosted the first meetings of Freemasons in the city. By the end of 1775, it would become the founding place of the United States Marine Corps.

These indispensable and multipurpose gathering places often hosted patrons for extended stays, offering more than food and lodging. An innkeeper was a de facto concierge, handling referrals to local services, collecting correspondence, and offering residents a place to entertain as well as lay their heads. Indeed, whenever Congress came to town, Philadelphia's inns had full beds and dining rooms, and a large number of the businesspeople running those establishments were women.

At the southwest corner of Fifth and Market Streets was an inn run by Mary House and her daughter, Eleanor Trist. Boarders there felt a part of Mrs. House's extended family, among them a Virginia planter and member of Congress by the name of Thomas Jefferson. On Arch Street, boarders found their way to the inn of Jane Port, and in Fore Street the home run by Sarah Yard.

"Mrs. Yard entertained Us, with Muffins, Buck Wheat Cakes, and common Toast. Buckwheat is an excellent grain, and is very plenty here," Congress's John Adams wrote during his stay the previous year, where he was sometimes joined by the Connecticut merchant and member of Congress Silas Deane. That May of 1775, Deane noted "an evening at Mrs. Yards with Mr. Hancock, Adams &c &c . . ."

Heading out of town toward Lancaster, the Buck Tavern, run by Mary Miller, hosted George Washington. Christiana Campbell and Jane Vobe were well-known tavern keepers in Williamsburg, Virginia.

These women sometimes inherited their inns and employed help— or enslaved people—to run these nonstop social hot spots. They were independent and essential. Up and down the East Coast were dozens of women keeping the motor of the growing colonies running smoothly.

Aside from Congress's arrival, Philadelphia was already abuzz with news of the events of Lexington and Concord. By the time word had reached the city on the twenty-fourth, Esther DeBerdt Reed had already experienced a shift in her own stance about what the British called the rebellion of the colonies. The town was bustling with accounts, both accurate or hearsay, and most of them were dreary. The situation was beginning to impact Esther's life more than she had ever anticipated, altering her ideas about family, love, and loyalty.

Esther had not intended for her life to be lived on this side of the Atlantic. She had grown up in a wealthy London family and one that prospered in transatlantic trade with the American colonies. She likely never anticipated that the very ocean that had bestowed so much fortune and privilege on her young life would be the same one that would keep her from her love, Joseph, and that would eventually come between her and her family.

Esther DeBerdt had met Joseph Reed when he was studying law at Middle Temple in London, a popular and respected institution that honed many of the top legal minds of the mid-eighteenth century. Esther was smitten by the young, intelligent man from the colony of New Jersey. It was not unusual for her father, Dennys, to entertain Americans in the DeBerdt home. He traded globally, and the colonies were a key part of his economic domain. Joseph had been to the house many times, and Esther looked forward to his visits. But when her father learned of their burgeoning romance, he forbade Esther from writing to Joseph once he had returned to America. He would not support a union of any kind between the two. But despite the times and her father's admonition, the pair continued to correspond, warming an attraction that built into a deep passion. That great Atlantic ferried letters back and forth between the two innamorati, bolstering and buoying their secret romance on its changing tides until 1770, when the courtship ended and their life as partners in marriage began.

But a life in London—their original goal—was not to be. The pair struggled to achieve the kind of financial stability they craved and the kind to which Esther was well accustomed. As a result, there was soon another Atlantic crossing, the one that brought Esther to her new life in Philadelphia. She now found herself not only on the other side of that great sea but also on the other side of a battle that threatened to upend her life.

Joseph's reputation as a fine lawyer with knowledge of American political sentiment led him to communicate with Lord Dartmouth, the British secretary of state for colonial affairs. Esther soon found herself engaged in a vibrant social life in the key colonial seaport. Joseph's aim was to familiarize Dartmouth with life and shifting loyalties in the American colonies, hoping that his advice would help England avoid events such as those that had transpired in April. Esther watched as Joseph became more embroiled in Philadelphia's military and political affairs, serving first as a lieutenant colonel in the militia and on the Committee of Correspondence, and, in 1775, rising to the position of president of the Provincial Congress.

In just the past year alone, the London-born-and-raised Esther had found herself amid the most well-known patriots of the day and had entertained Congressmen John Adams, Richard Henry Lee, Benjamin Harrison, and Silas Deane, and a Virginia plantation owner, engineer, and military veteran named George Washington. Washington had served in the First Continental Congress but recently assumed a leadership position of the military forces in the colonies, such as they were in early 1775.

Esther routinely impressed her guests as much as they may have impressed her.

Silas Deane wrote his wife Elizabeth, "On Tuesday We dined with Mr. Read, a Gentleman of the Law, very polite, & sensible, he married the Boston Agent Mr Deberts Daughter in London, and though small is of a most elegant figure, & countenance. She is a Daughter of Liberty zealously affected in a good Cause."

Esther may have never imagined herself as any such "daughter of liberty," but through the intersection of love, circumstance, and politics she most assuredly now was.

On Monday, June 12, 1775, Congress proclaimed the following:

> *This Congress . . . considering the present critical, alarming and calamitous state of these Colonies, do earnestly recommend, that THURSDAY, the Twentieth day of July next, be served by the Inhabitants of all the English Colonies on this Continent, as a day of public HUMILIATION, FASTING, and PRAYER . . .*

But before that day arrived, and just five days after Congress made their declaration, more fighting broke out, this time across the Charles River from Copp's Hill in Boston. This time planned and expected, this time bloodier.

Since Lexington and Concord, and after the British had retreated to Boston, where they found themselves surrounded by growing masses of militia, the situation in that city continued to deteriorate.

"My dear Son, What you feared is come upon us," Andrew Eliot, the minister of the New North Church, had written to his son in Connecticut on April 23, 1775. Andrew, who decided to stay in Boston, asked his son in Connecticut to help remove his Mother and other family members from the besieged city. "Such a Sabbath of melancholy and darkness I never knew—Our Congregation crowded with Strangers . . . A provincial Army in Roxbury—Dorchester & Cambridge College dispersed &—This Town a Garrison—every face gathering paleness—all hurry and confusion . . ."

Even before the battles at Lexington and Concord, which began this siege on the Massachusetts city, Sarah Winslow Deming, the wife of Captain John Deming, felt war encroaching on her life.

"Many a time have I tho't that could I be out of Boston, together with my family, & friends, I could be content with the meanest fare, & slenderest accommodations," she wrote her niece just days before the fighting broke out. "Out of Boston, out of Boston at almost any rate—away as far as possible from the infection of small pox, & the din of drums & martial Musick as its call'd, & horrors of war . . ."

Though essentially contained in Boston, the British still controlled the port, and reinforcements arrived by sea with troops set to assist their brothers-in-arms. The plan was to take the high ground to the north and south of the city, Dorchester Heights and Charlestown. Once again, the provincial government were forewarned, and the colonies' own soldiers, roughly 1,000 of them, made their way toward the peninsula of Charlestown and began the fortification of their position atop 62-foot-high Breed's Hill there. The troops constructed a rail fence and breastworks 160 feet long and 30 feet high to extend down the Mystic River. These were intended to repel the approach of soldiers on foot. But they were easily spotted by British forces on the warships *Somerset* and *Lively* and by sentries positioned in Copp's Hill. Just before the sun rose above the horizon on June 17, the British began to unleash their cannonade and bombardment. That afternoon, more than 2,000 British soldiers landed at Charlestown. Several hundred more arrived after an hour.

Despite their seeming advantage, the casualties piled up, most of them British. Directing the cannon and artillery fire for the colonists was Lucy's bookshop owner turned militarist, Henry. But the colonists soon ran out of ammunition and were eventually forced to retreat farther back to Bunker Hill. The British, despite losses greater than those of the colonists, took the peninsula. The colonists "lost" with 140 dead and 271 wounded. The British "victors" suffered 226 dead and 828 wounded. Charlestown was in flames.

The fallen hailed from every corner of life in the colony. Just over the neck from the peninsula were the roads to Medford and Cambridge. Locals established a makeshift field hospital in an expanse in Medford near South Street. There, Sarah Fulton and others worked to tend to the wounded, and New Hampshire's dead were soon buried in Medford's cemetery.

Dr. Joseph Warren, a well-known physician, early promoter of the smallpox vaccine, and now indomitable soldier, who had sent riders out to warn of the British advance toward Concord, rallied the troops at Breed's Hill, fought, and died in the battle.

On June 20, Abigail Adams wrote to John, her husband of eleven years, away in Philadelphia, where Congress was gathered, to confirm the news: "I wish I could contradict the report of the Doctors Death, but tis a lamentable Truth, and the tears of multitudes pay tribute to his memory."

She appreciated the news she received from her loyal correspondent, but at home in Braintree, Massachusetts, with their four children, she had a different perspective on events: "I rejoice in the prospect of the plenty you inform me of, but cannot say we have the same agreeable veiw here. The drought is very severe and things look but poorly."

With a centralized Continental Army just starting to take shape, there was no overall policy regarding enlisting nonwhite soldiers in battle. Militias did what they always did, relying on Black and Indigenous patriots as well.

The casualties among the colonial militia included Samuel Ashbow

Jr. and his brother John, of the Mohegan people. They had enlisted in May after Lexington and Concord. During this battle, they guarded the rail fence. Samuel died there and is believed to be the first Native American to perish in the Revolutionary War.

Black soldiers played crucial roles in the battle, many giving their lives in the process. Peter Salem, the formerly enslaved farmworker who had fought in Lexington, returned to fight in the redoubt on Breed's Hill, killing the British officer Major John Pitcairn, who had led troops to Lexington Green on that fateful day in April. Also in the redoubt were Cuff Whittemore—another veteran of Lexington and Concord—as well as Titus Coburn and a man named Salem Poor, whose gallantry during the battle did not go unnoticed.

Fourteen white officers would later sign a petition attesting to the bravery of the formerly enslaved Salem Poor, which they submitted to the General Court of Massachusetts Bay: "We declare that a Negro Man called Salem Poor . . . behaved like an Experienced Officer, as Well as an Excellent Soldier . . . Wee Would Only begg leave to say, in the person of this Sd. Negro, Centers a Brave & gallant soldier—the Reward due to so great and Distinguish a Character, We submit to the Congress."

There was none.

Charlestown burned. Inhabitants of Medford, Cambridge, Marblehead, Danvers, Salem, and other hamlets fled for safety. British general William Howe, then assisting General Gage, set up his headquarters in the now ash-ridden Charlestown and the British lines established around Bunker Hill remained. The human cost of the Siege of Boston continued rising. It would last well into the following year.

"The Spirits of the people are very good," Abigail wrote her husband, John. "The loss of Charlstown affects them no more than a Drop in the Bucket."

Farther south, at Mount Vernon in Virginia, the mistress of that vast plantation read a letter from her husband, then in Philadelphia:

"I am now set down to write to you on a subject which fills me with

inexpressible concern—and this concern is greatly aggravated and Increased when I reflect on the uneasiness I know it will give you," Martha read.

> *It has been determined by Congress that the whole Army raised for
> the defense of the American Cause shall be put under my care, and
> that it is necessary for me to proceed immediately to Boston to take
> upon me the Command of it. You may believe me, my dear Patcy,
> when I assure you in the most solemn manner that, so far from
> seeking this appointment, I have used every endeavor in my power
> to avoid it, not only from my unwillingness to part with you and
> the Family, but from a consciousness of its being a trust too far
> great for my Capacity and that I should enjoy more real happiness
> and felicity in one month with you, at home, than I have the most
> distant prospect of reaping abroad if my stay was to be Seven times
> Seven years . . . I shall feel no pain from the Toil or the danger of
> the Campaign—My unhappiness will flow from the uneasiness I
> know you will feel at being left alone . . .*

Martha had already lost one husband, Daniel Parke Custis, and two
young children. Now in her forty-fifth year, she was a twenty-eight-
year-old widow with two surviving children when she had married
George Washington sixteen years before. He had departed Mount Vernon earlier that year to take his place in Congress. But now, owing to
his experience in the French and Indian War, he had been assigned this
grave task and would not return for more than six years. She would go
to him often during that time. But George's assertion that she had been
left alone was not strictly true. She had her children, his relations, and
hers to help manage the plantation, as well as hundreds of enslaved
individuals—men, women, and children—who also toiled at Mount
Vernon's house, five farms, gristmill, and more.

And so, on June 19, the news Martha received was made public: The
Continental Congress had appointed George Washington "General
and Commander in chief of the army of the United Colonies and of all

the forces raised." This would affect not only Martha's life but Esther DeBerdt Reed's as well. Shortly after his appointment to lead the newly forming Continental Army, George Washington chose Esther's husband, Joseph, as his secretary and aide-de-camp. Less than a week after the events at Charlestown, Joseph left Esther and headed to the Continental Army headquarters in Cambridge, Massachusetts.

Esther wrote her brother, Dennis, the following day, her concerns evident, her position all too clear. The intensity and fervor of the times she now witnessed in the colonies alarmed her, especially considering the duties her husband now undertook. "The people here are determined to die or be free," she wrote. "They are now raised to a pitch it was thought they never could arrive at."

Joseph arrived in Cambridge on July 2 and took up residence with other officers and men already gathered in camp. Among them was Lucy Flucker Knox's husband, Henry.

Forced to leave behind his military library, the artillery enthusiast saw to the defenses in and around Cambridge, Charlestown, and, most significantly, the redoubt atop the hill in Roxbury, all from memory. Shortly after arriving at Cambridge with Joseph Reed, George Washington had inspected Knox's work at Roxbury and found it exemplary. Henry's new career as a military man was progressing rapidly.

Joseph's updates from camp in Cambridge sometimes chastised Esther for a lack of correspondence. Her husband desperately missed hearing from her and clearly relied emotionally upon her attentions. "My dear Hetty . . . I went to the post office this evening in full anticipation of receiving a letter from you . . ." began one such missive of July 26. "You will have received several from me . . . I did not think we should have lain inactive so long, but now it is settled into a plain kind of fog that life that is very tedious at times without you . . ."

She read of his sparsely furnished, twenty-foot-square room, and the comings and goings of the others in camp: "Our family is much reduced by the departure of General Lee who has taken the command of a part of the army and has his quarters 4 miles from us at Gen. Royall's."

Royall, for his part, had abandoned his home and, it would seem, those he had enslaved within it.

By the time Belinda Sutton shared her story with the Massachusetts legislature, sixty years had passed since she had last seen the Rio de Volta of the Gold Coast of Africa, what is Ghana today. She missed the land, the air, her family, and the mountains, which she recalled as "covered with spicy forests, the valleys loaded with the richest fruits, spontaneously produced . . ."

It was there that she had first lived. Much later in her life, she recounted those idyllic days and imagined the "compleat felicity" that would have been hers had she not, early in her life, witnessed "early impressions of the cruelty of men, whose faces were like the moon, and whose Bows and Arrows were like the thunder and the lightning of the Clouds . . . The idea of these, the most dreadful of all Enemies, filled her infant slumbers with horror, and her noontide moments with evil apprehensions! . . ."

Belinda remembered well the day she was captured, in the midst of praying to the deities, a divine force central to many West African religions. She described standing "in a sacred grove, with each hand in that of a tender Parent, . . . paying her devotions to the great Oris[h]a who made all things," when that dreaded horror came to pass and "an armed band of white men, driving many of her Countrymen in Chains, ran into the hallowed shade! . . ."

That would be Belinda's last free day in her West African home-land, when she was "ravished from the bosom of her Country, from the arms of her friends—while the advanced age of her Parents, rendering them unfit for servitude, cruelly separated her from them forever!"

Not yet twelve years old, Belinda now joined the estimated 12.5

million Africans whom, between 1525 and 1866, European enslavers forced to endure the Middle Passage, and among those who survived its inhumane brutality—and later shared their stories of it:

> *Once more her eyes were blest with a Continent—but alas! how unlike the Land where she received her being! here all things appeared unpropitious—She learned to catch the Ideas, marked by the sounds of language only to know that her doom was Slavery, from which death alone was to emancipate her.*

Belinda lived down the street from Sarah Fulton, in Medford, Massachusetts. Although Sarah and others considered Medford a hotbed of fervent Whigs, at this point in time there existed no haven from slavery in the colonies. The Royall family, who enslaved Belinda, were the largest slaveholders in Massachusetts throughout the eighteenth century. To date, the names of at least sixty individuals have been found in wills, account books, and other town records. Isaac Royall Jr., Belinda's enslaver leading up to the outbreak of the Revolutionary War, was born in Antigua, where his father, Isaac Royall Sr., had established a large plantation. The Royall fortune was built on trade: in sugar, in rum, and in humans.

Royall Jr. held various civic posts in town: representative to the colonial legislature; honorary general; overseer of Harvard College. Belinda was one of sixty-four individuals enslaved by the Royalls in Massachusetts. She bore children in this strange, cruel new land and witnessed them baptized far from the groves of Orisha.

And so, among Whigs and loyalists alike, the idea of what it meant to be free and independent was often as pale as those moonlike faces that haunted a young Belinda's dreams.

Sarah Fulton's town of Medford had, in the guise of Isaac Royall, shed a fleeing loyalist, and in the case of General Lee, gained a patriot general. Now the home of merchant Isaac Royall was no longer his own. The fates of those enslaved within it, Belinda Sutton among them, remained a mystery.

This new and growing army was in desperate need of supplies but had little in the way of money to obtain them. A broadside published in Cambridge on August 21, 1775, illuminated the dire situation:

WANTED *for the* CONTINENTAL ARMY.

One Million of Bricks.
Three Thousand Cords of Fire Wood.
Two Hundred Thousand Feet of Pine Boards and Scantling.
Five Hundred Bushels of Charcoal.
One Hundred and Fifty Tons of English Hay.
Twelve Hundred Bushels of Indian corn.
Twelve Hundred Bushels of Oats.
Three Hundred Shovels.
Three Hundred Spades.
Fifty Pick Axes.
One Hundred and Fifty Hand-Saws.
Five Thousand Bushels of Lime.
One Hundred and Fifty Tons of Rye Straw.

Those Persons who are willing to supply the Army with the Articles above-mentioned, may apply to the Quarter-Master-General, in Cambridge.

Additional broadsides posted about town pleaded for linen for bandages from the women of Lancaster. Significantly, other broadsides prohibited individuals from selling cider to soldiers.

Several months after Joseph's departure, Esther wrote her brother, Dennis, again. She had moved house to Perth Amboy, New Jersey, with her oldest daughter. She expressed frustration with each passing day and had resigned herself to a very prolonged separation from Joseph.

"He is yet there amidst all the confusion and horrors of War . . ." she wrote, "but I find the human mind can be habituated to almost anything, even the most disturbing . . ."

Yet the native Londoner still believed, at least then, in what Joseph was fighting for.

"I think the cause in which he is engaged so just, so glorious, and I hope will be so victorious . . ."

Her mind turned to the events earlier that year in Charlestown, wondering what effect, if any, "the Battle of Bunker Hill has both on our friends and our enemies.

"Where sleep all our friends in England? . . . Where sleeps The Winter of Justice of the English Nation? Will nothing rouse them, or are they so few in number, and small in consequence, that though awake, their voice cannot be heard in the multitude of our enemies?"

Earlier that year, Mary Katharine Goddard had gone public on the colophon of the newspaper she had effectively been running since arriving in Baltimore more than a year earlier: "Baltimore: Published by M.K. Goddard, at the Printing-Office in Market-Street, next Door above Dr. John Stevenson's." With an annual subscription cost of ten shillings, Goddard's paper also promised quality work to all who advertised within its pages: "All Manner of printing work is performed with Care, Fidelity, and Expectation . . . Notice, in a neat and correct manner."

Goddard's sideline in Baltimore—much as it had been earlier in Philadelphia and in Providence before that—also included the publishing of broadsides, an invaluable part of colonial public life.

Broadsides disseminated information about everything from pirate attacks to the latest sermon, to announce, to alert, to invite, and to warn. They were the key means of conveying up-to-date particulars of daily life and were posted in public spaces for all to see.

With war at their doorstep, the frequency of colonial newspaper editions steadily increased, and their circulations grew. The names of these early newspapers often reflected the manner by which they reached their readership: by "Post," by "Packet" (boat), or by "Courier." This convention stuck, and many newspapers carry these names to this day.

Newspapers shared not just news of the day but exchange rates, official decrees, the comings and goings of ships, and the people who had traveled to town aboard them. Like most if not all publications in the colonies, *The Maryland Journal, and the Baltimore Advertiser* featured ads offering rewards for runaway slaves. Most readers perceived no obvious conflict between these ads and the ongoing discussions of "freedom."

As a publisher, writer, editor, and printer, Goddard did not shy away from many of the arguments of the day and often embraced and amplified them. That same year, for instance, she printed a letter to the editor from one "Britannicus":

> *The British parliament claims a right to tax and bind the Americans in all cases whatsoever, when in reality, a British parliament has no more right to tax an American in anything than they have the right to tax the people in Japan; for by this means you are robbed of the democratical part of the constitution, the very essence of English liberty.*

However, in October of 1775, her responsibilities as a stationer and newspaperwoman grew significantly.

Earlier that summer, Congress had established a colony-wide postal system. The idea of a unified mail service had been proposed by Mary Katharine's brother, William, more than a year earlier in the *Essex Gazette* and several months later formally to Congress itself. Now, more than ten months later, a plan was enacted to adopt William's proposed postal system, but William would not be in charge—his perceived lack of reliability perhaps at issue. The job of postmaster general of this new Constitutional Post would go to the Philadelphia congressman and former printer Benjamin Franklin. He in turn tapped William Goddard as postal surveyor, scouting and inspecting delivery routes.

And in Baltimore, Mary Katharine Goddard was formally appointed that city's postmaster. She was now the first woman ever to hold the position of postmaster in the United Colonies.

Just off the Virginia coast at Norfolk, aboard the ship *William*, John Murray, the 4th Earl of Dunmore and royal governor of Virginia, decided to carry out at least part of the threat he had been making to the colonists for months.

He had sworn that he would free enslaved people and set fire to Williamsburg if the colonies rebelled. By June 8, 1775, his power drastically reduced, he had fled the Governor's Palace in Williamsburg and sought sanctuary on the *William*. There he remained, master of a floating city, and from that vessel on November 7, 1775, he issued a proclamation promising freedom to any enslaved individuals who abandoned their patriot enslavers in order to serve the Crown.

"As I have ever entertained hopes that an accommodation might have taken place between *Great-Britain* and this colony, without being compelled, *by my duty*, to this most disagreeable, but now absolutely necessary step . . ." the Proclamation began. In order to defeat "such treasonable purposes" so that "all such traitors, and their abetters, may be brought to justice, and that the peace and good order of this colony may be again restored . . . I do, in virtue of the power and authority to me given, *by his Majesty,* determine to execute martial law, and cause the same to be executed throughout this colony . . ."

Dunmore's proclamation gave hope to the enslaved and wrought some havoc in all of the colonies, despite the fact that Dunmore's jurisdiction was technically limited to Virginia. "I do hereby further declare all *indented servants, Negroes*, or others (appertaining to rebels) *free*, that are able and willing to bear arms, they *joining his Majesty's troops*, as soon as may be, for the more speedily reducing this colony to a proper sense of their duty, to his Majesty's crown and dignity."

This proclamation came roughly two weeks after the Continental Congress—in a series of meetings with George Washington—had reached a very different decision. Esther's husband, Joseph, had been on hand to record those October proceedings:

At Cambridge 18-22

> *Item seven on the agenda 7. Ought not Negroes to be excluded
> from the new Inlistment especially such as are Slaves—all were
> thought improper by the Council of Officers?*
> *Agreed that they be rejected altogether.*

> *Jos Reed secretary*

Just days after Dunmore's Proclamation—which soon made head-lines in the colonial press—Washington issued his own general order stating, "Neither negroes, boys unable to bear arms, nor old men unfit to endure the fatigues of the campaign are to be enlisted."

This announcement seemed to reverse the long-running practice of permitting all citizens to serve in militias. Indeed, since the Boston Massacre and Lexington and Concord, many free and enslaved Black seemed to have already been serving in, and dying for, the colonial cause.

Washington expressed his views again in mid-December.

> *If the Virginians are wise, that Arch Traitor to the Rights of Hu-
> manity, Lord Dunmore, should be instantly crushd, if it takes the
> force of the whole Colony to do it. [O]therwise, like a snow Ball in
> rolling, his army will get size—some through Fear—some through
> promises—and some from Inclination joining his Standard—But
> that which renders the measure indispensably necessary, is, the
> Negros; for if he gets formidable, numbers of th[e]m will be tempted
> to join . . .*

And so they did.

One of the hasty results of Dunmore's proclamation was the forma-tion of the Royal Ethiopian Regiment, which enlisted three hundred Black men within one month. The uniforms of this first Black loyalist fighting force reportedly carried the words "Liberty for Slaves." (This is based on illustrations, of course, and others have noted that Dunmore's flight and general lack of supplies likely made it challenging for new uniforms to be designed.)

In December, the Ethiopian Regiment and other loyalist troops fought with colonial troops from Virginia and North Carolina at Great Bridge, Virginia. Soon word of Dunmore's proclamation spread to other corners of the colonies as newspapers beyond Virginia's borders shared the news. Hope that freedom lay with the British seized many, no matter the colony in which they lived.

It is estimated that tens of thousands of enslaved individuals eventually fled to seek refuge with the British, whether to fight or merely escape amid the upheaval of war and the chaos brought about by the proclamation.

From the grounds of Mount Vernon, where he served as steward during the absence of his distant cousin, Lund Washington wrote the general: "Our Dunmore has at length Publishd his much dreaded proclamation—declareg Freedom to All Indented Servts & Slaves (the Property of Rebels) that will repair to his majestys Standard—being able to bear Arms—What effect it will have upon those sort of people I cannot tell—I think if there was no white Servts in this family I shoud be under no apprehension about the Slaves, however I am determined, that if any of them Create any confusition to make & [an] example of him, Sears who is at worck here says there is not a man of them, but woud leave us, if they believe'd they coud make there Escape—Tom Spears Excepted—& yet they have no fault to find[.] Liberty is sweet."

By the end of December at least one of Mount Vernon's enslaved had escaped. Others had gone before, and more would follow. Some enslaved at Mount Vernon were too young to know or take advantage of Dunmore's offer.

For now.

A couple of weeks later, in mid-December, another letter arrived for the commander in chief at his headquarters in Cambridge. This letter did not touch on slavery per se but rather was written by a formerly enslaved woman who remained in the employ of the Boston family that had once owned her:

SIR,

I Have taken the freedom to address your Excellency in the enclosed poem, and entreat your acceptance, though I am not insensible of its inaccuracies. Your being appointed by the Grand Continental Congress to be Generalissimo of the armies of North America, together with the fame of your virtues, excite sensations not easy to suppress. Your generosity, therefore, I presume, will pardon the attempt. Wishing your Excellency all possible success in the great cause you are so generously engaged in. I am,

Your Excellency's most obedient humble servant,
PHILLIS WHEATLEY
Providence, Oct. 26, 1775.

Celestial choir! enthron'd in realms of light,
Columbia's scenes of glorious toils I write.
While freedom's cause her anxious breast alarms,
She flashes dreadful in refulgent arms.
See mother earth her offspring's fate bemoan,
And nations gaze at scenes before unknown!
See the bright beams of heaven's revolving light
Involved in sorrows and the veil of night!
The goddess comes, she moves divinely fair,
Olive and laurel binds her golden hair:
Wherever shines this native of the skies,
Unnumber'd charms and recent graces rise.
Muse! bow propitious while my pen relates
How pour her armies through a thousand gates:
As when Eolus heaven's fair face deforms,
Enwrapp'd in tempest and a night of storms;

Astonish'd ocean feels the wild uproar,
The refluent surges beat the sounding shore;
Or thick as leaves in Autumn's golden reign,
Such, and so many, moves the warrior's train.
In bright array they seek the work of war,
Where high unfurl'd the ensign waves in air.
Shall I to Washington their praise recite?
Enough thou know'st them in the fields of fight.
Thee, first in place and honours,—we demand
The grace and glory of thy martial band.
Fam'd for thy valour, for thy virtues more,
Hear every tongue thy guardian aid implore!
One century scarce perform'd its destined round,
When Gallic powers Columbia's fury found;
And so may you, whoever dares disgrace
The land of freedom's heaven-defended race!
Fix'd are the eyes of nations on the scales,
For in their hopes Columbia's arm prevails.
Anon Britannia droops the pensive head,
While round increase the rising hills of dead.
Ah! cruel blindness to Columbia's state!
Lament thy thirst of boundless power too late.
Proceed, great chief, with virtue on thy side,
Thy ev'ry action let the goddess guide.
A crown, a mansion, and a throne that shine,
With gold unfading, Washington! be thine.

Would this act of correspondence with a Black female poet, coming on the heels of Dunmore's proclamation and the soldiers flocking to the Royal Ethiopian Regiment, shift Washington's views toward the enslaved, or did pragmatism compel the commander to reassess his own policies?

In either case—or perhaps a combination of the two—before 1775 came to a close, Washington had changed his mind about the Continental Army's enlistment guidelines.

On New Year's Eve he wrote the president of Congress, John Hancock:

> *It has been represented to me that the free negroes who have Served in this Army, are very much disatisfied at being discarded—as it is to be apprehended, that they may Seek employ in the ministerial Army—I have presumed to depart from the Resolution respecting them, & have given Licence for their being enlisted, if this is disapproved of by Congress, I will put a Stop to it.*

Congress did not disapprove.

The lasting results of both this decision and Lord Dunmore's would continue to create ripples of hope and disappointment, of dreams and of those dashed, surging as waves, crashing on each and every coast along the Eastern Seaboard of the colonies.

Standing in the Circle: Mount Vernon

A tricorne-capped man in colonial dress strolls through the dining room, playing all of your favorite hits from the 1770s on his fife. His name is Don Francisco, and when he is not entertaining diners and drinkers, he is part of a solemn procession and ceremony that occur daily here, a contrast in mood and setting to the convivial atmosphere in the Mount Vernon Inn Restaurant, on the grounds of George Washington's estate.

The smell of stewed meats and gravies hangs in the air, an olfactory introduction to a menu that includes shepherd's pie, fricassee, fried chicken, pot pies, chicken and waffles, and, this being the mid-Atlantic, crab cakes. In keeping with the practice of many historic towns and sites, some menu offerings are named in honor of those who lived here. Sip on a "Washington Apple," a mix of Crown Royal, Sour Apple Pucker, and cranberry juice. Or try Martha's Rum Punch, concocted with Myers's rum, Captain Morgan rum, and orange juice. Brunch, of course, offers two "Benedicts," one of eggs and the other of fried green tomatoes. Though not named for the infamous traitor, their presence on the menu feels more apropos than the "GW Burger" of Black Angus beef, available with a gluten-free bun.

The long, narrow room adjacent to the main dining room features a small bar where no one is drinking any fruity namesake drinks (though the George Washington porter and ale are popular). The familiarity with which the bartender and waitstaff greet many of the patrons is an indication that this spot is frequented by as many regulars as it is tourists. Less than an hour's drive from Washington, D.C., the site hosts those who have never been and those who stop by on a regular basis to enjoy the grounds or have a bite or a drink.

The day of my visit happens to be May 4. Don Francisco strolls up and says, "On this day in history . . ." and proceeds to play the theme from *Star Wars*. The Army veteran—and veteran of various Army bands—is a life member of the nonprofit Company of Fifers & Drummers, a sixty-year-old organization dedicated to preserving and sharing the history and music of the colonial era.

While chatting with Don, he reminds me about a ceremony that will take place elsewhere on the grounds that afternoon, and I plan to attend. Beforehand, I set out to see beforehand as much as possible of the site, once the home of Martha and George Washington and the hundreds enslaved on their property.

Mount Vernon's house, museum, and grounds are extensive, with farms including the Mansion House Farm, River Farm, Muddy Hole Farm, Dogue Run Farm, and Union Farm. Pioneer Farm allows visitors to explore Washington's agricultural operations. There is a gristmill and distillery. *Step back in time and experience life in the 18th century* . . . Tour the house. Walk the grounds and gardens. Watch a demonstration in the kitchen. Outbuildings abound, with "houses" of all kinds: icehouse, smokehouse, greenhouse, and salt house, which was not necessarily used to store salt, that all-important ingredient for preservation before the age of refrigeration. A peek inside the "necessary"—an elaborate wooden privy—provides a look into early sanitation practices. With small, removable waste drawers beneath each throne, the human refuse could be emptied into a single repository—a kind of early septic tank.

Various vantage points provide views of the Potomac River, whose waters embrace the estate. Prime sources of food for *all* who lived at Mount Vernon were shad and herring. Mount Vernon's ten miles of shoreline brought waters teeming with fish into enormous nets manned by the enslaved, said to bring in 1.5 million fish in just a few weeks. Salted fish and cornmeal were staples for the enslaved, the latter used to make "hoe cakes" (which are offered in the restaurant today, accompanied by vanilla bean butter and honey).

I wander the museum, and of all the extensive collection, interactive exhibits, and artifacts I am most drawn to the items and informational placards detailing Washington's lifelong and painful affair with dentistry.

Perpetually plagued by aching teeth, Washington tried everything available to a man of means in the mid-1700s. His first tooth was removed in 1756, when he was around twenty-four years old. By the time of his inauguration as president in 1789, a lone gnasher remained in his mouth. He ultimately owned eight sets of dentures, constructed primarily of hippopotamus ivory and human teeth.

The house itself sits at the top of a sweeping lawn and was added on to over the years. A technique called rustication was employed to create the building's facade. Constructed of pine, the planks were carved to resemble stone, then surfaced with sand to lend a textured, weathered look.

The entire estate was dilapidated and near ruin until Ann Pamela Cunningham founded the Mount Vernon Ladies' Association in 1853, galvanizing women across the country to the cause of preserving the home of the former president. Among those joining Cunningham's cause was influential magazine editor Sarah Josepha Hale, the oft-unacknowledged individual responsible for our modern-day Thanksgiving tradition. Hale used her platform—*Godey's Lady's Book*—to keep the Mount Vernon Ladies' Association mission in front of thousands of eyes. The association raised $200,000 (a whopping $5.7 million, give or take, today) in the first five years of its existence. It has come a long way since.

At first blush, Mount Vernon feels akin to many historic sites dedicated to the memory of a founder or framer: large parking lots, a welcome or "orientation" center, snack and gift shops. The George Washington Presidential Library is a tremendous resource for researchers, educators, and students of all types. The site, in its entirety, is evidence of Washington's curious and creative mind, and evidence of much more than that.

As years have passed, Mount Vernon—similarly to other sites with painful, complicated histories steeped in human bondage—has incorporated a focus on the history of enslaved people at Mount Vernon, an entirely different lens through which to experience the site.

Coming in on the Mount Vernon Memorial Highway, a historical marker commemorates Ona Judge, an enslaved woman who served the Washingtons at Mount Vernon and in Philadelphia, the city from which she self-emancipated. The museum highlights the lives of individuals such as William "Billy" Lee, whom Washington purchased in 1768 for £61. Lee traveled to

Cambridge, Massachusetts, with Washington in 1775 and remained at his side throughout the war. There was Moll, a nursemaid to the Custis children. Hercules Posey, the head cook. Charlotte, a seamstress. George inherited his first slaves at the age of ten. Upon marrying Martha, so-called dower slaves—acquired upon matrimony—added to the already increasing number on his plantation. Other individuals worked the estate on loan. George did not stop purchasing slaves until the 1780s. Over the years, 577 enslaved individuals lived at Mount Vernon. In 1799, at the time of George Washington's death, 317 people were enslaved on the property. A visit to the Women's Bunk Room in the Slave Quarters gives some idea of the day-to-day existence of those with no choice but to keep the estate running.

The bowling green—the dramatic formal lawn—leading up to the house was treasured by Washington. Our docent on the Enslaved People of Mount Vernon Tour tells us how much George Washington valued and sought to protect this verdant expanse. It took enslaved workers weeks to "mow" the lawn using hand tools. By the time they were finished, they practically needed to start all over again. But the manicured carpet was to be admired, never trod upon. This created a challenge for slaves, whose lives already required moving to and fro constantly on the property, without the burden of added steps to avoid the lawn. If they needed to get from point A to point B, a straight line and shortest distance was not an option for them. The docent tells us that on one occasion Washington noticed an errant footprint on the manicured stretch. He meticulously measured the footprint, determining the shoe size of the perpetrator in order to identify and, one assumes, punish them for their trespass.

After the tour, I encounter Don Francisco again. A group of us are walking through a wooded grove not far from George and Martha's tomb, along a path toward a small circle laid with brick and surrounded by a low wall and hedge. At the center stands a small granite monument. This is a cemetery. We are here to see not one grave but many. Bodies, the majority of which are unidentified, lie undiscovered beneath years of soil and memory.

Evidence and acknowledgment of the slave cemetery's existence long precede the current investigation into the burial ground that continues in earnest today. In 1833, a visitor to Mount Vernon wrote a letter describing the location and number of graves—they estimated 150 at the time—believed to be on the site.

In 1929, the Mount Vernon Ladies' Association placed a marker on the site commemorating the lives of those in the unidentified graves. In 1983, the organization erected a larger memorial, the centerpiece of today's ceremony. The small granite column was designed by Howard University School of Architecture students and reads:

In Memory Of
The Afro Americans Who Served As Slaves
At Mount Vernon
This Monument Marking Their Burial Ground
Dedicated
September 21, 1983
Mount Vernon Ladies' Association

Three low steps lead up to the memorial, reading, "Faith. Hope. Love."

In 1985, ground-penetrating radar was used to locate individuals, finding sixty-six. Technological advances have improved upon those methods in the years since, allowing archaeologists and their volunteers to locate grave shafts that indicate the remains lying beneath. For more than a decade, workers have been actively working to document those buried here and create a map indicating individual burial sites. As of 2022, eighty-six graves have been identified, and a map is in the works. William "Billy" Lee, Washington's onetime valet who was free at the time of his death, is believed to be interred here. Other individuals freed in George Washington's will in 1799 may have joined him. There are women. There are children. The remains, once located, are marked but never unearthed.

By around three o'clock, a large group gathers at this site for the twice-daily ceremony. The crowd is mixed in gender, age, and race, many sitting on a low wall around the site, others standing along the path. The docent with whom I was chatting picks me and two other individuals to read aloud brief selections before the wreath is placed on the memorial. At the end, Don Francisco plays the Black national anthem—"Lift Every Voice and Sing"—on his fife.

As solemn as the ceremony is, the ground surrounding us is perhaps the most moving. Beyond the limits of the path, strings mounted in quasi-rectangular shapes delineate the edges of what are believed to be the final resting place of a buried slave.

Stones cover the earth within some of these demarcated areas. The young hands of visiting schoolchildren have painted pictures on these stones and sometimes inscribed them.

One stone depicts the image of a family, while nearby another features butterflies and trees. The name "Alice" on a stone is decorated with a drawing of a spinning wheel. I see names like Nellie Quander. Hercules. Delia. The messages are simple: "Angels." "Thank you." "Love." Others are more specific and personal: "My ancestors were many stars with big hearts and huge souls."

Some of the outlined graves are completely covered, creating a kind of mosaic of these decorated pieces of rock. Other stringed outlines are waiting to be adorned. And many more strings have yet to be erected.

It is a somber walk as we leave this place. The house, gardens, demonstrations, and overall busyness of the grounds feel a jarring contrast. But the real jolt back to reality comes as I follow the rest of the tourists and exit through the gift shop.

"Huzzah!" screams one T-shirt as I enter the Shops at Mount Vernon. The stores carry a collection of items for anyone, history buff or not: books, jams, jellies, candles and Christmas ornaments, replicas of historic prints. There is jewelry; there are accessories. There are custom whiskies, wines, and brandies, and the barware and coasters to accompany them.

I drive past the research center as I leave. Among the archives and artifacts, the curators maintain and add to their online database of enslaved individuals, striving to give names and any distinguishing information as they continue to uncover—literally and figuratively—the site's uneasy history.

From here, I have the choice to head north toward the district named for the first president or south toward a mecca of colonial history: Williamsburg, Virginia. No matter which direction, each points to a past often forgotten or ignored, and in the best of cases our attempts to understand, honor, and own it. There is no moving past. Only through.

CHAPTER 7

Prelude to Independence: The Dawn of 1776

The first few months of 1776 saw rapid change and developments, both welcome and woeful, throughout the colonies. The loyalist stronghold of Norfolk, Virginia, for example, started the year engulfed in flames—set by British and Continental forces alike. To those who had been paying close attention to the events transpiring in and around Norfolk, the confrontation might have seemed unavoidable, considering all that had happened in the previous six months.

Sitting at the mouth of Chesapeake Bay and running alongside the Elizabeth River, a tributary of the James, Norfolk was a powerhouse port of the Eastern Seaboard and a crucial British stronghold.

Across the waters from the county of Norfolk and at the tail end of the James River sat Point Comfort, site of the first arrivals of enslaved Africans to English-occupied North America in 1619. And across from Point Comfort, where the James emptied into the Chesapeake, was a piece of land jutting into the bay created by a 1749 hurricane that caused the waters of the Chesapeake to rise fifteen feet above normal. In the process, roiling seas churned and deposited sand on the shoals, creating what became known as Willoughby Point.

Since the 1600s, two hundred or so acres had been in the Willoughby family that eventually enslaved the Dismal Swamp preacher Mary, inclusive of the original fifty-acre townsite of Norfolk. However, this latest fiery upheaval and its turbulent aftermath were causing Mary's enslavers to consider moving on, taking Mary with them.

"INTELLIGENCE EXTRAORDINARY," *The Virginia Gazette* had proclaimed a week before Dunmore fled to a ship in June 1775. "A certain nominal itinerant governor, who for some time past has been suspected of acting the part of an incendiary in this colony, is to take the field as generalissimo at the head of the Africans . . ."

Lord Dunmore had moved on board the HMS *Fowey*, sailed it down the James River to the Elizabeth River, and finally moored in Portsmouth at the Gosport shipyard, where he set up a headquarters of sorts, assembling troops and ships to attack the colonials. British forces made their way toward Hampton and Mills Creek. Not everyone in nearby Norfolk was happy with his presence, however, and Dunmore, in turn, was none too pleased with the media coverage the Crown and its representatives received in the local newspapers. By fall, Dunmore had decided to take journalistic matters into his own hands.

He had written Lord Dartmouth, secretary of state for the colonies, "The public prints of this little dirty Borough of Norfolk, has for some time past been wholly employed in exciting, in the minds of all Ranks of People the spirit of sedition and Rebellion, by the grossest misrepresentations of facts, both, public & private; that they might do no further mischief, I sent a small party on shore on Saturday last [Sept 30] at noon and brought off their press, tipes, paper, Ink, two of the printers and all the utensils, and am now going to have a press for the king on board one of the ships I have lately taken into his Majesty's service for the reception of the remainder of the 14th Regiment whose arrival I look for with great impatience every hour."

And so, from on board the HMS *William*, Lord Dunmore began printing his own *Virginia Gazette,* and it was from that vessel that he issued his now famous November 1775 proclamation promising freedom to those enslaved by American patriots if they were to come over to the British side.

The conflicts had continued. Dunmore and his forces raided patriot stores, farms, and military positions. A British victory at Kemp's Landing emboldened Dunmore to march into Norfolk proper. There he found a number of loyalists who welcomed his arrival. Not long after, however, another battle was in the offing, at the strategic location of

Great Bridge. Spanning the Elizabeth River about twelve miles south of Norfolk, Great Bridge was a main point of access between that city and North Carolina. There British troops—the Royal Ethiopian Regiment among them—encountered Colonel William Woodford and the 2nd Virginia Regiment and Culpeper Minutemen. The short fight—not even an hour—resulted in a decisive win for the colonials.

Reinforcements from North Carolina, among them Colonel Robert Howe and the 2nd North Carolina Continental Regiment, then headed for Norfolk to join forces with Woodford.

Patriot Colonel Thomas Elliott described Dunmore's force:

A List of the Naval Force, now in the Harbour of Norfolk, and in Hampton Roads, December 30, 1775, viz:

Ship Liverpool, *twenty-eight guns, Henry Bellew, commander; sloop* Otter, *sixteen guns, Matthew Squire, commander; sloop* Kingfisher, *eighteen guns, James Montagu, commander; sloop, eight guns, Robert Stewart, commander; Lord Dunmore's ship,* Eilbeck, *force unknown; six or seven small tenders of small force.*

The force of Lord Dunmore's, by account of Colonel Elliott: 120 Regulars; 120 Marines; 150 Negroes; 250 Liverpool.

From their watery vantage point off Norfolk, the British could see Continental troops marching back and forth along docks that had once been under the control of the Crown. Both sides exchanged threats and taunts and Dunmore threatened to attack. On January 1, after warning residents to evacuate, the British pounced.

The bombardment of Norfolk by the British and the chaos that ensued gave the Americans an opportunity to pin any wanton, infernal destruction on the British. Amid the cannonade, the British troops made for the shore to set fire to structures alongside the water. The resulting smoke and mayhem gave cover to the Continentals to unleash their own fiery havoc upon the buildings along the waterfront, making it appear as though their destruction were also the fault of the British.

"I cannot enter into the melancholy consideration of the women and children running through a crowd of shot to get out of the town, some of them with children at their breasts: A few have, I hear been killed," said Continental Colonel Robert Howe the day after the fiery rampage. "Does it not call for vengeance both from God and man?"

Dunmore sought to set the record straight in the pages of his *Virginia Gazette*. Of the nearly nine hundred structures destroyed, he claimed fewer than twenty had been at the hands of his troops.

"The Rebels cruelly and unnecessarily completed the destruction of the whole town, by setting fire to the houses in the streets back, which were before safe from the flames," Dunmore's *Gazette* reported on January 15, 1776.

Nevertheless, in February, more structures were destroyed and looted at the hands of both Continental and British troops. On the part of the Continentals, it was a further attempt to dissuade the British from reestablishing a stronghold in Norfolk.

Nearby, with ships in its sight, sat Willoughby Point, long home to the family that enslaved Mary. With Norfolk destroyed and numerous Black men and women fleeing to the British in hopes of freedom, it looked as though Mary's time preaching in Dismal Swamp might soon be coming to an end, as might her time with the Willoughbys.

"May that Being who blesses the universe with the rays of his benign Providence, bless you with a happy new Year, give You every joy & every wish necessary to your felicity . . ."

As Norfolk burned, the first week of the new year of 1776 saw Lucy Knox still in Worcester, Massachusetts, and ever separated from her "Harry," upon whom she had not laid hand nor eyes since mid-November. For the time being, Henry's words, inked in iron gall on wove paper, were the only tangible connection to the man who had been her husband for only six months. Her desire for real connection was likely more than just a longing for Henry, though neither of the pair of nascent lovers liked being away from the other during increasingly perilous times. However, no matter when Lucy and Henry were to be reunited, one thing was certain: In about one month their lives would irrevocably change.

Lucy, roughly eight months pregnant and alone, continued reading Henry's latest letter.

"With what raptures should I receive a Letter from my angels hands, I should think it one of the best forms of heaven," he wrote on January 5. "I would kiss [it,] I would put it in my bosom & wear it there 'til no part remain'd. Yet though it would be the last token of her love, it would not be the freshest in my memory, my Lucy is perpetually in my mind constantly in my heart."

Henry had written this letter to Lucy while in Albany, New York, where he was on his way back to Massachusetts after an arduous and icy mission that had taken him north to Fort Ticonderoga, New York, roughly ninety miles south of what is now the Canadian border. His mission had taken longer than he expected. He should have arrived at Cambridge already.

Lucy had last seen her husband during a short visit before he began his trek north to New York.

The capture of Fort Ticonderoga had been a key victory and also represented a potential windfall in supplies . . . if they could be transported south.

Before the Seven Years' War, vast swaths of the continent—from the Hudson Bay to the Mississippi and far to the west—were part of "New France." In 1755, the French constructed the star-shaped Fort Ticonderoga (originally called Fort Carillon) with bastions at each point. In 1759, the fort was taken by the British (with help, at the time, from American colonists fighting alongside them) and subsequently renamed "Ticonderoga," derived from an Iroquois term for "where the waters meet." The fort was, indeed, strategically located at the confluence of Lake Champlain and Lake George. Now it was back in the hands of the Americans, and securing that location helped to block British access to the Hudson River from the north.

And so the victory at Ticonderoga was not just a strategic victory; it also brought with it a very desirable arsenal. The only problem was,

George Washington needed that weaponry at Cambridge, about 225 miles away.

Enter newly minted colonel, artillery tactician, and erstwhile bookseller Henry Knox, tasked with retrieving the valuable munitions and transporting them to headquarters in Massachusetts. This, in the dead of winter.

Henry kept his pregnant wife apprised of his movements and trials, including in a missive written in December from Fort George, New York, where he shared a cabin and a bed with captured British officer John André. That twenty-five-year-old Renaissance man had been based at St. Johns in Quebec, where, in addition to any military responsibilities, he also indulged in his passion for painting and writing poetry. He had recently been released as part of a prisoner exchange and was being transported by Continental forces to Lancaster, Pennsylvania. Henry and John got on quite well. No doubt Henry found André's mastery of multiple languages and talents as a writer to be right up his literary alley, despite André's allegiance to the Crown.

Once at Fort Ticonderoga, the massive undertaking began. Henry had enormous sleds constructed in order to transport the bounty. On December 17, 1775, he had penned a letter to his commander in chief describing "42 exceeding strong sleds" and plans to have "80 yoke of oxen to drag them as far as Springfield . . ." (Along the journey, Knox employed both horses and oxen, depending on his needs, the terrain, and, of course, the price being asked by those from whom he procured the beasts.)

Scows, periaugers, oxen . . . The procession would transport cannon, howitzers, mortars, and more over ground and water, much of it frozen.

"I expect in sixteen or seventeen days' time," he continued, "to be able to present to your Excellency a noble train of artillery."

Sixteen or seventeen days turned into more of a month, but deliver a "noble train" Henry Knox did—though they would initially remain at Framingham, Massachusetts, where Abigail Adams's husband, lawyer and Continental Congress member John, saw the train with his own eyes. It was customary to describe cannon by the weight of the balls they were capable of firing, a convention Adams followed when he described the armored haul in his diary:

> *It consists of Iron—9 Eighteen Pounders, 10 Twelves, 6. six, four nine Pounders, Three 13. Inch Mortars, Two Ten Inch Mortars, one Eight Inch, and one six and an half. Howitzer, one Eight Inch and an half and one Eight.*
>
> *Brass Cannon. Eight Three Pounders, one four Pounder, 2 six Pounders, one Eighteen Pounder, and one 24 Pounder. One eight Inch and an half Mortar, one Seven Inch and an half Dto. and five Cohorns.*

Before the end of January, Henry arrived at the camp in Cambridge, his return to Massachusetts welcomed by a gratified military and a very pregnant, beleaguered Lucy. Martha Washington had joined George in Cambridge in December. After Henry's return, he and Lucy received an invitation to dine with the Washingtons. And not long after the couple were reunited, on February 26, a brand-new resident arrived on the scene: Lucy gave birth to a daughter, whom the couple named after her mother.

Just days later, another invitation emanated from a Georgian mansion on the Road to Watertown (present-day Brattle Street) in Cambridge. Formerly the estate of wealthy planter John Vassall Jr., it now served as headquarters for the Continentals and their commander.

The Vassall and Royall families were entwined through business, marriage, and their loyalty to the Crown. Like the Royall family, the Vassalls made their fortune running plantations—in their case, sugar plantations in Jamaica. The Vassalls had fled Cambridge as the Royalls had Medford. When the Vassall family left, at least seven people enslaved at the home stayed behind. One woman, Cuba, was originally enslaved to Isaac Royall Sr. when he brought at least twenty-seven peo-ple from Antigua, where Cuba was born.

Then Royall did "give and bequeath unto my well beloved Daughter Penelope" eight individuals, Cuba and her family among them. When Penelope married into the Vassall family, they moved to Cambridge. Cuba married Tony, an enslaved coachman. The couple had at least six children, several of whom were sold by the Vassalls or given away, in-cluding their young son Darby. Those remaining on the Road to Wa-tertown divided their work among a variety of enslaver properties. When Darby's new enslaver died at Bunker Hill, the six-year-old was able to rejoin his family.

There the enslaved family remained, elsewhere on the property, as the Vassall estate transformed into an American military hub. (Years later, a story emerged that young Darby Vassall had refused to work for the commander of the Continental forces, an enslaver in his own right.) The household and the times were awash in contradictions.

That same military commander was now sending a letter to a for-merly enslaved woman who lived just across the Charles River in Bos-ton. It was perhaps the only time the general had corresponded with a Black woman (or man, for that matter), a reflection of the hypocrisy and confusion around the concept of "freedom" that so defined the colonies. He was writing in response to a poem he'd been sent, one that clearly pleased him greatly.

Mrs Phillis,

> *Your favour of the 26th of October did not reach my hands 'till the middle of December. Time enough, you will say, to have given an answer ere this. Granted. But a variety of important occurrences, continually interposing to distract the mind and withdraw the attention, I hope will apologize for the delay, and plead my excuse for the seeming, but not real, neglect.*

Phillis read on as the general thanked her for the "polite notice" Phillis had made of him in the "elegant Lines" she had written; "the style and manner exhibit a striking proof of your great poetical Talents." He wrote that he might have had the poem published but was "apprehensive, that, while I only meant to give the World this new instance of your genius, I might have incurred the imputation of Vanity. This, and nothing else, determined me not to give it place in the public Prints."

At the close of the letter, Phillis noted an invitation.

> *If you should ever come to Cambridge, or near Head Quarters, I shall be happy to see a person so favoured by the Muses, and to whom nature has been so liberal and beneficent in her dispensations. I am, with great Respect, Your obedt humble servant,*

> *G. Washington*

And though Washington would not publish the poem, he did pass it along to Esther Reed's husband, Joseph.

"I recollect nothing else worth giving you the trouble of, unless you can be amused by reading a Letter and Poem addressed to me by Mrs or Miss Phillis Wheatley," Washington wrote his aide-de-camp. "In searching over a parcel of Papers the other day, in order to destroy such as were useless, I brought it to light again—at first, With a view of doing justice to her great poetical Genius, I had a great Mind to publish the Poem, but not knowing whether it might not be considered rather as a mark of my own vanity than as a Compliment to her I laid it aside till I came across it again in the manner just mentioned."

Esther's husband arranged to have a Pennsylvania newspaper publish Phillis's poem before spring was out. Her reputation in and around Boston, which had already taken her to London, was now spreading farther throughout the colonies and into Philadelphia. But more than balladry would be needed to keep spirits up and movements energized in what was shaping up to be a turbulent year, regardless of one's loyalties or station.

There was a question on everyone's mind, and Mercy Otis Warren was asked point-blank to answer it:

"Pray Madam, are you for an American Monarchy or Republic?" John Adams wrote her.

Mercy seemed to question his motive and whether or not he was patronizing her. Unsurprisingly, Mercy did not let that stop her from sharing her thoughts.

"And though the asking my opinion in So Momentous a question as the Form of Government to be prefered by a people who have an opportunity to shake off the fetters both of Monarchie and Aristocratic Tyrany, Might be Designed to Ridicule the sex for paying any Attention to political Matters," she wrote him, "yet I shall Venture to Give you a serious Reply . . .

"I have Long been an Admirer of A Republican form of Goverment, And was Convinced Even before I saw the Advantages Deliniated in so Clear and Concise A Manner by your Masterly pen, that if Established upon the Genuine principles of Equal Liberty, it was A Form productive of Many Excellent qualities, and Heroic Virtues in Human Nature, which often Lie Dormant for want of opportunity for Exertions, And the Heavenly Spark is smothered in the Corruption of Courts, or its Lustre obscurr'd in the Pompous Glare of Regal pageantry."

Spring arrived, and Lucy and her Harry could see the fruits of his ice-ridden labors to retrieve the armament from Fort Ticonderoga.

Beginning March 4, Continental forces moved stealthily south of Boston and began fortifying Dorchester Heights with Henry's "noble train" of artillery while distracting the British from their movements with attacks from farther north. With the redcoats' eyes fixed on Cambridge, troops wrapped wagon wheels with straw to help muffle the telltale clickety-clack sound of iron-shod wooden hoops against stone as they transported the artillery to Dorchester. By the time British commander General William Howe noticed the guns aimed in his direction from the south, his choices were extremely limited. A hope to remove the armament was decidedly quashed by a snowstorm. Rather than endure what they anticipated would be a brutal defeat, the British chose to abandon the colonial seaport. The Siege of Boston had finally come to an end.

March 17 would come to be known as "evacuation day," one that saw more than 10,000 troops and hundreds of loyalists leave Boston. Among those departing were Lucy's family, who boarded ships bound for England. She would never see them again.

This success further cemented Henry Knox in the minds of Washington, Congress, and other political and military leaders as an indispensable commander of the American artillery. But if Lucy had anything to say about it, she would never be left behind again, no matter where Henry's new responsibilities took him.

Isaac Royall Jr. had fled the Boston area months before the British mass evacuation. However, he was finding supporting himself more challenging once he was far from the comforts, connections, and properties that he had left behind. Around the time of the evacuation, Royall sent word back to Medford arranging to sell those he had enslaved in a bid to finance his new life.

> *Please to sell the following negroes: Stephen and George; they each cost £60 sterling; and I would take £50, or even £15, apiece for them. Hagar cost £35 sterling; but I will take £30 for her. I gave for Mira £35, but will take £25. If Mr. Benjamin Hall will give the $100 for her which he offered, he may have her, it being a good place. As to Betsey, and her daughter Nancy, the former may tarry, or take her freedom, as she may choose; and Nancy you may put out to some good family by the year.*

Belinda was not mentioned in this request, and her location at that time or where she might have gone during and after the siege remains a mystery.

But she would resurface in Boston soon enough.

Now that the winter encampment at Cambridge had ended, Lucy received word from Henry: "Certain it is they (the enemy) are packing up & going off bag & baggage—how far or where is yet uncertain—if to New York my Dear Lucy must prepare to follow them—as we are Citizens of the World any place will be our home & equally cheap . . ."

He signed off writing Lucy to "kiss your heavenly babe & bless it for me."

As it turned out, war and the headquarters of the Continental Army were indeed heading south. Henry's description of the pair being "Citizens of the World" during this new phase of the couple's life together would prove prescient. For, indeed, it would be many years before Lucy, Henry, and their family would have a stable home of their own.

For now, Lucy was a new mother separated by an ocean from her family and by miles from her Henry, who, by April, was already in New York City, where the Continental Army was setting up its new base of operations. If there was a way to join those descending—many military wives among them—upon New York, Lucy was determined to find one.

Yet, even before the Continental Army made themselves at home on the island of Manhattan, the shifting focus of the war was already impacting that city's inhabitants, patriot and loyalist alike.

CHAPTER 8

Manahatta

By the time the Continental Army headed to New York, it was already a city of roughly 25,000 people—one of the largest in the colonies—and a booming maritime hub, the "nexus of the Northern and Southern Colonies, as a Kind of Key to the whole Continent," as Massachusetts congressman John Adams described it in a letter to George Washington in January.

Manahatta, Manna-hata, Manahata, Manahatin, Manhattes . . . For more than a century, maps had featured Anglicized variations on these names for this land. What these varied spellings had in common was that they were all derived from terms the Lenape had long used to describe their "hilly island" or "place for gathering wood to make bows."

These are the "Lenapehoking," the lands of the island's original inhabitants, the Lenape. (The word "Lenape" means original people.) Today, most Lenape—or Lenni-Lenape—are part of the Delaware Nation. The numerous confederacies, tribes, and bands and the dialects that they spoke were—and are—often confused, conflated, and misrepresented. European mapmakers viewed tribes and trails as interchangeable and identified the landscapes accordingly by laying out the routes they intended to seize and control. Maps and the nomenclature they contained wielded tremendous power.

The Lenni-Lenape were a nation that extended north along the Hudson, east onto Long Island, and south past what is now Philadelphia and into Delaware. Confederacies consisted of individual tribes who, for example, spoke the same language. Tribes in turn comprised individual bands. The Wappinger were a large confederacy of Algonquian-speaking indigenous people of the eastern regions of North America. Dialects also united various factions, and the Lenape consisted of speakers of Munsee, Unalachtigo, and Unami. For example, the Wecquaesgeek were a Munsee-speaking people.

The Lenape, part of the Algonquian people, had lived in the region for thousands of years prior to 1607, when Henry Hudson, in the employ of the Dutch East India Company—the first publicly traded multinational company—first sailed the river that would eventually bear his name.

In the 1620s, another firm—the Dutch *West* India Company—seized upon this island to build a colony from which they could export beaver skins, among other resources. And they were powerful, even endowed with governmental powers, including maintaining their own military force, minting money, and essentially operating as a colonial state in their own right.

The Dutch eventually gave way to the British, and in 1664 "New Amsterdam" became "New York." Not long after, the Lenni-Lenape living on Staten Island experienced their own deceitful exchanges with Europeans. Executed April 13, 1670, a "contract" between the governor-general of New York and "Aquepo, Warrines, Minqua-Sachemack, Pemantowes, Quewequeen, Wewanecameck, and Mataris, on the behalf of themselves as the true Sachem owners, and lawful Indian proprietors of Staten Island and of all other Indians any way concerned therein on the other part . . ." ultimately stated that the above-named Lenni-Lenape sachems sold Staten Island to King Charles II of England. They were given a year to vacate the lands and promised never to attempt to reclaim them or attack those living there.

The contract read in part:

The payment agreed upon for the purchase of Staten Island conveyed this day by the Indian Sachem Proprietors is

Four hundred fathom of wampum
Thirty Match Coats
Eight Coats of Duzzens made up
Thirty Shirts
Thirty Kettles
Twenty Guns
A Firkin of Powder
Sixty Barres of Load
Thirty Axes
Thirty Howes
Fifty Knives

Six Lenape youth also signed the document, as a sign that generations to come would continue to honor the pact: "The mark of Rokoques, about 6 years old, a girl. The mark of Shinguinnemo, about 12 years old, a girl."

The inclusion of girls in this engagement is significant if not mandatory. The Lenape are (like the Cherokee, for example) matrilineal. Everything passes from generation to generation through the mother, including leadership roles. As the English intended for Staten Island to pass down from the British king to *his* heirs, the involvement of subsequent generations of leaders was likely necessary. For the Lenape, that could mean the inclusion of girls and/or women, something that was unheard-of in the English culture. What was unheard-of on the part of the Lenape was buying or selling land.

The "wampum" mentioned as part of this interaction is a perennially misused term. The beautiful artifacts were—and still are—used to symbolize promises or agreements as well as serving ornamental purposes.

For Indigenous peoples, wampum was a treasured and important part of life. "A white string of beads" was commonly mentioned as part of exchanges during talks between the English and many different Indigenous representatives. When John Verelst painted Theyanoguin, a Mohawk leader who traveled to the British royal court of Queen Anne in 1710, he depicted him holding wampum, intended to symbolize the Mohawk alliance with the Stuart monarch. Quahog clams, familiar to those in colonies like New York, Connecticut, Rhode Island, and Massachusetts, contained purple interiors, making them even more valuable and providing a contrast in color and therefore meaning.

The European colonists, however, saw wampum differently and decided to use it among themselves and set it as actual currency. By 1650, the shell-borne beads were officially recognized by the Massachusetts Bay Colony as legal tender and exchange rates were set. In a sense, the Europeans took a long-standing, meaningful, and often spiritual object and reduced it to cash.

In the mid-1770s, ships dotting the waters around Manhattan came and went to locations as nearby as Brooklyn and also oceans away. Oysters abounded in the surrounding waters, long prized by the Lenape. (Before being purchased by its namesake, Samuel Ellis, the site of one of America's prime entry points for immigrants was referred to as one of the Oyster Islands by the Dutch, as was the current home of the Statue of Liberty.) The shipping industry was a major source of employment as well. Workers loaded and unloaded the ships, fashioned sails, and served as pilots, carpenters, and stevedores. Those filling these roles included free and enslaved Black workers. Though the slave market on Wall Street had closed in 1762, slavery continued in the British colony. By the middle of the eighteenth century, as many as 20 percent of the population of New York was enslaved, and more than 40 percent of households had at least one enslaved individual under their roofs.

The lower point of the island was humming with industry and arrivals from the world over. In the spring of 1776, it was also buzzing with news of the arrival of the Continental forces as well as British ships. The city was divided about which they preferred.

Lorenda Holmes probably never imagined that her loyalty to England would land her under house arrest and accused of participating in a supposed plot to assassinate the commander of the American forces. Yet, even before she was embroiled in that conspiracy, her life and her well-being had already been turned upside down by the increasing number of rebel troops arriving in the city she now called home.

Lorenda had been living with the family of Jacob Walton, a prominent loyalist merchant, landowner, and member of the New York Assembly. Walton had a grand country home at Horn's Hook, just north of Blackwell's Island—called "Minnehanonck" by the Lenape and "Roosevelt Island" by Manhattanites today—which provided a view of the East River and a treacherous confluence of waters known as Hell Gate. The Continentals wanted Walton's strategic view.

She had lived there, Lorenda later wrote, for years in the "most perfect tranquility" until New York became "a seat of War where all the Rebel Troops were brought." In March, Lorenda was identified as a loyalist, along with the rest of the Waltons. With the impending arrival of the Continental forces, shifting tides and limited tolerance for Crown-leaning residents forced the Walton family to leave the city in April of 1776. General Charles Lee—a former British officer who joined the Continentals—essentially told Walton to get out so that the Continentals could move in. (The remnants of the property form part of the foundation of Gracie Mansion, modern-day home of New York City mayors.)

Lorenda, in turn, moved in with her aunt on Great Dock Street near "La Bourse," or the Royal Exchange, which sat near the intersection of Broad and Dock Streets, and slightly northeast of the military hospital and the Battery at the southern tip of the island. It wasn't long before soldiers moved into Lorenda and her aunt's home as well, and the two women found themselves turned out into the street. The pair decided to seek refuge at the home of some like-minded friends, the Mortier family.

The two headed north out of the city, past the end of Broad Way and west of the Negros Burial Ground located in an area once called the Palisades. From there, it was a path over a ditch through Lispenard's Meadows. This trail linked the city of New York to a tiny rural village just north of the city called "Greenwich," roughly two miles from the southern tip of the island. The area is still known as a village today, though it is no longer little and a far cry from the rural colonial estates and farms occupied by people like the late Abraham Mortier. When the former British tax master died in 1775, he left his widow the estate and home, also known as Richmond Hill House. The twenty-six-acre parcel was originally leased from Trinity Church, and the house and lands were bordered by what are now King, Varick, Charlton, and Mac-Dougal Streets. Columned and pilastered with an elevated position, the home did not want for ornament or sweeping views of rolling farmland and the Hudson River.

Lorenda's tenure there would not be a long one. Come spring, she found herself embroiled in the loyalist cause, pressed into service on a bizarre mission that found her wading into the dark, cold waters of the East River.

At the time, His Majesty's Ship *Asia*, under command of a Captain George Vandeput, was offshore in the East River opposite Burling Slip near Bedloe's Island. About two miles below the *Asia* sat the ship *Three Sisters*, having just arrived from Boston with orders and letters from General Thomas Gage—onetime commander of British forces in America and former military governor of Massachusetts—to friends in the city. But the American forces positioned sentinels onshore to ensure that no communication would pass between the ships themselves and between the vessels and Manhattan.

Lorenda resolved, however, at the "hazard of her life" to get herself on board to retrieve those letters. So one evening she decided to take a stroll to Burling Slip, just above the docking site of the Long Island Ferry. She could see the *Asia* . . . and the Continental sentinels posted along the shore could see her. Undaunted, handkerchief in hand, Lorenda began signaling the British ship. The sentinels threatened to fire on Lorenda, but she kept waving the cloth in hopes of getting Captain Vandeput's attention—which, incredibly, she did.

Vandeput sent a boat to retrieve Lorenda and positioned his own troops on the ship's deck. As the boat approached her, Lorenda leapt into the water to reach it and injured her side in the process. Somehow the sailors pulled her aboard the *Asia*, where she told Vandeput her mission. He dispatched her in a longboat to the *Three Sisters*. Now it was near 9:00 p.m., the black water surrounding her and her escorts as the longboat pulled alongside the *Three Sisters*. There, Lorenda retrieved the letters and placed them in a pile of Holland, a fine linen of high quality. With the captain's assistance, Lorenda fashioned the post-bearing cloth into a petticoat. She put it on under her clothes and was taken by boat and promptly deposited on the shore of Long Island.

Ferry services were legion along the East River. Sites like Fulton Ferry Landing were booming, often transporting animals and produce from farmers on Long Island to the markets of Manhattan. That night the Brookland Ferry carried Lorenda back to the city, and there she headed to the home of one Mrs. Mann, whose husband had been a junior officer under British general Gage. Lorenda passed the letters to Mrs. Mann. Her job was done. Almost.

Mrs. Mann told Lorenda that she also had *goods* on board the ship that she had initially left behind after vacating Boston. Lorenda approached Sons of Liberty leader and provincial congressman Colonel Alexander McDougall, of the 1st New York Regiment, for permission for the pair to retrieve Mann's property from the ship and promised she would not retrieve any more communiqués while on board. McDougall agreed—provided the pair submit to a strip search. After enduring that humiliation, it was irritating to find that McDougall did not live up to his word. He subsequently took Mann's property as his own, and Lorenda, thinking she'd had enough of espionage, seemed to consider leaving the city for good. For the time being, however, she headed north, to East Chester. Any future forays into Manhattan would have to wait. For now, at least.

By mid-April 1776, Martha Washington, Henry Knox, and George Washington, along with other officers and their wives, had arrived in New York City, where the Continental Army established their headquarters at No. 1 Broadway, the Kennedy House.

Captain Archibald Kennedy, a former British naval officer and an exceedingly wealthy landowner, had fled his grand house in the city and taken his family to New Jersey as the tensions between the British and the Americans increased. The two-story home, complete with a cupola and a drawing room reported to be fifty feet long, was situated on a corner near the Bowling Green, where the grand equestrian statue of King George III stood. The Kennedy House was conveniently located near the Battery and Fort George and was a short walk from one of the central hubs of downtown activity: the Queen's Head Tavern.

Samuel Fraunces (or Francis or Frances, depending on who was writing) was a West Indian man who had come to New York in the 1760s and ran several successful taverns. In 1762, he purchased the property at 49 Great Dock Street at the corner of Broad Street—the former site of a dance hall run by Henry Holt. It stood three stories, had dry cellars and fourteen fireplaces, and was convenient to the ferry. Its tile-and-lead roof had already seen its own form of action in the war, when an eighteen-pound cannonball fired from the HMS *Asia* pierced it in the summer of 1775.

In an ad in the *New York Gazette*, Fraunces informed potential patrons that he had "fitted up said Tavern in a very commodious Manner for their Reception and Entertainment." He offered weekly board for "gentlemen who choose it," as well as families. His gustatory offerings included oysters, "all sorts of pickles," "alamode beef," pastries, sweetmeats, jellies, and more, including "necessary articles to set out a des[s]ert." He pledged to "Make it his chief Study to furnish every Accommodation in the most genteel Manner, with the utmost Decorum and Acknowledgement."

Though he ran other successful businesses, the Queen's Head or "Sign of the Queen" (or simply "Fraunces's") became a magnet for those friendly to the fight for independence, and the site played key roles in it, offering space and sustenance for military officers, their guests, and other patriot-minded patrons. The tavern hosted meetings of the Sons of Liberty. New York's Provincial Congress met upstairs in the tavern's Long Room. And it served as the site of a court-martial in April of 1776.

The night he arrived in town, George Washington noted in his diary that he had dined at "Sam's." To many who knew him, the tavern keeper was also referred to as "Black Sam," and on a separate occasion Washington also recorded in his accounts, "Saml Frances, Alias Black Sam for Dinner."

Washington originally quartered at the residence of colonial governor William Tryon, who had taken refuge aboard the HMS *Duchess of Gordon*, which, like the gunship *Asia*, sat in New York Harbor. However, Washington soon joined his wife, Martha, and moved into the home belonging to the loyalist Mortier family. From this spot atop Richmond Hill, Washington conducted the business of war and assembled around him a staff befitting a Virginia gentleman and general. Naturally, some of those working there, mingling, moving, and bustling about, did so in a bid to gather information on his movements and plans. There, starting in April, the general and Martha employed a housekeeper named Mary Smith.

Someone who had not yet arrived in New York City in April with the troops, the Washingtons, and other officers was Lucy Knox, and she wasn't happy about it.

Lucy wrote her beloved from her home in the Cornhill neighborhood of Boston, where she cared for their three-month-old daughter. She noted that while other officers' wives had gone to the city on the Hudson, she remained in Massachusetts.

"I should long before this have indulged myself in the pleasure of writing to him who is allways in my thoughts, whose image is deeply imprinted on my heart, and whom I love too much for my peace . . ." she began. "Is my Harry well. Is he happy. No, that cannot be when he reflects how wretched he has left me . . ."

She mentioned the "scenes and gaiety" she imagined she was missing out on in New York, and the "tender infant" whom Henry must surely miss; little Lucy had been christened the Sunday prior.

Her tack appeared to work. In early May, Henry responded and told Lucy to "prepare for your Journey with as much haste as convenient." In advance of her departure he instructed her to "sell Romeo—he never will be of any service to you" and said she should travel with "Billy," who would serve as her guard. He reminded Lucy to pack the couple's linens and spoons.

Later that month, Lucy joined Henry at No. 1 Broad Way, presumably linens and spoons safely in tow. The Kennedy House—and former site of Mrs. Kocks's tavern—was not just the headquarters for the Continental Army and where Henry maintained the headquarters of the artillery; it would now become a temporary home for these two "citizens of the world."

Lucy and Henry were finally together, but as May wore on, Henry and his fellow officers understood that trouble was likely coming—from across the sea, from up the coast, and from the waters in and around New York Harbor. And soon more trouble would come from increasingly turbulent waters farther south.

Mary's life preaching in the Dismal Swamp had ended, but her travels were just beginning. The burning of Norfolk resulted in a number of loyalist families abandoning their lives in and around the port city and joining the British flotilla offshore. Norfolk, though in charred shambles, was now firmly in the grasp of American hands.

Earlier in the year, not long after the fiery upheaval in Norfolk, Lord Dunmore had given instructions to fortify Tucker's Mill Point (or simply Mill Point, and eventually known as Hospital Point). The location sat just across the river from gutted Norfolk and a few miles to the northwest of Portsmouth. The exiled Dunmore and his fleet moved there from the chaotic ashes of Norfolk. Mary and her daughters, Patience, Hannah, and Zilpha, ranging in age from four years to twelve years old, would soon find themselves among them.

In April, the Virginia Committee of Safety had let Mary's enslaver, John Willoughby, know that, as the loyalist that they believed him to be, he had to move away from shore and ordered that those enslaved by him be taken by militia.

The patriot press kept a keen eye on Willoughby's movements. He was either an ardent loyalist or the coerced collateral damage of Dunmore's last days in charge.

Amid news of marriages, deaths, troop movements, stolen bay horses, a congressionally proclaimed General Fast throughout the colonies, and the arrival to town of a "famous doctor" who "bleeds, and draws teeth," the Friday, May 10, 1776, edition of *The Virginia Gazette* reflected on Willoughby's choice to make for the British ships. "Col. John Willoughby, of Norfolk county, with his son, and between 60 and 70 negroes, have gone on board Lord Dunmore's fleet . . ." the newspaper reported, adding that the Whig community had already given Willoughby the benefit of the doubt as to where his loyalties might lie, to the Crown or to America. No one was looking the other way now, however. Willoughby had, according to the *Gazette*, "voluntarily, and without any compulsion, gone over to our enemies, thereby marking himself a vile apostate, and *black* traitor."

While Dunmore had given the plantation owner a commission as lieutenant of the county, Willoughby had long insisted that he was "compelled" to side with the British government; in other words, it was not his choice. Witnesses came to his defense, touting Willoughby's allegiance to the colonies, and he was restored to the "former good opinion of his countrymen."

Willoughby was wealthy enough that news of his actions made its way up the coast to the Pennsylvania newspapers as well. One week later, the *Gazette* sang a different tune. The editor wrote he was "exceedingly sorry for having bestowed unmerited epithets upon gentlemen that do not deserve them, but who rather merit the commiseration and thanks of their country."

With so many individuals acting out of the desire to ensure the continuation of their way of life, it was difficult to discern who was truly a friend to the Crown and who was merely trying to appease the power that be at any given time. In good standing or not, reputation repaired or marred, Willoughby saw much of the enslaved population of his plantation flee to the British ships. The colonial militia, it seems, did not take possession of all of them. Exactly how many made it to the

British lines, how many took other routes to freedom, it is difficult to say. His son, John Willoughby Jr., would later claim that eighty-seven individuals abandoned Willoughby Point.

Mary and her three daughters were among them, eventually making it to Tucker's Mill Point, the latest Dunmore and loyalist stronghold. By then there were barracks. The number of Black recruits continued to rise. There were also fellow Methodists and a religious community for Mary to join.

An outbreak of typhus aboard one of the ships in Dunmore's fleet, the *Otter*, and the eventual eruption of smallpox—which took a particular toll on Black residents of Tucker's Mill Point—greatly depleted the ranks of Dunmore's Royal Ethiopian Regiment.

It was time to move on yet again, and the seafaring group of military, loyalists, and those enslaved who had abandoned their bondage in and around Norfolk departed Tucker's Mill Point. Ships—close to one hundred of them—sailed out of the Elizabeth River, up through the Chesapeake Bay, and on to Gwynn's Island, a small island off the Virginia coast roughly sixty miles due east of Richmond. They arrived in late May.

In their wake, the British left Tucker's Point dotted with hundreds of graves of typhoid and smallpox victims. As the flotilla moved north, the surrounding waters became the final resting place for still more dead, unceremoniously tossed overboard night after night, sinking into the depths or washing ashore, much to the horror of Virginia's residents.

For Mary, Willoughby Point—if not the Willoughby family—was now behind her. Mary's journey would soon take her even farther away from the swamp that had once served as her pulpit.

The Continental forces were woefully ill-prepared to manage the influx and threat of maritime traffic. The seas had become a massive thoroughfare, a refuge for some, treacherous and foreboding for others.

Guarding the comings and goings of ships fell to those who stood vigil along the shorelines. Their lamps could not go out. Ever.

As night crept over the Atlantic, the gloaming gave way to darkness, engulfing the shoreline and the seafarers striving to arrive safely there. The lights led the way through murk, fog, and tempest, the promise of a safe mooring inherent in their steady glow.

There were no days off for Hannah Thomas. She occupied her post at the Gurnet Point lighthouse off the coast of Plymouth, Massachusetts, 7 days a week, 365 days a year. She could never step away. This she had done since she lost her husband. He had joined the Continental Army, as so many in their community in and around Plymouth had done, but it was not musket fire that had ended his life but rather that other menace, smallpox.

The lighthouse had stood on the Massachusetts shore for eleven years, since 1768. It boasted the very first twin lights in the colonies, and Hannah was the first woman in those colonies to *wo*-man this facility or any other.

The lights stood at either end of the residence Hannah shared with her three children: thirty feet long, fifteen feet high, and fifteen feet wide. Each of those structures looming over the shore contained two lamps, each with two flat-wick lamps. The glow from burning whale oil at Gurnet Point had replaced the feebler light cast by tallow candles, and the distinct double beacons visually distinguished Hannah's location from the nearby Barnstable Light.

Each night, Hannah ensured that all the wicks remained lit, and while the whale oil burned brighter than its predecessor, its burning also generated more smoke and enough black, powdery soot to blacken the windows. Several times a night, Hannah ascended the steps to the top of the seaboard structures, trimmed the wicks, and wiped clean the wooden-framed and begrimed panes of glass. Every morning, she snuffed the lights out, cleaned the precious lamps, and prepared for the next night's vigil.

The sea was life to the colonies. It provided fish to eat, transported wares to sell, and carried goods to sustain a fragile population. But the seas also brought danger, now headed to New York, where trouble and treachery were already brewing on this island amid the roiling waters of rebellion, and those most in peril hadn't seen it coming—or could have ever suspected who might be involved.

CHAPTER 9

A Plot Is Afoot

Later that spring, Lorenda left East Chester and headed back south to New York City. But by the time she arrived in mid-June, she realized that New York had a new resident: the rebel commander George Washington. The general had moved into a grand house near Greenwich. As it happened, her aunt, Mary Smith, was currently serving as Washington's housekeeper.

On this trip to Manhattan, Lorenda once again carried letters intended for friends of the Crown, in this case the Ryan family. When Lorenda arrived at her destination, she was greeted by a house in a state of complete disarray and confusion. The Ryans were anxiously biding their time, waiting for what they imagined to be the inevitable: to be overtaken by rebels. Mr. Ryan decided to head north for Harlem, while Mrs. Ryan begged Lorenda to stay with her. Lorenda agreed. While it is unclear how long Lorenda remained with the Ryans, what they feared soon came to pass: A mob surrounded the Ryan home. Not long after, Continental soldiers burst in, swords drawn, and proceeded to drag Mrs. Ryan from her bed. However, the rebel intruders appeared pleasantly surprised to discover Lorenda on the premises.

"Oh, we have got the damned Tory and the penny post at last!" they shouted upon spotting her. No sooner had they seized Lorenda than they ordered her to strip, hoping to locate any letters this notorious messenger might be carrying. Mortified, Lorenda had no choice but to comply. The men promptly dragged the unclothed Lorenda through the house and into the drawing room, which faced the busy New York City street. They forced her to stand in front of the window, in plain sight of onlookers, naked, while they hunted through her garments. Lorenda would later write that she suffered "no wounds or bruises from them only shame and horror of the mind."

By five o'clock in the afternoon the mob was off to root out more loyalists. Yet again, Lorenda managed to flee. She headed north through Lispenard's Meadows and arrived at a home to which she had fled in the past—the Mortier house at Richmond Hill, where George Washington had recently taken up residence. She sought to rejoin her aunt, Mary Smith. In recent days, however, Smith had been outed as a loyalist and "taken up" on June 23 for her part in a widespread British conspiracy to oust Washington and the Continentals from New York. We don't know how Lorenda was greeted by Continental soldiers upon arrival at the house, but she was permitted to see her aunt, whom she found in very poor condition, now a prisoner in the place she had come to call home. Mary Smith and her son Horatio were confined to a single room and slept on the floor. Now, with her aunt's sympathies revealed, Lorenda's own actions and loyalties were under heightened scrutiny. As such, Lorenda's movements around the house were limited as well. Washington, she later recalled, "ordered her a prisoner at large that was to walk no further than within the lines of his Body Guards."

These soldiers were members of Washington's recently commissioned Life Guards. Washington had recruited them in March while still in Cambridge. In establishing the force, he instructed his commanding officers to choose four men from each regiment of the Continental Army, all of whom met the following criteria: Physically, Washington wanted soldiers who stood between five feet, eight inches and five feet, ten inches tall. (Standing an estimated six feet, two inches himself, perhaps Washington desired a slight edge in the height category.) He also required that the recruits for his personal protection unit be "handsomely and well made" and at all times maintain a "clean and spruce" appearance. Of course, "sobriety, honesty, and good behavior" were a must. To command "His Excellency's Guard," Washington chose Captain Caleb Gibbs. The motto of the Life Guards was "Conquer or Die."

That choice was about to be made rather clear now, in June. Clearly, a plot *was* afoot, and spies truly were everywhere. There had been more than one right under Gibbs's nose—but Lorenda would turn out to be the least of the general's worries.

After just a few days under house arrest at Richmond Hill, Lorenda encountered a young soldier by the name of Thomas Hickey. Sergeant Hickey was an Irishman who had originally fought with the British. After being taken prisoner at Bunker Hill, Hickey deserted to the Continental Army. He now served as one of Washington's Life Guards under Captain Caleb Gibbs.

Rumors and hearsay were in ample supply at Richmond Hill—not to mention in the bustling city to its south. One rumor was that the British would attempt to assassinate or kidnap General Washington in a bid to distract and demoralize the Continental forces. If the rebels could be reduced to panicked chaos at news of an attack on or the loss of their commanding general, British troops might be able to exploit the resulting pandemonium and set fire to rebel magazines. Havoc would give the British an upper hand as they prepared to land large numbers of their ships at New York.

Word of the conspiracy spread. Accusations flew in every direction, pointing equally to the upper echelons of New York government.

On the orders of George Washington, the loyalist mayor of New York City, David Matthews, was arrested for aiding the British as they prepared to take the city. Matthews was believed to be in league with the British governor of New York, William Tryon, as a part of the supposedly far-reaching plot to upend Washington's tenure in Manhattan. And now the long arm of the conspiracy had reached Washington's most trusted protectors: A chief suspect was none other than Sergeant Thomas Hickey.

"This poor lad was taken off his post," Lorenda wrote, "the crime alleged against him was that of accepting two shillings sterling from some Gentleman Loyalist."

Hickey's trial took place June 26, and the verdict issued in short order. Details of Hickey's ordeal were elaborated upon in the trial transcripts and ultimately came down to—just as Lorenda had heard—accepting loyalist bribes. A member of Washington's own Life Guards accepting monies, no matter how little, in exchange for details of, say, the commander's movements and vulnerabilities could not go unpunished. After a short and not-so-sweet trial, Hickey was sentenced.

One day after the trial, on June 27, 1776, George Washington approved Hickey's sentence, which would be carried out the following day, June 28. That day Washington issued the following:

By His Excellency GEORGE WASHINGTON, Esq., General and Commander-in-Chief of the Army of the United Colonies:

To the Provost-Marshal of the said Army:

Whereas Thomas Hickey, a soldier inlisted in the service of the said United Colonies, has been duly convicted by a General Court-Martial of mutiny and sedition, and also of holding a treacherous correspondence with the enemies of said Colonies, contrary to the Rules and Regulations established for the government of the said troops; and the said Thomas Hickey, being so convicted, has been sentenced to death, by being hanged by the neck till he shall be dead; which sentence, by the unanimous advice of the General Officers of the said Army, I have thought proper to confirm: These are, therefore, to will and require you to execute the said sentence upon the said Thomas Hickey this day, at eleven o' clock in the forenoon, upon the ground between the encampments of the Brigades of Brigadier-General Spencer and Lord Stirling; and for so doing this shall be your sufficient warrant. Given under my hand this twenty-eighth day of June, in the year of our Lord one thousand seven hundred and seventy-six.

GEORGE WASHINGTON. Head-Quarters, New-York, June 28, 1776.

News spread of Hickey's imminent hanging just off Bowery (in a field near what is now known as Chinatown), as hangings were often publicly attended affairs. On June 28, 1776, an estimated 20,000 on-lookers turned up, among them Continental soldiers who were ordered to attend—to serve as witnesses to a fatally cautionary tale. The conspiracy was, indeed, traced up the ladder to include colonial governor William Tryon and Mayor David Matthews. Though Hickey was hardly alone in the conspiracy, alone he stood on the gallows before a crowd of thousands.

"I die in the Twenty-eighth year of my age," Hickey said before the fatal drop. "And may the Lord have mercy upon my soul." That moment, as the support beneath his feet disappeared and the noose snuffed the breath and life from his body, Thomas Hickey became the first person in the history of what would become the United States of America to be tried and executed for the crimes of mutiny and sedition.

That same day, Washington had other pressing business to attend to: It was clear that Mary Smith could no longer continue serving in his home.

"Having occasion to part with my Housekeeper, a Mrs Thompson somewhere in your Neighbourhood, is recommended to me as a fit person to supply her place," Washington wrote a Colonel James Clinton on June 28. "I therefore give you the trouble of forwarding the Inclosed Letter to her, & beg of you to hasten her to this place or an answer, as I am entirely destitute, & put to much inconvenience for want of discharge the duties of this Office."

Time has a way of embellishing facts, like some patina of lore covering the copper-clad truth that lies beneath. This was indeed true in the case of the widespread plot against George Washington, which was far from over. Over the years a popular story cropped up, one that had legs well into the twenty-first century: a cunning scheme to poison the general's peas.

Peas were a food staple for Continental troops. At the winter encampment at Cambridge, an order described rations for "all Troops of the United Colonies." In August of 1775, Congress had authorized rations for troops. It is a fascinating list of what was regarded as a reasonable diet for American soldiers during the era. But since funds for the Continental forces were always tight, the included items represented more of a wish list than an ironclad reality.

> *Corn'd Beef and Pork, four days in a week.*
> *Salt Fish one day, and fresh Beef two days.*
> *As Milk cannot be procured during the Winter Season, the Men*
>   *are to have one pound and a half of Beef, or eighteen Ounces*
>   *of Pork Pr day.* [Earlier in 1775 Congress had authorized
>   "One pound of fresh beef, or 3/4 of a pound of Pork, or one
>   pound of Salt Fish, pr diem."]
> *Half pint of Rice, or a pint of Indian Meal Pr Week.*
> *One Quart of Spruce Beer Pr day, or nine Gallons of Molasses to*
>   *one hundred Men [per] week. Six pounds of Candles to one*
>   *hundred Men Pr week, for guards.* [Congress authorized
>   three pounds per one hundred men.]
> *Six Ounces of Butter, or nine Ounces of Hogs-Lard Pr week.*
>   [Congress did not authorize rations of butter or lard for
>   troops.]
> *Three pints of Pease, or Beans Pr Man Pr Week, or Vegetables*
>   *equivalent, allowing Six Shillings Pr Bushel for Beans, or*
>   *Pease—two and eight pence Pr Bushel for Onions—One and*
>   *four pence Pr Bushel for Potatoes and Turnips.*
> *One pound of Flour Pr Man each day—Hard Bread to be dealt*
>   *out one day in a week, in lieu of Flour.*

According to a popular account, conspirators had enticed a female servant in Washington's home to dump arsenic in his peas—a vegetable rumored to be a favorite of the general. But as one version of the story goes, this woman had a change of heart at the last second. One delicious embellishment to this particular tale describes her dramatically hurling the peas into the yard, where chickens snacked upon them and promptly keeled over.

In other versions of this story, a plot to poison Washington was uncovered, and a female servant bravely intervened to save him. The heroine was Phoebe Fraunces, daughter of "Black Sam," proprietor of the Queen's Head Tavern.

Lore began to grow up around Phoebe, who was, in fact, rumored to be a servant at Richmond Hill (despite scant evidence). One version of the story—cited in the Fraunces Tavern Block Historic District Designation Report, originally filed in New York in 1978—identifies Phoebe as the *lover* of Thomas Hickey—unlikely, since Phoebe, born in December 1765, would have been ten years old at the time. Nevertheless, a children's book was penned about Phoebe Fraunces and her supposed lifesaving role in foiling Washington's assassination.

Thomas Hickey's role in the plot against Washington and his subsequent demise has been thoroughly researched. Nowhere in that extensive record is there any mention of poisoned peas.

However, the peas do appear in the later writings of Lorenda Holmes.

Years after the war concluded, in an attempt to settle her aunt Mary Smith's estate and recover losses she claimed as a result of her loyalty to the Crown, Lorenda described her briny postal adventures and additional exploits in at least one lengthy document filed with the British government.

"The Memorial of Lorenda Holmes, late of New York" was penned by Holmes and addressed "To the Right Honorable the Lords of His Majesty's Treasury," and a copy was sent to the Commissioners of Claimants.

In both America and England, petitions for pensions and other financial restitution can sometimes prove fruitful when seeking to piece together the activities of women and enslaved people. Individuals seeking funds from the government for service in the military—either directly, in the form of quartering troops, or, in Lorenda's case, suffering losses while acting as a courier—provide not only their full names (which are often overlooked in favor of the names of their husbands or enslavers) but their backgrounds and activities as well.

Here is the version of events related to the plot to assassinate Washington as written by Lorenda in 1789.

The evening after Thomas Hickey was hanged for sedition and treason, Captain Caleb Gibbs, commander of Washington's Life Guards, summoned Lorenda. In his role as head of the guard, Gibbs was also responsible for overseeing the household alongside Washington's housekeeper: Lorenda's recently outed loyalist aunt. Gibbs and someone whom Lorenda described simply as an "Indian chief" approached her. Gibbs drew his sidearm.

Had Lorenda been in the kitchen while dinner was being prepared? Gibbs demanded to know.

No, she had not, Lorenda answered.

Gibbs left Lorenda alone, but not for long. About an hour later, Gibbs was back, hurling more accusations at Lorenda and her aunt, Mary Smith. Gibbs marched the women into the kitchen at gunpoint and ordered them to sit. On the table in front of Lorenda was a plate of green peas. Gibbs ordered her to eat.

What if the peas were poisoned? Lorenda wondered. Poisoned not by her but *for* her?

Lorenda leaned forward over the table, scooped up the potentially deadly vegetables, lifted the spoon to her lips, and swallowed.

Nothing happened. Nothing at all.

Apparently cleared of the crime of attempting to poison the Continental commander, Lorenda and her aunt later demanded that Washington tell them the names of their accusers. Washington refused, saying that it was not "customary" to "give up informers." He had, he said, "many letters against" the pair.

On the strength of this evidence, Washington banished the two women from the premises. Lorenda would one day wax philosophical about the outcome: He did "save our lives as well as he could because he did not think his safe," she wrote. Once again, in the "dead time of the night," Lorenda and Mary Smith found themselves evicted from a house, with little choice but to make their way south. Washington provided the pair with the "countersign" (password) that enabled them to enter New York City. For this gesture, Lorenda later noted "Mr. Washington's humanity."

Lorenda had heard that the HMS *Phoenix* and another British ship of war were moving up the "North River." Since the time of the Dutch, this was a popular name for the *southernmost* portion of the Hudson River. The Dutch, who had ruled southern Manhattan or "New Amsterdam" between 1624 and 1664, before losing it to the British, had dubbed the body of water the "Noort Rivier." It was later renamed for explorer Henry Hudson, who "discovered" it in 1609. The river's existence, vitality, and treasured role in the fertile region predated Hudson and others by nearly 10,000 years. The Lenape called it "Muhheakunnuk," the "River That Runs Both Ways."

No matter the direction it was running, the river's waters now carried a massive amount of British forces. Lorenda took advantage of the resulting "horror and confusion" at the approach of the British ships to make her escape. Mary Smith, her son, and three enslaved individuals boarded one, fleeing for Long Island. Lorenda, however, was once again off to East Chester, several miles north of Manhattan, northeast of what is now the Bronx. It was a roughly twenty-five-mile journey to her destination. She set off first on foot, then traveled aboard a privateer vessel that eventually set her onshore at Rodman's Point. Exhausted, she then made her way along Pell's Neck and finally to Old Estate, East Chester.

She was tired. She was hungry. The small spoonful of untainted peas had hardly sufficed. But her service to the Crown's cause was not done and her knowledge of this region would prove handy once again.

Lorenda had shown herself to be resourceful, flexible, mobile, clever, determined, and even cunning when she needed to be. But her greatest disguise was that she was a woman and thus not taken seriously enough early on by those who should have been paying closer attention.

By late June, Lorenda was gone from the city on the Hudson, but not for good. She still had unfinished business with the rebels. Pell's Point would come into play before the year was out, and Lorenda would have her part to play in the theater of war once again.

In addition to the ships already parked in the waters in and around Manhattan, many more British were making their way en masse toward New York. British general Sir William Howe and about 130 ships and thousands of British troops were on their way from Halifax in Nova Scotia. They would eventually skirt their way through the waters off Long Island and finally anchor off Staten Island in early July. As British and Hessian ships were already converging upon New York, more British troops were due to arrive from points south. On the very same day as Thomas Hickey's demise, June 28, 1776, British general Sir Henry Clinton began making his way up the coast after suffering an unexpected, rather stinging loss.

General Clinton had hoped to seize control of one of the colonies' most important ports. But instead the general and his forces were now headed north to New York, leaving the waters of Charles Town Harbor in South Carolina behind. Things had not gone as planned in that southern stronghold.

The British press blamed an obstinate daughter.

Shades of Indigo: South Carolina Low Country

The ragged-edged square of cloth in my hands is a disappointment. I followed the directions as I made my first attempt at old-school dyeing. The process was simple enough. The strangers standing around me smile, pleased at their results. The fabric in my hands is indeed seeped with color, but the blue dye has bled beyond the limits I set for it, like a brand-new periwinkle T-shirt after a hot turn in the washer.

I decide to give it another go. I fold and twist the cotton swatch and bind it at intervals with rubber bands. I then lower it into the vat of inky, midnight blue liquid, using a piece of string. After waiting several minutes, I tug the string, remove the fabric from the watery tub, and hang it from a nearby line with a clothespin. I wait for the results, seeking shade while my experiment hangs in the summer sun.

I am at Middleton Place, just outside Charleston, South Carolina, on a hot June day. Here the Cooper River opens up into the Atlantic, and the salt and fresh water that once washed over endless fields of rice flows, ebbs, and mixes in a timeless rhythm.

I feel a shift in mood as I hop in my car and move beyond the sultry streets of Charleston's old historic district toward the harbor and the Atlantic. Moving out over the water and bridges of Charleston and the Intracoastal Waterway, I encounter salty swatches of mussel-encrusted banks populated by bottlenose dolphins arcing over the surface of the water, the odd alligator revealing its snout above it, a cold-blooded beast in a hot town. As soon as I catch sight of the ocean, I am immediately moved to roll down the car window. The humidity settles on my skin like a wet lap dog.

Here the landscape tells its own tales: Lines of "barrier islands"—so called for their position between the coast and the expanse of the Atlantic—were in earlier times punctuated by prisons and pesthouses for the quarantined, potentially afflicted with the bane of colonial life, small-pox. Broad tracts of what remains of colonial plantations sit along the waterways, visual nods to the once lucrative crops, perpetual reminders of a legacy steeped in power and pain.

This is the Low Country. Echoes of the Gullah Geechee society strive to remain, and do, thanks to those dedicated to preserving their colorful and bittersweet cultural roots. Remnants of these can be seen as I drive down Highway 17, known as the "Sweetgrass Highway." This stretch of road is named for the local reed that has been used for hundreds of years on this continent and in Africa to craft baskets. The Black women who sell these useful and ornate wares by the roadside have been trained by generations of creatively dexterous hands that came before them.

This was the home of Arthur Middleton, signer of the Declaration of Independence, a member of a family that played pivotal roles in colonial government. Another former resident, Arthur's grandson Williams Middleton, would become one of the signers of another significant document in American history: the South Carolina Ordinance of Secession, which would effectively seek to dismantle the very union that his ancestors sought to fortify.

Middleton Place boasts grand vistas. The gnarled branches of the live oaks are strewn with spindly strands of pale, greenish-gray flora that blow and billow in the breeze like gossamer, organic window treatments. Horses graze, the occasional goat strolls by, and oxen and sheep are among the animals I spot in the distance as roosters wander freely among tourists eager to soak up the grandeur while being simultaneously presented with the painful, uneasy history of one of Charleston's most historic plantations.

Like Mount Vernon, Middleton Place no longer shies away from the history of slavery that is an inextricable part of its grounds; quite the opposite. One of the tours available to visitors is "Beyond the Fields: Enslavement at Middleton Place." This experience discusses the harvesting and production of rice, the process of working with indigo, and the lives of those captive residents of the plantation upon whom those crops depended.

Enslaved people contributed far more than physical work to the success of this and other plantations. Enslavers benefited from their knowledge of cultivation, exploiting both their bodies and their minds for profit.

Many varieties of plants arrived in the colonies aboard the same ships that transported enslaved individuals. Some grains and seeds were carried by the enslaved themselves, often braided into their hair. Others were like botanical stowaways, the seeds of as-yet-unseen crops lining the hulls of the vessels of the Middle Passage, landing on the East Coast of North America and occasionally finding some new life in the soil on the far side of the Atlantic. By the seventeenth century, crops commonly found on the western coast of the African continent, such as millet, okra, field peas, peanuts, yams, and, of course, rice, became staples of the colonial diet and a vital part of the economy.

One clay pot's worth of a combination of these humble staples became known as a "pilau" (pilaf). The ingredients provided ample nourishment, and the right seasonings made them sought after and embedded them in the nascent culinary traditions of the Carolinas.

Prominently displayed on the property is a panel listing the names of hundreds of individuals enslaved by the Middleton family for generations. The site also hosts an annual family reunion, which has for many years welcomed *all* Middleton descendants, white and Black alike.

But I am not at Middleton Place to delve into the life of Arthur Middleton or to learn about any particular person per se but rather to discover how a humble plant is transformed into the "I" of our mnemonic rainbow device, ROYGBIV, otherwise known as *Indigofera suffruticosa*. Indigo.

Standing near the clothesline, I notice a small shrub poking its way out of the sunbaked dirt, small and green with almost frond-like branches dotted with tiny salmon-colored buds. There is nothing blue about it, but this foreign arrival to North America brought with it the ability to transform a bland ecru cloth into one of the hues of the rainbow. A nearby display describes the botanical journey of the dried, banana-shaped seedpods. When harvested, they are clinging to desiccated stalks, but they're later processed and pressed into cakes—also on display—that yield the magical blue dye that once captivated the globe.

I finally unhinge the clothespin from the line and remove the rubber bands from the damp fabric. As I unravel the handkerchief-sized square, what emerges is a deep-blue creation surrounded by rings of paler hues, like denim only brighter, bordered by streaks of untouched white emanating from the center. My square is reminiscent of poorly executed do-it-yourself tie-dye, all courtesy of a plant-based colorant that helped fuel the colonial economy vital to Charleston, specifically, and the revolution as a whole.

Not far from Middleton Place, a short drive down Long Point Road in Mount Pleasant, is the Charles Pinckney National Historic Site. Snee Farm Plantation was one of the homes of this South Carolina political player, who not only signed the Constitution but is often considered to be one of its more unheralded authors.

Archaeological digs have unearthed evidence of enslaved quarters, a cotton gin, the original plantation house, and a kitchen. A panel titled "Indigo and Its Beginnings in South Carolina" sits on the property.

But I am seeking a family connection of Charles's, so I hop back in the Toyota and take off on the twelve- to fifteen-mile (depending on the route you take) drive to where the Wappoo Plantation once stood, due west of downtown Charleston. I make a right off of what was once the King's Highway—now Highway 17—just past the Early Bird Diner at Mama's Used Cars, and onto Betsy Road. A short drive down this residential road, and soon after crossing Pinckney Park Drive, Betsy Road dead-ends at 300 Lord Calvert Road. Here, two small stone columns flank a driveway lined with live oaks dripping with moss and leading to a modern home with a wide, inviting porch running its length—fairly anticlimactic. It takes me a minute to ensure that I am at the right spot, because the plantation no longer exists. There is, however, a marker.

The column to the right of the driveway displays a metal placard erected by the Charleston Federation of Women's Clubs in 1976. It reads: "This marker commemorates where indigo seed was planted by Eliza Lucas in 1741."

CHAPTER 10

Planter. Mother. Patriot.

I have the business of 3 plantations to transact, wch requires much writing and more business and fatigue of other sorts than you can imagine, but least you should imagine it too burthensom to a girl at my early time of life, give mee leave to assure you I think myself happy that I can be useful to so good a father."

She did not ask to be responsible for three plantations while her father was away in the West Indies. But she was.

She did not need to rise hours earlier than most women of her class and privilege in order to read and study and therefore become less reliant on those around her—those who sought to dismiss her. But she did.

She did not know that she would become instrumental in revolutionizing a crop new to America, impacting a colony and an economy at a time when financial support was becoming more crucial in the face of increasing conflict and instability. But she did.

Eliza Lucas had begun her life much farther afield, in the British Caribbean, on the island of Antigua. Eventually she; her father, George; her mother, Anne; her sister, Polly; and her cousin Fanny arrived in the Low Country and settled outside Charles Town. The port city was about seventeen miles overland from their home—a scant six by way of the river.

But Eliza's father would not remain in the colonies. Business, political opportunities, and a military commission in the British West Indies called him back to the Caribbean. Regardless, he had plans for the family lands he was leaving behind, and he told Eliza he was relying on her to ensure that those plans were executed properly.

At her father's behest, Eliza took up the challenge and began investigating new crops that already enjoyed robust harvests and sales on Antigua but were not readily found in the colonies. In her father's absence, Eliza was to supervise overseer William Murray at Garden Hill, a 1,500-acre tar and timber plantation on the Combahee River. She would also supervise George Starrat and the family's 3,000-acre rice plantation on the Waccamaw, which also produced beef, pork, and lime. Finally, she personally would directly manage the 600 acres of the Wappoo Plantation, where she lived, along with the twenty persons enslaved there.

Eliza began experimenting with ginger, lucerne (now more commonly known as alfalfa), the hearty and nutritious cassava tuber, and, most importantly, indigo, a plant revered for the rich blue color it bestowed upon receptive fabrics. Her father wrote of the high demand for indigo in London if Eliza could successfully cultivate and process the crop from seed to harvest to dye lot.

She was sixteen years old.

In addition to seeds and tubers and marching orders, Eliza's father sent her assistance in the form of one Nicholas Cromwell, a man who, supposedly, had the know-how to guide Eliza in this new venture. However, Eliza was immediately suspicious of Cromwell's intentions and withholding behaviors and chafed at what she referred to as his "churlishness." But she had no choice but to heed his counsel—for the time being, in any case—in what was a daunting undertaking.

The process of transforming indigo from plant to dye was as tedious as it was malodorous. Planted in April, with a first cutting in July and perhaps another toward the end of August, the indigo plant was harvested when its flower was nearly ready to burst. Enslaved workers bundled stalks, which went straight to processing.

One of the first steps was the steeper: Large stones and chunks of wood were employed to keep the plants submerged in water. After about one day, the once flowering plant began to rot in place, turning the water into what looked more like a green rather than a blue liquid. This pigment was, in fact, indigo.

The second step was a vat called the "beater." The water at this stage approached the stench of sewers. Here, enslaved workers mixed the reeking, murky liquid with paddles, stomping on the plant and poking it with poles, removing detritus along the way. All of this added the necessary oxygen that, molecule by molecule, churn by churn, nudged the mixture closer to a truer blue.

Once the water drained off, what remained was a kind of mud that was bagged, squeezed, and hung to dry. This smoother, drier substance was malleable and could be encased in boxes, resulting in "indigo bricks." Those bricks were in turn cured, packed, and shipped off to the Europeans, who could scarcely get enough of them.

The smell of the vats repelled humans and attracted flies. No one wanted to be near the vessels if they could help it, but Eliza did the best she could to gain a mastery of the process, desperate to learn and make this investment a success for her father and family.

"I observed him as careful as I could," Eliza wrote a friend about her attempts to learn from Cromwell. But that did little good in the face of Cromwell's disingenuous guidance and what the young woman came to view as outright sabotage. Eliza believed Cromwell was, in fact, employing a technique to destroy her dye's colorfastness. Once applied to the targeted fabric, the dye produced according to Cromwell's direction faded quite easily, making it useless to anyone who might be inclined to buy it.

Cromwell's motives made sense to Eliza. Her father was paying him well, so there was little cause to step away from this wallet-fattening post. However, Cromwell himself had a strong incentive to see the Lucas family's venture fail. After all, if South Carolina could grow and sell indigo and develop a booming trade with London in particular, what use was there for his own supply of the dye back in the Caribbean? Any potential success on Eliza's part represented a potential undercutting of Cromwell's own position in the market.

After nearly four years of Cromwell's supposed "help," Eliza had yet to see a decent indigo crop turn into a colorfast, long-lasting, vibrant dye, let alone a profit.

Yet, where some ventures lay fallow, others began to unexpectedly bloom. By twenty-one years of age, Eliza's growing prominence gained her the attentions of Charles Pinckney, a recent widower, lawyer, landowner, and member of the Governor's Council. His courtship of her followed soon after the death of his wife—a woman with whom Eliza herself had been acquainted—inviting some measure of scandal. Eliza's father was unable to provide the kind of dowry he wished for his daughter, but Charles was not to be deterred.

"[I am] sensible Sir how unequal this sum is to your Fortune and Figure," George Lucas wrote Charles Pinckney, "[but] as it is not in my power at present to do more without leaving [my other] children destitute, I thought proper to lay the naked facts before [you] . . . and if as your letter speaks, you think fit to [marry my daughter] I shall think my self extremely happy in your alliance."

The pair married and Eliza was delighted.

"It must be a great satisfaction to you as well as to myself," she wrote her father, "to know that I have put myself into the hands of a man of honor, whose good sense and sweetness of disposition gives me a prospect of a happy life . . ."

Soon after the marriage, Nicholas Cromwell departed Wappoo, likely feeling confident that he had safeguarded his own colony's hold on the indigo trade. In his place, Eliza's father sent Patrick Cromwell, Nicholas's brother, who proved to be a very different sort of man.

Patrick openly shared with Eliza all he knew of the crop itself as well as the dyeing process. Shortly after his arrival, the Lucas indigo crop improved and Eliza's efforts at long last achieved a rich blue colorfast dye lot. Eliza and Charles shipped it off to the South Carolina agent in London and awaited word. The agent soon responded with lavish praise: Eliza's dye was as good as that of the French, to whom London paid approximately £200,000 annually. If Eliza could get a piece of that trade, it would change everything.

One planted acre might produce fifty to eighty pounds of the plant, whose dye was all the rage in Europe during the eighteenth century. Fifteen enslaved individuals could plant and tend roughly fifty acres of indigo, and another twenty-five could take the plants through the processing, and so, with all things going reasonably well, fifty acres could bring 2,500 pounds of indigo dye.

Though colonial America saw indigo production at different points in the seventeenth century—English colonists and French Huguenots had cultivated the colorful crop in and around Charles Town—by the early eighteenth century evidence of it was quite rare. Eliza saw the height of the new indigo trade and played a key role in its revival.

She tested every variety she could get her hands on and began growing indigo at her husband Charles's plantation, Belmont, as well, increasing their blended family's potential dye output. The Lucas-Pinckney venture additionally benefited from Charles's ability to act as their sales agent in the colonies and abroad, owing to the fact that he, unlike Eliza, possessed the necessary Y chromosome to do so.

Having long been science-minded and curious, Eliza expanded her early agricultural investigations beyond indigo. Before Charles entered the picture, she had experimented with oak and fig trees and seeds for various crops, including ginger, cassava, alfalfa, and cotton. After marriage, Eliza decided to explore the potential for producing silk at Belmont. She sent off for silkworm eggs and placed an ad in the newspaper for "a handy wench, who is a very good seamstress." In 1755, she tasked enslaved children with gathering mulberry leaves to feed the worms.

The pair freely shared their successes and techniques with others. In various editions of *The South-Carolina Gazette*, Charles penned articles about the cultivation of indigo, as well as about sericulture (silkworm rearing and silk production) under the name "Agricola," the Latin word for farmer.

Though not a robust business, the result of the initial foray into the silk business resulted in a gold damask robe à la française. And in 1755 the Pinckneys gifted Augusta, Dowager Princess of Wales, a piece of silk damask dyed a deep indigo blue. Silk production would continue into the 1760s, with "nearly fifty bushels of cocoons" in play by

1766. Despite this, the success of Eliza's silk experiment was still quite touch and go.

Throughout her life and especially during her youth, Eliza's business endeavors and evident success—along with her rigorous mind and daily schedule—attracted attention, but not always of a positive sort. Her work and leisure activities were hardly de rigueur for the average eighteenth-century woman. Eliza rose before the sun, read for two hours, and then went for long walks. Her neighbors took note, and one in particular frowned upon her behavior.

"An old lady in our neighborhood is often quarreling with me for rising so early as 5 o'clock in the morning," Eliza wrote a friend in the days before marrying Charles, "and is in great pain for me lest it should spoil my marriage, for she says it will make me look old long before I am so." This same busybody also frowned upon Eliza's penchant for reading.

"I can't help running a parallel between the above lady and my valuable and worthy friend Mrs. Woodward," Eliza continued, "who incourages me in every laudable pursuit."

Eliza's laudable agricultural pursuits soon became economically successful ones to boot, and she expanded her plans and project to include those who had never been given any choice in enabling her to achieve it. Eliza taught her sisters and several enslaved women working on the plantation to read and write. Her aim was start a school for all of the enslaved children of Wappoo, ideally training the older ones to eventually teach as well.

"If I have my papa's approbation (my mama's I have got) I intend [them] for school mistresses for the rest of the negro children—another scheme you see," she wrote of the potential project.

Eliza's growing indigo venture increasingly depended upon the enslaved worker whom the Pinckney family called "Mulatto Quash"—John Williams—a carpenter who lived at Wappoo. John had been baptized an Episcopalian. However, when Eliza's father transferred ownership of John to Eliza, he said he would be known as "Quash" from that point forward. And as the Pinckney family's reliance on John grew and evolved, Eliza and Charles began paying him for his efforts on their behalf, including £200 per year for three years to supervise the construction of their house in the city of Charles Town proper, and separately for the decorative trim work and carvings John created for the new home. Soon thereafter, Charles released John from his enslavement—"for good and faithful service"—and Eliza was present when he received his manumission papers.

Within three years of Eliza's first successful batch of indigo dye, South Carolina exported 135,000 pounds of indigo to England alone, transforming the colony's economy. The dye that Eliza and others in the region produced was slow to bleed and boasted a fastness that would soon serve a weather- and war-worn flag of a country now in the midst of an identity crisis and in the early stages of yet another war.

Eliza became the mother of three children: Charles, Harriott, and Thomas. (George, Eliza's second child, died in infancy.) On April 4, 1753, she and her husband, Charles, had taken the family to London, where the children attended school and Charles acted as the trade agent for their indigo consortium.

Trade between England, France, and Spain suffered due to political conflicts, which worked in the favor of the colonial growers. Combining the success of the indigo crop with this interruption of commerce fed the revived market for South Carolina dye.

Wars had come and gone and would come again in Eliza's lifetime. King George's War arrived in the mid-1740s. The French and Indian War—often referred to as the "Cherokee War" in the Carolinas—had threatened the safety and security of the Pinckney home and business as violent encounters with the Cherokee on lands that had long been in Indigenous hands before the arrival of Europeans cost lives, property, and crops on both sides. The Pinckney family departed London on March 12, 1758, roughly a year later than originally planned, due to concerns about the ongoing hostilities. They arrived back in South Carolina on May 19, 1758. They inspected their lands, much of which was now swarming with mosquitoes. Pox tore across the Low Country in a virulent, unceasing rampage.

And, indeed, the look of the plantations and lands upon their return was uninspiring. Much had been neglected due to fear of Cherokee attacks and a general lack of attention. After their time in London's milder climate, the heat of the Low Country proved taxing. Charles left Belmont and went to Charles Town to join Eliza at their home in the city . . . but not before he was bitten by malarial mosquitoes.

For Eliza, the return to the colonies had certainly been jarring, but her greatest loss turned out to be far more horrific. Charles never recovered from his illness, and their happy marriage thus came to an abrupt and tragic end on July 12, 1758, just fourteen years after it began.

It pained Eliza to share this news with friends, but she soon reached out to a Mrs. Branfill Evance, who, along with her husband, watched over Eliza's sons, who were yet attending school in England, while Eliza and her daughter, Harriott, were in America.

"My dear friend," Eliza wrote, "till now I surely was the happiest of mortals till the last dismal, fatal month. Oh! dreadful reverse of what I was. Think if you can what is my distress when I tell you the beloved of my soul! all that was valuable and amiable in man! my dear, dear Mr. Pinckney is no more. Great God soport me in this terrible affliction! For 'tis heavy indeed! I beg you, my dear Mrs. Evance, to take care of my dear fatherless babes, to comfort their tender hearts; and let them be a little while at home with you upon this meloncholy occasion . . . Poor dear creatures!"

For Eliza, the security provided by her wealth and privilege may have ameliorated some of the gut-wrenching trauma that accompanies the loss of a spouse. But there was no true barrier to her ongoing grief—not in her adopted land of Carolina, not while struggling against fixed ideas of what it meant to be a lady in that day and time, and not while held within the emotional grasp of those children she loved and an increasingly frustrating monarchy, both of which were an ocean away.

Upon his death, Charles's estate left Eliza with four houses in Charles Town, one in England, and nine plantations. She raised her children while managing the affairs of thousands of acres as tensions grew between the Crown and the colonists. That ongoing friction would soon impact her business, her life, and the lives of her children.

By the time the revolution was gaining momentum, indigo—along with rice—had helped form part of the backbone of the economy of South Carolina. In 1775 alone, more than 1 million pounds of indigo sailed from the port of Charles Town. But the increased animosity and now violence between the colonies and England was proving detrimental to that trade. When Congress sought to enact non-exportation measures in 1775—which would halt the shipment of goods to England—the majority of the South Carolina delegates threatened to leave Congress unless indigo and rice were exempted from the ban. The result: Rice was indeed exempted from the ban. Indigo was not.

Hanging like rows of hurricane-worn umbrellas on the humid horizon stood the palmetto trees. The sabal palmetto, or cabbage palm, as it has long been known, now serves as the state tree of South Carolina and is emblazoned on the state flag. Native Americans cooked the hearts (which reportedly taste of cabbage) and used the plants' berries to take the edge off of both headache and fever. The tree fronds were used for thatching and weaving. Those narrow palmetto trunks, which are so easily swayed by strong offshore Atlantic winds, convey to the eye a deceptive fragility. But they prove surprisingly resilient, much like the people who walked beneath and among them for centuries.

On the other side of the Charles Town peninsula from Eliza's Wappoo Plantation, across the Ashley and Cooper Rivers, sat Sullivan's Island, a central hub for the importation of enslaved people. The first Africans to the area may well have arrived in 1526, brought by a Spanish expedition from the Caribbean. However, with the arrival of the English and their settlement in what is now South Carolina in 1670, the plantation economy took root. An estimated 49 percent of people enslaved from West Africa entered the colonies through South Carolina ports. From there, they were shipped as cargo to locations as far away as Massachusetts or as nearby as Savannah. The island also served as a quarantine site, or lazaretto, for anyone arriving by sea. If not left quarantined on the ship itself, anyone believed to be diseased or possibly contagious was held in a pesthouse on the island until fear that they might spread contagion had passed.

The westernmost tip of Sullivan's Island was not quite four miles overwater from the tip of the Charles Town Peninsula. The island's namesake, Provincial Congress appointee Captain Florence O'Sullivan, arrived at the island now bearing his name with the first wave of English settlers in 1670. He had, decades earlier, been placed in charge of a project to establish a signal cannon on the island to warn Charles Town of incoming ships.

In 1776, thirteen years after the signing of the Treaty of Paris, which ended the Seven Years' War, Charles Town–born Colonel William Moultrie was overseeing the building of a fort on Sullivan's Island, one just shy of completion but which, by the end of June, was desperately needed. The largest threat yet to the colonies was coming fast by sea with the speed of a well-funded royal fleet. The combined forces were under the command of Commodore Sir Peter Parker and Major General Sir Henry Clinton.

The British aimed for Sullivan's Island, intending it as a base from which to take the all-important port city of Charles Town. Eliza's sons had returned to the colonies from London. Charles was now a noted statesman in South Carolina's Provincial Congress, a London-educated lawyer who had graduated from the prestigious Middle Temple. But he was a true colonial now and, like his mother, dedicated to building an independent life on the unexplored side of the Atlantic.

In June 1776, alongside other nerve-wracked and undersupplied soldiers, Charles awaited the coming British ships, knowing full well that his mother, mere miles away, would be concerned for him. He took to paper and ink while the hours passed and the British approached.

"Lest my honored mother should be alarmed by hearing exaggerated reports of the fleet off the bar, I snatch a few minutes from the duties of my station to acquaint her of the particulars of it," he wrote to Eliza. "We are preparing to receive them properly when they do come over. Our men are in fine spirits and I doubt not will behave as they ought to do on the occasion."

On June 28—the same day that Thomas Hickey met his demise in

New York—the British arrived with nine ships of war and 270 cannons with plans of breaking the bones and spirits of 400 Continental soldiers, who were equipped with just 31 cannons and 30 rounds of powder—much of which would need to be saved for their muskets should the British make it ashore.

The nearly completed fort stood ten feet high, with double walls spaced sixteen feet apart. The spaces between those walls were filled with earth and sand. The walls themselves were made of local palmetto logs.

The attack lasted nearly ten hours, but despite their advantage in number and weapons, the British simply could not take Sullivan's Island. What happened must have seemed like some sort of illusion: The British cannonballs struck those fortress walls and appeared to bounce right off them.

Those spongy palmettos proved remarkably resilient that day, taking every bit of cannon fire that the British could spew at them. Bending, yes; breaking, *no*. Splintering but not faltering, seeming at the brink of destruction, yet never cracking in two. It was a display of a deceptively fragile flora's grit and grace under immense pressure, as if bracing itself for what was to come in the years to follow.

The bombardment lasted but a day, but it would not be the last Charles Town would endure at the hands and arms of the Crown. Defeated and battle-worn, the British masts faded into the summer horizon. The British general Clinton left, defeated, and headed to New York to join the British and Hessian forces amassing there.

News of the events at Sullivan's Island soon reached England, where a London paper reported the surprising news of their force's inability to take the island and Charles Town. A cartoon depicted a proper southern woman in profile, a bow upon her bosom, with cannons, flags, and ramparts emerging from her voluminous and upswept hair. The caption read: "Miss Carolina Sulivan, one of the obstinate daughters of America, 1776."

Though it was June of 1776, it felt as if war had been in the offing for years, an inevitable result of the recent and increasingly fervent talk of a declaration of independence from England. Now fifty-four years old,

Eliza watched and waited as her world was upended and her two sons were now counted among those who would risk all for freedom from the Crown.

Eliza, like so many others, found her life, her family, and her livelihood were increasingly at risk. Thomas now served as a captain in the 1st South Carolina Regiment, and Charles would soon head north to act as aide to General George Washington. Charles's wife, Sarah Middleton Pinckney—Eliza's daughter-in-law—was the sister of Arthur Middleton, who was in Philadelphia with other members of the Continental Congress, preparing to debate, adopt, and sign one of the most controversial documents in history. From her home in South Carolina, Eliza could do little more than protect what she had, stay safe, and work to survive as she anticipated letters, news, and some sort of resolution to this growing conflict.

The British may have left, but they would return, and when they did, they would not be so handily dismissed. Those within and without the city of Charles Town itself would long feel their painful presence.

Up and down the East Coast, in the wake of those warships and in every corner of the colonies, there were women, like Eliza, caught up in the turmoil of the time, those who would stand fast, those who would remain obstinate. Like the palmetto, they would certainly bend and undoubtedly suffer as they absorbed hit after hit.

Bend beneath the weight of the times, perhaps, but not break. Not ever.

CHAPTER 11

Shades of Freedom: July 4, 1776

On Thursday, July 4, 1776, the temperature in Philadelphia was a pleasant seventy-six degrees. News throughout America spoke of nothing *particularly* momentous that day, insomuch as everything felt of tremendous import, the stakes of choices made in daily life rising increasingly high. Most quotidian happenings felt noteworthy during war, even though news of any developments often arrived days, weeks, or more after they occurred. Dispatches from the far reaches of the conflict—from Canada to Florida—arrived via post, public notice, or word of mouth. Setbacks and gains may well have been reversed by the time colonists received news of them. Updates from the other side of the Atlantic might arrive months after the fact.

The front page of *The Maryland Gazette* on July 4 reported news from Lisbon that had transpired in February. There was news out of London dated March 31. Reports from Hartford, Philadelphia, Boston, and New York reached the mid-Atlantic colony more quickly and were only a few weeks old, some accounts dating from as recently as mid-June. Among local items were the "Proceedings of the Convention of the Province of Maryland" held at Annapolis, the settling of estates of the deceased, a reward for a strayed bay horse ("about 14 hands"), and advertisements seeking weavers and waitstaff. The newspaper's printer, Frederick Green, advertised for supplies to keep his publication up and running, ensuring his readership remained informed: "THREE PENCE per pound is given for fine white LINEN RAGS, and one penny per pound for course, by the Printer hereof."

Commanding center stage of *The Pennsylvania Evening Post* ("Price only Two Coppers") were the proceedings of that colony's Provincial Conference of Committees, which was held at Carpenters' Hall. Much of the minutes of that meeting was colonial housekeeping, such as the division of existing counties into various districts. Elsewhere in the paper, the proposed sale of a "lively active" Irish boy who had four years and two months to serve of his indenture was announced next to a report from Canada that the Continental Army had retreated to Île aux Noix, an island in the Richelieu River in Quebec not far from Lake Champlain. Word from New York dated July 3 was that a ministerial fleet had arrived at Sandy Hook from Halifax—130 sails' worth—and had taken at least three officers prisoner.

All of this—the loss, the struggle, the growing naval threat to the seaboard—was newsworthy, to be certain. But there was not—not yet—any printed news of the document recently approved by Congress. But two days later, on July 6, *The Pennsylvania Evening Post* would become the first publication in America to print, on its front page and in its entirety, an edict that would change the course of history on the North American continent.

In the *Post*'s home city of Philadelphia, in that very same Carpenters' Hall, members of the Second Continental Congress had, within the first few days of July, hotly debated and finally agreed upon the language that would come to define a new nation: the Declaration of Independence.

In June, Congress had tasked a "Committee of Five" to shape the language of a document that would declare, in no uncertain terms, independence from England. The phraseology and arguments would come to outline, define, and ultimately imbue the concepts of freedom into whatever new government happened to grow out of the ongoing war. Among the members of the Committee of Five were Abigail's husband, John Adams, Pennsylvania's Benjamin Franklin, Roger Sherman of Connecticut, and Robert R. Livingston from New York.

Rounding out the Committee of Five was a senator from Virginia named Thomas Jefferson. Jefferson was not alone in drafting the declaration, though chief among his tasks was massaging much of that language.

The entire document went through several iterations. The "truths" referred to in the second paragraph, for example, changed from "sacred & undeniable" in a draft version to "self-evident" in the final one.

Jefferson sat in the second-story parlor of a suite of rooms he rented from Joseph Graff, a bricklayer of German descent. He lived there from May 23 until September 3, 1776, with more than two of those weeks dedicated to the parsing of the Declaration's language.

As to the original citizenry of the North American continent, the Declaration of Independence stated: "[King George III] has excited domestic insurrections amongst us, and has endeavoured to bring on the inhabitants of our frontiers, the merciless Indian Savages, whose known rule of warfare, is an undistinguished destruction of all ages, sexes and conditions."

The first draft of the Declaration also included, among other things, language regarding the institution of slavery. As the conceit of the document laid out evidence of the various ways in which the Crown tyrannized the colonies, the section penned about slavery seemed to heap all blame for the institution's existence and continued practice throughout the colonies on King George III. The passage read:

> *He has waged cruel war against human nature itself, violating it's most sacred rights of life & liberty in the persons of a distant people who never offended him, captivating & carrying them into slavery in another hemisphere, or to incur miserable death in their transportation thither. [T]his piratical warfare, the opprobrium of infidel powers, is the warfare of the CHRISTIAN king of Great Britain. determined to keep open a market where MEN should be bought & sold, he has prostituted his negative for suppressing every legislative attempt to prohibit or to restrain this execrable commerce . . .*

The passage continued, referencing the promise of freedom offered to those enslaved individuals willing to leave their lives of bondage and lend their support to the Crown:

> *. . . and that this assemblage of horrors might want no fact of distinguished die, he is now exciting those very people to rise in arms among us, and to purchase that liberty of which he has deprived them, by murdering the people upon whom he also obtruded them; thus paying off former crimes committed against the liberties of one people, with crimes which he urges them to commit against the lives of another.*

This was an astounding passage, given that forty-one of the eventual fifty-six signers of the Declaration of Independence owned enslaved people. In 1776 alone, fourteen children were born into slavery at Jefferson's Monticello plantation in Virginia. Two of those babies born in 1776 would not live out the year. More than six hundred individuals were enslaved by Thomas Jefferson during his lifetime, two-thirds of them at Monticello. One of those enslaved at Monticello, fourteen-year-old Robert Hemmings, served Jefferson during his stay in Philadelphia, sleeping in the garret of the town house where Jefferson lodged. Robert arranged for trips to the barber, waited on Jefferson, and served all the expected roles of a valet while Jefferson focused on writing. Hemmings had ten siblings at Monticello, born to his mother, Elizabeth Hemings. An eleventh would arrive in 1777. Robert's younger sister, then three-year-old Sally Hemings, would go on to bear five children with Thomas Jefferson.

However, that substantial paragraph describing the "execrable commerce" of slavery did not survive the debates in Congress and was struck in its entirety.

Later in July, Abigail wrote her husband, John. As a member of not only Congress but also the Committee of Five appointed to draft the Declaration of Independence, John had input as to the document's content.

Abigail did not pull any punches in her correspondence, routinely making her views about any new government quite clear to a husband who was playing a crucial role in its creation.

"Remember all Men would be tyrants if they could," she had written just a few months earlier. "If perticuliar care and attention is not paid to the Laidies we are determined to foment a Rebelion, and will not hold ourselves bound by any Laws in which we have no voice, or Representation."

She was no less clear about her thoughts on enslavement in the colonies: "I wish most sincerely there was not a Slave in the province," she wrote her husband in 1774. "It allways appeard a most iniquitious Scheme to me—fight ourselfs for what we are daily robbing and plundering from those who have as good a right to freedom as we have. You know my mind upon this Subject."

Nevertheless, when Abigail wrote John in July, she was excited about the latest news her husband had shared regarding the Declaration of Independence. She felt great pleasure at the "prospect of the future happiness and glory of our Country." She also felt "gratified" that "a person so nearly connected with me has had the Honour of being a principal actor, in laying a foundation for its future Greatness. May the foundation of our new constitution, be justice, Truth and Righteousness."

Abigail did allow herself least one significant lament, however:

"I cannot but feel sorry that some of the most Manly Sentiments in the Declaration are Expunged from the printed coppy. Perhaps wise reasons induced it."

Knowing her feelings on the subject of slavery, it would appear that Abigail was referencing the excision of that topic from the final draft. She had indeed received letters from her husband dated the third, fourth, and seventh of July, but whether one of those missives included that earlier draft of the Declaration mentioning slavery remains unknown.

Though the crucial vote in Congress to approve the Declaration of Independence came on July 2—and no one actually signed the Declaration on July 4—"IN CONGRESS, JULY 4, 1776. THE UNANIMOUS DECLARATION OF THE THIRTEEN UNITED STATES OF AMERICA" is emblazoned across the top of the historic document.

Congress sent the amended copy of the Declaration to printer John Dunlap on July 3 and requested that Dunlap run off two hundred copies—twenty-six of which are still in existence—of the broadside to be disseminated throughout the thirteen colonies. These were likely published on July 4. These broadsides were then sent to all the states, members of the press, and personal correspondents.

The only two names listed on that initially published copy of the Declaration of Independence were those of the president of Congress, John Hancock, and Charles Thomson, that body's secretary.

A master penman by the name of Timothy Matlack was later hired to hand-letter a formal document for the congressmen to sign. This "engrossed" copy of the Declaration of Independence—with all the flourishes and eventually individual signatures—was soon drawn up by Matlack. The signing of *that* document by fifty-six members of Congress—at least seven of whom were not even elected to Congress until *after* July 4, 1776—did not begin until August 2. The last of those signers, Thomas McKean, would not sign until years later, as his military duties during a time of war kept him otherwise occupied.

Lucy Knox was in neither Philadelphia nor New York when news of the Declaration broke. Henry had insisted she leave New York and go to stay in Connecticut.

On July 4, Henry wrote his brother that Lucy had "gone to Fairfield."

He had written his brother, "Billy," in June that Lucy was "very unwell." He hoped that it was due to the care of the baby, whom Henry described as being "in very fine health."

Word of the Declaration would eventually reach Lucy's ears in Connecticut, as well as those of Elizabeth and Phillis Wheatley in Massachusetts. The hometown newspaper of Philadelphians Elizabeth Drinker and Esther Reed, *The Pennsylvania Evening Post*, would be the first newspaper in the colonies to print the Declaration in its entirety. Mary Katharine Goddard would soon follow suit.

The following year, and for hundreds that followed, the commemoration of July 4 would grow and change, as would the legacy of that document—and the communities it both welcomed and excluded.

CHAPTER 12

Two Weeks (or So) in July

Nanye'hi took the salt and threw it into the kettle along with the branches of the yaupon in preparation of the White Drink. Not everyone gathered at the council meeting agreed upon the right course of action for the Cherokee. There was much disagreement among those individuals whom the Declaration of Independence referred to as "merciless savages" as to the best way to protect and keep the fast-disappearing lands that had long been theirs.

While July 4 remains etched in American memory as one of the most significant moments in the nation's history, other days that month were equally or even more impactful, depending on your point of view.

July 8, for example, was certainly, for at least one nation, one of those days.

On that day, in Chota, Nanye'hi, her uncle Attakullakulla, her cousin and Attakullakulla's son, Dragging Canoe, and his father, Oconostota, met for a council of war. The time had come to decide what to do about the increasing numbers of white settlers who had moved with their families to land along the Holston River and elsewhere.

Following the Seven Years' War, the British king had decreed that no white settlers should move beyond the boundary that ran along the spine of the Appalachian Mountains: the Proclamation Line of 1763.

But that king was an ocean away. In defiance of that decree, white people continued coming in droves. Unrest along the frontier and farther inland continued as Indigenous nations saw more of their lands encroached upon by settlers who ignored the boundaries established by the British.

It was as if these people refused to obey the law, or they had forgotten. But how could the Cherokee and other nations forget? They felt the power of the British still. The suffering of those who sided with the French during the Seven Years' War was seared in their collective memory.

But now, as this new war grew in its size, scope, and violence, the Cherokee and their alliance with the English took on greater importance. If the British managed to beat back the colonists, the reverberations might be felt by the Cherokee themselves, as those whites who trespassed on Cherokee land were in violation of the Proclamation Line of 1763. This was regarded by the British as an act of defiance of the Crown—and by the Cherokee and other Indigenous peoples as yet another invasion of their lands.

This trespass was not limited to lands on the East Coast. In May 1776, a war chief of the Shawnee named Cornstalk had traveled from Detroit with representatives from the Shawnee, Lenape, Ottawa, and Iroquois to meet with the southern Indigenous peoples, including the Cherokee, Muscogee, Chickasaw, and Choctaw, to discuss allying with the British against the white American settlers, whom they referred to as "Long Knives." The British at Fort Detroit, under the leadership of Lieutenant Governor Henry Hamilton, encouraged and armed the Indigenous peoples in the area to support British efforts to control the territory.

Many Indigenous people in the area and elsewhere believed that an alliance with the British was the only way to stem the flow of settlers seeping deeper into the fabric of their homelands. At that meeting with Cornstalk and other Indigenous representatives, Dragging Canoe accepted war belts from the Ottawa and Iroquois.

These belts consisted of wampum, mollusk shells sanded and shaped by a bow drill and strung together into designs rife with symbolism and meaning. The manner in which these belts (for holding in one's hand, not for wrapping around one's waist) were woven determined what messages they conveyed. Wampum commemorated events and might be strung together into belts that would aid in recalling tribal history or community stories. Wampum was used to ceremonially mark everything from a birth to a treaty. The fact that the belts were physical objects containing history, law, tradition, and more meant that they could be passed down within a nation or community, generation after generation.

The Penn Treaty Belt, for example, represents a meeting between the Lenape and William Penn in 1682. The Hiawatha Belt represents the union of the five original Haudenosaunee nations of the North: the Onondaga, Oneida, Mohawk, Seneca, and Cayuga. (The Tuscarora joined the Haudenosaunee Confederacy in the early eighteenth century.) Woven together, the wampum of the Hiawatha Belt visually and physically connect representations of the individual nations, symbolizing a union between them under the Great Law of Peace. (The original belt, which is more than 1,000 years old, was returned to its origin at Onondaga Lake in central New York in 2017.)

Belts of wampum were clasped and "read" at ceremonies, used to recite law and tradition, and especially employed during diplomatic meetings to discuss treaties. They were tangible representations of alliances and events, such as the meeting between the Cherokee and British that took place in September of 1768 to discuss boundary lines yet again. (This was just five years after the establishment of the Proclamation Line of 1763.) The records of this meeting refer repeatedly to wampum in the form of belts and, in many other instances, to "a string of white beads."

At those 1768 meetings, Oconostota had addressed the white settlers and Cherokee present regarding the treaty at hand and the boundary lines to which it referred. After indicating a readiness to sign the proposed treaty, Oconostota said: "Afterwards I shall cut such a deep ditch around our Lands, that whoever shall attempt to cross it will be in danger of falling in. I make not the least doubt but the Great King will give the necessary orders for preventing Encroachments by his people and if we find any White people settling upon our side of the Line we will tye them and carry them to you."

He then noted the "Great King's Goodness in ordering a Line to be marked between the white people's lands and our Hunting Grounds, it will preserve peace between us and them . . .

"The Land is now divided for the use of the Red and White people and I hope the white Inhabitants of the Frontiers will pay great attention to the line marked and agreed upon."

At this break in the diplomatic discussions, the notes suggest that an item was passed from one party to the other: "A Belt of White Whampum."

Wampum also played an important role in the council meeting taking place in Chota on July 8, 1776.

The principal topic of debate was how to proceed against the settler incursions into Cherokee land. That "ditch" to which Oconostota referred had indeed been crossed. Again. For Dragging Canoe, it was one time too many.

He wanted to assemble warriors to attack white settlements to the north along the Holston River. Along with the leadership of two other warriors, Old Abram and the Raven, the plan was to execute a three-pronged attack. Dragging Canoe would move on Eaton's Station, a post at the Long Island on the Holston River; Abram, to Nolichucky and the Watauga settlements; the Raven—"Savanukuh"—to Carter's Valley and points west.

Nanye'hi did not favor attacking these newcomers. She wanted to seek a peaceful solution to her people's troubles. The elder Cherokee men, Attakullakulla, Oconostota, and Ostenaco, agreed with her. Her cousin Dragging Canoe, however, did not. And he was not alone.

In a sense, this was a drama that had become irritatingly common, and there was not a lot of agreement on how to deal with expansionist visions of the settlers—whether or not they were loyal to the Crown— in a time when allegiances shifted as rapidly as boundary lines.

The night of the council meeting, each of the Cherokee acted in many ways in accordance with their roles within the Cherokee clan system. Nanye'hi was of the Wolf Clan—"Aniwahya"—who were charged with protection and security. Dragging Canoe was Red Paint

Clan—"Aniwodi"—sorcerers, conjurors, and those permitted to make the red paint in times of war. Each clan sought the well-being of their people in its own way.

Dragging Canoe's mind was made up. In the council, he struck the war pole. Nanye'hi, in her role as Ghigau, prepared the White Drink, part of an important ritual and purification process that might also include other ceremonial observances such as scratching and going to water. "Scratching" meant that warriors raked a comblike object over their skin until blood flowed. "Going to water" was, among other things, a form of purification; it involved an immersion in flowing water and was an example of the continued significance of rivers and streams in the lives of the Cherokee.

Nanye'hi took salt from her pouch and scattered it at the feet of the chiefs before tossing it into the brewing concoction of branches and leaves of the yaupon shrub. The yaupon was, and is, the only naturally caffeinated plant species of North America. Lastly, she waved her swan wing, symbolic of her important role among the Cherokee, over the war kettle.

The decision was made. Dragging Canoe, Old Abram, and the Raven would gather about two hundred Cherokee and attack the Watauga settlements.

Nanye'hi had made a decision of her own: She would devise a way to warn the settlers of the danger coming their way.

One day after Nanye'hi prepared the White Drink, in another province of the war, shelling rained down on those British encamped at Gwynn's Island off the coast of Virginia, along with Lord Dunmore. Among those enduring the attack of the Virginia patriots were what remained of Dunmore's own British troops, the Queen's Own Loyal Virginia Regiment, and the Royal Ethiopian Regiment, along with people such as the preacher Mary, and other civilians who had fled their homes and plantations in Virginia and elsewhere.

Dunmore's beleaguered troops stood little chance. When the

Virginia artillery opened fire on July 9, their aim was true enough to send a splinter into Dunmore's leg, and shatter the precious china he had cherished enough to bring with him when he fled Williamsburg.

News of the Declaration had not yet reached the British loyalists fleeing the embattled Gwynn's Island, nor the patriots attacking it.

The fleet moved on once again, this time into the Chesapeake Bay. It, too, would eventually make its way up to New York. However, most of the individuals on those ships had no idea New York City was their ultimate destination. Meanwhile, on the island of Manhattan, Washington's troops were instructed to gather to hear the news that would forever alter the political landscape.

Washington's orders read as follows:

> *The Honorable the Continental Congress, impelled by the dictates of duty, policy and necessity, having been pleased to dissolve the Connection which subsisted between this Country, and Great Britain, and to declare the United Colonies of North America, free and independent STATES: The several brigades are to be drawn up this evening on their respective Parades, at six OClock, when the declaration of Congress, shewing the grounds & reasons of this measure, is to be read with an audible voice.*
>
> *The General hopes this important Event will serve as a fresh incentive to every officer, and soldier, to act with Fidelity and Courage, as knowing that now the peace and safety of his Country depends (under God) solely on the success of our arms: And that he is now in the service of a State, possessed of sufficient power to reward his merit, and advance him to the highest Honors of a free Country.*
>
> *The Brigade Majors are to receive, at the Adjutant Generals Office, several of the Declarations to be delivered to the Brigadiers General, and the Colonels of regiments.*

And so it happened. Continental troops gathered in the Commons in Lower Manhattan. The area was located about one mile north of the southern tip of that valuable seaport, in the vicinity of the park in front of New York City's present-day City Hall. On July 9, 1776, this was not to be the site of a military exercise but rather a public reading. George Washington had ordered the newly accepted Declaration of Independence to be read to the troops and any civilians who gathered nearby.

According to Washington's aide-de-camp, Lieutenant Colonel Samuel Blachley Webb, the reading itself was initially well received by those within earshot: "Agreeable to this day's orders, the Declaration of Independence was read at the Head of each Brigade; and was received by three Huzzas from the Troops—every one seeming highly pleased that we were separated from a King who was endeavoring to enslave his once loyal subjects. God grant us success in this our new character."

As the reading progressed, individuals heard for the first time both the declaration of "unalienable rights" as well as the litany of complaints against the Crown that the document laid out: "The history of the present King of Great Britain is a history of repeated injuries and usurpations, all having in direct object the establishment of an absolute Tyranny over these States. To prove this, let Facts be submitted to a candid world . . ."

As the gathered crowd listened, it grew in size, number, and ire as other New York residents joined the throng. The reaction to these words—words so recently adopted by Congress and in public circulation only five days—soon morphed from patriotic enthusiasm to unbridled rage.

Mobs swarmed the streets, forging a path of destruction along the way. Individuals—believed to include Sons of Liberty and soldiers, among others—stormed the chambers of the New York City Council. Once inside, they tore down a painting of King George III and did the same to his coat of arms.

Soon enough, the rabble's attention turned toward the statue of King George III standing in the Bowling Green. Though the fifteen-foot-tall sculpture looked opulent from a distance, its golden exterior was truly only skin-deep. Under the gilt was a hollow carving fashioned entirely of lead. The figure of the king mounted upon his steed was itself mounted by rioters, roped, and yanked down off of its noble pedestal.

In his report, Lieutenant Colonel Webb would later recall: "Last night the Statue of George the third was tumbled down and beheaded—the troops having long had an inclination so to do, tho't this time of publishing a Declaration of Independence, to be a favorable opportunity—for which they received the Check in this day's orders." And the General Orders out of the Continental Army's headquarters in New York City the following day, July 10, 1776, revealed Washington's distaste for what had transpired: "Tho the General doubts not the persons, who pulled down and mutilated the Statue, in the Broadway, last night, were actuated by Zeal in the public cause; yet it has so much the appearance of riot and want of order, in the Army, that he disapproves the manner, and directs that in future these things shall be avoided by the Soldiery, and left to be executed by proper authority."

The statue of King George III lay in pieces. After His Highness's metallicized likeness toppled to the ground, it was seized upon by members of the rabble. The lead beneath the gilt was, after all, more precious than the golden exterior.

Parts of the statue disappeared in their entirety, George's massive head among them. (The Crown's crown was rumored to have been paraded through town on a pike and eventually turned up in London.) Rather than disappearing into a nearby metalsmith's shop, massive pieces of the sculpture set off on a much longer journey. Soldiers, industrious friends of the patriot cause, and a Connecticut congressman seized upon pieces from the razed statue. They collected as many chunks as they could and transported them overland. Then they transported them on a vessel across the waters of Long Island Sound—carefully dodging British ships—and finally landed on the shores of Connecticut at Norfolk.

From there, patriots loaded remnants onto oxcarts and continued on the final leg of the trek, to Litchfield, Connecticut, and the residence of the congressman Colonel Oliver Wolcott.

Laura Wolcott was at home in Connecticut with her children, fifteen-year-old Laura, eleven-year-old Mariann, and nine-year-old Frederick.

(Oliver Jr., sixteen years old at the time, was studying at Yale College and would soon serve in the military during 1777 and 1779.) Laura was active in the Litchfield community, maintained the home and farm while her husband was away at Congress—with assistance from their enslaved workers—and instructed her children, teaching them to read and write quite early on in their young lives.

She regularly received letters from her husband in Philadelphia with updates, concerns, and encouragement.

"The Ladies, I hope," he had written her about the various boycotts, "will still make themselves contented to live without Tea for the good of their country."

She missed Oliver, and he missed her. He wrote that he wished "to return to the Pleasures of a domestick rural Life . . . Here I see little except human Faces which I know not, and numerous Piles of Buildings which have long since satiated the Sight, and the street rumble is far from being musical. But as I was not sent here to please myself, I shall cheerfully yield to my Duty."

Laura had also read the news her husband sent earlier in 1776 about the state of the yet-to-be-formed union.

"My Dear," Laura read in March, "I feel much concerned for the Burden which necessarily devolves upon you; I hope you will make it as light as possible. You may easily believe from the Situation of publick Affairs, that the critical Moment is near, which will perhaps decide the Fate of the Country . . ."

But little could have prepared Laura for what Oliver would ask of her now . . . and few could have imagined just how spectacularly she would rise to the occasion.

Connecticut's state motto, *Qui Transtulit Sustinet*, translates to "He who transplanted still sustains." Those bits and remains and shards of riotous animosity uprooted from Bowling Green and transplanted to Litchfield had yet to see their last participation in the ongoing war.

Laura, her children, and others in the Litchfield community would soon transform the detritus of this violent act into a much-needed boon for the colonial troops. She and her community would indeed endure and sustain.

The Hidden City

Standing at the north end of Bowling Green, all eyes focus on a chunky slab of horned, snorting bronze on four hooves: the *Charging Bull*.

Though the bull has only been here since 1989, tourists line up daily to get a picture of artist Arturo Di Modica's creation. Visitors from the world over elbow their way through like-minded shutterbugs, seeking the 7,100-pound sculpture's best angles—namely, the view from behind, where the animal's masculine attributes are on full display, offering undeniable visual confirmation that this is indeed a bull and not a cow.

Few take note of the small park sitting just nearby—the first public park established in New York City. Even if people pass through or spend time sitting in the compact green space, the vast majority don't give the low fence surrounding it a second thought. This is the very same fence that surrounded this very same green more than 250 years ago and the only surviving remnant of the July 9, 1776, riot. The statue-less pedestal stood, barren, for decades until it was finally removed in 1818. The portion of the fence that still remains dates to its original installation in 1771. Before the mob got to it, the fence's spikes sported decorative finials shaped like small crowns. Those went the way of the statue itself, ripped from their metal moorings, never to be seen again.

I have come to Manhattan in search of Revolutionary War history, which at first glance seems like a tall order. Lower Manhattan and the Financial District do not often spring to mind when one thinks of walking in the footsteps of anything other than stock market history.

There is not much to see, for example, at Number One Broadway, the former site of not only the headquarters of the Continental Army but also the temporary home of Lucy Knox and her husband, Henry. The building standing there now, completed in 1887, is a recently renovated bastion of gleaming office and retail space.

Heading north on Broadway, or Greenwich Street, as Lorenda might have done on her way to the Mortier residence, there are no more Lispenard's Meadows to traverse, though you can stop into a TriBeCa wine bar called Terroir offering the "Anthony Lispenard" charcuterie plate—four cheeses, four charcuterie, and "yummy condiments"—named for the family that once owned these lands and whose descendants drained the acreage that would become TriBeCa itself.

The Mortier residence—or, as it is better known, Richmond Hill House—is no longer there. Richmond Hill remained a grand estate after Washington's (and Lorenda's) tenure there, serving as home to president John Adams and Broadway musical namesake Alexander Hamilton. It would have been located in the vicinity of Varick Street near the corner of Charlton.

A historic marker once commemorated the approximate location of the Richmond Hill House. It hung on the side of a CVS pharmacy in SoHo at the corner of Spring Street and Sixth Avenue. A faded outline is all that remains of the metal placard, now barely discernible on the exterior wall of the CVS, just to the right of the drugstore's entrance.

A bit farther west, however, at 326 Spring Street between Washington and Greenwich, is the Ear Inn, an establishment, building, and location with a unique history that predates Lorenda's adventures in the neighborhood.

On the exterior of the pub, beneath a lamp, a hand-painted pale blue line trickles down the facade. Above it is written, in freehand, "Hudson River shore 1766 2012," commemorating both the shoreline during the Revolutionary Era and the high-water mark for Superstorm Sandy. On the sidewalk out front, giant metal dock cleats wrapped in rope rise from the concrete. "*Watch your step!*" a plaque beneath your feet warns.

The Ear Inn is located in the James Brown House. Brown was reputed to be a Black Revolutionary War soldier and aide to George Washington during the war who flourished in the tobacco trade, enabling him to count the future president as one of his neighbors. Details of his life continue to be debated. Is that oarsman seen in Emanuel Leutze's famed painting *Washington Crossing the Delaware* a depiction of James Brown?

Maybe.

The neon sign hanging above the pub's entrance now reads, "EAR Est. 1817 A.D.," but don't let that number fool you. This Federal-style structure has been around a lot longer than that and has served as a brewery, board-inghouse, speakeasy, and more in its day. It has been a continuously oper-ating watering hole for longer than most any other establishment in New York City. So why 1817? That was the year that the ever-expanding "New York City" finally reached—and swallowed up—the village known as Green-wich, thus landing the bar in the city's record books. The modern-day pub is also reportedly haunted by a salty sea dog of a ghost named Mickey.

After Prohibition, the sign hanging over the entrance read simply "BAR." In the 1970s—in order to avoid the red tape inherent in renaming a historic structure—the rounded protrusions of the *B* were sloshed with paint, mag-ically transforming the word "BAR" into "EAR," and thus it remains.

A commemorative copper marker embedded in the sidewalk (courtesy of the Carlsberg Brewing Co.) reads, "Original Shoreline Marker 1766 A.D. You are standing on the former Hudson River shore." These days, if you want to reach the water, it's a two-block stroll and a jaunt across the West Side Highway to get to Pier 34 and Hudson River Park, which sit atop part of the Holland Tunnel.

Shifting shorelines aside, much of the arrangement of the streets of Lower Manhattan remains unchanged from 1776 and even long before.

When cartographer Bernard Ratzer mapped his "plan of the city of New York" and "most humbly inscribed" it to His Excellency Sir Henry Moore, 1st Baronet, "captain general and governour in chief, in & over the Province of New York & the territories depending thereon in America, chancellor & vice admiral of the same," Pearl Street was where Pearl Street still is, minus the piles of oyster shells.

Everyone who was anyone in the eighteenth century wanted a hat fash-ioned from beaver fur, and the Lenape traded beaver pelts with the Dutch and eventually the English for various goods. The market was so hungry for these cuddly rodents that they were nearly hunted to extinction. The trade ended, but not before it lent its name to the thoroughfare still known as Beaver Street.

The roadway dubbed "Bowry Lane"—from the Dutch word *bouwerie*, meaning farm—was also labeled as the "Road to Boston," but it's still the same old Bowery, minus the rural acreage and plus a lot more big-box stores, boutique hotels, and boho chic.

Burling Slip, where Lorenda launched her daring run into the waters of the East River, is long gone. But, as mentioned, modern-day maps line up quite well with those of the mid-1700s. Burling Slip would have been at the intersection of Front Street and John, where the East River once lapped against Manhattan's shoreline. Thanks to a landfill process originally intended to make it easier for ships to load and unload, John Street now stretches farther, under FDR Drive, straight to Pier 16 and the South Street Seaport.

The painstakingly restored 1885 tall ship *Wavertree* docks there now, maintained by the South Street Seaport Museum, its flags welcoming tourists and available to visit. The museum manages a small fleet of historic ships, which host educational programs and can be chartered for a sail or rented out for private events. The museum experience as a whole, and the *Wavertree* specifically, offer a welcome islet of history amid a sea of tourist attractions. Standing on the deck of the graceful ship and looking out across the water toward Brooklyn was about as close to Lorenda's swim as I was able or willing to get. The museum and the restored ship give a good sense of the role that New York played in the maritime world and the role those surrounding waters played in the life of New York.

With each step you take upon the New York City asphalt, strip away the skyscrapers, shift your lens, and mentally peel back the layers beneath your feet, decade by decade, century by century.

———

However, as much as I enjoy strolling through Manhattan and imagining Lorenda Holmes stalking past the bourse on her way to Burling Slip to fetch the post, or darting through the fields to that faraway rural village called "Greenwich," where Martha Washington and Mary Smith were living—very possibly passing by Lucy Knox's temporary home along the way—these imaginings merely scratch the surface of the thousands of years of history beneath my feet.

When the Dutch sailed into town, they took advantage of all that the Lenape had already put into place, including their trading routes, and re-named them. One of the most significant of those routes was the Wick-quasgeck Trail, which headed north and eventually became known as Broadway.

Broadway originally ended at State Street, an area called "Kapsee," meaning sharp rock place. Wall Street is named for an actual wall that be-gan to take shape during the Dutch reign over Manhattan. It was built by workers enslaved by the Dutch in an attempt to keep the British *and* those original Indigenous people literally at bay.

Farther north along Broadway and Bowery sits Astor Place. On this spot, representatives from the major Native American tribes, including the Canarsie, Munsee, and Sapohannikan, met regularly. This was originally called "Kintecoying," or "Crossroads of Three Nations." Farther west, Mi-netta Lane in Greenwich Village took its name from a creek the Native Americans called "Manetta." The street ran adjacent to what had been the stream, and was later called "Negroes Causeway" by the British.

Heading farther south, however, the island tapers. It is still surrounded by the water that so shaped its fortunes, with bridges in every direction. Florentine navigator Giovanni da Verrazzano explored the eastern coast of what is now the United States and Canada in the sixteenth century for King Francis I of France. He initially went ashore somewhere around Cape Fear, North Carolina, before turning his attention north. When arriving at the waters of what became New York Harbor, Verrazzano, in his letter to the French king, pronounced it a "very agreeable place." Here, in 1524, the Lenape encountered the Italian seaman who had beaten Henry Hudson to the area by a good eighty years. The structure that spans those waters and connects Brooklyn to Staten Island is the Verrazzano-Narrows Bridge (which many movie buffs—myself included—associate with an acrophobi-cally climactic scene from *Saturday Night Fever*).

No visit to colonial-era New York City is complete without a visit to Fraunces Tavern on Pearl Street. That thoroughfare once ended at the Battery, then the island's southernmost tip, and is named for the post-shucking remnants of the bivalves that piled up and were sometimes crushed and used to pave the streets of the growing city. Pearl Street pays cartographical homage to the indispensable oysters. In fact, the marine history of New York City was literally embedded in the thoroughfares trod upon each and every day by the city's residents.

Fraunces Tavern has a variety of rustic, historic nooks, bars, and dining rooms, some of which are named for revolutionary "big-Whigs," including the Marquis de Lafayette and George Washington. The museum upstairs is well worth the price of admission and features rotating exhibits in addition to paintings, etchings, and display cases of objects ranging from powder horns and dinnerware to bells, badges, bayonets, and broadsides. You can also step into the Long Room, where George Washington bid farewell to his troops in 1783.

It is less than a five-minute stroll from Fraunces Tavern back to Bowling Green. Along the way I pass the Alexander Hamilton U.S. Custom House, now home to the Smithsonian's National Museum of the American Indian. Within those 199-year-old walls you can step further back into the muddled and reclaimed history of the island on which you stand.

To Bowling Green again, the site of so much upheaval for hundreds of years and one of the oldest public gathering places. Negotiations, council meetings, preaching, trade, riots . . . Bowling Green as seen it all.

Just across the street at the northeast corner of Battery Park stands a monument commemorating one of the more mythically embellished events ever to grace U.S. history books. The stone flagstaff depicts a Dutchman and Lenape exchanging a belt. This monument in Lower Manhattan marks the supposed "sale" of Manahatta to the Dutch in 1626 for a sum Peter Minuit reported as "60 guilders worth of trade."

This exchange was not, however, a sale. The Lenape could not sell something that they did not believe they owned. Yes, there was an exchange of goods, but that was to be expected when two groups came together to share, for example, hunting rights to the lands they cohabited. The Lenape most likely considered their transaction with Minuit—then director general of New Amsterdam—to be an exchange of gifts in light of their new relationship on this land.

The monument itself is riddled with inaccuracies. The Lenape is dressed like a Plains Indian—the pervasive "Hollywood" image of any and all Indigenous peoples. The legend reads:

In testimony of ancient and
unbroken friendship this flagpole
is presented to the city of New York
by the Dutch people 1926.

That friendship did not survive the 1600s, let alone last until 1926. It was as broken as the statue of the next ruler who sought to take the island of Manahatta as his own.

As for the remnants of Manhattan itself, they remain. While it is common in New York City to tilt one's head to the skies and the edifices that scrape them, rather turn your attention to the ground beneath and the memories it holds, encased in the pearl of old.

CHAPTER 13

Choices, Consequences, and an Island Lost

On July 10, news of the riot in Bowling Green on the ninth had not likely reached the offices of *The Maryland Journal, and the Baltimore Advertiser* and its publisher, postmistress Mary Katharine Goddard. Even so, there was a key piece of news that Goddard had yet to share with her readers.

Each day, the front page of Goddard's newspaper proclaimed to the world—as the *Providence Journal* had—that these pages contained "the FRESHEST ADVICES, both FOREIGN and DOMESTIC."

"Freshest" advices for any publisher at the time meant receiving news days if not weeks after they occurred and still needing to report it to and contextualize it for your readership. But this day, the "freshest advices" on the domestic front stood on their own, no contextualization necessary as words that would forever impact the nation greeted Goddard's readers: "THE THIRTEEN UNITED STATES OF AMERICA, Have declared INDEPENDENCY."

In the July 10, 1776, edition of the newspaper was the full text of the Declaration of Independence.

This would not be the last time Mary Katharine Goddard printed the Declaration of Independence. The next time she did, she would insert herself as indelibly as any ink in a history that spans 250 years and counting.

"Sunday the 21st of last month . . . a large party of Indians attacked the Watauga fort, in which were 150 men," *The Virginia Gazette* reported in early August. "They fired on a great number of women who went out at day-break to milk their cows, and chased them into the fort, but providentially did not kill one of them."

The newspaper went on, reporting on the results of the attacks led by Dragging Canoe, the Raven, Old Abram, and the warriors who had joined them. The report indicated that, after the initial attacks, the Cherokee had "retired with considerable loss, as was supposed from the quantity of blood found."

The subsequent information, provided by a Colonel Fincastle, indicated that the Cherokee attacked more than once—with even more mixed results.

"But they returned to the attack, and were besieging the fort six days after, as a messenger who was slipped out informed our men . . ." This occurred along the Holston River, which switchbacked its way through Cherokee lands in what is now eastern Tennessee.

The plans of the Cherokee leaders failed in large part because they were greeted at two of their targets by hundreds of armed colonists who had the element of surprise on their side.

The reason behind it all was even more surprising than the attack. After the council meeting at which Dragging Canoe had announced his intent to attack the settlements, Nanye'hi alerted the three white men being held as captives by the Cherokee in Chota. One was Isaac Thomas, a survivor of the Cherokee attack on Fort Loudon, who had been trading with the Cherokee. He was being held in Chota by order of Dragging Canoe, along with at least two other men, William Fawling and Jarrett Williams. Nanye'hi informed the men of Dragging Canoe's plans and his intended targets. She then helped the three to escape, which allowed them to forewarn the settlers at Watauga and elsewhere, especially women and children. The "messenger" to whom *The Virginia Gazette* newspaper article referred who had "slipped out" and managed to "inform our men" may very well have been someone acting on Nanye'hi's tip.

Once word was out, John Sevier, a leading member of the Wataugan settlement, was forewarned—and therefore forearmed. White traders and their families quickly made their way to safety, and the militia assembled for a fight.

Settlers and militia killed at least thirteen of Dragging Canoe's party, and Dragging Canoe himself was injured in the ambush and subsequent fighting. Cherokee attacks along frontier settlements in the Carolinas had begun earlier that spring of 1776 in an ongoing and bloody conflict that would come to be called the Cherokee-American War (or Dragging Canoe's War). The losses suffered by the Cherokee during those failed raids at the end of July were notable not solely for the suffering endured but also for what appeared to be a growing schism among the Cherokee leadership and Nanye'hi's role in how those doomed attacks unfolded.

Though the advance warning served its purpose, not all settlers escaped without incident. Two of the people who fled but were subsequently captured by the Cherokee were a young boy named Samuel Moore and a woman, Lydia Russell Bean. Lydia's husband, William, was one of the first white settlers in the area. Lydia was likely among the women who had gone out to tend to the cows when the attack began. The Cherokee brought the prisoners Bean and Moore to Toqua, an Overhill Cherokee town on the Little Tennessee River.

Toqua was an important ancestral site of the Indigenous peoples of the Mississippian Period (1000–1540 CE) containing an architectural and culturally significant feature: a platform mound. For thousands of years, Indigenous cultures throughout the area constructed these monumental earthen mounds, which often stood along rivers. According to Henry Timberlake, who visited Toqua in 1761, the town had two mounds, the larger of which stood twenty-five feet high and upon which sat the council house. As the highest point of these communities, platform mounds were often visible from the flowing waterways below and might be used for burial sites, ceremonies, or, in the case of Moore and Bean, a pyre.

Upon arriving in Toqua, Samuel Moore was quickly burned at the stake atop one of the town's mounds. Next, standing atop the mound, a bound Lydia Bean awaited her excruciating fate. Her captors built the pyre whose flames would soon engulf her.

When Nanye'hi arrived at Toqua, she was too late to rescue young Samuel Moore. However, there was time to intercede on Lydia Bean's behalf.

The power of her swan's wing could include the potential to free the condemned, an influence that Nanye'hi, in her role as Beloved Woman, now wielded in order to spare the life of Lydia Bean. This action would spark speculation for centuries after. What compelled her to save someone who was *not* Cherokee? Was Nanye'hi acting, in her role as Ghigau, also as a "protector"? Was there some other purpose or outcome she envisioned for herself or her people? Answers to these questions have evolved over the years, and Nanye'hi's choices would have even more impact on her people in the years to come.

Whatever the reason, Nanye'hi saved Lydia's life and took her to live with her family. There, under Nanye'hi's apparent protection, Lydia came to instruct the Cherokee woman on how to tend dairy cows and how to make butter and cheese from their milk. Nanye'hi perhaps envisioned the importance of animal husbandry to her community, and for doing so she would be credited with introducing dairy farming on a larger scale to the Cherokee.

As for the Cherokee attacks on the Watauga settlements, the August 1776 article in *The Virginia Gazette* spoke proudly of the actions of the settlers and the militia, noting the number of Cherokee killed and prisoners and weapons seized, noting, "It is worthy of our observation, that in these several skirmishes with the Indians, in all of which we did more execution than in some of the principal actions of the last war, we lost not a man." This and other successes against the Cherokee the article attributed to "Divine Interposition in our favor."

The choice Nanye'hi made cost the Cherokee people. Her ties to the settlers appeared to strengthen as the power of the Cherokee in the region weakened. Future scholars would note that, in her role as a member of the Wolf Clan, she was expected to ensure the care and protection of the vulnerable: the sick and wounded, women and children, and captives as well. It mattered not if they were Cherokee. In her role as Ghigau, she could act as a peacekeeper and decision-maker. She would bless food and drink. She also had the responsibility to help protect Cherokee land and water from being tainted by the blood of warfare—even if white people sought to claim them as their own. Taken all together, this was a huge responsibility. Within this context, perhaps, her choices made a certain kind of sense and were neither anti-Cherokee nor pro-American.

Nevertheless, as fall progressed, the original inhabitants of these lands would see their place in it dwindle even more.

Lucy Knox—at Henry's insistence—had recently arrived in New Haven, Connecticut, far from the riot that erupted beneath the windows of her former abode in Lower Manhattan. Once settled, she wrote her brother-in-law, William, about her well-being and to report that her young daughter, Lucy—not yet a year old—was healthy and doing well.

When Lucy received her reply in mid-July, the news William shared was a mix of the potentially urgent and the predictably mundane. He was doing his best to shop for Lucy—seeking corsets with bells, among other items—and reported that he had some tea to send along. He then shared the news from Boston, gleaned from the usual hodgepodge of firsthand experiences, written reports, and hearsay:

> *We hear by a person two months from England, by the way of the West Indies, who arriv'd at Nantucket some few days since, that all the Foreign Troops except the last division (which was at Spithead & expected to imbark very soon] had sail'd for america, so that we may expect them immediately . . . Yesterday an [acco.t] arrived in town of the intire defeat of Genl. Clinton by Genl Lee at Charlestown S. Carolina . . .*

He continued with mentions of neighbors and friends and business associates, whom Lucy in her relative isolation surely missed, before signing off, "Kiss little Lucy for me."

A week later, Lucy received a letter from her poor, dear Harry, still in New York and perpetually disappointed in the frequency (or lack thereof) of Lucy's correspondence. He noted that he had been expecting Lucy to have already written him a letter, but she had not, and to his "great mortification was disappointed."

"What was the matter," she continued reading, "did you miss the post or was so fatigu'd with your Journey that you could not find an opportunity to write to your Harry? I do most earnestly beg you to be more attentive for the future peace of your friend, & lover . . ."

He then pleaded with Lucy to get the smallpox vaccine, as deaths from that highly contagious disease continued to plague the colonies. Lucy, for her part, seemed reluctant to undertake the inoculation, which brought with it a mild-to-severe experience with the malady before one's body developed an immunity to the virus. Henry knew this, adding, "This matter my dearest is left entirely at your own will . . ."

Henry, the highest-ranking artillery officer in the Continental Army, shared what details he could of the ongoing war:

> *The enemy have sent no more flags since I wrote you they appear to be waiting for a Reinforcement—My Lord Dunmore has been twice beat—once at Gwyns Island and again at Powtomack, I suppose he with Clinton lord Cornwallis and the whole Southern Crew will [not] be able to make head [again] In that Climate therefore we shall leave them here which together with the Hessians and other hard nam'd people will to be sure make a most Motley band of nations Colors and Languges.*

He closed the letter in his usual gushing manner, "Adieu, My dearest Life."

The letter in Lucy's hands included a postscript, referring to the date the letter was written—July 25: "Your [Harry's] birth day. I hope you will remember him in your petitions," Henry had added, perhaps in an attempt to see if guilt might impel Lucy to write more often.

His plea must have worked. Lucy sat down to write him on July 29. She spoke of her difficulties in her travel to New Haven but insisted she did indeed like her temporary home, which she was sharing with the wife of another Continental officer. Conversely, she did not like Catharine Greene very well but did not get into any details about her distaste for Continental general Nathanael Greene's wife. Henry wanted any troubled waters calmed, if at all possible, for the sake of his own working relationship.

Greene was one of Washington's most trusted commanders. He had been raised in a devout Quaker family in Rhode Island, and, as a result of his support for the war against the Crown, the Society of Friends expelled the oft-called "Fighting Quaker." After establishing a militia—the Kentish Guard—in Rhode Island and serving with Washington during the Boston campaign, Greene became a brigadier general in the Continental Army. He had established himself as a go-to leader. In fact, Greene's fast rise through the ranks of the American military was not entirely unlike Henry Knox's.

Henry was certainly over the moon with this fresh correspondence from his beloved but had some advice for his wife. "I dont know your reason," Henry responded in his next missive, "beware of busy bodies, they are the greatest pests of society. I have a great Respect and friendship for [Catharine Greene's] husband it is impossible it should mature if you and she are at variance therefore for the sake of me smother any little matter which you may think an Injury."

Lucy admitted to Henry that she was worried about smallpox. However, she had not yet decided to avail herself of the painful inoculation, which often resulted in much illness before it prevented any. The variola virus that caused smallpox had torn through North America more than once in the early eighteenth century, resulting in aches, pains, pustules, and death. Europeans brought the disease to North America, and the British forces knowingly infected Native Americans with the gruesome pestilence during the French and Indian War, almost like some early form of biological warfare.

Inoculation—such as the one mandated by Washington for his troops—involved taking a small sampling of the disease in the form of pus from an infected individual and injecting that into a healthy person by way of a small incision.

Puritan reverend Cotton Mather—an ardent participant in the Salem Witch Trials—was instrumental in spreading this inoculation method in the Boston area during a 1721 outbreak of the disease. But neither Mather nor Dr. Zabdiel Boylston, the doctor he recruited to begin inoculating the people of Boston, had developed this remarkably effective and preventive treatment. Rather, Mather learned of this method of inoculation from a man who had procured the knowledge in his homeland of West Africa, where it had long been practiced. That man, responsible for bringing this healing approach to the attention of Mather, was a man named Onesimus, whom Mather enslaved.

Henry complained of his own physical ills and fatigue as well as the sweltering weather in New York and a sun "hot enough to roast an egg." This roasting had resulted in a rash erupting on Henry's arms, for which he had been bled with leeches. He advised Lucy, on behalf of their doctor, to drink tamarinds and water. Lucy, for her part, demanded written permission from Henry to return to him once she was inoculated.

And if Lucy promised not to go to Boston, Henry wrote, he promised to send her a dozen bottles of her favorite wine.

As for Dunmore's latest strokes of bad luck, the man himself was working to decide what steps to take next with his seafaring village of the king's loyal soldiery and subjects.

"Since Writing your Lordship of the 26th of June at Gwins Island, we have again been obliged to Shift our quarters," Lord Dunmore wrote Lord George Germain, secretary of state for the American Department, on the thirty-first of July. From the midst of the Potomac, aboard a ship now bearing his name, Dunmore described the attacks his fleet had suffered on the ninth and the subsequent decision he had made in light of his embattled state.

*I have taken the opportunity of Advising all those who have put
themselves under the protection of His Majesty's Ships, to proceed
to such place of Safety, as they shall think proper; some go immediately to Great Britain, others to the West Indias, and others to St
Augustine, by which means we shall be disencumbered of every
thing but the Ships of War and Transports; but where we are to go,
or what we can do next to render Service to His Majesty I own I
am puzzled to know . . .*

Captain Andrew Snape Hamond of the *Roebuck* could not have
agreed more, especially about reducing the burdens and obligations
Dunmore had taken on by the boatload since leaving Virginia's waters.

"The great number of familys inhabiting Vessels," Hamond wrote,
"ill provided with all Sorts of materials, that have ever since the destroying of the Town of Norfolk put themselves under the protection
of His Majesty's Ships, have been found to be so great an inconvenience
to his Majesty's Service that it is become absolutely necessary that they
should be sent to a place of Security."

The enslaved woman preacher Mary, still among those vessels,
would not be so easily "disencumbered," nor would others who had
fled to those ships on the basis of the thin British promise of freedom
from enslavement.

On August 6, Captain Hamond wrote to Captain George Montagu:

*The Sickly and weak State of the Troops under Lord Dunmores
command, as well as the bad condition of the Transports have
determined His Lordship and my self to proceed with them to
New York; being clearly of opinion that remaining within the
Capes without power of Acting against the Rebels only tends to
bring disgrace on his Majesty's Arms, and give Spirits to the
enemy.*

While part of Dunmore's ninety-or-so-ship fleet headed south, the
Roebuck and other ships headed north to join the growing numbers of
British on Staten Island and in the waters surrounding Manhattan.

Harry Washington, an enslaved man from Mount Vernon, had sought refuge aboard the forty-four-gun HMS *Roebuck* captained by Hamond. He had escaped Washington's Mount Vernon for a *second* time and came on board in July. His work at Mount Vernon—including at the Dismal Swamp, where Mary had been preaching—would serve him and the British well in the coming months and years.

Lord Dunmore's Ethiopian Regiment, decimated by disease and exhaustion, essentially disbanded once Dunmore's fleet landed on Staten Island. But the vision of a Black fighting force was not gone for good. When Dunmore's countryman General Clinton headed down the East Coast toward Charles Town in the spring of 1776, he stopped in North Carolina, where he picked up seventy or so Black men and enrolled them in the service of the Crown. On his return north after failing to secure that southern port city, he recruited still more. A new, better armed, trained, and organized unit of Black soldiers, free and enslaved, had joined the British. These fighting men—including Harry Washington—would be known as the Black Pioneers, and the scant remaining members of the defunct Ethiopian Regiment would join them.

Clinton, like Dunmore, now was headed to New York. The British presence in the area had been felt since the spring, with more and more ships amassing on Staten Island as July wore on and August arrived.

On the second day of that month, Congress began signing the engrossed—hand-lettered—copy of the Declaration of Independence, adding their signatures to what was widely regarded as a document treasonous to the Crown. If this additional act of defiance was viewed by patriots as a boon to their cause, it was one of the few if any that late summer and early fall. "Independence," such as it was, had gotten off to a rocky start, even if fervor for its realization endured.

New Hampshire congressman and eventual signer of the Declaration Josiah Bartlett wrote fellow New Hampshire representative John Langdon from Philadelphia, saying, "Governor Dunmore and his ragamuffins it is said have left Virginia and are supposed to be going to join General Howe. I think we may expect that some important event will soon take place at or near New York—God grant it may be favorable to the United American States."

It was not.

In his letters, Henry Knox had derided the king's mercenaries as a "Motley band of nations Colors and Languges," Hessians, and "scoundrells" in a bid to quell Lucy's nerves. However, the Hessians to whom he referred would prove rather troublesome and dangerously effective. A little more than half of the more than 30,000 German troops hired by Britain to fight in the American Revolution hailed from the principality of Hesse-Kassel, resulting in the whole lot of hired guns being referred to as "Hessians." This was not the first instance of German troops being employed to fight for other nations, and as a result they were more experienced than many of the volunteers and militia comprising the Continental forces. The Hessian role in this war was a significant one.

News that the British were closing their grip ever tighter on New York spread throughout the colonies. In Philadelphia, Quaker diarist Elizabeth Drinker paused a moment after logging the requisite notes about her children's activities and visits from acquaintances to write: "Augt. 13. An Account this afternoon of 104 sail of Vessels having joined Lord How."

Dunmore, Clinton, and members of their respective fleets were among those who had already arrived in New York to join the amassing ships Lucy had read about in her letters from Henry and her brother William, and which Elizabeth Drinker wrote about in her diary. General William Howe—along with a daunting four hundred ships and 32,000 men—had been on Staten Island since early July. By August 20, British ships made the short jaunt toward Long Island.

The Battle of Long Island confirmed the fears of anyone with patriot sympathies: It was a rout, with General Washington and his troops soundly beaten by Howe and his British, Hessians, and "scoundrells" alike.

Inclement weather on the twenty-ninth allowed the Continentals to flee to Manhattan, but the British were not far behind. On September 15, 4,000 British troops landed at Kips Bay on the eastern shore of

Manhattan (the East Thirties today) and continued to exert their dominance over the patriot troops.

Washington and his men fled north and west to Harlem. There, on September 16, the Americans clashed with the British again and, though barely hanging on, managed to notch a small but important victory at the Battle of Harlem Heights. The British retreated, but they weren't going very far. And so September 1776 saw the British not only land in force on the island of Manhattan but settle in for what would be a very lengthy stay in the second-largest city of the American colonies.

When the Crown executed its siege of New York City, Harry Washington and the Black Pioneers were there. Mary, as far as we can determine, was somewhere in that city as well. Perhaps she stayed with Dunmore's "ragamuffins" on Staten Island, perhaps she ended up in Manhattan, but wherever she landed, she managed to find work, likely for the British Army, and would not depart New York for years to come.

With hardly a moment to catch its breath, New York City found itself gasping once again when an event known as the Great Fire erupted on September 21, likely starting at the Fighting Cocks Tavern near White Hall Slip at the southern tip of the island. No matter the origin of the inferno, by the time the meager and understaffed bucket brigades had managed to get the flames under control, nearly five hundred buildings had burned. (Some estimates suggest as many as 1,000 structures went up in smoke that day.) Washington himself had considered burning New York City intentionally, believing the destruction would make the city less appealing to the British. No matter who was to blame, burn Manhattan did, and riotously so.

In the lands of the Cherokee, September 1 brought Continental commanders General Griffith Rutherford and Colonel Andrew Williamson to their towns, and mayhem came with them.

The goal of these expeditions was to cripple the Cherokee so badly that it would render them incapable of allying with and supporting the

British. With that intent, American forces forged a path to strike and demoralize the Cherokee of the Lower and Middle Towns.

Rutherford and his contingent of nearly 2,000 soldiers had started at Davidson's Fort at the head of the Catawba River. From there he had departed the fort and headed west. At the Swannanoa Gap, he and his troops crossed the Blue Ridge Mountains. Among his troops was a Pennsylvania-born Scots-Irish preacher named James Hall. Hall drew some of the first blood during the violent expedition when he mistook an enslaved person for a Cherokee and shot him dead. Rutherford eventually set up camp on the banks of the Little Tennessee River in Noquisiyi (then called Nuquassee and later referred to as Nikwasi). During their encampment, Hall stood upon a great mound of the Middle Cherokee town to preach.

Colonel Williamson had begun his march in South Carolina in July, initially focusing on the Lower Cherokee towns. By mid-August, he reported burning crops and homes in Oconee, Tugaloo, Estatoe, Seneca, Tomassee, and Keowee, encountering Dragging Canoe and the British agent for Indian relations, Alexander Cameron, along the way.

The two military men—Williamson and Rutherford—and their troops eventually joined forces in the Middle Towns of the Cherokee. Between them, by the end of September, at least thirty-six Cherokee towns had burned to the ground.

That was enough to bear—but it was not over.

In October, an expedition led by Colonel William Christian of the Virginia militia swept through the Cherokee Overhill Towns of eastern Tennessee. Though they confronted opponents—led again by Dragging Canoe and the British agent Cameron—Christian and his men quashed their adversaries, sending the outnumbered Cherokee farther into the mountains. Christian reported that his troops had burned Tellico, Chilhowee, Citico, and Tuskegee.

Along the way, these forces burned not only towns but also large swaths of life-sustaining crops, confiscated arms, and availed themselves of valuable deer hides. They also helped themselves to prisoners, free and enslaved alike. All who lived in the path of their onslaught suffered as the patriot Americans cut a swath through Cherokee land that would forever impact that nation and its people.

The facts surrounding this campaign of intimidation and destruction are many. But legends, too, grew up around the fiery events of that fall, one of which concerned Nanye'hi. Of the Cherokee towns that fell that fall, only Chota, Nanye'hi's home, was spared. A legend would later emerge of a belt that hung from a crossbeam in her home in Chota. The ills befalling the Cherokee, the legend goes, were due to the fact that the Cherokee had strayed from their true path. If the Cherokee followed a path that adhered to tradition, and as long as that belt survived, all would be as it should. The belt caught fire, but not the home in which it hung. Yet the belt survived—as would, according to the legend, the Cherokee themselves.

In every corner of this so-called New World, from New York City to the lands of the Cherokee and beyond, it seemed, inhabitants were struggling for their own version of freedom. The Indigenous peoples, those who were enslaved, the Continentals, the British—all sought to establish, or at least protect, their communities and their ways of life. They were all, each in their own way, burning for independence.

The world was on fire.

CHAPTER 14

Three Women, One Friend, Shifting Tides

A fire of fever had come for the young woman then known as Jemima Wilkinson. Illness in that time came in many and highly contagious forms. Dysentery. Smallpox. Measles. Malaria. On October 5, 1776, one such noxious ailment seized Wilkinson in the twenty-fourth year of their life.

This life-threatening fever lasted for five days. She lay near death, on the verge of succumbing to the powers of a malady that had already claimed many lives in the close-knit Quaker community. The doctor could do little to help her. She was expected to die.

The child first known as Jemima Wilkinson was born in Cumberland, Rhode Island, in 1752, the eighth of twelve siblings born to Jeremiah, a farmer, and Amy. Growing up, she had always attended Quaker meetings. Her mother had died when she was only eight years old. By the time she had reached her early twenties, a group that practiced a new way to worship caught their attention: the New Light Baptists.

The evolution of devotion and exaltation that emerged in the First Great Awakening appealed to Wilkinson during the early 1770s, when she was in her early twenties, and she felt a strong pull toward it. Though she might not have known it at the time, she was, in fact, on the verge of an extraordinary awakening of her own, one that would transform her relationship not only with God but also with the established societal and religious practices of her entire world.

Now, less than six years later, Jemima lay near death. But five days after the deadly fever appeared, it vanished. But someone *had* departed this life. The patient rose from bed and announced to the family members gathered that Jemima had, in fact, died.

Yet the patient had been resurrected, brought back to the living world by God. However, upon waking, they were no longer the same. Yes, their family had once called them by the name Jemima Wilkinson. But the new person who was reborn and brought back to this world announced that they were neither female nor male. This being, who would now be known as the Public Universal Friend, had come back for a reason. They would serve God in the manner they saw fit.

The Friend changed not only their name but also their appearance, wearing clothing commonly associated at the time with men *and* women. Sometimes skirts. Other times ties or vests. Their tresses, too, were a reflection of their new life: short and trimmed in front and on top, while curls fell down along their back. If anyone called them by the name used in their previous life, they simply did not respond.

Though religious doctrine dictated that Quakers remain apart from war, the Friend's brother had, nonetheless, joined the Continental forces. Religious belief kept many from taking sides, but that did not render these devout individuals, no matter the nobility of their intent, immune from the suffering that engulfed their world. The Friend sought to ease that suffering, to comfort others, through their preaching.

And so, at the next Quaker meeting they were well enough to attend, the Friend rose and stepped outside of the meetinghouse. Standing beneath a nearby tree, they were moved to preach. Some of the others at the meeting were moved to listen.

Soon after the Friend's rebirth, they also referred to themselves as the Comforter, a reference to biblical passages in the Gospel of John, specifically, and in other books. John 14:16, 14:26, and 15:26 refer to a "Comforter" sent by "the Father," and "which is the Holy Ghost, whom the Father will send in my name, he shall teach you all things, and bring all things to your remembrance, whatsoever I have said unto you" (John 14:26 KJV).

The Friend's transformation and awakening came, as many non-conformist stances often do, with some sacrifice. While there were those congregants compelled to hear what the Friend had to say, the larger community of which the Friend had long been a part—the same one that had welcomed them since they were a child—shunned them. And in time the Friend's family found themselves expelled from meetings as well.

The Friend's transformation had come with a purpose. They were on a new mission, which was revealed to them during their brush with death. They decided to travel, speak God's word, and share their experience, their rebirth, with anyone who would listen. Over the next several years, the Friend and their followers would travel throughout southern New England, initially establishing a base in Rhode Island. As the Friend continued to preach, they amassed a following hungry for their message.

Not surprisingly, the Friend's eschewing of the gender role assigned to them at birth often put them at odds with women as well as men. Even though the Great Awakening brought with it more expansive ideas about who may preach the word of God, acceptance was a knotty, thorny road to travel.

Multitudes flocked to hear the Friend speak—not always with the most open of minds or the best of intentions. They frequently came to gawk, often focusing on the Friend's mode of dress, hair, and manner. They came to judge for themselves this preacher's devotion. Crowds of attendees were rife with detractors who viewed the Friend as threatening and immoral. However, some came to see this embodiment of spirituality that flew in the face of everything they had come to know about what it meant to be a man or a woman as a positive development. Many others truly wished to experience redemption or salvation during trying and violent times. And in those savage times, the Friend also comforted prisoners who were about to lose their lives, as well as the executioners who were about to take those lives. While the Friend had been inspired by the New Light Baptists, they had now become a beacon for others, sharing a new, individualistic way of being oneself in a rapidly changing world.

On October 16, just days after the Public Universal Friend's "death" and rebirth, the British officially assumed control of the island of Manhattan. After victories on Long Island and at Kips Bay, they shifted part of their divided but well-fortified attentions to just north of New York City.

In the midst of this upheaval, waiting for her next opportunity to do her duty on behalf of the Crown, was Lorenda Holmes.

The British Army had landed roughly 4,000 troops at Frog's Neck (now known as Throggs Neck) near West Chester and from there ventured to Pell's Point (now Pelham Bay Park), about three miles to the north. Roughly seven and a half miles to the north was East Chester, where Lorenda had been living since the chaos that erupted in New York City allowed her to flee Manhattan. She was now in a unique position to help the loyalist cause yet again.

A man named Crickston approached Lorenda with a mission. Sixteen gentlemen originally from Boston wished to join the British troops but knew nothing of the area. Lorenda, however, knew the paths overground and through the woods well. She guided them south until they were near enough to the shore to "swim across to the British Army." She succeeded in her duties without incident . . . initially.

As Lorenda made her way back to East Chester, Continental troops captured her and brought her to the provost. Once again she was searched, but the Americans could find nothing in her possession to prove her guilty of any crime. They released her and she continued back to the home where she was staying.

The autumn night was a raucous one, with fires visible and the sounds of artillery booming in the distance. It was cold that night, and Lorenda had walked for miles. A fire back home in the hearth helped to keep her warm. But then, at nearly eleven o'clock that night, American troops burst into the house. Lieutenant Philip Pell, an officer with the New York Volunteers, and the soldiers under his command immediately seized Lorenda.

Pull off your shoes! Pell commanded. He then ordered one of the soldiers present to gather up a shovel's worth of hot coals from the fire.

The men then pressed Lorenda's right foot to the searing embers. "That will learn you to carry off loyalists to the British Army!" The excruciating pain tore through Lorenda as the flames scorched her flesh.

They may have been done with Lorenda, but the men were not done with the rest of the loyalists in the village. The next morning, the fighting between the British and the Americans intensified. Her wounds still painfully fresh, Lorenda watched as rebels plundered the village. Soldiers drove off two milk cows and a few hogs from the house where she was staying and reduced her papers to ashes. Some were hers; others were documents that had been entrusted to her care. Her foot was in such a dolorous state she could do little to rescue them.

The British made their way to White Plains, where they routed the Americans. When they passed back through East Chester, Lorenda and a number of other loyalist civilians decided to accompany them. Joining the troops, traveling with them in exchange for a little work, was often viewed as a means to ensure one's safety. Many loyalists in Virginia had done this when they joined Lord Dunmore's fleet. Mary, who had been enslaved to the Willoughbys, Harry, who had been enslaved to George Washington, and other individuals had done so for safety and the promise of freedom. And now, after all she had been through, Lorenda tagged along with the British troops, hoping for some measure of protection after all she had suffered in her support of Crown rule. She struggled as she marched south with them through growing cold, bitter weather, and on a burned and blistered foot. British forces were to engage the enemy at Fort Washington, which sat high above the Hudson River.

Already at Fort Washington was a patriot named Margaret Corbin.

Though on opposite sides of the war, these two women had much in common. They were both committed and willing to suffer—and perhaps die—for a cause in which they believed. They both lived at a time when violence and suffering knew no gender. They both rose to the occasion when the moment asked it of them.

American forces had been camped there for months. And in the wake of the disastrous Battle of Long Island not quite three months earlier, the British demanded the Continentals surrender. The Americans did not.

By the time fighting broke out at Fort Washington on November 16, 1776, twenty-five-year-old Margaret had been married four years. She had been born into a Scots-Irish family on the Pennsylvania frontier. When she was quite young, she survived a raid by local Indigenous people. Her father did not, and her mother was taken captive. Margaret and her younger brother were raised by her uncle.

John Corbin, Margaret's husband, had enlisted with the Pennsylvania artillery at the beginning of the war. He served as a matross, whose job it was to assist artillerymen during battle with the loading, firing, and sponging down of cannons. After each firing, for example, the matross stepped up and inserted a damp sponge on a rod into the cannon barrel to wipe it free of debris and extinguished any flaming remnants. When John was garrisoned at Fort Washington, Margaret followed him.

The term "camp follower" is used to describe those who were not soldiers enlisted with the army or the militia but who traveled and encamped with them. They were not just women. There were also children, enslaved individuals, and men who were not fighting. Some, like Lorenda, sought safety among the troops. They were invaluable to the units with which they traveled, performing numerous necessary duties, including nursing, cooking, laundering, and mending.

They were not mere "followers." In countless instances, they emerged as leaders.

Margaret and John were positioned with the Fort Tryon redoubt, north of Fort Washington proper, a two-gun battery under the command of Colonel Moses Rawlings.

John loaded cannons. Margaret, who dressed as a man in order to stay comfortable or to remain inconspicuous on the battlefield, went with John as he prepared for battle. On that day in November, when the fighting began, cannon fire rained from the frigate *Pearl* to the west, and from a team of British artillerymen to the north firing twelve-pounders, and still more ordnance flew in from the east. The Americans were under attack on three sides. Margaret stood alongside John, helping him load and sponge the cannons.

Then John fell. He lay on the ground next to Margaret, dead, and she assumed his post and kept fighting. She stepped in and did what was required, just as many women before her, Nanye'hi among them, had done.

While tending John's cannon, Margaret soon became the target of Hessian fire and found herself on the wrong end of three musket balls and grapeshot.

Finally, the Continental Army had no choice but to retreat. The British took prisoners after their win, the wounded among them, though some were left on the cold field to wait for medical attention— if it came.

The Continental forces suffered a tremendous loss at Fort Washington, where nearly 8,000 British and Hessians had taken on roughly 3,000 American troops defending the outpost. Yet, despite these lopsided numbers, the Americans suffered fewer wounded and casualties. The British tallied 86 casualties and more than 350 wounded, while the Continental forces counted 59 dead and just over 100 injured. However, the British marched away with more than 2,800 American prisoners.

George Washington and his closest commanders managed—just barely—to escape across the river to New Jersey. Four days later, on November 20, General Cornwallis and 5,000 troops landed north of Fort Lee, New Jersey. General Nathanael Greene, upon hearing of Cornwallis's impending attack, ordered the abandonment of Fort Lee. The Continental retreat farther into New Jersey continued.

The Battle of Long Island. The Battle of White Plains. Fort Washington. Fort Lee . . . The New York campaign had been an utter calamity for the Americans.

After the smoke cleared at Fort Washington, Margaret's left arm hung in tatters, and her chest and jaw had taken a brutal beating as well. Though Margaret's injuries were eventually tended to in some manner, her arm would never be functional again. The British paroled Margaret and other wounded Continental soldiers who, it was obvious, would never be able to raise up arms against them. She and some other soldiers who would never see combat again became part of what was known as the Invalid Corps, established in the spring of 1777. Her whereabouts between the Battle of Fort Washington and her surfacing as part of the Invalid Corps are unknown. We can only imagine Margaret's plight. She had lost her husband. She had lost the use of her arm. She would never fight for the cause of American liberty ever again. Yet she would soon tend to those who did.

As for Lorenda, after the victories at Forts Washington and Lee, Lorenda and other loyalists who had been sheltering from the cold in meager huts as the battles played out were granted safe passage to return to New York City. However, even though the British had taken over Manhattan, that did not mean animosity toward them had been greatly diminished. New York—and many other cities—remained divided, and the anger of those loyal to the patriot cause was nothing if not more fervent in this post-Declaration world, where patriotic colonists found themselves forced to live under the thumbs of their foes. Whether New York City was controlled by Continental forces or those of the British, loyalties—and loyalists—were always going to be living among those friendly to the patriot cause, and vice versa.

Once back in New York, Lorenda once again saw her aunt Mary Smith, who had lost nearly all of her possessions. Seeing that the city remained a hostile place—especially for someone with Lorenda's history of actions on behalf of the Crown—she decided to sail for England. England was not the land of her birth, nor the country she had called home her entire life. Nevertheless, England was where her loyalties lay. It was the nation for which she had risked and suffered, and it now became her only destination. She gathered what little she could take with her and boarded a ship bound for London, forever to "quit her native soil for that of England."

After taking Newark on November 28, General Cornwallis and the British pushed farther into New Jersey in pursuit of George Washington and his embattled—and underfunded—Continentals.

Their movements did not go unnoticed.

In Quaker-settled Burlington, New Jersey, twenty miles north of Philadelphia, on the opposite side of the Delaware River, Margaret Morris was on her way back from visiting a friend when she heard that the English fleet was closing in. Margaret was a healer and purveyor of medical advice. Now she heard that some in the nearby areas were preparing to burn their towns in advance of the British arriving.

"When I heard the above report," Margaret wrote, "my heart almost died." A widow with four children, Margaret lived with her sister, Sarah, in this riverside town. "On my journey home I was told the inhabitants of our little town were going in haste into the country and that my nearest neighbors were already removed. When I heard this, I felt myself quite sick. I was ready to faint . . . I thought of my own lonely situation, no husband to cheer, with the voice of love, my sinking spirits. My little flock, too, without a father to direct them how to steer. All these things crowded into my mind at once and I felt like one forsaken."

A regiment of Hessian troops had been encamped in Morris's town, and the colonial Pennsylvania militia was nearby. A clash seemed imminent.

The next day, news arrived that the British Army was bearing down on Burlington. That same day, Washington crossed the Delaware for the *first* time—from New Jersey into Pennsylvania. And there he waited, desperate for reinforcements.

"Every day begins and ends with the same accounts," Margaret wrote, "and we hear today the Regulars [British soldiers] are at Trenton." This key city, where the colony's freeholders met annually, lay about twenty miles north of Burlington, just around a bend in the Delaware River. Margaret's neighbors were leaving. Her brother did the same.

Esther DeBerdt Reed, too, had been in Burlington. During the war, she would move several times to keep her children safe while Joseph was away with the Continental Army. By this point, Esther's mother, Martha, was with Esther and her children: Martha, Joseph, Esther, and eight-week-old Theodosia. Burlington had seemed safe. No longer.

On December 10, Esther, her mother, her children, and her husband Joseph's sister Polly fled to Evesham, New Jersey, in the Pine Barrens of that state. The trip was about twenty miles and would take at least five hours, even in good weather. However, Esther and her family were making the journey during a cold that would linger in that region, drastically impacting Continental troops in just two weeks' time. She wrote her brother Dennis of her travels, saying, "You cannot have any adequate idea of the scenes we have passed . . . One day's escape from an army of foreigners." She wrote of being "within a few hours march of them."

The day after Esther departed, on the eleventh, Margaret Morris received word that Hessian soldiers had arrived in nearby Bordentown, while others had entered Burlington.

"About 10 o'clock in the morning of this day, a party of about 600 [militia] men marched down the main street," Margaret wrote. "As they passed along, they told our doctor and some other persons in the town that a large number of Hessians were advancing and would be in town in less than an hour." Once they did, American ships patrolling the Delaware fired on them.

Quill in hand, Margaret recorded what information she was able to gather: "A cannonade was continued till almost dark in different directions, sometimes along the street, sometimes across it. Several houses were struck and a little damaged, but not one living creature, either man or beast, killed or wounded . . . While all this tumult was in town, we, on our peaceful bank, ignorant of the occasion of the firing, were wondering what it could mean, and unsuspecting of danger, [and] were quietly pursuing our business in the family, when a kind neighbor informed us of the occasion and urged us to go into the cellar as a place of safety. We were prevailed on by him to do so, and remained there till it ceased."

Margaret, her children, and her sister found themselves in the middle of the war, terror on all sides. However, Margaret and her family were not the only ones residing on their property: Dr. Jonathan Odell, an Episcopal clergyman and loyal to the Crown, was a "poor refugee" hiding in an "augur-hole" (secret room) in Margaret's home.

When American sailors arrived, they combed the area for Hessians and loyalists, then announced they were going to set fire to the town. Margaret begged them not to burn her house down. They were surprised it was still standing. They had seen candles burning in her home the night before and had assumed Hessians lurked inside. They had trained their munitions on Margaret's house more than once.

"I told them my children were sick, which obliged me to burn a light all night. Though they did not know what hindered them from firing on us, I did; it was the guardian of the widow and the orphan who took us into his safekeeping and preserved us from danger . . ."

But that was not the end of it. On December 16, her son took a spyglass to get a better look at the ships on the river. The sailors noticed.

"A loud knocking at my door brought me to it," Margaret wrote. "I was a little fluttered and kept locking and unlocking that I might get my ruffled face a little composed." When she finally opened the door, she was greeted by "half a dozen men, all armed . . ."

Her diary entries, so detailed and harrowing, conjure a vivid scene of the terrifying day-to-day existence of anyone in the path of war.

"Bless me, I hope you are not Hessians," Margaret said.

"Do we look like Hessians?" asked one of them rudely.

"Indeed, I don't know."

"Did you ever see a Hessian?"

"No, never in my life, but they are men, and you are men and may be Hessians for anything I know, but I'll go with you into Col. Cox's house, though indeed [the person you saw with a spyglass] was my son at the mill; he is but a boy and meant no harm. He wanted to see the troops."

The patriots were beating the bushes for Tories. And she was hiding one. She walked ahead of them. They searched in every possible spot, finding no Tories at all. ("Strange where he could be," she wrote.) "We returned—they greatly disappointed—I, pleased to think my house was not suspected."

Days passed; reports arrived of ships coming and going, of violent engagements and pillaging, and of troop movements across the Delaware.

Meanwhile, Washington had established a headquarters at a two-story house belonging to William Keith, situated at the south side of Jericho Mountain in Pennsylvania, not far from Coryell's Ferry. Continental Army generals Horatio Gates and John Sullivan, along with their troops, were to join up with him. The British troops and the Hessians who fought alongside them were making themselves comfortable in and around New Jersey and New York, settling in for the oncoming winter, impacting the lives of people like Margaret throughout the colonies. The Hessians were encamped primarily in western New Jersey, in Delaware River towns such as Bordentown, Princeton, Margaret's home of Burlington, and Trenton—just across the Delaware from where the Continental troops were encamped.

Congress, for their part, had headed south. After successfully seizing control of New York, the British had set their sights on the home of the Continental Congress and the de facto capital of America: Philadelphia. Congress did not want to stick around to see how that played out, especially after the debilitating losses the colonies had suffered in November. After adjourning on December 12, the governing body moved south to Baltimore, reconvening in the Maryland city on December 20. The Declaration of Independence relocated as well, making the trip to Baltimore by wagon, stuffed in a cloth bag with other important congressional documents. Once in Baltimore, Congress began meeting at Henry Fite's house, a six-year-old, three-story brick building located just a few blocks away from Mary Katharine Goddard's print shop and post office.

Goddard's responsibilities and value to the new government grew. In addition to her responsibilities as a newspaper publisher, she printed broadsides for Congress. Along with her responsibilities as Baltimore postmaster, she handled Congress's mail. She also continued to sell stationery, including blank books like the one she sold to Massachusetts congressman John Adams.

Sitting in Bucks County, Pennsylvania, on Christmas Eve 1776, George Washington had something on his mind. He sat down to write a letter to his "Brothers of Passamaquoddy":

"I am glad to hear by Major Shaw, that You Accepted of the Chain of Friendship which I sent you last February from Cambridge, & that you are determined to keep it bright and unbroken . . ."

That "chain" began to be forged nearly eleven months earlier, when ambassadors of the Caughnawaga, St. Johns, and Passamaquoddy peoples visited Washington at his Continental Army headquarters in Cambridge, Massachusetts. One of the chiefs present, Jean Baptiste (Ogaghsagighte), said they had been sent by the five tribes of Canada to "inquire into the cause of the Quarrel between the people of England & Our Brothers in this Country . . ." Jean Baptiste let Washington know that he and his fellow chiefs were willing to respond if called upon to support the American cause.

The Passamaquoddy were Indigenous peoples of the Wabanaki Confederacy, from what is now Maine and New Brunswick, Canada. And now, on the eve of one of the most significant military maneuvers of Washington's career, the general was reaching out to them, longing to be assured of their support.

"Brothers—I have a piece of News to tell you which I hope you will Attend to," he wrote, speaking of attempts of "Our Enemy the King of Great Britain" to "stir up" Indigenous communities throughout the colonies against the patriot cause. He noted that "our Bretheren of the Six Nations and their Allies the Shawanese and Delewares . . . kept fast hold of our Ancient Covenant Chain." He also mentioned the Cherokee, writing that they were "foolish enough" to side with Britain and "take up the Hatchet Against us." Washington then proceeded, perhaps as a veiled threat of sorts, to spell out the colonists' response: "Our Warriours went into their Country, burnt their Houses, destroyed their Corn, and Oblidged them to sue for peace and give Hostages for their future Good Behaviour.

"Now Brothers never lett the King's Wicked Councellors turn your Hearts Against Me and your Bretheren of this Country, but bear in Mind what I told you last February and what I tell you now."

Washington signed off, "In token of my Friendship I send you this from my Army on the Banks of the great River Delaware this 24th Day of December 1776."

Christmas morning came, but troops waited until nightfall to begin their long-planned passage across the river, availing themselves of several embarkation points. McConkey's Ferry saw the most traffic that night, and in addition to soldiers, fifty horses and eighteen cannons—watched over by Lucy Knox's "Harry"—had to make the watery trip as well. Flat-bottomed vessels called Durham boats as well as ferries made up the fleet that carried the troops across the frigid waters of the Delaware.

"A part of the army consisting of about 2,500 or three thousand pass'd the River on Christmas night with almost infinite difficulty," Lucy read in a letter from Henry written two days later, "with eighteen field pieces. Floating Ice in the River made the labour almost incredible however perseverance accomplishd what at first Seem'd imposible—about two OClock the troops were all on the Jersey side—we then were about nine miles from the object, the night was cold & Stormy It haild with great violence the Troops march'd with the most profound Silence and good order . . ."

Upon entering the town of Trenton, Henry wrote Lucy that "the hurry fright & confusion of the enemy was [not] inlike that which Will be when the last Trump shall sound" and to his eyes looked like "a scene of war of Which I had often Conceived but never saw before."

The crossing was a success, if behind schedule, and, for his part, Henry Knox—who also had to arrange for the transport of prisoners and captured munitions *back* across the Delaware—was promoted to brigadier general. "I should blush to mention to any other than to you my dear Lucy," Henry wrote. "The General has done me the unmerited great honor of thanking me in public orders in terms strong & polite."

The day after the crossing was accomplished, Margaret Morris received word that Esther's husband, General Joseph Reed, had written his brother about the events of the twenty-fifth.

Insightful Quaker that she was, she mused in her journal on the military events themselves as well as their larger spiritual implications:

"Can we call ourselves Christians while we act so contrary to our Master's rules? . . . [I]nstead of good-will, envy and hatred seem to be the ruling passions in the breasts of thousands."

On the final day of 1776, Mary Katharine Goddard printed a letter in the pages of *The Maryland Journal, and the Baltimore Advertiser.* Written by George Washington at Newtown, Pennsylvania, it was ostensibly addressed to John Hancock, president of Congress, but was clearly meant for public consumption.

"I have the pleasure of congratulating you upon the Success of an Enterprize, which I had formed against a Detachment of the Enemy lying in Trenton, and which was executed yesterday Morning," the commander in chief wrote regarding the Continental force's crossing of the Delaware and procession north to attack the Hessians based in Trenton. The letter waxed on, spelling out the details of the events that had transpired on the twenty-fifth and twenty-sixth.

After months of humiliating losses and retreats, Washington had finally delivered a victory that seemed to validate Congress's faith in him and stoked the courage of the patriot cause when it was needed most. He wrote Alexander McDougall of crossing the river with more than 2,000 men to attack three regiments of Hessians.

"Our Men pushed on with such Rapidity," Washington wrote, "that they soon carried four pieces of Cannon out of six, surrounded the Enemy and obliged 30 Officers and 886 privates to lay down their Arms without firing a Shot. Our Loss was only two Officers and two or three privates wounded. The Enemy had between 20 and 30 killed."

Finally, he added that he hoped "the late Success at Trenton on the 26th and the Consequences of it, will change the face of Matters not only there but every where else."

And so with this, the tumultuous year of 1776 drew to an end. A new year of revolution and upheaval dawned, its outcome more hopeful, yes, but guardedly so. For the printer Mary Katharine Goddard, the document she would commit to print the following month would mark her most public and notable achievement yet in service to the new nation.

CHAPTER 15

In Ink. In Stone. In Metal.

After Congress hied it from Philadelphia and headed to Baltimore—Declaration of Independence and other documents in tow—one of the items on their agenda was to share "an authenticated copy of the Declaration of Independency, with the names of the members of Congress subscribing the same," and to have that authenticated copy "sent to each of the United States . . ."

In CONGRESS, January 18, 1777.

ORDERED, THAT an authenticated Copy of the DECLARATION OF INDEPENDENCY, with the Names of the MEMBERS of CONGRESS, subscribing the same, be sent to each of the UNITED STATES, and that they be desired to have the same put on RECORD.

By Order of CONGRESS,
JOHN HANCOCK, President.

The representatives got to work in the space they rented from Henry Fite—£60 for three months—located at the west end of Market Street at, aptly, the corner of Liberty.

They spent their working days in a long room equipped with two fireplaces. Outside the meeting space—which would later be referred to as "Congress Hall"—members of Congress found Baltimore to be expensive, dirty, and muddy.

Along with the authenticated copy of the Declaration, Congress sent each state a message from president of Congress John Hancock:

> *As there is not a more distinguished Event in the History of America, than the Declaration of her Independence—nor any that in all Probability, will so much excite the Attention of future Ages, it is highly proper that the Memory of that Transaction, together with the Causes that gave Rise to it, should be preserved in the most careful Manner that can be devised.*
>
> *I am therefore commanded by Congress to transmit you the enclosed Copy of the Act of Independence with the List of the several Members of Congress subscribed thereto—and to request, that you will cause the same to be put upon Record, that it may henceforth form a Part of the Archives of your State, and remain a lasting Testimony of your approbation of that necessary & important Measure.*

This particular printing was different than the broadside that had been circulated in the summer of 1776. For the first time, this document listed the names of fifty-five of the fifty-six men who ultimately inked their names at the bottom of the Declaration of Independence. (Thomas McKean, busy at war, had yet to sign.) More than just words, this printing was a very public act for those men . . . and for one woman.

At the bottom of the authenticated, history-making copy of the Declaration were the following words:

"BALTIMORE, in MARYLAND: Printed by MARY KATHARINE GODDARD."

The names of those who had signed the Declaration were now made public—as well as the name of the printer of that treasonous document—encouraging patriots throughout America to be bolder and to stand publicly for what they believed. Those who sought to avoid taking sides in the ongoing war between England and her former colonies—the Drinker family among them—were finding it more difficult to do so without suffering the consequences.

The winter of early 1777 brought many troops to and through Philadelphia. Barracks were in short supply for the many colonial militia in the city; the Council of Safety ordered them housed in the private homes of families who had not joined up to fight the British in some way. The Drinker family had had five American soldiers quartered with them for that very reason. Quakers also bore the brunt of the requisition requests. Elizabeth noted in her diary on June 5 that "an Officer with 2 Constables call'd on us for Blankets, went away without any—as others had done 3 or 4 times before."

And sometimes, as in the case of fellow Quakers Mark Miller and Thomas Redman, a refusal to join the patriot cause landed one in jail. Quakers suffered punishment if they did not agree to "taking the test"—pledging loyalty to the new nation. But joining in the war effort was a violation of the Quaker peace testimony. Those who did might find themselves disowned by the Quaker community. The choice was one between religion and country, a choice that many who had envisioned America as a place of liberty hoped they would not have to make. And the stakes were ever higher.

Winter turned to spring and the impact of the Revolutionary War—and the British—was keenly felt farther north in the Hudson River Valley. When the royal governor of New York, Major General William Tryon, invaded Connecticut in April, he had his sights set on Danbury and its store of rebel supplies. Twenty or so miles northwest of Danbury was the town of Carmel, New York, where militia were on high alert.

Sybil Ludington was the first of twelve children born to Henry and Abigail Ludington. Colonel Ludington led the 7th Dutchess County Militia of New York and was also a respected resource for a new congressionally established network dedicated to rooting out traitors: the Commission for Detecting and Defeating Conspiracies. The commission was established "to devise ways and means for preventing the dangers which may arise for the disaffected in this State," meaning loyalists, spies, and informants. One of the key appointees of this commission was Nathaniel Sackett. Sackett collaborated with Sybil's father to gather intelligence for George Washington, and mention of Henry Ludington appears several times in George Washington's papers. In his work with Sackett, Colonel Ludington was often ordered to apprehend and confiscate the papers of suspected loyalists. The responsibility was not without its risks, and the threat to the Ludington family was real. In 1776, a fellow by the name of Jonathan Stokum was apprehended after threatening to burn down the Ludington home.

Colonel Ludington was a go-to leader in the Hudson River Valley. At the end of March 1777, for example, Continental general Alexander McDougall had written Washington from Peekskill, New York, that he had sent word to "Col. Ludington of the Militia of Dutchess to March as many Volunteers as he could raise into that Fort." But it was a summons received by Colonel Ludington roughly one month later that, stories would later claim, concerned Sybil.

On April 26, 1777, a rider arrived at the Ludington household with a mission to alert Colonel Ludington that General Tryon's forces had landed on the coast of Connecticut between Fairfield and Norwalk a day earlier and were marching to Danbury intent on seizing the cache of supplies there. Colonel Ludington needed to muster his troops. However, the rider was too exhausted to continue summoning members of Ludington's militia. So—and here is where the story gets interesting—sixteen-year-old Sybil allegedly saddled up and rode off on horseback into the night in her father's place to rally his men.

The events that April were a part of the larger British strategy to cut off New England from the rest of the colonies. In order to accomplish this, the Crown also planned to dispatch separate armies toward Albany. One, under the command of British general John Burgoyne, headed south from Canada, through the Hudson River Valley, and eventually to Saratoga. Another, under the command of General Barry St. Leger, was going to join Burgoyne in Albany after taking Fort Stanwix, in what is now Rome, New York.

But before Saratoga could be reached, on August 6, 1777, upstate New York saw one of the bloodiest battles of the war, in a village now known as Oriskany.

Fort Stanwix was under attack. Patriot militia under the command of Continental general Nicholas Herkimer set off to provide relief. Along the way, they camped outside Oriska, New York, a village of the Oneida people. A leading member of the Oneida, and one who summoned other Oneida to the patriot cause, was Han Yerry Tewahangarahken—"He Who Takes Up the Snow Shoe"—of the Wolf Clan.

Oriska sat roughly fifty miles northeast of present-day Syracuse, New York, and just under twenty miles due east from the lake bearing the name of the Indigenous people who came to America's aid and helped to thwart British forces.

The British initially learned of the patriot troop movements from a Mohawk woman named Mary ("Molly") Brant, whose brother, Joseph Brant—Theyendanegea—led the Mohawk fighting force. The Mohawk, or Kanien'kehá:ka, were a strong and influential people among the Iroquois Confederacy, and key allies with the British during the war. Molly Brant—also known as Konwatsi'tsiaienni or Degonwadonti—was a clan mother of the Mohawk and played a significant role in that relationship. Molly had also been in a common-law marriage with Sir William Johnson, an Irish immigrant who had served as Superintendent of Indian Affairs for the Crown. Though Johnson had died in 1774, Molly's position within the Mohawk and her ability to help gather intelligence maintained and solidified her prominent status with the British. British officer Alexander Fraser later wrote of "Miss Molly Brant's influence," describing it as "far superior to that of all their Chiefs put together."

That influence had now come into play. After encountering Oneida warrior Tegahsweangalolis (Paul Powless) on his way to Fort Stanwix, the Oneida and Mohawk were aware of the others' movements.

Roughly five hundred Native Americans, predominantly Mohawk and Seneca people, joined with the British. With this advance notice, British troops ambushed Fort Stanwix. This battle represents the only one in which Americans and Oneida allies fought against the British and their Mohawk allies. The Oneida were the only Haudenosaunee nation to side with the Americans in the Revolutionary War, and this battle saw two peoples of the Six Nations Confederacy battling each other.

Members of Han Yerry's family fought alongside him, including his wife, Tyonajanegen, whose name meant "Two Kettles Together." As Molly Brant had forewarned the British, Tyonajanegen helped spread the news that the British, Mohawk, and Seneca were attacking Fort Stanwix. She—like so many other women, white, enslaved, and Indigenous alike—took up arms to fight and loaded her husband's weapons after he was wounded.

Though considered a strategic victory for the Continental militia—St. Leger eventually retreated back to Canada—the battle took at least five hundred lives. This would not be the last time that George Washington and the Continentals would rely upon the help of the Oneida people.

After the bloody encounter, Mohawk laid waste to Oriska, and other Haudenosaunee/Iroquois destroyed the beautiful farm, livestock, and home that Tyonajanegen and Han Yerry had built near there. Later during the war, Molly Brant would risk her life to feed and shelter loyalists. She was driven from her home as a result.

These two Indigenous women, Degonwadonti and Tyonajanegen, both fought to preserve their lands and their way of life in the best ways they knew how. Both of them paid a price for standing up for what they believed in.

St. Leger's retreat meant that the British general would not join up with Burgoyne in Albany as planned. This in turn impacted the outcome of what is considered by many to be the turning point of the Revolutionary War: the Battle of Saratoga.

Laura Wolcott was most likely not expecting the fruits of the July 1776 riot in New York City to reach her at home in Connecticut. But part of it surely did, in the form of mangled hunks of metal that once resembled King George III.

Laura's husband, Oliver, not only was a member of Congress and a signer of the Declaration of Independence but also was a judge, had been the first sheriff of Litchfield County, was a commissioner of Indian affairs, and had also served as a commander in the Connecticut militia. This meant he was away quite a bit, leaving Laura, with the help of those enslaved to her and her children, to maintain their home and farm.

"My distant Situation does not diminish my Regard for you and my Family . . ." he had written on the occasion of their anniversary earlier in January of 1777. "I am not able to give you the least Advice in the Conduct of my Business . . . I only wish that the cares which must oppress you were less. But if the present Troubles shall terminate in the future Peace and Security of this Country (which trust will be the case), the present Evils and Inconveniences of Life ought to be borne with cheerfulness."

In the wake of the Bowling Green riot, Wolcott had arranged for the chunks of the toppled statue of King George III to be taken overland and by water and overland once more to his home in Litchfield. There, in the family's apple orchard, where Wolcott had erected a shed, an axe reduced the metal into more manageable pieces. Then Laura, her children, and others in the community got to work melting the metal and molding it into bullets.

Soldiers were constantly desperate for ammunition, and George Washington was reported to have instructed his own troops in camp that if they had nothing else to do with what little spare time they had, they should be tending to their personal rounds of powder and ball. In addition to their flintlock muskets and other personal and military supplies, soldiers carried cartridge boxes. Bullet molds were used by soldiers and civilians alike, who melted down everything from teapots to leaden window casements. Handles of a bullet mold could snip the ends of the cooled metal, and soldiers might then smooth out the bullets with whatever they had available. They then rolled the bullets with gunpowder in a piece of oiled paper. When it was time to load, soldiers would tear the paper with their teeth and dump the content into their gun barrels.

Amassing the remnants of a lead-filled statue as large as that of

King George was a boon, and Oliver kept meticulous notes regarding the bullets cast over the fire behind the Wolcott house. He carefully noted who did what, the children perhaps competing with each other to see who could produce the most, and in some cases where the bullets were destined. According to Oliver Wolcott's own record:

Laura recorded 8,378 cartridges.

Daughter Mary Ann logged 5,762 cartridges, to which Wolcott added a note: "Not sent to the court house 119 packs, out of which I let Colonel Perley Howe have 3 packs."

Young Frederick Wolcott contributed 936, and amounts were also listed for other individuals by name as well as "sundry persons." The grand total of ammunition the Wolcotts and their neighbors generated from the statue came to 42,088. King George's own likeness had given much-needed firepower to a cause that would soon face one of its most significant and tide-turning battles yet.

In September of 1777, General Oliver Wolcott would lead hundreds of militia troops to join with General Horatio Gates and heralded officer Benedict Arnold at Saratoga, New York.

The handiwork of his wife and children would travel with him.

In addition to their efforts in the Hudson Valley, the British continued to set their sights on the colonial capital of Philadelphia. But the war and its many casualties were increasingly affecting the home of the Quaker diarist Elizabeth Drinker even before Howe and his fleet arrived.

The one-year anniversary of the signing of the Declaration of Independence had been celebrated in grand—if not long-planned—form. Homes and businesses lit their lamps in a patriotic glow of solidarity. Congress celebrated at City Tavern. Thirteen-gun salutes erupted from various armed ships afloat in the Delaware, some of them, as John Adams had written his daughter Abigail, "beautifully dressed in the colors of all nations, displayed upon the masts, yards, and rigging." Crowds on land celebrated as well, "all shouting and huzzahing, in a manner which gave great joy to every friend to this country, and the utmost terror and dismay to every lurking tory."

But there was also a degree of terror for anyone who did *not* opt to join in the celebrations by lighting their lamps or closing their establishments in support of the patriot cause—Quakers among them. Those shops paid the price.

"1777 July 4—the Town Illuminated and a great number of Windows Broke on the Anniversary of Independence and Freedom," Elizabeth Drinker wrote in her diary. And three days later she jotted down a more prosaic observation: "July 7. This is the seventh day of the seventh month. 1777."

Beyond the ongoing harassment she and her community experienced as pacifists and Quakers, the encroaching British presence impacted all residents of Philadelphia.

In early September, things took a turn for the worse as the British approached and the simmering American hostility toward Quakers hit home.

> *1777 Sepr. the 2 third Day—HD. Having been, and continuing to be unwell, stay'd from meeting this morning. he went towards Noon into the front Parlor to copy the Monthly meeting minuits— the Book on the Desk—and the Desk unlock'd, when Wm. Bradford; one [Bluser] and Ervin, entred, offering a Parole for him to sign—which was refus'd. they then seiz'd on the Book and took several papers out of the Desk and carried them off; intimating their design of calling the next morning at 9 o'clock; and desireing HD to stay at home for that time, which as he was unwell, was necessary; they according calld the 4th, in the morning and took my Henry to the [Massons] lodge—in an illegeal, unpredesented manner—where are several, other Friends with some of other proswasions, made prisoners . . . I went this Even'g to see my HD. Where I mett with the Wives & Children of our dear Friends and other visitors in great numbers—upwards of 20 of our Friends call'd to see us this Day—my little Henry very low and Feverish.*

On the fifth, Elizabeth went again to the lodge, alone, calling it "a day of great distress." Her husband and others sought some sort of official reprieve from their arrest and confinement.

"Henry and the other captives sent Remonstrances to the Continental Congress and more citing no charges," Elizabeth wrote. Congress referred it to Pennsylvania's Supreme Executive Council, which responded that it had no time to hear these claims. Both entities passed the prison buck back and forth, and denied the twenty-two men their right of habeas corpus. The fate of Henry and the others hung in the balance.

With each passing day, Philadelphia grew more chaotic with the approach of the British and Henry's situation worsened at the hands of the Americans.

Elizabeth wrote on September 9: "My self Sally and little Molly went this Afternoon to the Lodge, during my stay there, word was brought from the Conscil that their Banishment was concluded to be on the Morrow, the Waggons were preparing to carry them off—I came home in great distress, and after doing the necessary for the Child went back near 10 at Night, found the Prisoners finishing a Protest against the Tyrannical conduct of the Present wicked rulers . . .' tis now near 11 o'clock, I have just heard a cannon go off."

The "wicked rulers" were engaging the soldiers of the Crown, and two days later Elizabeth noted, "The Town is in great Confusion at present a great fireing heard below it is supos'd the Armies are Engag'd, 'tis also reported that several Men of War are up the River . . ."

But, worse, she heard that the wagons holding her Henry and others were about to depart.

"I quickly went there; and as quickly came away finding great a number of People there but few women, bid my dearest Husband farewell, and went in great distress to James Pemberton's, Sally with me the waggons drove off about 6 o'clock and I came home at Dusk . . ."

On the twelfth Elizabeth wrote that "Washingtons Army has been routed, and have been seen coming into Town in Great Numbers . . ."

The "routing" referred to the Continental defeat at Brandywine, as British general Howe inched ever closer to the seat of the new American government. Part of the Continental retreat was led by the nineteen-year-old Frenchman the Marquis de Lafayette, who had just arrived in Philadelphia in July to volunteer his services in support of the American cause. Shot through the calf, he nevertheless managed to persevere in his duties and maintain some sense of order among the Continental forces.

"The slain is said to be very numerous," Elizabeth continued, "hundreds of their muskets Laing in the road . . ."

Elizabeth watched as neighbors fled town, and on September 19 she awoke to the news that "the English were near; we find that most of our Neighbors and almost all the Town have been up since one in the Morning[.] The account is that the British Army cross'd the [S]weeds-Foard last night, and are now on their way heather; Congress, Counsil &c are flown, Boats, Carriages, and foot Padds going off all Night; Town in great Confusion . . ."

And that same day, much farther north, more chaos erupted, and another woman who had traveled across the Atlantic to seek out her husband found herself in the middle of it.

Of Those Both Missed and Mythical

Driving into Baltimore, I certainly get a patriotic feeling. Cal Ripken Way, named for that legendary Baltimore Orioles shortstop, is strewn with American flags the day I motor along on my way to 125 East Baltimore Street, the reported location of Mary Katharine Goddard's original offices. I had read of efforts to commemorate this building with a plaque of some sort. This seems the least that could be done for the only woman to ever grace the Declaration of Independence with her name.

I continue north on South Howard Street and hang a right on Baltimore (which would have been Market Street in 1777). I had read about a campaign to erect a marker denoting the location of Goddard's print shop. As I approach the block between Grant and South Calvert—where the proposed marker denoting the location of Goddard's print was supposedly located—I start scanning the sides of the brick buildings. Looking for parking, I pass by the Baltimore Mini Mart and stop in front of a takeout joint called American Fish & Chicken, whose windows are decorated with photos of fried platters of fowl and seafood, each of which somehow appears indistinguishable from the others.

I walk back toward 125 East Baltimore to take a closer look. The building had recently been occupied by a Rite-Aid and was now completely shuttered. (I am reminded of the now-missing "Richmond Hill" placard on the side of the CVS in New York City and momentarily ponder why neglected historic building sites might appeal to drugstore chains.) I peek in the windows, walk the perimeter, and see nothing at all to commemorate the site and its role in American history.

As for "Congress Hall," the Henry Fite House was destroyed in the Great Baltimore Fire of 1904. In its place now is the CFG Bank Arena.

I hurry back to my car, which is double-parked in front of the fried-food shop. Once in nearby Washington, D.C., I decide to take my Goddard fangirling self to the Smithsonian National Postal Museum on Massachusetts Avenue. For the philatelically inclined, this massive museum is a delight from an architectural as well as a content perspective.

One of the exhibits includes a walk through the "woods," allowing visitors to experience what the delivery of communications entailed long before the advent of the stagecoach. Axe cuts on tree trunks marked the Indigenous trails connecting the 268 miles between New York and Boston in the late seventeenth century. This would eventually become known as the King's Best Highway and, even later, as U.S. 1. Correspondence might finally be dropped at taverns or other centers of community activity, yet more proof of the importance of boardinghouses and inns, many of which were run by women. A placard discussing the life of Mary Katharine Goddard is here. Unfortunately, the image they have of her is not actually her but more likely an actress named Ann Brunton Merry.

There are four virtual exhibitions available on the museum's website, entitled "Women on Stamps." The first part focuses on "Pioneering Women and Early Government Leaders." Martha Washington has been on three different U.S. stamps over time and was the first *American* woman to ever grace postage. (The first real-life woman was Queen Isabella of Spain.) The United States Postal Service has since honored other colonial-era female celebrities, including Abigail Adams, Betsy Ross, and Molly Pitcher.

One notable absence from this esteemed group is the first female postmaster of the United States and the only woman whose name appears on the Declaration of Independence. Yes, it's true: Mary Katharine Goddard has never been featured on a postage stamp.

However, someone who *has* had that philatelic honor bestowed upon her is Sybil Ludington.

Listen, my children, and you shall hear
Of a lovely feminine Paul Revere
Who rode an equally famous ride
Through a different part of the countryside,
Where Sybil Ludington's name recalls
A ride as daring as that of Paul's

—Berton Braley, "Sybil Ludington's Ride,"
This Week magazine, April 1940

———

Standing in the parking lot behind a Mobil gas station, now 258 miles away from Baltimore, I have a view of what was once a training ground for Colonel Ludington's 7th Dutchess County Militia. It is now a view of I-84, just off Exit 58: Ludingtonville Road.

I am here thanks to a map posted at the Old Baptist Burial Ground in Carmel. This Eagle Scout project includes the names and contributions of individuals buried in the historic cemetery. Although Colonel Ludington is not buried there, some of his militia members are. The signage at the cemetery reads:

"As you travel toward Storyville on Route 52, on the small area of grass and marsh at the corner of Ludingtonville Road, there stands a sign commemorating the location Colonel Ludington trained his Militia. In the distance, there can be observed Interstate 84, which runs through what used to be Colonel Ludington's Home."

Across the way from the Mobil station is Gappy's Pizza, and in front of it is a historic marker reading, "SIBYL LUDINGTON rode horseback over this road the night of April 26, 1777, to call out Colonel Ludington's regiment to repel British at Danbury, Conn."

This marker was erected in 1935, one of several in the area—the earliest dating to 1932—that guide visitors along the route that Sybil followed that April night. Which April night depends on which marker you're standing in front of. The marker at the site of the former Ludington home—the future Ludington Mill Site & Museum—says April 25. These markers and the others like it detail the forty-mile trek young Sybil supposedly took in April

1777 to call her father's militiamen to arms. However, prior to the 1930s, no specific "route" of Sybil Ludington's was ever described in any detail.

And that begins the first of many complications with the story of Sybil Ludington. In her lifetime, Sybil never mentioned the heroic events and contributions to the patriot cause since attributed to her—even when, as a widow, she (unsuccessfully) applied for her husband's pension. Her "legend" appears to have first appeared in an 1880 book written by someone with a relationship with the family. In 1907, Colonel Ludington's grandchildren—Sybil's niece and nephew, Lavinia and Charles H. Ludington—published a more elaborate memoir written by Willis Fletcher Johnson titled *Colonel Henry Ludington: A Memoir.* That book describes her ride and compares Sybil to Paul Revere. In an 1854 letter discovered by local historian Vincent T. Dacquino, author of four books focused on Ludington, Sybil's nephew Charles H. Ludington recalled the ride.

Still, the story didn't catch on in 1854—only twenty-two years before the nation's centennial—even at a time when other stories about other unsung women were cropping up. The late 1800s—within the years following the Revolutionary War's centennial—saw organizations dedicated to honoring that moment in history and tracing ancestors who had played a role. Both the Daughters of the American Revolution and the Colonial Dames of America were founded in 1890, the National Society of the Colonial Dames of America in 1891. Stories of that era and other moments in history began to take on lives of their own. Sybil's was not among them. Interestingly, the book *Industrial Chicago: The Lumber Interests*, written by George W. Hotchkiss and published in 1894, mentions Sybil's ride and describes Sybil and her younger sister Rebecca guarding the house, muskets in arms, while their father was away. If you're wondering why a Revolutionary War heroine is mentioned in a book about lumbermen, it helps (a little) to know that Sybil appears in the section entitled "Personal Sketches of Lumbermen," in which Nelson Ludington, grandson of the colonel, is featured.

A newspaper article in *The Putnam County Courier* titled "Putnam County's Feminine Paul Revere" appeared in 1929, two years after the alleged 150th anniversary of Sybil's ride. By 1934, roadside markers commemorating Colonel Ludington and Sybil started to appear in the region.

The "Dutchess County" edition of the American Guide Series, compiled by members of the Federal Writers' Project, describes the path along which Sybil "galloped." Those markers, spotted by author Erick Berry, resulted in a book called *Sybil Ludington's Ride* in 1952.

The route I and others have since traversed was never described in detail in any book, any article, or the letter from Charles Ludington. The marker indicating where the historic ride supposedly began and ended is located beside a nondescript, run-down structure in need of a paint job. A kid's bike lay against the back of the house, near a few old plastic lawn chairs. I peek in the windows at the front of the building. One ledge features a random collection of small canvas bags containing Easter bunnies and plastic eggs. Crockery sits beneath a straw wreath on another window ledge, draped by a gingham curtain. A notice proclaims the building "under surveillance." The sign in front reads: "Town of Kent Future Ludington Mill Site & Museum."

In the region, not one but two statues have been erected in Sybil's honor, not to mention a street named after her—"Sybils Crossing"—leading past the Kent Police Department and to a small municipal complex containing the Kent Justice Court, the Recreation and Parks Department, and the Kent Public Library. A tiled mural on an interior wall of the library features a tile depicting Sybil's ride.

The larger of the two statues, erected in 1961, stands high on a pedestal in Veterans Memorial Park, a wide expanse of green alongside Lake Gleneida in the town of Carmel. It is a lovely park to visit, and Sybil sits tall above it all, on horseback, riding crop in her hand, defiant and proud. A smaller casting of that statue stands at the Danbury Public Library. Sybil's name has been celebrated in musicals, in board games, in road races, and on PBS. Sadly, Ludingtonville, named for her father, Henry Ludington, went the way of so many hamlets when Interstate 84 came into existence.

Sybil's grave lies in Patterson, New York, and its stone is a simple one, bearing no reference to any roles she may have played during the war for American independence. A more recently erected marker reads: "LUDING-TON GRAVES: Here are buried Colonel Henry Ludington, of the Dutchess County Militia, and his daughter Sybil, who rode to call them."

Of course, the fact that there is little evidence to support the story of Sybil's ride certainly does not mean that it did *not actually happen.*

History evolves. Documents are uncovered. Maybe Sybil didn't think what she did was all that extraordinary; certainly, many people rose to all sorts of occasions during those days. Perhaps she didn't want to boast about her actions, which—within the larger context of the war and the countless sacrifices that many individuals made—may have seemed de rigueur in her view.

I want to believe that Sybil Ludington's ride took place. But more than that, finding out whether it did or not almost—*almost*—doesn't matter. I know that it absolutely *could* have, and that other young women in her boots might have done the same under similar circumstances. There may very well be a hundred Sybils out there we do not know about. Maybe the story took on such a life of its own and has persevered as long as it has because we need it to. In a canon rife with the contributions of white males to the creation of our nation, most of us know there is more left unsaid and unwritten. We resonate with stories like Sybil's because we sense deeply their feasibility. We hunger for them.

It doesn't take much time spent in the historical records surrounding the Revolutionary War—or any other conflict or significant moment in history, for that matter—to become acutely aware that "history" is made by the meek alongside the leonine; out of necessity more than out of some zeal for glory. And lives nobly lived do not always end as such.

Every once in a while, newly discovered historical archives and family records enable researchers to piece together a story, transforming it from that which is supposed to that which can be substantiated.

———

About forty miles northeast of Ludingtonville, crossing the state line from the lands of Sybil and into Connecticut, lies Litchfield, where I hoped I might lay eyes on a painting depicting one of my favorite stories of the American Revolution.

I walk into the lobby of the Union Savings Bank on North Street with no idea what I would find there. The two-story, columned, butter-yellow building stands in the historic center of Litchfield, and I had not alerted the institution to my arrival. If there were to be any confusion or surprise as to the reason for my visit and rather unusual request, I wanted to witness it firsthand. I was there not to open an account but rather to ask about the whereabouts of an oil painting.

Describing the small New England town of Litchfield, it is easy to lapse into clichés—quaint, charming, picturesque, walkable—but some clichés exist for a reason, and Litchfield is all of those things. There are antique shops and cafés surrounding the Litchfield Town Green, and it is a fantastic place to visit for lovers of colonial history.

The Union Savings Bank is just off that green, and its lobby houses just a handful of tellers. I am on the receiving end of a line of pleasant yet perplexed expressions after I ask about the painting I seek: Laura and Mariann Wolcott, along with assorted Litchfield townspeople, sitting around an open fire, molding bullets.

The famous bullet-making episode was memorialized in a 1935 oil painting by artist and illustrator James Calvert Smith, and that painting was rumored to be in the Union Savings Bank.

The young, smiling tellers first greeted me cheerfully in that bank teller *How can I help you?* kind of way—I am the only customer in the small space—but their helpful expressions morph into blank stares when I ask about the painting, each looking at the others, with no one saying a word.

A voice booms from down the hall. One of the managers knew *exactly* what I was talking about. I explain a bit about my book, and he shares that the bank had been undergoing some renovations. He thinks the painting might be in storage. He disappears up a small spiral staircase and soon descends with the artwork. We walk into a small conference room, where he allows me to examine the painting up close. The figures in the painting are young, cutesy white women—the sort you would have found depicted in the magazines of the 1930s—a white man chopping lead, some Continental officers conferring over documents, a girl with a doll and a boy sporting a wooden toy sword, and one Black man, presumably one of the enslaved people of the community. The women depicted are scooping molten lead, wielding bullet molds—single serving or "gang" versions, which mold multiple bullets at once—using scissors to trim off the excess lead "spurs," and depositing the precious ammunition in what looks like a small treasure chest. They all smile beatifically, seemingly enjoying this tedious—and toxic—undertaking.

I appreciated the banker hunting down the artwork, and he clearly appreciated it being in the bank's possession. As I leave, he is returning the piece to its upstairs storage. I wonder why a painting with such historical significance isn't in the hands of a museum or the local historical society—where I was next headed.

Leaving the bank, I cross the town green, bordered by North, South, East, and West Streets. At the corner of South Street, just off the grassy expanse, is the Litchfield Historical Society. The site houses a museum and shop, archives, and an extremely helpful group of employees and docents. I wander through the museum—very manageable and highly recommended—which contains paintings of various members of the Wolcott family, among other antiquities, artworks, furnishings, and clothing.

From the museum, I walk less than five minutes down South Street to the Tapping Reeve House and Litchfield Law School, which is managed by the Litchfield Historical Society. The Reeve site is truly fantastic. If you enjoy a trip back in time to look at a large moment in history—like the colonial era—through a small lens, this is an ideal outing. In this case, that lens is a small school that impacted individual lives and the history of a young nation.

Opened in 1774, the Litchfield Law School—the first independent law school in America—drew legal-eagle hopefuls who traveled from far and wide to study the laws that would shape an as-yet-unsecured republic. (In 1792, Litchfield would also become the home of the Litchfield Female Academy, a renowned institution for female education in the early years of the United States.)

Tapping Reeve was an associate of the noted lawyer Theodore Sedgwick, resident of Sheffield, Massachusetts, and worked with the Massachusetts attorney on at least one rather high-profile case. Sedgwick's home was roughly a four-mile walk from the home of Colonel John Ashley, where the enslaved woman Elizabeth lived. Those four miles would change Elizabeth's life.

Catty-corner across the way from the Tapping Reeve House and near the intersection of South and Wolcott Streets is the still-standing home of Oliver and Laura Wolcott, built in 1754.

I stand on the sidewalk and study the Wolcott house, which remains in private hands. A lovely line of greenery impedes virtually any view of the backyard, which served as command central for the production of tens of thousands of bullets.

I decide not to trespass and am left with only the imagery of the painting now back in storage at Union Savings Bank. But of greater interest to me than the orchard itself, or the bullets molded there, was their ultimate destination more than one hundred miles to the north and slightly west of their origin in the fires of Litchfield.

———

Days earlier, as I headed north out of Manhattan on the trail of Ludingtons and Wolcotts, I decided to stop off at two locations to commune with the memory of Margaret Corbin: the Met's Cloisters in Upper Manhattan, and West Point, New York, where a monument dedicated to Margaret Corbin stands in the cemetery on the campus of the United States Military Academy.

The first of the sites memorializing Corbin's actions during the Revolutionary War is a temporary sculpture by artist Zaq Landsberg on the grounds of the Cloisters. Humans have long sought to memorialize their idols in marble, metal, and stone. Usually gallant, often on horseback—as in the cases of Sybil Ludington and King George III. But Landsberg's artistic interpretation is quite different—more like a sarcophagus—and feels more intimate and approachable. Though this legendary museum, part of the Metropolitan Museum of Art and devoted to European medieval religious art, is perched high above the Hudson River, the Corbin sculpture itself is just a few feet tall, inviting visitors to come near, walk around it, interact with it, touch it. Corbin lies there, her stone visage oddly serene, near the battle post where the Continental Army lost Fort Washington and where she lost her husband and use of her left arm.

But Corbin's remains are not interred inside this lovely monument, so I venture farther north to my next stop: West Point, New York.

Sitting on a plateau high above the west bank of the Hudson River, West Point was a strategically valuable post during the Revolutionary War. By the time Congress approved the Declaration of Independence, this location was one of four sites along the Hudson tasked with preventing the British from navigating the crucial waterway.

Margaret Corbin likely came to West Point as part of a unique military corps. On June 23, 1777, Congress established an Invalid Regiment and elected Colonel Lewis Nicola to be its commander. The unit comprised eight companies "to be employed in garrison and for guards in cities and other places where magazines, or arsenals or hospitals are placed, and to serve as a military school." The Invalid Regiment served in the Philadelphia area as well as in Fort Mifflin, Allentown, and Easton, Pennsylvania; Bordentown and Trenton, New Jersey; and Boston. In 1781, the Invalid Regiment was sent to West Point, which was intended "not only to be a retreat for those who suffered in the service, but also, a recruiting corps and military school."

West Point offers a guided tour that explores its history as both a military outpost and a training ground for some of the United States' most decorated military leaders. The guided outing brings visitors to the West Point Cemetery, a historic site on the grounds of the Old Cadet Chapel, which is the oldest military post cemetery in America. It is also the site of a monument dedicated to Margaret Corbin.

The tour bus stops, and our small group goes inside the historic chapel before exiting to walk through the cemetery. Our knowledgeable and enthusiastic tour guide points out many a famous grave site: General George Armstrong Custer. General "Stormin' Norman" Schwarzkopf. General Ying-Hsing Wen, the first Chinese cadet admitted to West Point in 1905. From the Revolutionary War forward, the cemetery marks time in the cadence of tombstones lining its solemn grounds.

But the tour guide has made no mention of Margaret Corbin before herding us back toward the bus. I abandon my husband among the cemetery's stones, commanding him to prevent the bus from departing without me. I and one other gentleman—who, like me, had studied a map detailing where Corbin's monument stood—run to get a glimpse of it.

Corbin's monument is of white granite, with a bronze tablet gracing the facade, which features an inscription extolling Corbin's actions at Fort Washington beneath a relief of a woman firing a cannon. Here, in 1926, the bones of Margaret Corbin were relocated from their former resting place in Highland Falls, New York, 150 years after that November 1776 battle.

Unfortunately, we now know that the bones beneath this monument do not belong to Margaret Corbin. More than ninety years after Corbin's remains were exhumed and relocated and the monument I visited was erected in her honor, construction work disturbed the site. Twenty-first-century forensic analysis followed, and the verdict was clear: Not only was the skeleton not Corbin's; it was that of an as-yet-unidentified *man* from the same era.

Nonetheless, it is the only monument dedicated to a woman veteran on the grounds of West Point. In 1976, West Point admitted their first female cadets. And that very year West Point established the Margaret Corbin Forum. It still exists today.

Margaret Corbin's final resting place remains a mystery that may not ever be solved. However, her monument and her legacy, if not her bones, remain.

CHAPTER 16

Melted Majesty

I left Wolfenbüttel on the 14th of May, 1776, at five o'clock in the morning," the baroness wrote, "and in spite of my ardent longing to see my husband again I could only have a heavy heart from the full realization of the magnitude of my undertaking, especially as I had been told repeatedly about the dangers connected with such a voyage."

That was well over a year ago now, and the decision she made was merely the first step in what would be a very long journey toward a very uncertain future. That future, the baroness hoped, would at least reunite her family.

Friederike Charlotte Luise Riedesel had married Lieutenant Colonel Friederich Adolf Riedesel, a baron, when she was sixteen and he was about twenty-four. War had tainted everything in the lives of the Riedesels. The baron had served in North America during the Seven Years' War. While he was home recovering from his wounds, he stayed with Charlotte's family and she nursed him back to health. They fell in love and married, and now they were in the midst of war again.

In 1776, their principality of Brunswick-Wolfenbüttel, in what is now Lower Saxony, Germany, signed a treaty with King George III, agreeing to fight on his behalf. Charlotte's husband accepted a post as a general in the British Army, commanding 4,000 Brunswick troops. Charlotte, in essence, was serving as well. She understood the life. Her father had served in the Prussian Army and she had traveled with him as a girl. Now, at age thirty-one, Charlotte had her own daughters, aged six and younger—Augusta, Frederika, and Caroline—traveling with her to America. "It took all my courage and tenderness, therefore, not to renounce my only wish, my resolution to follow him."

By the fall of 1776, she and the girls were lodged on the coast of England, waiting. Waiting for news. Waiting for passage across the Atlantic. Waiting for life to return to normal.

She sat down in front of the fireplace to write Friedrich a letter. The children lay in a bed beside her, fast asleep. The father they missed and the husband to whom she wrote was there in spirit. The bracelet Friederich had given her always adorned her wrist; if she gazed at it, it was almost as though he were looking back at her. It was as near as they could be for the time being.

"Unfortunately, I had to follow you when I was able to do so. I am not, therefore, setting out with the dangers of the hurricane season," she wrote her husband on September 19, 1776. But she had long feared the other perils that awaited her on the other side of the ocean.

Months earlier, when she had first left her homeland, she had written in her journal: "I was told not only of the dangers of the sea, but that we might be eaten by the savages; that people in America ate horsemeat and cats; but all of this was less frightening than the thought of going into a strange country where I did not understand the language. However, in the meantime I was prepared for everything, and the thought of following my husband and fulfilling my duty sustained me throughout the entire journey."

The baroness's plan to join Friederich in North America had taken longer to execute than she had anticipated, and she had received word that General Riedesel and the British and German troops were now marching south from Canada to New York.

"If you but knew how I suffer!" she wrote him. "When I think of the six or seven months when I shall not be able to have your precious news, I wish I were dead."

She used her time in England to perfect her English, but expenses mounted during her long wait, and she still was not aboard a ship. As the descendants of noble families, the Riedesels were hardly impoverished, but expenses had to be kept well under control until the American rebellion her husband fought to quell was settled.

She knew winter was approaching, further delaying her departure. "I am more miserable than ever," Charlotte wrote General Riedesel. "Up to now the hope, yes, the possibility of joining you sustained me. Now it is not only the sea but the ice which separates us."

She closed her letter by describing the image that sustained her and gave her hope until they could be reunited—*if* they could be reunited.

"Here I am in front of a fireplace, your portrait on my bracelet, which I always wear, in front of me, the children asleep in a bed beside me, and my heart, oh, that is with you. Oh, do not forget me, pity me, love me always, as I love you. Your faithful wife."

The baroness finally reunited with her husband in Canada on June 15, 1777. General Riedesel was with British general John Burgoyne and more than 7,000 men. The combined troops were moving steadily south through Canada and New York State. The British had retaken Fort Ticonderoga and took Fort George and Fort Edward, all of which sat along the valuable Hudson River.

When General Burgoyne's troops mobilized for their next maneuver, the baroness was determined to go with them and to keep her family together. That meant accompanying the troops on the next leg of their journey. The baron arranged for a carriage to transport his family.

Charlotte's experience as the child of a military man informed her experiences now as the wife of one, and her journal entries reveal a direct, clearheaded woman who was unafraid to confront men in authority when they made rash decisions that would impact her, her young family, and the other civilians traveling with the troops.

"When the army marched again, it was at first decided that I was to stay behind," she wrote in her journal, "but upon my urgent entreaty, as some of the other ladies had followed the army, I was likewise finally allowed to do so. We traveled only a short distance each day and were very often sorely tried, but nevertheless we were happy to be allowed to follow at all. I had the joy of seeing my husband every day."

She was traveling with only a small selection of her summer attire and sent the rest back home. Initially, though tiring, the journey south to a small American village called Saratoga proceeded well enough. "We had high hopes of victory and of reaching the 'promised land,'" she wrote, "and when we had crossed the Hudson and General Burgoyne said, 'Britons never retreat,' we were all in very high spirits."

The wives of the other officers were among the troops as well, and they knew the British troops' movements and plans. She quickly perceived that this situation presented a security threat that everyone around her appeared to accept as normal.

"Even the Americans were acquainted with all our plans in advance, with the result that wherever we came they were ready for us, which cost us dearly."

Exactly one year after writing her husband from her seat before the fireplace, his portrait dangling from her bracelet, she was now truly in the midst of war.

"On September 19 there was a battle," she wrote, "which . . . forced us to halt at a place called Freeman's Farm."

Freeman's Farm was near the Hudson River in Stillwater, New York, just to the southeast of the village of Saratoga. Loyalist John Freeman had abandoned his home and fled to Canada and was now returning as part of Burgoyne's forces.

"I saw the whole battle myself," the baroness wrote, "and, knowing that my husband was taking part in it, I was filled with fear and anguish and shivered whenever a shot was fired, as nothing escaped my ear.

"I saw a number of wounded men, and, what was even worse, three of them were brought to the house where I was."

Two of the wounded individuals were the husbands of other women traveling with the baroness. One of them, a Major Henry Harnage, had been shot in the stomach, but it was believed he would survive. The other soldier was carried to a bedroom near to the baroness. When she heard moans emanating from the room, she crept in to inquire after him. There, she learned that the officer was named Young and was not yet twenty years old. By sheer coincidence, this soldier's family had shown great kindness to the baroness while she was still in England.

The house was so sparsely furnished that Young was lying on a pile of straw. "He had lost a great deal of blood, and the doctors wanted to amputate his leg," she wrote, "but he would not let them, and now gangrene had set in." She arranged to get the young man pillows, blankets, and a mattress and visited him every day. "In the end the amputation was attempted, but it was too late, and he died a few days later. As he lay in the room next to mine, the walls being very thin, I could hear his groaning until the end came."

The British held their ground at Freeman's Farm, a battle that saw both sides changing their grasp of the upper hand. The battle was technically a victory for the British; however, Burgoyne lost nearly six hundred troops to General Gates's Continental forces, who lost closer to three hundred. In expectation of the next battle, Burgoyne marched his troops into the upstate wilderness, waiting and hoping for the arrival of British general Henry Clinton and his reinforcements from New York City.

The baroness, her three children, and her two maids "followed the army right in the midst of the soldiers." She found the overland travel through the woods "magnificent" but saw hardly a soul, "as all the people had fled before and had gone to strengthen the American army under General Gates.

"This was a great disadvantage for us, because every inhabitant is a born soldier and good marksman; in addition, the thought of fighting for their country and for freedom made them braver than ever."

As for the British troops, they "sang and were jolly, burning with the desire for victory."

Victory would prove elusive.

Just days after the Battle of Freeman's Farm, Elizabeth Drinker got more alarming news about her city, while there was little to no news about her Henry, who remained imprisoned with his fellow Quakers in Winchester, Virginia, nearly two hundred miles southwest of Philadelphia.

"It is reported and gains credit, that the English have actually cross'd [the] Schuylkill [River] and are on their way towards us," she wrote on September 23, "all the Bells in the City are certainly took away, and there is talk of Pump handles and Fire-Buckets being taken also, but that may be only conjecture; things seem upon the whole to be drawing towards great confusion, May we be strengthen'd and supported in the time of tryal . . ." The impending arrival of the British continued the following day, with fresh rumors of Philadelphia being set ablaze, though Elizabeth knew "not what to believe . . ."

Then, on September 26, anticipatory dread became tangible fear.

"Well, here are the English in earnest, about 2 or 3000, came in, through second street, without oppossition or interruption, now plundering on the one side or the other."

After eluding Washington at Brandywine, Howe and the British had taken control of Philadelphia. Harry Washington, the enslaved man who had escaped Mount Vernon, and other members of the Black Pioneers were with them, hoping that by siding with the British their own freedom from bondage in America might be gained.

In seizing the capital of the rebel government, the Crown hoped to gain the support of loyalists in that booming, strategically precious city. The day after the British entered the city, Elizabeth kept watch on the developing chaos.

"About 9 o'clock this Morning the Province, and Delaware Frigets, with several Gondelows came up the River, with a design to fire on the ~~town~~," Elizabeth wrote, "they were attac'd by a Battry which the English have erected ~~at the upper lower end of the town~~ the engagement lasted about half an hour when many shots were exchang'd; one House struck, but not much damaged; no body, that I have heard, hurt on shore; but the people in General, especialy downwards, exceedingly Allarm'd, the Cook on board the Delaware, 'tis said, had his Head shot off, another of the men wounded, She ran a Ground, and by some means took fire, which occasion'd her to strike her Color's, the English immediately boarded her . . . [P]art of this scean we were spectators of, from the little Window in our Loft . . ."

That day also saw Congress on the move yet again. The legislative body first headed west to Lancaster, Pennsylvania, but found it too overcrowded. By September 30, they had convened in York, Pennsylvania, and would remain there nearly nine months.

By October 3, news of Freeman's Farm had reached Elizabeth, though details were scarce.

"'Tis repoarted to day that Gattes has beat Burgoine, also that Burgoine has beat Gattes; which is the truth we know not, prehaps nither . . ."

With the Battle of Brandywine lost and the British in Philadelphia, Washington and the Continental Army set their sights on a British encampment outside Philadelphia at Germantown. The sounds of the battle and the resulting casualties impacted the city.

"The heaviest fireing that I think I ever heard, was this Evening, for upwards of two hours, thought to be the English troops, engaged with the Mid-Island Battry," Elizabeth wrote on the sixth, "—an Officer call'd this Afternoon to ask if we could take in a Sick or Wounded Captain; I put him off by saying that as my Husband was from me, I should be pleas'd if he could provide some other convenient place, he hop'd no offense, and departed . . ."

Some Quaker meeting houses served as hospitals, and Elizabeth strove to continue to attend meetings. While hope for her Henry's freedom seemed, for the moment, lost, and the promise of American independence felt out of reach in the capital of the states, events farther north would soon offer reason for a touch of optimism for some, even if they brought turmoil to people like Baroness Riedesel.

The baroness, her children, and the others traveled about an hour behind the troops, but she still went to visit her husband in camp every morning and he often came to dine with her in the evenings. She was preparing to move into a newly erected twenty-square-foot home nearer the British camp. She had never seen nor heard of an abode of this sort before, but this so-called log cabin would enable her husband to live with her.

But it was not to be. On October 7, the British troops broke camp and left their followers behind while they went ahead on a reconnaissance.

"This moment was the beginning of our unhappiness!" she would later write.

She fully expected the soldiers to return. In fact, she went about the whole day planning for a dinner party she was hosting at her temporary residence.

"On my way back to the house I met a number of savages in war dress, carrying guns. When I asked them whither they were bound, they replied, 'War! War!'"

By the time she was in the house, the sound of gunfire grew louder and louder. The second battle of Saratoga—at a location known as Bemis Heights—had begun.

"It was a terrible bombardment, and I was more dead than alive!"

"Toward three o'clock in the afternoon, instead of my dinner guests arriving as expected, poor Brigadier General Simon Fraser, who was to have been one of them, was brought to me on a stretcher, mortally wounded."

She had already set the table for dinner but it was moved to make room for a bed for the general. "I sat in a corner of the room, shivering and trembling," she later wrote, describing her vigil.

There was little she or anyone could do for Fraser. She had seen this before, in the case of Major Henry Harnage: A bullet had torn through the abdomen. But Fraser's condition was much more serious.

"Oh, fatal ambition! Poor General Burgoyne! Poor Mrs. Fraser!" the baroness heard General Fraser lament before dying. She wondered what—or who—would come through the door next. "The thought that perhaps my husband would also be brought home wounded was terrifying . . ."

The hall and rooms of the house were all full of sick soldiers. At some point in the night, Fraser was moved to Charlotte's own bed.

"Finally toward evening I saw my husband coming; then I forgot all my sorrow and had no other thought but to thank God for sparing him!"

The baron ate a quick meal with some of the other men behind the house. The mood was somber as Charlotte's husband shared with her the news that the battle was going poorly. She and the children should be ready to leave, if necessary, at a moment's notice.

By three in the morning, the baroness received word that Fraser was near death. She gathered her children and waited in the hall. Soon after, Fraser died in Charlotte's room. His body was washed, wrapped in a sheet, and placed back in her bed to await burial. There was talk of a retreat, and in the afternoon of the next day flames erupted from the small log cabin that was to be her temporary home. The rebels were close.

Despite the engagement, Burgoyne had Fraser buried. From a distance, the baroness witnessed the hastily executed service, which took place around 6:00 p.m. She and the children would flee immediately after the funeral.

"Cannonballs constantly flew around and over the heads of the mourners," she recalled. "Also flew about where I stood, but I had no thought for my own safety, my eyes being constantly directed toward the hill, where I could see my husband distinctly, standing in the midst of the enemy's fire."

The following evening, October the eighth, the baroness and others departed, traveling through a skin-soaking rain on their way to the village of Saratoga, halting twice along the way on the order of General Burgoyne. Charlotte was not pleased. Finally, by the evening of October 9, they arrived at Saratoga (today known as Schuylerville).

The baroness felt that nearly an entire day had been wasted and asked a General Phillips why the caravan had not continued on. The baron had told her that the troops would cover their retreat and follow behind them. General Phillips was awed by her tenacity.

"Poor woman, I admire you!" he said. "Thoroughly drenched as you are, you still have the courage to go on in this weather. If only you were our commanding general! He thinks himself too tired and wants to spend the night here and give us a supper."

Charlotte was aware of Burgoyne's penchant for a "jolly time," often involving food, drink, his mistress, and champagne.

The following day, Friday, October 10, the retreat continued but didn't get very far before the group of soldiers and followers stopped yet again. Provisions were scarce, and the baroness gave what she could to hungry British soldiers, some of them also wounded, who came to her, pleading. Then her own supply ran out as well. She had had enough. She flagged down an officer who was passing by and told him that he needed to inform Burgoyne directly of this lack of provisions for wounded soldiers.

Burgoyne came to call on the baroness. He "thanked me most pathetically for having reminded him of his duty." She asked for his pardon for intruding into what she knew was "not a woman's business." She nevertheless could not stand by and watch soldiers suffer from hunger as well as wounds when there was food to be had.

Burgoyne apologized to his officers, and, despite his thanking her, Charlotte wrote: "I believe in my heart he never forgave me for this interference."

The retreat began again, but by two o'clock or so that afternoon, the sounds of cannon fire and muskets filled the air. The baron sent word for the baroness to go to a nearby house to seek shelter. When she reached the farmhouse, she saw "five or six men on the other side of the Hudson, who were aiming their guns at us." She threw her three children to the floor of the carriage and herself on top of them. Gunfire erupted. She looked up to see the shattered arm of an already wounded soldier who was trying to seek shelter in the farmhouse as well.

The rebel forces continued firing at the house, and the baroness, her children, and others ran to the cellar, where Charlotte huddled in a corner with her young ones. "And thus we spent the whole night. The horrible smell in the cellar, the weeping of the children, and, even worse, my own fear prevented me from closing my eyes."

The next morning the bombardment continued but was coming from the opposite side of the farmhouse. The Americans were surrounding them. The cellar was becoming steeped in urine and feces, and the baroness knew the group of refugees would succumb to sickness if they did not clean their surroundings. She seized control of the situation, ordering everyone who could to scrub down the cellar with vinegar. After that, Charlotte essentially triaged their situation: She arranged for one-third of the cellar to be devoted to the convalescence of the most severely wounded men; another area was designated for the women; and everyone else would occupy the final third of the cramped subterranean refuge.

Over the next six days they sequestered themselves in the farmhouse. A temporary ceasefire allowed for some time to be spent upstairs and for her husband to spend the night in the house. The time in the cellar was brutal. The smell of human waste combined with that of oozing, festering wounds. The baroness could hear cannonballs rolling across the floor above them. One poor soldier, awaiting the amputation of his leg, lost his *good* limb to a cannonball that tore through the house.

The group soon ran out of water, and soldiers found themselves under fire when they tried to leave the farmhouse in search of it. One brave woman among them took it upon herself to go fetch water from the river. She returned unscathed, as the Americans did not harm her "out of respect for her sex."

There were moments of levity and comfort amid the terror and wretchedness. One soldier imitated the mooing of a cow and the bleating of a calf to soothe the baroness's youngest to sleep. When a Major Thomas Bloomfield suffered a bullet wound that smashed through both of his cheeks, the pus resulting from the infection nearly choked him. Charlotte insisted that he keep some of her Rhine Valley wine in his mouth, hoping the alcohol might help heal the wounds. It did just that. The infection disappeared and, she noted, "I gained another friend."

Finally, on October 17, 1777, the worst of their ordeal was over. General John Burgoyne, his troops outnumbered nearly four to one, surrendered to General Horatio Gates. The baroness, her husband, and their children stayed with American general Philip Schuyler and his wife, Catherine, at their home near Albany before they moved on to Boston. It would be several years before the Riedesels traveled back across the Atlantic. Burgoyne later complained that the loyalist troops serving under him were just like the British men lampooned in two recently penned plays, *The Adalateur* and *The Group*: self-serving. Those plays had been published anonymously. They had been written by Mercy Otis Warren.

Much of those American munitions exploding over the field of battle at Saratoga had made quite the long journey. American negotiations with France had proven invaluable, and it is believed that the French supplied a majority of muskets and cannonballs used at Freeman's Farm and Bemis Heights. However, it is also believed that thousands of the lead bullets loaded into those muskets were not only American but cast by citizens of Litchfield, Connecticut.

Those crucial days in Saratoga, bullets flew, fashioned by the hands of Louisa Wolcott, her daughter, Mariann, and others, blasting English troops with what Oliver Wolcott later referred to as "melted majesty," a reference to the downed statue of King George III.

Flags waved in Saratoga and beyond in celebration of what was considered a major victory for the Americans. On June 14, Congress had passed a resolution describing the flag that would represent the new nation: "Resolved: that the flag of the United States be made of thirteen stripes, alternate red and white; that the union be thirteen stars, white in a blue field, representing a new Constellation."

The *creator* of that initial design is debated, but many of those newly designed flags would be sewn by a widow in Philadelphia working to keep her husband's upholstery business going. The "blue field" Congress described was infused with indigo now readily available thanks to the industrious undertakings of Eliza Pinckney and others in the southern colonies.

Small moments joined together as one. The individual actions of the often nameless and thankless few were like mere stones dropping into a sea of turmoil. Yet they created ripples that gathered into a wave of change and influence. The tide, America hoped, might be turning.

Mary Katharine Goddard received a letter bearing the date of October 7. She read the report and decided, though it was unofficial and unconfirmed, to publish it in her paper the following day.

"We have received various Reports, and a private Letter, with an imperfect Account of an Attack made by General WASHINGTON on the Enemy last Saturday Morning," Goddard wrote. "No Account is yet received by Congress,—Take the Substance as follows."

The unidentified correspondent wrote Goddard, "They marched all night," "and about Five o'Clock on Saturday Morning the Left and Centre Divisions of our Army surprized the Enemy's Picquet, which was advanced from Distance beyond Germantown, who, after a very feint Resistance, were compelled to retreat; being reinforced, they were beat into Germantown . . ."

The account continued, relating troop movements, advances, and setbacks. "We killed great Numbers of the Enemy.—Our Loss, though greatly inferior to theirs is considerable."

The Battle of Red Bank followed the fighting at Germantown, and Elizabeth Drinker noted its unfolding in her diary. She awoke on October 21 to the excruciatingly painful sound of cannons. Explosions shook the glass panes of windows on the upper floor of her house as she looked through them at a fleet of ships burning near the New Jersey shore. The Americans had deployed fortifications known as cheveaux-de-frise to deter British coming up the Delaware. These massive sections of timber, anchored by stones and peppered with iron spikes aimed downstream, would hopefully skewer the hulls of British ships making their way up. But this was to no avail.

"The Americans had set their whole Fleet on fier, except one Small vesel and some of the Gondelows," she wrote. "There is talk of Washingtons making an attack on the City before Morning—this has been a Day repleat with events, very hazey weather, my Head Aches."

"This day will be remember'd by many," she wrote on October 23, "the 2500 Hessians who cross'd the River the day before yesterday, were last Night driven back 2 or 3 times, in endavouring to Storm the fort on Red Bank, 200 slain and great Numbers wounded, the fireing this Morning seem'd to be incesant, from the Battry, the Gondelows . . . The Hessians and other of the British Troops are encamp'd in the Jersyes, this Night, we can see their fiers for a considerable distance along the shore . . ."

By this time Elizabeth's husband, Henry, had already been gone six weeks. "The thoughts of the approaching cold season, and the uncertainty when we shall meet again, is at times hard to bare; yet at other times I am sustain'd with a Lively hope, that I shall see that time, and perhaps it may be sooner than we seem to expect . . ."

November brought the fall of the American Forts Mifflin and Mercer, and the Continental forces ceded control over the Delaware River. Robberies and plundering were a persistent and troubling consequence of the violent chaos erupting in and around the city, with both the American and British troops in such close proximity.

"These are sad times for Thieving & plundering, tis hardly safe to leave the door open a minute," Elizabeth lamented, commenting on the "gloomy aspect" of the current situation.

Though she and many other Quakers had no intention to join the patriot cause, the British command of Philadelphia presented its own challenges. Loyalists now felt free to be out and about in the city. They flaunted fashions and behaviors that Elizabeth did not appreciate.

Hairdressers, for example, promoted London and European styles, marked by a mountain of curls held high on the head, which was a look associated with Toryism. Elizabeth commented on a friend stopping by wearing the "most ridiculous Headdress that I have yet seen . . ."

It was soon clear that the British planned to stay for the foreseeable future.

"Gen. Howe intends its said to winter with us,—I hope he is a better man, than some people think him," she wrote.

And though the British did not appear to be leaving Philadelphia, Elizabeth soon would be. The American soldiers were headed twenty miles south to their winter encampment site at a place called Valley Forge. For the sake of her husband, Elizabeth Drinker would soon make a visit there.

She would not be alone.

CHAPTER 17

Forged in the Valley

Officers. Volunteers. Women. Children. European. Indigenous. The enslaved. The free.

They arrived on foot and on horseback, marching and struggling, their horses suffering alongside them, at what would become the fourth-largest city in colonial America. Mud and muck greeted those underfunded and overtired entering Valley Forge. Many walked. A poor woman lay crushed and dead beneath an overturned wagon on the way in. It was December 1777, and this mass of humanity was a day's march away from Philadelphia, which was now under British control. Congress had fled the capital city yet again. Loyalist residents rejoiced and patriots scattered.

Washington and Congress had chosen this site for the winter encampment, wanting a location that might offer some protection for the areas outside America's capital of Philadelphia. Winter often brought temporary respite from ongoing battle for both sides of the war—Washington's crossing of the Delaware being a notable and successful exception. This location kept open the option for the Continental forces to launch a winter military campaign should they choose to. Upward of 12,000 soldiers marched into Valley Forge in December, and four hundred others—most of them women—followed. The total number of people encamped at Valley Forge would peak at nearly 20,000 during the army's six-month stay, including at least seven hundred people of African and/or Native American descent.

Cold and wind proved painfully challenging as those encamped there that winter sought to build small cabins to replace their tents, between 1,500 and 2,000 in total. Supplies were short—they had been for some time now—and morale was low: no shoes, tattered clothing or a lack of it, few provisions, and even less hope. An assessment of the beef supply for the thousands there deemed it not safe for consumption.

Just four days after the troops' arrival at Valley Forge, Washington wrote Congress saying, "Unless some great and capital change suddenly takes place . . . this Army must inevitably . . . Starve, dissolve, or disperse."

"To see Men without Clothes to cover their nakedness, without Blankets to lay on, without Shoes, by which their Marches might be traced by the Blood from their feet, and almost as often without Provisions as with them, marching through frost and Snow, at Christmas taking up their Winter Quarters within a day's March of the enemy, without a House or Hutt to cover them till they could be built and submitting to it without a murmur, is a mark of patience and obedience which in my opinion can scarce be parallel'd," George Washington later wrote.

The Schuylkill River flowed to the north, and the camp was flanked to the west by the aptly named Mounts of Misery and Joy.

Living near the banks of the Schuylkill, Elizabeth Stephens, her husband, David, and two of their three children, Maurice and Abijah, did not know what to expect when the Continentals arrived.

British and Hessian soldiers had come through months earlier, disrupting Elizabeth and David's bucolic life. Now thousands of Continental soldiers and the hundreds more who followed them transformed the Stephenses' small corner of Pennsylvania into a mini-metropolis overnight.

The Stephenses now had houseguests: Brigadier General James Mitchell Varnum and six members of his staff had moved into the Stephenses' small home. The parlor became a bedroom, and the kitchen, the warmest room in the house, saw more than three times its usual inhabitants throughout the day. In addition to the daily responsibilities that went along with maintaining a 150-acre farm, the Stephens family now had military tête-à-têtes occurring in their home. Though their workload remained the same, the space in which to perform it shrank significantly.

The family of Isaac Potts, too, would watch as their home transformed into a military headquarters—that of George Washington. Near to where Valley Creek met the Schuylkill River, the two-story stone house had attic space, a roomy basement, and a detached kitchen. With all the comings and goings of military and family alike, it was not enough.

The remaining thousands scattered throughout the more than 7,000 acres that made up Valley Forge. They took to tents and other available shelters as huts of clay, straw, and wood, fourteen by sixteen feet, went up around them. There were trenches for training and latrines for relief. A tent and log city burst forth from the farmland—but more slowly than many would have liked.

"We are still in Tents—when we ought to be in huts," wrote surgeon Albigence Waldo of the Connecticut Line on Christmas Day 1777. "The poor Sick, suffer much in Tents this cold Weather. But we now treat them differently from what they used to be at home, under the inspection of Old Women and Doct. Bolus Linctus. We give them Mutton & Grogg and a Capital Medicine once in a While, to start the Disease from its foundation at once. We avoid Piddling Pills, Powders, Bolus's Linctus's Cordials and all such insignificant matters whose powers are Only render'd important by causing the Patient to vomit up his money instead of his disease."

Hungry soldiers foraged for food. "Fire cake"—a batter of water and flour cooked over a fire—provided little nourishment, and even this was hard to make when fresh water was scarce. Soldiers fanned out into the surrounding woods, hunting wild game and seeking out provisions sold by those residing close by—if they accepted Continental currency, the value of which fluctuated wildly. Most civilians, no matter their allegiance, preferred British money. Ideally, a soldier in the Continental Army had a daily ration of twenty-four ounces of protein, a pound of bread, and two ounces of alcohol, which, at the time, was likely more palatable—and safer—than water. But this ideal was not achievable at

Valley Forge, where soldiers often subsisted on only five hundred calories per day.

"Foraging" for food might also mean stealing from the stores and livestock belonging to people like the Stephenses. Some families took it upon themselves to try to hide what they had lest they become as starved as their new neighbors. Reports of thieving of food and livestock abounded. They had seen the same when the British had passed through earlier in the fall, destroying a local sawmill and the "forge" that gave this location its name. Grain. Turkeys. Potatoes. Sheep. Rum. Gin. Whether British or Continental, area residents had seen it "foraged."

Though locals had been ill-used by the successive waves of troops, many still felt inclined to be generous. Women arrived in camp offering goods for free, such as food or socks they had knitted. But it was never enough. Socks did little good without shoes to cover them.

Once-fertile fields became training grounds. Farmers watched as their remaining winter crops succumbed to the marching and training of a largely volunteer force much in need of them.

"Half-cock firelock! Handle cartridge! Prime! Shut pan! Charge with cartridge! Draw rammer! Ram down cartridge. Return rammer! Shoulder firelock! Poise firelock! Cock firelock! Take aim! FIRE!"

The shouts of the soldiers carried over the once quiet farmland. A red-faced, intemperate, yet highly effective Prussian general and baron by the name of Friedrich Wilhelm von Steuben was credited with transforming the bedraggled Continental force into a disciplined fighting force. His technique and approach—derived from his own experience under Frederick the Great, king of Prussia—were committed to print in *Regulations for the Order and Discipline of the Troops of the United States*, which von Steuben wrote with the assistance of Washington's young aide, Alexander Hamilton.

What little spare time soldiers had might be spent playing the mouth harp or playing cards, marbles, or "long bullets," a game in which cannonballs were essentially used for bowling, like some exhausting wartime version of bocce.

But it was not just the soldiers who had descended on the Stephens, Potts, and other families of Valley Forge. Just as the baroness and her family had traveled with the British troops, hundreds of women and children came with the Continental Army. Some traveled to be near their soldier spouses and fathers. Others came along for perceived safety. Still more provided temporary—and sometimes compensated—companionship, as alluded to in this poem written by one soldier:

> *What! Though there are, in rags, in crepe,*
> *Some beings here in females shape*
> *In whom may still be found some traces*
> *Of former beauty in their faces*
> *Yet now so far from being nice*
> *They boast of every barefaced vice.*
> *Shame to their sex!*
> *Tis not in these one e'er beholds*
> *These charms that please.*

No matter their role in the community, Washington was not a fan of the mostly female throngs that followed his troops.

"The Multitude of women in particular, especially those who are pregnant or have children, are a clog upon every movement," he had written the summer before arriving at Valley Forge. Now the "clog" had grown more numerous. But that same clog helped keep the camp—and those living and training in it—alive. They sewed, cooked, nursed the sick and injured, and performed one of the more crucial roles of camp life: laundry.

Cleanliness, to the extent it was attainable, was key to maintaining some semblance of health within a crowded encampment where illnesses of all sorts could easily run rampant through the cramped huts and tents. It was nearly impossible to keep the ragged clothing clean, though indigo could be used to enliven and whiten yellowed clothes. Those performing these duties came from all walks, and the extent of their contributions can be challenging to quantify. Some women came with their families, like Mary Geyer, a forty-two-year-old laundress who arrived with her rifleman husband, Peter, and eleven-year-old drummer son, John. Maria Cronkite, whose husband, Patrick, was with the 1st New York Regiment, also laundered clothes. Valley Forge was not the first battlefield Maria had seen, nor would it be the last. She traveled and worked for the army until the war ended and her husband was discharged. Clean clothes and bed linens were a crucial means of disease prevention in a world where lice combs traveled alongside dominoes in soldiers' kit bags.

The deadly smallpox, too, remained a serious concern, though Washington had already mandated inoculation for all Continental soldiers shortly after the Battle of Princeton in early 1777.

"Necessity not only authorizes but seems to require the measure," Washington wrote Dr. William Shippen Jr., adding that "should the disorder infect the Army in the natural way and rage with its usual virulence we should have more to dread from it than from the Sword of the Enemy."

Shippen now served as the surgeon general of the Continental Army and was influential in the establishment of the medical profession in the new nation. He was also instrumental in establishing training in the field of midwifery, upending what had long been a respected realm of women's work and income in the process.

The Valley Forge encampment had a critical need for nursing, for everything from dysentery and typhus to the more general "camp fever"—any illness that could spread virulently in a crowded, filthy environment. The smallpox inoculation offered relief but came with an inherent downside: Anyone who received the treatment would be out of commission for likely a month's time. These sick needed care, and that carried with it the possibility of transmitting illness to the caregiver. At times, the desperate need for clothing resulted in the pilfering of a patient's clothing while they lay recovering, leaving them without anything serviceable to wear when it was time to return to duty.

Despite the crucial roles they played—cooking, nursing, laundering, mending—the women of Valley Forge were not necessarily remembered well by the men encamped there. Soldiers wrote in diaries and letters ridiculing everything from the women's appearance to their dialects. One of Washington's aides wrote that nurses at the Valley Forge encampment were drawn from the population of "camp whores," a group this aide believed had grown in number as the encampment wore on. "Lusty wench." "Miserable dirty hussy." "Whore." "Caravan of wild beasts." For his part, Washington did not want any women to be seen walking alongside the men as they marched through a city. So they were sent on side-street detours to keep them out of sight. But no matter how much they were criticized or reviled, they were even more relied upon. Nevertheless, the letters and reports of soldiers and officers contained various derogatory descriptions of many of the women who helped keep Valley Forge running—unless, however, they were "ladies" accompanying Continental officers.

Early 1778 saw arrivals of this ilk at Valley Forge. Twenty-four-year-old Catharine "Kitty" Greene arrived in January to be with her husband, General Nathanael "the Fighting Quaker" Greene, who served as quartermaster general of the Continental Army at Valley Forge. She initially lived with her husband in a log hut, but the pair eventually moved to Moore Hall, a two-story stone house that belonged to a Tory judge. Charming and attractive, the French-speaking Kitty fell ill while at Valley Forge, eventually learning that she was pregnant again. (Her two other children stayed behind with family in Rhode Island.)

George Washington had arranged for Martha to come to camp, and she arrived in early February. By now Martha had become accustomed to this life. She had joined her husband at Cambridge in the winter of 1775 and at Morristown, New Jersey, in the spring of 1777. She would join him again in December 1778 at Middlebrook, New Jersey (where Kitty Greene would also join Nathanael), and once more at Morristown between 1779 and 1780. From December 1780 through June 1781, Martha would stay with him at New Windsor, New York.

Lord and Lady Stirling (Sarah Livingston Alexander and Major General William Alexander) arrived with their daughter, Catherine—Lady Kitty—and several servants. They lodged with Reverend William Currie, who owned a nearby farm. Alice Lee Shippen, wife of Dr. Shippen, arrived from Virginia. Two of her brothers, Richard Henry Lee and Francis Lightfoot Lee, were signers of the Declaration of Independence. Her nephew, Henry "Light-Horse Harry" Lee, also came to Valley Forge. He would later have a son, Robert E. Lee, who would fight to see the union for which his father fought divided in two.

Moore Hall continued to fill up with Washington's officers, among them General Clement Biddle and his wife, Rebekah. Judge Moore and his wife saw their living space limited to a few rooms on the upper floor. (After the army left, William Moore would file for losses incurred while the military resided there, including silverware, a large copper Dutch oven, shingles, and a "fine cow.")

All of these people—high-ranking officers, aristocrats, patrician landowners, and their families—descended upon homes in the area, and it was incumbent upon the commander's wife to entertain them. With the help of an enslaved worker, Hannah Till, and Till's husband, Isaac, a cook, Martha Washington orchestrated activities at the Potts house. "The Generals apartment is very small," Martha lamented of the cramped quarters overrun with aides and cooks and enslaved servants, most of whom likely slept in the attic or wherever there was floor space.

Hannah was not well liked by George Washington. She had been "leased" to Washington—a practice common among enslavers and those who considered themselves to be against the abhorrent business—by Reverend John Mason, a Presbyterian minister from New York. Later in life, Hannah granted interviews to journalists, during which she said that she considered Washington a moderate individual in his demeanor and habits, although she did recall the general once calling her "a colored fool."

Washington also loaned Hannah out for six months to work for the Marquis de Lafayette, whom Hannah found to be "truly a gentleman." Years later, after Hannah had earned her freedom and was living with Isaac on South Fourth Street in Philadelphia, Lafayette paid off the mortgage on their home. She lived to the age of 104.

The staff at the Potts home also included the ever-dutiful William Lee, Washington's devoted valet, and Margaret Thomas, a free Black woman who worked as a laundress and seamstress. (Margaret would later live with Isaac and Hannah Till in Philadelphia until she was able to join William Lee at Mount Vernon. Washington was not in favor of their match but would not deny William Lee's wish.)

Housekeeper Elizabeth Thompson—who replaced Washington's housekeeper Mary Smith in New York City after it was revealed that Smith and Lorenda were ardent loyalists and not to be trusted—rounded out the household entourage Martha relied upon when she played hostess to the other officers' wives and visitors.

The food was certainly better at headquarters than in the rest of the camp, but often not by much. Isaac and Hannah did what they could with what they had, and they were sometimes able to avail themselves not only of donations from local residents but also of goods confiscated from captured British ships.

Martha and those working for her arranged grand dinners and theater performances. Guests sang songs over cups of tea. Noted artist Charles Willson Peale, a member of the Sons of Liberty and the Pennsylvania militia, painted portraits of some of the luminaries in residence at Valley Forge, once charging $56 for a small depiction of Washington. Several of the wives made a point of sitting for him.

But not all "entertaining" was of the diversionary sort. In April of 1778, Martha Washington welcomed a group of distraught Quaker women to headquarters who sought freedom for their imprisoned husbands.

Elizabeth Drinker had traveled with her fellow Quakers Mary Pleasants, Susanna Jones, Phoebe Pemberton, and Molly Pemberton Pleasants, hoping to get to see their detained husbands, who had finally been moved to Lancaster. A crowd of Quakers had seen the women off as they left in their carriage with "4 Horses, and two Negroes who rode Postilion" and a minister riding alongside them. In Philadelphia, Elizabeth had seen enough of soldiers, especially in Henry's absence. At the end of 1777, a British officer, Major John Cramond, moved into her house along with his aides and servants. Elizabeth was at first reluctant to permit him to stay but realized he was far more civilized than many of the other soldiers she had encountered and might provide some measure of protection in the absence of her husband.

She had only recently watched as another British officer took away a friend's servant. On January 13, she noted in her diary that "it is 17 years this day, and the same day of the week since my marriage with my dear Henry." Rumors about her husband were all she had, and on January 27 she heard that Henry and the others might be moved farther away, to Staunton, Virginia. Congress offered them again their "liberty" if only they agreed to the "test." Elizabeth believed this to be "all sham, as they know they will not do it."

In late February, a letter was presented to Congress arguing that Henry and the others be released. Elizabeth recounted that those reasons were presented "on the score of Humanity, justice and good Policy; but all in vain. Those are things they seem unacquainted with . . ."

March came and went, with rowdy crowds of Irish soldiers on the seventeenth passing by her home, where she was still forced to quarter troops. By the end of that month, she was alarmed by both the lack of correspondence from Henry and the dire situation of the family finances. "Our Hay is out, and I believe I must sell our poor Cow . . ." she wrote on March 25.

Now, a month later, Elizabeth and the other desperate Quaker women approached the first picket guard at Valley Forge. She told the guards they meant to go to headquarters; escorts were sent with them to the Potts House. The group arrived at headquarters at around one thirty in the afternoon and requested an audience with George Washington to plead for the release of their husbands. Martha Washington—"a sociable pretty kind of woman"—initially received them. The general eventually arrived and "discoursed with us freely, but not so long as we could have wish'd as dinner was serv'd in, to which he had invited us."

The crowd at dinner consisted of "15 of the Officers besides the General and his Wife." Elizabeth described the meal as an "eligant dinner, which was soon over; when we went out with the General Wife up to her Chamber, and saw no more of him,—he told us, he could do nothing in our busyness further than granting us a pass to Lancaster, which he did . . ."

Washington noted in his own letters that the women wanted permission to pay a visit to Congress in York, Pennsylvania, to make the case for their husbands' freedom. He described them as "much distressed" and added, "Humanity pleads strongly in their behalf."

Elizabeth and the others arrived at Lancaster, where good news awaited them: The exiled Quaker men were being brought to meet them there. The court of public opinion had found in their favor.

"I can recollect nothing of the occurances of this Morning," a relieved Elizabeth wrote on April 25 after finally seeing her beloved Henry. He had arrived in "just time enough to dine with us; all the rest of our Friends came this day to Lancaster; HD much hartier than I expected, he looked fat and well."

Not long after Elizabeth rejoiced at being reunited with her Henry, those encamped at Valley Forge in early May rejoiced at the news that the French were officially allying with the Americans against the British. England had declared war on France in February, so this was not unexpected. Washington nonetheless shared official news of the alliance with his troops, and celebrations of the news included sermons in the morning, a review of the troops on the Grand Parade, a firing of muskets in a feu de joie, a banquet in the evening with many cheers throughout the day for the French King Louis XVI, and the requisite huzzahs for America.

Several days later, on May 11, a production of the play *Cato*, written by Joseph Addison, was performed. The work was one of Washington's favorites: the tale of the Roman statesman who dared to defy the Greeks.

But even before America officially struck her alliance with France, the Marquis de Lafayette had already contributed much to the patriot cause, and not solely on the field of battle. The young Frenchman had recruited Indigenous allies while in upstate New York, convincing them to aid the beleaguered troops at Valley Forge. On May 15, 1778, a group of forty-seven Oneida and Tuscarora arrived at Valley Forge, bringing much-needed food and supplies with them. Han Yerry, who had fought in support of the Continentals at Oriskany, was among those who made the arduous journey south and would dine with Washington in his home. Atayataghlonghta—also known as Colonel Louis Joseph Cook—was a part of the delegation. The following year,

Congress would give Cook a commission as a lieutenant colonel, making him the highest-ranking officer of both Black and Indigenous descent.

The Native American group that arrived at Valley Forge bearing white corn included at least one woman, Polly Cooper, who soon began teaching soldiers and civilians alike at the city-sized encampment how to better forage edible plants in the surrounding woods and how to cook them. The underfed soldiers had to be dissuaded from eating the corn supplied by their generous Native American allies in its raw form, which would have had a disastrous effect on their digestive systems.

Polly helped to shell the ears of corn and grind it down, then demonstrated how to make soups and more from the combination of grain and foraged items. When her fellow Oneida departed with 2,200 Continental troops on a scouting mission, Polly stayed behind and continued to nurse the ill and wounded and share her knowledge of roots and medicinal plants. Martha Washington, oral tradition indicates, later brought Polly Cooper to Philadelphia, where she bought her a shawl to thank her for all she had done at Valley Forge.

Not one to be left behind, late May finally brought twenty-two-year-old Lucy Knox to Valley Forge to be near her "Harry." Henry's correspondence had continued virtually unabated and often carried numerous lines in which he sought to convince Lucy of how distraught he was at their separation due to his growing responsibilities to the Continental Army.

One letter in particular, which Lucy had received several months earlier, in December, began as it often did with professions of not only his love but his emotional suffering.

"I have in every letter which I have written to you lamented with the utmost sincerity the cause of my being absent so long from You . . ." he wrote. "In short [he added in a letter that was anything but], my Lucy no man on earth seperated from all that he holds Dear on earth has ever suffer'd more than I have suffer'd in being absent from you whom I hold dearer than every other object . . ."

He had been "unhappy at the contents" of Lucy's most recent missive and reiterated that he would remain unhappy "until heaven shall bless me with your society." (Again, fewer of Lucy's letters have survived than Henry's, but one can surmise she had recently castigated him over his long absence.)

He was concerned that answering her letters in an even *more* direct manner might be "improper least it might miscarry."

Lucy reflected on her own wider distress at the ongoing conflict in a letter to her sister, saying, "How horrid is this war, Brother against Brother—and the parent against the child."

Lucy arrived at Valley Forge in late May of 1778 with two-year-old Lucy in tow after having been escorted from New Haven to Valley Forge by General Benedict Arnold, a hero of Saratoga. She and little Lucy took up residence in her Harry's hut in the midst of all the army's activities. She had become close with Martha Washington and had finally, after much urging from Henry, gotten her smallpox inoculation. She soon earned a reputation as a card player to be reckoned with, and her girth continued to expand over the years along with reports of her vivacity, a feature noted by everyone from Abigail Adams's daughter "Nabby" to other social acquaintances. Lucy sported precisely the kind of hairdo that Elizabeth Drinker detested: high upon her head, with a hat teetering atop it all. (The only existing image of Lucy Knox is a silhouette of her that features a skyscraper of a headdress nearly as high as Lucy herself.) Major General François-Jean de Beauvoir, Marquis de Chastellux, who would serve as the chief liaison between the French military and George Washington, later wrote in his journal that Lucy's "attire was ridiculous without being neglected; she had made of her black hair a pyramid which rose a foot above her head; this was all decked out with scarves and gauzes in a way that I am unable to describe."

Twenty miles away, in Philadelphia, the mood was shifting as it appeared the British run of the city was coming to an end. The French had allied with the Americans. Saratoga was a painful loss. Now they had intelligence indicating the imminent arrival of the French fleet. The British felt the wiser course was to retreat from Philadelphia and New Jersey and consolidate their forces in New York. But that didn't prevent the loyal subjects of the Crown from throwing a gala celebration in honor of General William Howe, who was resigning. (William's older brother, Admiral Richard Howe, would return to England in November.)

The affair was not to be missed. The coveted ticket bore images of a shield, flanked by flags, which pictured a sun rising over ocean waves. A banner proclaimed, "Luceo discendens, aucto splendore resurgam." [I shine as I descend; I rise with increased splendor.] What looks like a spying moon waits to ascend. At the top were the words "Vive Vale." At the bottom, simply "Ticket for the Meschianza." British officer John André had organized the grand fete and even designed costumes for part of the festivities, which included a revival of the medieval sport of jousting. The Knights of the Blended Rose, dressed in red, pink, and white, competed against the Knights of the Burning Mountain, clad in black, orange, and gold. Each officer fought on behalf of a lady chosen by André himself.

Refreshments and dancing inside Walnut Grove, the Wharton estate on Fifth Street, followed the joust, and once night fell, fireworks lit the sky above. Then guests adjourned to a 180-foot-long tent flanked with mirrors and overflowing with candles. The enslaved men who had to serve the nearly four hundred guests wore Asian-inspired flowing garments, bracelets, and silver collars. The costumes alone cost £12,000, while other expenses for the event itself ran a mere £3,312.

Boats sailed along the Delaware River in the late afternoon carrying dignitaries both military and civilian. Along the watery procession's route, Philadelphians gathered wherever there was room—"the wharfs, the shipping, the balconies and the tops of houses," according to the *Royal Pennsylvania Gazette*. The music, pomp, seventeen-gun salute, and gala gathering were in great contrast to the suffering of the time and the war that loomed above all.

Elizabeth Drinker was not impressed by the show of wealth and frivolity amid such suffering.

"This day may be remembered by many, from the Scenes of Folly and Vanity," she wrote on May 18, "promoted by the Officers of the Army under pretence of shewing respect to Gen. Howe, now about leaving them—the parade of Coaches and other Carriages with many Horsemen, thro' the Streets . . . [G]reat numbers of the Officers & some Women embark'd in three Galleys, and a number of boats, and pass'd down the River, before the City, with Colours display'd, a large Band of Music, and the Ships in the Harbour decorated with Colours, saluted by the Cannon of some of them; it is said they landed in south park, and proceeded from the waterside to Joseph Wharton's late dwelling, which has been decorated and fitted for this occasion—in an expensive way, for this Company to Feast, Dance, and Revel in,—on the River Sky-Rockets and other Fire Works, were exhibited after Night.

"How insensible do these people appear, while our Land is so greatly desolated, and Death and sore destruction has overtaken and impends over so many."

It was quite the last huzzah and hurrah for the British, but now it was time to leave. British general Henry Clinton had been appointed on March 8, 1778, to replace the departing general Sir William Howe and head up British forces in North America. Clinton's job was evacuating the mass of the military under his command from Pennsylvania to New York by way of New Jersey. On June 18, Elizabeth had much different news to report:

> *Last night it was said there was 9000 of the British Troops left in Town 11,000 in the Jersyes: this Morning when we arose, there was not one Red-Coat to be seen in Town . . . [The last of them] had not been gone a quarter of an hour before the American Light-Horse enter'd the City, not many of them, they were in and out all day . . . A Bell-Man went about this evening by order of one Coll. Morgan, to desire the Inhabatants, to stay within doors after Night, that if any were found in the street by the Partrole, they should be punish'd—the few that came in today, had drawn Swords in their Hands, Gallop'd about the Streets in a great hurry, many were much frightn'd at their appearance.*

The day after the British departed Philadelphia, the Continentals decamped from Valley Forge. George Washington installed Benedict

Arnold, who had just weeks earlier signed his "oath of allegiance" to America, to be the military commander of the capital city.

As the British made their way through New Jersey, Continental forces were hot on their trail. Along the way, American militia attacked British troops at every turn, whether ambushing camps or shooting from the windows of their homes. "Each step cost human blood," German captain John Elwald wrote in his diary of the incessant assaults the British and Hessian forces suffered at the hands of lurking militia.

Meanwhile, the organized, confident army leaving Valley Forge in spring 1778 was very different from the bedraggled one that first arrived. General von Steuben's training proved so effective that Congress soon approved his "Blue Book" for use by the American military, which employed the manual for more than three decades. On June 28, that army met the British at the Battle of Monmouth Court House in New Jersey. Esther DeBerdt Reed's husband, Joseph, was with them.

Joseph had proven himself an excellent officer and cavalryman. But that meant he remained far from Esther and his family, who were now in Flemington, New Jersey, and theoretically out of harm's way. But it was not only war and her husband's absence that brought pain and grief to Esther's life. Just a month earlier, in May 1778, Esther had given birth to a son, naming him Dennis. The following day, her nineteen-month-old child, Theodosia, died of smallpox.

"The loss I have sustained in my little circle," Esther wrote a friend, "I find sits very heavy upon me . . . I cannot help reflecting on my neglect of my dear lost child. Too thoughtful and attentive to my own situation, I did not take the necessary precaution to prevent that fatal disorder when it was in my power. Surely, my dear friend, I ought to take blame to myself."

Joseph was able to attend his child's burial in Flemington. He then returned to his military duties. In Monmouth, he narrowly escaped death himself, when he had his horse shot out from under him. It was not the first time he had almost met his end while fighting.

The heat of battle at Monmouth was both figurative and literal: Temperatures soared that day. "One of the hottest I ever felt," Henry wrote Lucy Knox the day after the battle. Though not an outright victory for the Americans, it felt like one to Henry and others.

"The Britons confess they have never received so severe a check," Henry claimed, describing British deserters, and a lopsided number of casualties that favored the Americans. "Indeed upon the whole it is very splendid—the Capital Army of Britain defeated; and oblig'd to retreat before the Americans who they despise so much."

One of the fighters present on the victorious battlefield at Monmouth left an impression that would be etched into popular history for more than 250 years, almost eclipsing the battle itself. Her tale spawned one of the most well-known if inaccurate monikers in American history. She would come to be known as "Molly Pitcher."

CHAPTER 18

Colonial Dames

I am heartily tired with my journey and almost so with human nature. I daily discover so much baseness and ingratitude among man-
kind that I almost blush at being of the same species, and could quit
the stage without regret was it not for some few gentle generous souls
like my dear Peggy, who still retain the lively impression of their mak-
er's image, and who with smiles of benignity and goodness make all
happy around them."

Sitting in her grand home in Philadelphia, Margaret "Peggy" Shippen read the latest letter from her beloved beau, a military man then
encamped at Raritan, New Jersey. The youngest of four sisters, the
comely Peggy caught the eye of many a suitor in America's capital. Her
father, Edward, was a noted legal mind, and Peggy enjoyed the trappings of Philadelphia high society no matter who controlled the city.

During the time that the British held sway in Philadelphia, Peggy
had caught the eye of a British officer named John André. Upon their
withdrawal after Valley Forge and the British defeat at Monmouth, she
accepted the flirtations of a dashing young *American* general and military governor who next presided over the city. She awaited his return
to Philadelphia as he bemoaned his treatment by the emerging—and
elected—colonial powers. Peggy continued reading the letter from her
beloved: "Let me beg of you not to suffer the rude attacks on me to give
you one moment's uneasiness they can do us no injury. I am healed

with the greatest politeness by Gen Washington and the officers of the army, who bitterly excoriate mr reed and the council for their villainous attempt to injure me . . ."

The above-mentioned Reed was Joseph, Esther's husband. Rumors of Peggy's suitor's impropriety during his tenure as military governor of Philadelphia were on Reed's radar, and Joseph intended to get to the bottom of things, especially as he had recently assumed a powerful—and more permanent—role in the governing of Philadelphia and beyond.

"Appearances of great rejoysing all day: on choosing a President," Elizabeth Drinker had written of Joseph Reed in December of 1778. "President" referred to the then-highest position in the American state of Pennsylvania. ". . . ringing of Bells and fireing of cannon," Elizabeth noted in her usual perfunctory manner, "moderate weather."

How stories of the American Revolution were captured and how widely they were shared often came down to whose pen had the most power. Elizabeth Drinker noted Betsy Ross's valued upholstery services in her diary. Her record provides valuable insight into, among other quotidian details, what it was like to be a Quaker in the nation's capital during the Revolutionary War. Yet, centuries later, lost stories continue to come to light, often confided to humble diaries, unassuming letters, and ever-present commonplace books. Connections emerge, insights are broadened, and the historical record gains a deeper, richer texture.

Some, like Mary Katharine Goddard, shared their writings in newspapers and broadsides as well. "Our best beloved they are gone, / We cannot tell they'll ever return," begins a poem published by Molly Gutridge of Marblehead, Massachusetts. Little more is known of this woman, but her poem "A New Touch on the Times: Well Adapted to the Distressing Situation of Every Sea-port Town," published as a broadside in 1779, sheds light on the day-to-day trials she experienced during the ongoing conflict.

Gutridge laments, among other things, the lack of men—"They could not do by day or night, / I think that man's a woman's delight"—as well as the cost of getting by:

> *It's hard and cruel times to live,*
> *Takes thirty dollars to buy a sieve.*
> *To buy sieves and other things too,*
> *To go through the world how can we do,*
> *For times they sure grow worse and worse,*
> *I'm sure it sinks our scanty purse . . .*
> *All we get is but rice,*
> *And that is of a wretched price . . .*

She ends her verse with a plea familiar to anyone who endured the time:

> *Then gracious GOD now cause to cease,*
> *This bloody war and give us peace!*
> *And down our streets send plenty then*
> *With hearts as one we'll say Amen!*
> *If we expect to be forgiven,*
> *Let's tread the road that leads to Heaven,*
> *In these times we can't rub along.*
> *I now have ended this my song.*

Often unassuming forms of writing played important roles in the functioning of colonial society. The work of cookbook authors shed light on day-to-day life and often provided vital information. In addition to "receipts" for foods in times of scarcity as well as abundance, they provided recipes for balms and household cure-alls. For example, in addition to calf's foot jelly, quaking pudding, and countless cakes, Sarah Fayerweather's cookbook offered a remedy for common ailments such as "bilious cholick," a form of intestinal distress suffered by adults. The remedy involved a mixture of lime juice, brandy, molasses, castile soap, and hog's fat (served hot, naturally). One concoction involved pounding a head of garlic and mixing it into a glass of wine. "If the patient throws up the first dose as is often the case," Fayerweather advised, "repeat it."

A groundbreaking cookbook by a British woman, Hannah Glasse, was originally published in England in 1747, but its success spawned later pirated editions that made their way to the colonies. The 1774 issue included a justifiably boastful subtitle: *The Art of Cookery, Made Plain and Easy: Which Far Exceeds Any Thing of the Kind Yet Published*. This version of Glasse's tome included tips on preparing food for the sick and a section designed especially for ship captains titled "How to Make All Useful Things for a Voyage; and Setting Out a Table On Board a Ship." Keeping in mind the length and challenges of keeping food at sea, she advised shipmen on how to make "catchup to keep for twenty years" and a method for keeping artichoke bottoms dry.

In her address to the reader in the 1774 edition of her book—published after her death—London-born Glasse begins:

"I believe I have attempted a branch of Cookery, which nobody has yet thought worth their while to write upon . . . ," noting that she wrote with those in domestic service in mind.

"I have not wrote in the high polite style, I hope I shall be forgiven; for my intention is to instruct the lower sort, and therefore must treat them in their own way."

She warned against following the French lead in cooking without first considering why.

"Have heard of a cook that used six pounds of butter to fry twelve eggs; when every body knows (that understands cooking) that half a pound is full enough, or more than need be used: but then it would not be French. So much is the blind folly of this age, that they would rather be imposed on by a French booby, than give encouragement to a good English cook!"

Women writers shared and encouraged each other's work and published by whatever means necessary. Philadelphia, notably, in addition to being a political hub, was the seat of female literary prowess. There, Quaker and poet Elizabeth Graeme Fergusson hosted a salon often attended by notable Philadelphia residents, both men and women, as well as her niece, ward, and fellow poet Anna Young Smith.

Commonplace books might include such poetry but also important dates, recipes, letters, and other personal writings—not always one's own. Philadelphian Milcah Martha Moore's commonplace book featured the poetry and prose of women she knew in addition to her own. Among these pages was the writing of Elizabeth Graeme Fergusson and her travels, as well as Moore's cousin Hannah Griffitts. Moore's own sister was Margaret Morris, whose detailed account of the war in and around Burlington, New Jersey, during December 1776 was kept, according to Morris, "for the amusement of a sister." *Milcah Martha Moore's Book* was eventually published in the 1790s.

Businesswoman Susanna Wright, who raised hemp, flax, and indigo, was also a part of this literary circle, and her writing seemed to sometimes reflect her thoughts on women's prescribed role in society, a role she clearly defied in her own life.

> *But womankind call reason to their aid,*
> *And question when or where that law was made,*
> *That law divine (a plausible pretence)*
> *Oft urg'd with none, & oft with little sense.*

Wright served as a mentor to Milcah Martha Moore's cousin Hannah Griffitts, who in turn wrote under the name "Fidelia" in Moore's commonplace book. Griffitts authored, among other poems, "The Female Patriot":

> *Since the Men from a Party, on fear of a Frown,*
> *Are kept by a Sugar-Plumb, quietly down.*
> *Supinely asleep, & depriv'd of their Sight*
> *Are strip'd of their Freedom, and rob'd of their Right.*
> *If the Sons (so degenerate) the Blessing despise,*
> *Let the Daughters of Liberty, nobly arise,*
> *And tho' we've no Voice, but a negative here.*
> *The use of the Taxables, let us forebear . . .*

And then there were those like Baltimore's Mary Katharine Goddard, who devoted their lives to sharing the written word. In addition to her daily contributions as an editor and publisher, she published her own almanac. This handy reference included insightful writings, calendars, notes, and diagrams describing the positions of planets in the night sky, the dates of eclipses, poetry, court reports, and a "cure" for dysentery.

From professional printers and poets to cookbook authors and diarists, these voices help to fill in what frankly still remains an incomplete record of the female experience during this era. Their contributions are invaluable historical breadcrumbs in the quest to better understand a war that seemed to have no end.

By the end of 1778, as America awaited the naval support of the French allies, British general Henry Clinton sent troops over land and water to overtake South Carolina, hoping once again to eventually lay claim to its key port city of Charles Town. In late December 1778, a fleet arrived at Savannah, Georgia, and the city fell into British hands. In January of 1779, nearby Augusta fell as well but was retaken by Continental forces a few weeks later.

Much of the war through 1779 began to feel like a test of wills and endurance to see which army could outlast the other. Often what constituted a "victory" became difficult to determine as fighting in the northern parts of the colonies resulted in no major wins for either side. For people on the margins of society, life often meant quickly adapting to changing rules imposed by whichever military force was suddenly in charge.

In March of 1779, anticipating increased need for support in the South, former president of Congress Henry Laurens suggested raising Black regiments to protect South Carolina. George Washington disagreed, though Black regiments had already served at Valley Forge, and Black Pioneers had been with the British in New York and Philadelphia. One suggestion mentioned was to grant those Black soldiers who served $50 and their freedom. Nevertheless, the congressmen of South Carolina and Georgia—two states that would benefit from the recruitment—decided against it. Generals Nathanael Greene and Benjamin Lincoln, who were tasked with leading American forces in the South, supported the idea but continued to receive pushback from Washington and other members of Congress.

On June 30, 1779, Clinton added a wrinkle to this ongoing debate.

His Phillipsburg Proclamation stated that no one could lay claim to any enslaved individual who had found their way to British lines. These claims, and attempts to recapture the people whom some colonists considered their "property," would nevertheless continue throughout the war.

The proclamation read in part:

Whereas the enemy have adopted a practice of enrolling NEGROES among their Troops, I do hereby give notice That all NEGROES taken in arms, or upon any military Duty, shall be purchased for the public service at a stated Price; the money to be paid to the Captors.

But I do most strictly forbid any Person to sell or claim Right over any NEGROE, the property of a Rebel (Patriot fighting the British), who may take Refuge with any part of this Army; And I do promise to every NEGROE who shall desert the Rebel Standard (Patriot flag or side of the fight), full security to follow within these Lines, any Occupation he shall think proper . . .

The lives of Black individuals throughout the colonies continued to vary greatly. What little progress may have appeared on the surface, however, did not equal progress in practice and sometimes contradicted decisions made by Congress and Washington. In early 1778, Rhode Island had passed the Slave Enlistment Act, which sent Black troops to Valley Forge and elsewhere. Yet proposals put forth by Laurens and others to recruit a regiment of Black soldiers in the South stalled. Also in 1778, the Lenape people and the Americans had signed the first-ever treaty between the United States and an Indigenous tribe. But the Stockbridge-Munsee alliance with the Americans cost them dearly during a standoff with the British just north of New York City at the end of August 1778, and they lost their sachem, Daniel Nimham, and his son, Abraham.

Phillis had an eventful 1778. Though John and Susannah Wheatley had emancipated Phillis upon her return from London, she continued to work for their family. When Susannah Wheatley died in 1774, Phillis wrote her friend Obour, "I was a poor little outcast & a stranger when she took me in: not only into her house but I presently became a sharer in her most tender affections." Now, in March 1778, John Wheatley had died. He left no provision for Phillis in his will. Through it all, Phillis continued writing.

In April 1778, not quite a month after John Wheatley's death, Phillis announced her plans to marry John Peters, a free Black man. Peters worked as a grocer and had a store on Queen Street not far from the Wheatley home. Phillis moved there after the pair's marriage on November 26, 1778. That same year, she wrote two poems, one entitled "Ocean" and the other "On the Death of General Wooster." The former was presumably about her trip home from England and the latter about the celebrated American general David Wooster, who had died in early May 1777 after being wounded at the Battle of Ridgefield in Connecticut.

During this time, Phillis's fame had reached such a level that she herself became the *subject* of a poem, one written by Jupiter Hammon of Hartford, Connecticut. Entitled "An Address to Miss Phillis Wheatly, Ethiopian Poetess, in Boston, Who Came from Africa at Eight Years of Age, and Soon Became Acquainted with the Gospel of Jesus Christ," the lengthy verse refers to her by name in four instances.

Where and when and how enslaved individuals might seek to emancipate themselves varied, depending on a variety of circumstances. Unlike Mary, Judith Jackson had *not* sought refuge with the British in 1775 after Lord Dunmore issued his impactful proclamation granting Black men and women protection and eventual freedom should they join in service of the Crown. However, in May 1779, when the British sent ships from New York to the Chesapeake Bay to raid stores in Virginia destined for Washington's troops, Judith saw her chance. She took her six-year-old child and fled Norfolk and her enslaver, John Clain. Judith, like many individuals who escaped slavery, ended up in British-controlled New York City. There, Judith laundered, cooked, and cleaned for the Royal Artillery Department. Though she received money for her work, the reception of Black females into the British ranks was often not welcoming, though their contributions were crucial. Judith's experience of "freedom" was undoubtedly a fraught and stressful one.

For Native Americans throughout the colonies, lands continued to shrink—either by direct force or by "treaties" forced upon them, often after violence was used to convince them of the wisdom of supporting the patriot side of the war.

In June of 1779, the same month as the Phillipsburg Proclamation, Spain declared war against Britain. What had begun as a tax dispute between largely white American colonists and Great Britain had grown into an international conflict. By the end of that month, former royal governor of New York William Tryon, along with 2,600 loyalists and regulars, attacked New Haven and Norwalk. Throughout that summer, New York and Pennsylvania saw confrontations between Continentals and Native American forces supporting the British along the frontier.

Washington's personal history of fighting in the North American French and Indian conflict meant that he was keenly aware that Indigenous forces, teamed with the British, could turn the tide against him. At every opportunity, he sought to remind Native peoples to whom they should owe their allegiance.

Continental forces sought to drum this message home again and again. In spring 1779, when it was discovered that British agents were supplying the Chickamauga with arms, food, and other supplies via Florida, a militia leader by the name of Colonel Evan Shelby wrote the governors of Virginia and North Carolina warning them of the danger brewing in their backyard. But Patrick Henry of Virginia and his counterpart in North Carolina, Richard Caswell, were not in a position to devote resources to rooting out the perceived threat.

Colonel Shelby took it upon himself to enlist a company of five hundred volunteers who mounted an attack on the Cherokee, British, and Chickamauga via the Holston River. Eleven towns were decimated in the battles that followed, with Shelby's men salvaging the British supplies left behind and burning what they could not carry.

On May 29, 1779, *The Virginia Gazette* reported this story, mentioning as well that this expedition into the Cherokee lands resulted in what Shelby described as peaceable talks with the "great warrior" Oconostota. He later wrote to Virginia governor Patrick Henry that he was pleased that the Native Americans were "reduced to a Sense of their Duty and a Willingness to treat for peace with the united States which I flatter myself will ease us in some measure from the Calamities incident to an Indian War."

After the violent expedition, *The Virginia Gazette* reported that "fugitives were flying to Chota, and our people in pursuit on horseback."

Farther north, New York and Pennsylvania continued to see confrontations between Continentals and Native American forces supporting the British along their frontier. Washington had ordered General John Sullivan to put an end to it.

"The immediate objects are the total distruction and devastation of their settlements and the capture of as many prisoners of every age and sex as possible," Washington had instructed Sullivan earlier in the year. The commander wanted "the total ruin of their settlements" so that the lands, crops, and more "may not be merely overrun but destroyed."

This Sullivan did. From June to October of that year, he and those fighting with him cut a savage swath through Ontario County, burning homes and crops alike in nearly forty villages. Hearing of the brutal destruction heading their way, many of these Iroquois people fled to the presumed protection of British forts. But not all.

In September, Sullivan and his troops came upon an unexpected sight: a Native American woman emerging from the destruction of a Seneca village.

The appearance of this woman, Madam Sacho, shocked Sullivan and the troops alike. She spoke to the general through an interpreter, indicating that there had been a debate about whether to flee or to stay and fight. Women exerted great influence in Native American communities—like Nanye'hi's influence over the treatment of Cherokee prisoners and Molly Brant's influence within the Mohawk community to secure support for the British. But any influence Madam Sacho wielded had not been enough to convince the warriors of her community to stand their ground.

There had been a younger woman in the village as well who had stayed behind with Madam Sacho, but she had been shot dead in the attacks by Continental forces. The treatment of women encountered during Sullivan's bloody campaign was not limited to death. An Onondaga chief later asserted the abduction of young women by American troops "for the use of their Soldiers" before being executed "in a more shamefull manner."

When the troops departed, Sullivan left Madam Sacho with food. His compassion seemed odd, after having laid waste to the surrounding orchards and crops and his troops destroying roughly 160,000 bushels of corn alone throughout the forty or so towns their expedition annihilated. The irony of his behavior was not lost on his soldiers, one of whom noted in his diary, "We destroy all their houses & fruit trees this afternoon which Seems to us a pity."

Madam Sacho's memory survives, in diaries and letters, and she appears in the records as old, haggard, and disheveled. The written evidence of this woman seeming to emerge from the destruction and detritus of hastily destroyed crops, where embers and ashes were all that was left of the longhouses and ravaged communities. She had chosen to stay in the community she knew, where corn, before it was reduced to cinders, had waved in the breeze, waiting to be harvested that fall. She had fought to survive.

During the war, choices often carried with them far-reaching consequences. Madam Sacho had made her choice. Nanye'hi had made choices that impacted the future and safety of the Cherokee. The Baroness Friederike Charlotte Luise Riedesel chose to follow her husband across an ocean into a war zone and to aid those she encountered amid the terrors of Saratoga. Elizabeth Drinker chose to fight for the freedom of her imprisoned husband. The Public Universal Friend chose to throw off the cultural chains imposed upon them by society. Margaret Corbin and others like her chose to pick up their husbands' weapons and battle in their stead.

And in the spring of 1779, the young Philadelphia debutante Peggy Shippen also made a choice: to follow her heart. She married her dashing American general. That seemingly happy choice and the choices that followed would eventually lead her far from her home in Philadelphia and into a scandal that would rock the colonies. Peggy had chosen to love and marry a soldier named Benedict Arnold.

London-born-and-raised Esther Reed, too, had made a choice. After coming to America from London, she eventually chose to see the world through patriotic eyes. She and Joseph welcomed another baby in May of 1779, whom they chose to name George Washington Reed. Martha Washington attended the child's christening.

The day after Christmas in 1779, British general Henry Clinton turned a laser focus on the South. He and Admiral Marriot Arbuthnot sailed from British-held New York City. Eight thousand five hundred troops, fourteen warships, and ninety transports were going with them. Charles Town was in their sights.

The next two years would prove to be critical ones. Sides were taken, as were risks.

Americans and British alike were growing weary of war. But Esther's commitment to the cause of independence did not flag. Now she would share her sentiments regarding the country of her heart, if not her birth, openly and widely, with whoever might care to read them.

As it happens, many did.

Chasing Molly, Finding Betsy

Arriving at the Valley Forge National Historical Park amidst pleasing weather makes it difficult to imagine the bleak conditions of those who endured living there in December of 1777. The distance to Philadelphia is a short one, about twenty miles, and a clear reminder even today of just how close the British troops occupying that city were to their enemies.

Pulling into town, both I and my car need fuel. I have a general rule of thumb when hunting down a place to eat while on a research trip:

1. Is it haunted?
2. Are any menu items named after historic figures, objects, or events? (Examples: Benedict Arnold pie, lead bullet stew . . .)
3. Does this site and/or eatery jibe with my book's theme? (I know it seems as though this should be No. 1, but it is not.)
4. As such, is there evidence of any historical figures who are not both male and white?

There are a variety of dining choices in and around Valley Forge, all of which claim to be haunted: Black Powder Tavern, the General Warren, and the Rising Sun Inn. (This last one was tempting because a similarly named Rising Sun Inn plays a role in my last book, *We Gather Together*.) Black Powder Tavern on Valley Forge Road in Wayne, Pennsylvania, wins out.

This watering and dining hole has been around since 1746 and reportedly sated the appetites and slaked the thirsts of George Washington, the Marquis de Lafayette, and others. "Black Powder" is a nod to the legend that Valley Forge's Prussian military training guru, Friedrich Wilhelm von Steuben, stashed black powder munitions belowground during the 1777–1778 Valley Forge encampment.

Today the tavern is a popular site, with as many locals as visitors stopping by. The outdoor patio is topped with a black awning and the interior space is akin to most "taverns" in twenty-first-century America: dark wood on the surfaces, baseball on the television, ales on the bar. Libations include the "21st Amendment Hell or High Watermelon" wheat beer that nods to the Prohibition Era, if not the revolution. Yards Brewing Co. offerings included beers named for Thomas Jefferson and George Washington.

I start off my meal with "Lafayette's Onion Soup" and move on to the potpie. Though not named for any particular historical figure or event, meat pies have their own fascinating history, with culinary ancestors harkening back to the Roman Empire, when the celebratory pastries housed live birds, which flew forth when the crust was pierced like some sort of culinary jack-in-the-box. During the Elizabethan Era the pastries were referred to as "chicken peepers"—gooseberry-stuffed chicks plucked, dressed, and baked into the pie. The evening has satisfied items one through three on my checklist. As for number four, no luck yet.

The Valley Forge mural in the game room of my hotel captures the conflicting—perhaps overlapping—desires of visitors to the area. Flanking the foosball table, the artist's rendering features George Washington mounted on horseback in front of the King of Prussia Mall, with Philadelphia's skyline rising above all.

The next morning I head to Valley Forge National Historical Park and its twenty-six miles of trails. These paths are traveled by visitors and locals alike, and on a nice day area residents out dog-walking, cycling, and running bob and weave their way through map-wielding tourists on the paths that encircle what was the camp where roughly 12,000 soldiers and around four hundred women and children spent the winter of 1777–1778.

The Visitor Center at Valley Forge was newly renovated and dedicated in February of 2022. One of the aims of this makeover was to shine a light on the contributions of all of those "others" who lived and worked at Valley Forge. This is clear from the moment you enter the building: Images of women and children—white, Black, and Native American alike—greet visitors just beyond the entrance. Nursing. Mending. Tending. Cooking. Guarding and spying. Selling provisions to soldiers. A fair amount of the center's ground-level display describes the countless ways that those who followed the troops contributed to the maintenance—and survival—of those who fought.

The exhibits are a refreshing departure from the usual top-down view of history, though the nuts and bolts of the military significance of the encampment and its cause célèbre, George Washington, are prominently featured. It is a refreshing juxtaposition.

The soothing voice of Laura Linney takes you through the nineteen-minute live-action historical film, entitled *Determined to Persevere: The Valley Forge Encampment*. The short movie provides a solid overview of life at Valley Forge and highlights the contributions of Black soldiers, domestic staff, camp followers, and Native Americans, including Polly Cooper.

Over the years, historians have debated the extent of Cooper's contributions, believing them to be exaggerated. The Oneida Nation does not. The shawl supposedly gifted to Cooper by Martha Washington is now in possession of the Oneida Nation.

Once you exit the visitor center, the outdoor site visit begins. Driving is an option, but biking is a lovely way to interact with Valley Forge at one's own pace, and bike rentals are available. Mind the weather, though: Under a blazing midday sun the trek can be much more exhausting and sweaty.

Along the route, there are various stops, including replicas of the small cabins fashioned of wood, clay, and straw that would have housed as many as twelve soldiers at once—along with any family members. The reproductions contain three bunks, one atop the other, on your left and right, and a wood-burning fireplace in the middle. Farther along the route, the Valley Forge Station, a small train depot dating to 1911, now houses exhibits. On my visit, I pass a storyteller standing on the station platform who offers to perform his one-man show entitled "Once upon a Nation."

We bike down to the Isaac Potts House, site of Washington's headquarters, near the confluence of the waters of the Schuylkill and those of Valley Creek. Potts was an ironmaster—one of those living in the vicinity of the forge—but his aunt, Deborah Hewes, lived in the house at the time of the encampment. She rented the two-story, garret-topped structure to Washington for £100 in Pennsylvania currency. Now open to visitors, the main section of the house remains much as it would have appeared that bleak winter, when up to twenty-five people may have lived there, including family, domestic workers, and military staff. The somewhat habitable attic-like garret floor is likely where both free and enslaved servants slept.

The same park ranger who assisted me at the visitor center is now doing his duty at Washington's headquarters. I am *that* tourist, the one who keeps asking questions on top of questions about sources behind the history being presented. The wealth of information provided by everyone working at the center is more than adequate and leaves me—or any other visitor—with plenty to dive into further after leaving the park.

Near the house is a statue of George Washington. He is standing in front of a plowshare, a walking stick in his right hand, while his left rests atop a bundle of thirteen fasces, symbolizing the unification of the Thirteen Colonies. (This imagery harkens to the use of thirteen arrows in the official seal of the United States. This, in turn, was inspired decades earlier by the continent's original Indigenous inhabitants, who used bundled arrows as a sign of unity among what were then the Five Nations of the Iroquois.) The paths leading from the Washington statue are lined with cherry trees, a botanical nod to the "I cannot tell a lie" myth.

Washington is far from the only Valley Forge alumnus with a statue in his honor. There are many throughout the park, dedicated to various individuals and brigades. The Joseph Plumb Martin Trail is named for a veteran whose personal writings, *Narrative of Some of the Adventures, Dangers, and Sufferings of a Revolutionary Soldier*, provides valuable insight into what life was like for a soldier during the Revolutionary War. Not far from General Varnum's headquarters—still standing, though not open to the public—is a statue of the Prussian military maestro Baron von Steuben. Nearby is a monument to Varnum's Brigade, which comprised units from Connecticut and Rhode Island. Among these was the 1st Rhode Island Regiment, which counted a number of Black soldiers among its ranks. A short jaunt down

Route 23, past the Washington Memorial Chapel, is the Patriots of African Descent Monument. Erected in 1993, it is the only monument in the Northeast United States dedicated to Black Americans and their role in the revolution. A rectangular stone features a bronze bas-relief depicting uniformed soldiers facing front and in profile, holding bayonets.

———

Back in the car, it is a short drive (depending on traffic) to the City of Brotherly Love, and few cities scream "American Revolution" as loudly as Philadelphia.

Much of the city's storied role in the war for American independence from Britain can be enjoyed on foot. Stroll the expansive Independence Mall, flanked by the National Constitution Center, Independence Hall, and Christ Church Burial Ground—all of which are worth more than a quick visit. Dive into colonial life, walking the same cobblestoned streets that Elizabeth Drinker, Peggy Shippen, and Esther Reed did, where countless women-run boardinghouses once stood or continue to stand. Stop by Carpenter's Hall, where the Continental Congress routinely gathered, and Independence Hall, site of the adoption of the Declaration of Independence. Near the visitor center sits an enclosure featuring the famously cracked Liberty Bell. If you don't wish to endure the lines, miniatures are available for sale, as are copies of the Declaration of Independence, the Constitution, and the Bill of Rights. These are good references for any American to keep on hand as a refresher, no matter their station or level of education. More than one elected official has made what I have come to regard as the "Declatution" mistake: conflating the words and meanings of the two most significant documents in American history.

Many historic sites dot the streets of Philadelphia, including one dedicated to perhaps the city's most notable resident, Benjamin Franklin, and there is a plethora of colonial-inspired beer available when you need a cool respite during a summer visit. At the celebrated City Tavern—now, sadly, shuttered due to COVID—I imbibe a brew made from Thomas Jefferson's own recipe. There are other taverns worth a visit, including the Tun Tavern and the delightfully named Man Full of Trouble. In every direction there are museums, cemeteries, and more tricorne hats than you can shake a fife at.

The Museum of the American Revolution is one of my favorite sites to visit—one that strives to celebrate disparate voices from every corner of the Revolutionary War era. In their possession is a part of the statue of King George III that was torn down during the riot at Bowling Green, a tiny reminder of the monument that was melted down on the Wolcott family property to be used for ammunition. The museum also offers viewings of George Washington's war tent. The three-hundred-square-foot portable abode has separate "rooms" of a sort, creates a footprint measuring forty-five feet by thirty-six feet when its guylines are spread taut, and boasts a roomy, twelve-foot "ceiling" at its highest points—perfect for the six-foot-two-inch Washington. The flax-linen structure dates to between 1777 and 1778. It was not the only tent to be fashioned for General Washington, as the wear and tear of the field took its toll. The tent on display at the museum creates quite an impression, sporting scalloped edges lined in crimson, giving it almost a "big top" feel, as if the Continental circus were pulling into town. It allowed Washington to remain in and among the troops—even when he had other, more permanent quarters—something that he considered important while in the field.

The tent in the museum's possession remained in the Washington family until 1909, when Reverend William Herbert Burk, an Episcopal priest and founder of the Washington Memorial Chapel on the grounds of Valley Forge, purchased it and made it a part of a history museum he established at the former winter encampment. The Valley Forge Historical Society served as the predecessor of the Museum of the American Revolution. Burk was a lifelong collector of Revolutionary War artifacts, and he and collectors like him brought to light remarkable and tangible pieces of American history and used them to shed new light on the past. The short film shown in the museum's theater just prior to the revelation of the actual tent provides a surprisingly effective buildup, and when the curtain is pulled back onstage for the big reveal, the moment does not disappoint.

———

Just blocks away from the museum stands the home of noted seamstress Betsy Ross. I consider the Betsy Ross story one of the motivations for writing this book, as it speaks to a question that routinely occupies the minds of many writers and historians: Why do we remember certain people while neglecting others, and moreover, why do we *misremember* so many individuals when their factual stories are fascinating in their own right?

Betsy—whose name was Elizabeth Griscom Claypoole at the time of her death—was long identified as the woman who created and sewed the first American flag. The day I visit, her house stands draped in bunting, adorned with many Stars and Stripes. Tourists traipse through a self-guided tour of the tiny house, peeking at trinkets in the gift shop and congregating in the courtyard where Betsy and her third husband, John Claypoole, are buried. Betsy died in 1836 and was initially buried in the Free Quaker Burial Ground on Fifth Street. So who is in the courtyard? you might ask. It is she. Twenty years after her *initial* burial, her body was moved to the Mount Moriah Cemetery. And finally, in 1975—on the eve of America's bicentennial—Betsy was moved to the courtyard of the home you see today. (There is also a rumor that she was later moved to Basking Ridge, New Jersey.) However, the house and museum on Arch Street are very possibly *not* the original Ross house but rather next door to where it once stood and may have, ironically and mistakenly, been torn down to lessen the fire hazard it posed to the home you visit today—then believed to be hers. Still with me? In any case . . .

The house on Arch Street has been a tourist destination for decades despite the fact that there is no solid evidence that Betsy Ross created the *first* American flag. She very likely sewed more than a few. What scant clues there are as to who came up with the design point in the direction of Francis Hopkinson, a signer of the Declaration of Independence from New Jersey, but even his role in the creation of the flag is unclear. Quite the Renaissance man, Hopkinson—an artist and a composer as well as a congressman—did design the Great Seal of the United States. He once submitted a bill to the Continental Congress for what he claimed to be his role in the design of a flag—the only person in history to have done so.

Betsy's story has been dissected over the years. Did George Washington, in fact, stop into her shop and ask her to sew a flag for him, as she reportedly later told her family? This was not that outrageous a claim. It was not unusual for Washington himself to seek out supplies for the perpetually undersupplied Continental Army. Betsy was the niece by marriage of the congressman and Declaration signer George Ross, so it is not unreasonable to think that Washington knew of her talents as a seamstress. It is known also that she sewed flags. Did she sew the very first American flag? Possibly, but there is no proof. We know that Hopkinson was partial to six-pointed stars, while the U.S. flag features five-pointed versions that, reportedly, were easier for seamstresses like Ross to snip in a hurry. And a folded paper star pattern linked to Betsy's family was discovered in Philadelphia in 1922. But what of it? Though her role as seamstress of the *first* American flag is likely not true, her role as an integral part of colonial Philadelphia history is. This thrice-widowed upholsterer managed to keep a successful business going during the war. She took custom orders and helped Philadelphians furnish their homes with beds, chairs, draperies, and the like. The house is an inspirational site to visit for that reason alone and can deepen an understanding of the sacrifices and determination it took to endure and thrive while the world around you fell into chaos.

In this sense, even if definitive evidence never emerges with respect to Betsy Ross's part in the flag story, she's still a role model and stand-in for the countless individuals whose stories were never shared, accurately or otherwise. Sybil Ludington, whether or not she really rode out to raise the alarm and gather her father's militia, stands for every young woman who stood up for what she believed, defending home and family.

And whether or not the name "Molly Pitcher" refers to a specific individual, the story of a woman—more than a few—serving on a battlefield alongside her husband or in his stead is a factual one.

———

Molly Pitcher she stood by her gun
And rammed the charges home, sir;
And thus on Monmouth bloody field
A sergeant did become, sir.

Pennsylvanian Mary Ludwig Hays had followed her husband, William, to battle. During the Battle of Monmouth Court House, William manned a cannon while Mary assisted him, toting water from a spring to sponge it down.

When her husband fell, *wounded*, Mary nobly stepped in to take over.

No, wait. She *demanded* of a passing officer that she be able to "avenge" her husband's death. As a result, George Washington gave her a lieutenant's commission on the spot.

Hang on: He gave her a sword.

Wait, strike that: It was a gold coin.

An 1837 article in *The Baltimore Sun* purported to tell the story of "Molly Pitcher . . . an interesting account of this courageous woman, and of her daring exploits during the revolutionary war." It cited an article from the *New Brunswick (NJ) Times*, and all seemed to stem from a conflation of previous related stories. In 1826 an article entitled "Recollections of Washington" had appeared in *The United States Gazette* (Philadelphia). George Washington Parke Custis, step-grandson of George, penned this collection of stories, one of which was the tale of "Captain Molly," describing the deeds of a woman at Monmouth. Custis gave no source for the story, but it clearly caught on. The exact same article from *The Sun* was reprinted in 1838 and 1840 in different newspapers in different parts of the country. Many of the subsequent articles presumably borrowed from a Molly Pitcher story that appeared in the exhaustingly titled 1841 tome *A Popular Cyclopedia of History, Ancient and Modern, Forming a Copious Historical Dictionary or Celebrated Institutions, Persons, Places, and Things; with Notices of the Present State of the Principal Cities, Countries, and Kingdoms of the Known World: To Which Is Added a Chronological View of Memorable Events, as Earthquakes, Volcanic Eruptions, Storms, Conflagrations, Diseases, Famines, Inventions, Discoveries, Battles, Treaties, Settlements, Origins of Religious Sects, etc.*

This book is more commonly—and concisely—referred to as "Durivage's Historical Cyclopedia." Arranged alphabetically, it shares the story of Molly Pitcher in a section describing the Revolutionary War and the Battle of Monmouth.

The brave actions of a woman fighting alongside her husband at Monmouth would also be described in the diaries of at least two Revolutionary War veterans, neither of whom refers to the woman by any name and certainly not by the name that sometimes still "carries water" today.

In 1848, though the legend still had not been investigated by reputable historians, Nathaniel Currier created a hand-colored lithograph titled *The Women of '76. "Molly Pitcher" The Heroine of Monmouth*, which was published by Currier & Ives sometime in the late nineteenth or possibly early twentieth century. The caption reads:

> *Her husband falls . . . she sheds no ill timed tear,*
> *But firm resolved . . . she fills his fatal post.*
> *The foe press on she checks their mad career,*
> *Who can avenge like her a husband's ghost?*

In around 1856, Currier's artistic interpretation was followed by yet another illustration, this one an oil painting by the Irish artist Dennis Malone Carter, entitled *Moll Pitcher at the Battle of Monmouth*. Then, sometime between 1860 and 1880, Carter gave us yet another: *Moll Pitcher Being Presented to George Washington*. All of these helped cement the idea of "Molly Pitcher" as a specific individual in the collective American memory, a testament to the power that art—whether poems or paintings—can have on cultural memory.

By the 1890s, the story was already being dissected, refuted, and defended. "No imaginary heroine was Molly Pitcher, but a real, buxom lass, and a strong, sturdy, courageous woman," insisted the author of an article printed on July 3, 1897. Identifying Molly Pitcher as Mary Hays, the in-depth analysis of the story appeared in *The Sentinel* of Carlisle, Pennsylvania, where Hays was buried.

The following year, an article titled "Molly Pitcher Again" in the *Monmouth Democrat* out of New Jersey stated, "The claimant recognized by us (she buried at Carlisle, Pa.) seems to be ahead so far in the controversy . . . ," the controversy being about the identity of the "real" Molly Pitcher. In 1912, *The American Catholic Historical Researches* printed its own "Molly Again" notice, which was much more brief and much less supportive: "How happy people can be when in delusion—when celebrating an event that never occurred," the article stated. "The alleged Molly wasn't Irish and no Molly manned a gun at Monmouth and so was not by request of Washington made a Lieutenant nor given a pension for life.

"Molly Pitcher, Betsy Ross and Lydia Darragh ought by this time [to] be abandoned by our over-patriotic but ill-informed."

Lengthy treatises have since been written about Molly Pitcher's origin story, and—without getting too deep into those fascinating and thoroughly plowed weeds—suffice it to say that over the years two *prime* candidates have emerged as potential muses for the Molly Pitcher story: Mary Hays (McCauley) and Margaret Corbin.

Both were from Pennsylvania. Both served in artillery units with their gunner husbands under a Captain Thomas Proctor. Both were referred to as Captain Molly—and neither as Molly Pitcher—during their lifetimes.

As for the name itself? "Molly" at times served as a nickname for Margaret and Mary. "Pitcher" is believed to have been a common cry of soldiers on the battlefield shouting for water to slake their thirst or sponge down the embers in hot cannons. One can imagine a beleaguered militiaman in the midst of battle tending to his cannon and bellowing to his beloved or whoever might be within earshot, "Molly! Pitcher!"

However, this story—of a woman going off to battle with her husband and picking up his weapon after he falls wounded or dead next to her—feels familiar because it probably was a common occurrence. The details recall the experiences of not only Margaret Corbin and Mary Hays, but also of Nanye'hi and likely others whose names we will never know because recorded history tends to put almost as much focus on disproving the stories of women—and Native and Black Americans—as it does on unearthing and recording them in the first place. And false stories *should* be disproved. However, it is interesting how women whose tales have been intertwined and mingled and augmented and polished often demand as much or more attention from our twenty-first-century minds as actual women who lived, breathed, and left behind verifiable sources.

I couldn't help but think about this while driving into Valley Forge, approaching from the south along I-81. I passed Exit 3 in Antrim Township and encountered Molly Pitcher Highway. I was reminded of her again when heading south on the New Jersey Turnpike. Near mile marker 71 is the Molly Pitcher Service Area, featuring Shake Shack, Subway, Panda Express, and the always unavoidable Starbucks.

Traveling through New Jersey, there are as many Molly options as there are Molly candidates: the Molly Pitcher Inn in Red Bank. A Molly Pitcher burger. A Molly Pitcher Cheese Board and potpie. Molly Pitcher Amber Lager, at the time produced by Red Tank Brewing of Red Bank, New Jersey.

Was there a Molly Pitcher? In name, no. In actions, undoubtedly. And very likely not just one. Rather than asking, "Who was the real Molly Pitcher?" perhaps the better question is, "Who wasn't?"

CHAPTER 19

Tides Turn South

For years, Esther seemingly contented herself with sharing her feelings on the conflict between America and her home country of England in letters with her closest confidantes. She longed to share her ideas and passions with a larger audience. She sensed that what she had seen, heard, and learned over the last several painful years would resonate with others beyond her social circle, perhaps even spur them to action.

> *On the commencement of actual war, the Women of America manifested a firm resolution to contribute as much as could depend on them, to the deliverance of their country. Animated by the purest patriotism, they are sensible of sorrow at this day, in not offering more than barren wishes for the success of so glorious a Revolution.*

What Esther DeBerdt Reed wrote was nothing short of a manifesto rallying women to the cause of revolution. She reached back in time, finding inspiration in the lives of countless women who had gone before her:

> *Our ambition is kindled by the same of those heroines of antiquity, who have rendered their sex illustrious, and have proved to the universe, that, if the weakness of our Constitution, if opinion and*

manners did not forbid us to march to glory by the same paths as the Men, we should at least equal, and sometimes surpass them in our love for the public good. I glory in all that which my sex has done great and commendable. I call to mind with enthusiasm and with admiration, all those acts of courage, of constancy and patriotism which history has transmitted to us . . .

By the time Esther's article appeared in *The Pennsylvania Gazette* on June 21, 1780, the first part of the year had seen an extraordinarily brutal winter encampment at Morristown, New Jersey, the inability of Continental forces to retake Savannah, and the Crown's Southern Campaign getting into full savage swing.

The General Sir Henry Clinton and his troops made their way to Johns Island, one of the barrier islands along the coast of South Carolina, crossed the Stono River to James Island, and finally headed up the west bank of the Ashley River. Clinton's sights were fixed on Charles Town, of course—the same port city that the British had failed to take in June 1776.

By May 12, Charles Town, South Carolina, was in British hands. General Clinton forced the surrender of the Charles Town garrison's 5,500 troops. Three weeks later, Clinton sailed back to New York, leaving General Charles Cornwallis in charge of the city specifically and the British campaign in the southern states more broadly. Cornwallis's task: dig in, move inland from the coast, and deliver the South.

In her lengthy article, Esther touched on those aspects of the fighting that had reached her ears. "The situation of our soldiery has been represented to me," she mentioned, before extolling the contributions of the troops, reminding those who were fortunate enough not to be in the midst of conflict to be grateful. Next she addressed the new nation's fighting men directly:

"We know that at a distance from the theatre of war, if we enjoy any tranquility, it is the fruit of your watching, your labours, your dangers." Those who fought conferred by their actions certain privileges that were enjoyed by civilians: the ability to "live happy" with one's family, to be able to harvest crops "in peace," and to be able to care for one's child "without being afraid of feeling myself separated from it, by a ferocious enemy." For all of these comforts, Esther assured the beleaguered military men, "it is to you that we owe [them]."

"Brave Americans, your disinterestedness, your courage, and your constancy will always be dear to America, as long as she shall preserve her virtue."

More than mere opinion and thanks, Esther's words expressed a call to action. She challenged women to "wear a clothing more simple; hair dressed less elegant," and questioned who would not be willing to forgo "vain ornaments" knowing that "the valiant defenders of America will be able to draw some advantage from the money which she may have laid out in these."

Since before the first shots were fired at Lexington and Concord, women throughout the colonies had banded together to fight with their pocketbooks and their spirit. Now, nearly a decade later, Esther's essay reminded them of how far they had come and how they could not now abandon the fight. Armed or not, women had been battling for what they believed in for years. And it was time to do so once again:

> *The time is arrived to display the same sentiments which animated us at the beginning of the Revolution, when we renounced the use of teas, however agreeable to our taste, rather than receive them from our persecutors; when we made it appear to them that we placed former necessaries in the rank of superfluities, when our liberty was interested; when our republican and laborious hands spun the flax, prepared the linen intended for the use of our soldiers.*

Esther signed her essay, which found its way into newspapers throughout the East Coast, "By An AMERICAN WOMAN."

Far from mere "sentiments," Esther's influential broadside hit a patriotic nerve. Esther had been in America for roughly ten years, but the cause of patriotism resonated within her. She was also the first lady of Pennsylvania now, as Joseph had been elected to lead that state, and as such she was in a position of greater standing and influence. Sarah Franklin Bache, daughter of Pennsylvania statesman and inventor Benjamin Franklin, chose to help Esther with her efforts. Together they launched the Ladies Association of Philadelphia.

A reported 1,645 women joined the cause, many even going door-to-door to solicit donations. The money would be dedicated to the soldiers, who were perpetually in need of clothing and food. Donations ranged from humble offerings like a pair of leather breeches to the largess of the Marchioness de Lafayette, who donated one hundred guineas in hard currency.

Esther's husband, Joseph, wrote George Washington to describe and celebrate his wife's efforts:

"The Ladies of the place have also caught the happy contagion," he wrote, letting the general know that Esther would soon "have the honor of writing to you on that subject. It is expected she will have a sum equal to one hundred thousand pounds to be laid out according to your Excellency direction . . . in such a way as may be thought most honorable and gratifying to the brave old soldiers who have borne so great a share of the burthen of this War."

Washington responded, "I very much admire the patriotic spirit of the Ladies of Philia., and shall with great pleasure give them my advice, as to the application of their benevolent and generous donation to the soldiers of the Army."

However, not everyone was in favor of Esther's approach.

Philadelphia's Anna Rawle wrote a friend, "Of all absurdities the Ladies going about for money exceeded everything; they were so extremely importunate that people were obliged to give them something to get rid of them." She lamented "a number of very genteel women" who "paraded about streets in this manner, some carrying ink stands, nor did they let the meanest ale house escape . . .

"I fancy they raised a considerable sum by this extorted contribution, some giving solely against their inclinations thro' fear of what might happen if they refused."

Nevertheless, the example of the Ladies Association of Philadelphia spread well beyond the borders of Pennsylvania. Similar efforts soon sprang up in New Jersey, Maryland, and Virginia. From Massachu-setts, Abigail Adams waxed lyrical about the efforts. She wrote her husband's lawyer and legal secretary, John Thaxter:

"Yet virtue exists, and public spirit lives—lives in the Bosoms of the Fair Daughters of America, who blushing for the Languid Spirit, and halting Step, unite their Efforts to reward the patriotic, to stimulate the Brave, to alleviate the burden of war, and to shew that they are not dis-mayed by defeats or misfortunes. Read the Pennsylvania papers, and see the Spirit catching from state to state."

On July 4, 1780, Esther wrote General George Washington to up-date him on her organization's progress:

"The Subscription set on foot by the Ladies of this City for the use of the Soldiery is so far completed," she began, "altho it has answered our Expectations, it does not equal our Wishes." She nevertheless viewed it as "proof of our Zeal for the great Cause of America, & our Esteem & Gratitude for those who so bravely defend it—The amount of the Subscription is 200,580, Dolls. & £625.6.8 in Specie, which makes in the whole in Paper Money 300,634 Dolrs." (This amount was esti-mated to be about $7,500 in gold at the time.)

She noted that the Ladies Association of Philadelphia was "anxious for the Soldiers to receive the benefit" of their efforts, and finally asked his opinion on how best to use the funds raised.

Washington's reply was "Course linnen" to be fashioned into shirts for the soldiers.

Esther wrote in response, suggesting that cash money—as depreci-ated as Continental currency might well be—might convey a better "thank you" for the soldiers' service. But Washington thought the clothing would prove less problematic.

"I have my apprehensions (from the peculiar circumstances of our Army) that a taste of hard money may be productive of much discon-tent, as we have none but depreciated paper for their pay."

While some "provident Soldiers" might make good use of "the gen-erous bounty of two hard dollars in specie," Washington thought it might pose too great a temptation to those whose "propensity to drink-ing, overcoming all other considerations, too frequently leads them into irregularities, & disorders which must be corrected. A Shirt would render the condition of the soldiery in general much more comfortable than it is at present."

"Course linnen" shirts it was. By August, Esther was purchasing the fabric. A brigade of women would sew the shirts themselves. The military, now more stretched than ever, would make good use of them, as the Southern Campaign was taking a brutal toll on both sides of the ongoing conflict.

"Ah! my foreboding soul! what I feared has indeed taken place. S. Carolina grows under the British yoke; her sons and daughters are exiled, driven from their native land; and their pleasant habitations seized by the insulting victors."

So wrote a twenty-three-year-old widow named Eliza Yonge Wilkinson as she watched in horror as the British took over Charles Town and the surrounding areas, including the barrier islands she and her family called home. In addition to taking more than 5,000 troops, the British seized artillery, tens of thousands of rounds of ammunition, 49 ships, 120 boats, staples like milled flour, necessities like rum, and valuable Low Country crops such as rice and indigo.

With a city to control and troops to house, feed, and outfit, the British now also had to see to the *additional* troops they had *captured*. They soon realized that they needed to fan out into the countryside to find supplies. This led to some of the worst examples of looting and violence seen in the course of the war.

Eliza's husband, Joseph Wilkinson, had died just six months after they married; their only son died shortly after birth. During the British occupation, she spent time at Yonge's Island, which bore the name of her Welsh immigrant father and plantation owner Francis Yonge, and across the Wadmalaw River at an island of the same name, where her brother's plantations stood.

Both of Eliza's brothers were away fighting, while she and others in Charles Town and the surrounding Sea Islands endured "violence and oppression, and sword law."

"Oh! . . . who can forbear to execrate these barbarous, insulting red coats?" Eliza Wilkinson wrote a dear friend. "I despise them most cordially, and hope their day of suffering is not far off."

She endured the occupation of her city with a resolute vigor. She took it upon herself to not only correspond with but also visit those Continental soldiers incarcerated aboard the noxious prison ships just offshore.

One officer advised her "to take care whom I speak to," she wrote a friend, "and not to be very saucy; for the two Miss Sarazens were put in [the] Provost [dungeon], and very much insulted for some trifle or other. Did you ever hear the like!"

Once a handy site for confiscated tea and a meeting place for the South Carolina Provincial Congress, the Provost, or Exchange, had been built roughly ten years earlier and stood at the foot of Broad Street. The British quartered troops there and used it as a prison during their occupation. (Continental general William Moultrie had cached in the northeast corner of the basement 10,000 pounds of gunpowder, which the British would never find.)

Among those imprisoned at the Provost during the British occupation were common thieves, outspoken women, and—briefly—three signers of the Declaration of Independence: Arthur Middleton, Edward Rutledge, and Thomas Heyward Jr.

While some individuals—the signers, for example—were held in the main Provost building, a number of prisoners were housed in the building's dank dungeon. The "two Miss Sarazens" of whom Eliza wrote were the sisters Mary and Catherine, who were confined in the dungeon for vocally supporting their patriot brother, the silversmith Jonathan.

Prisoners were also held on notoriously harrowing prison ships. Robert Sheffield, a survivor of a prison ship, would later describe the intense heat, which prompted some prisoners to go about without clothing. This helped to "get rid of vermin," he told the *Connecticut Gazette*, "but the sick were eaten up alive. Their sickly countenances, and ghastly looks were truly horrible; some swearing and blaspheming; others crying, praying, and wringing their hands; and stalking about like ghosts; others delirious, raving and storming,—all panting for breath; some dead, and corrupting." Sheffield was among the lucky survivors. It is estimated that 12,000 prisoners of war died on prison ships during the war, many from disease and starvation.

Although the bulk of these ships were moored off the coast of New York City, where dead bodies tossed overboard would wash up on-shore, they also floated in the waters around Charles Town. In light of the fate of the Sarazen sisters, Eliza's visits and writings were not with-out risk. Throughout the region, she and others—whether or not they wore their patriot leanings on their sleeves—always suffered the threat of harassment and theft. Troops plundered the homes of Eliza and her family, absconding with the shutters from the windows. She dreaded the day when trouble would return to her doorstep, and that ever-present threat was woven throughout her writings.

"Bless me! here is a whole troop of British horse coming up to the house; get into my bosom, letter;—how I tremble!" she abruptly wrote in the midst of one of her missives.

The outspoken young woman, who believed women should have a voice in political proceedings, wanted a record of her words preserved. So she diligently copied all the letters she wrote to others by hand into a blank quarto book.

"What will the men say if they should see this?" she wondered aloud on paper. "I am really out of my sphere now."

Traveling by water up the Wadmalaw River to the Stono and then finally onto Wappoo Creek, it was a short trip to Eliza Pinckney's Wap-poo plantation and eventually Charles Town. The fortunes of the in-digo plantation owner's life had shifted dramatically over the course of the war.

The Pinckney family had already noticed upheaval as the British grasp on the region tightened. British raids were common, and the South remained ravaged by smallpox. Eliza had considered leaving—others certainly had upon hearing of the approaching troops—but in-stead stayed.

A year earlier, in 1779, Thomas Pinckney had informed his mother about troubles at his plantation. After a British raid, he complained, the only enslaved individuals who were left on his Ashepoo plantation were sick women and children who "pay no attention" to the orders of the overseer and "who are now perfectly free & live upon the best produce of the plantation."

Eliza echoed her son's sentiments. The Revolutionary War, she claimed, had allowed those enslaved by the Pinckney family and elsewhere to "do now what they please every where." With at least twenty men and women enslaved at her Wappoo plantation, she complained that they "behaved so infamously" and that "even those that remain at home [were] so Insolent and quite their own masters . . ."

As the British streamed into Charles Town and the surrounding areas, enslaved workers fled the plantations to seek freedom with them. The British were struggling to maintain control of the city of Charles Town; seeing to the housing, feeding, and care of those who sought safety behind their lines proved nearly impossible to manage. Additionally, disease thrived in the crowded, unsanitary, and sweltering conditions. Seeking to avoid the same sort of disastrous results that Lord Dunmore had incurred years earlier when inviting the Black population to flee their enslavers and join the British, Lord General Cornwallis ordered that those abandoning nearby plantations and joining the British troops be quarantined first. Variola (smallpox), however, needed fresh hosts and found plenty of them in the quarantine camp. The lack of fresh water and decent shelter, cramped surroundings, and, in the summer months, rising temperatures served as a recipe for increased transmission of the brutal disease.

Where Dunmore had inoculated and employed the Black troops as soldiers, Cornwallis opted for quarantine and preferred that all Black individuals serve as laborers, as laundresses, or in other nonfighting roles. The only hope of making it out of quarantine was to buck the odds and survive it.

A man named Boston King, who escaped enslavement, was one of the "fortunate" ones.

"I was seized with the small-pox, and suffered great hardships," King later wrote, "for all the Blacks infected with that disease, were ordered to be carried a mile from the camp, lest the soldiers should be

infected, and disabled from marching. This was a grievous circumstance to me and many others. We lay sometimes a whole day without
any thing to eat or drink . . ."

The horrific circumstances were well known throughout Charles
Town.

"As the smallpox was in the British camp," Eliza Pinckney wrote
her son that fall, "thousands of Negroes dyed miserably of it."

Though the British controlled Charles Town—and had enjoyed a
very one-sided win on August 16, 1780, when they roundly defeated
Continental forces at the Battle of Camden, in the midlands of South
Carolina—the rural areas remained unruly and treacherous, and Continentals and militia employed tactics beyond what the British were
accustomed to in open warfare.

Francis Marion, a forty-eight-year-old patriot commander, was only
five feet tall and weighed in the neighborhood of one hundred pounds.
But the veteran of the French and Indian War and the Battle of Sullivan's Island packed a punch. His rather effective tactics thrived on am-
bushes, "hit-and-run" assaults, especially attacks on supply lines. Local
connections supplied intelligence, and his troops' knowledge of the terrain undermined the British at every turn. Later that year, Dragoon
lieutenant colonel Banastre Tarleton would pursue Marion through
twenty-six miles of backwoods and swamps. "As for this damned old
fox," Tarleton later wrote, "the Devil himself could not catch him."

Marion—now dubbed the "Swamp Fox"—fought twelve battles employing his effective if unorthodox methods, and as such is considered
by some to be the godfather of guerrilla warfare.

While the Crown managed to keep a tentative hold on the South, it
knew if it could upend the Continental hold on the Hudson River to
the north, Britain would have a massive strategic advantage. To that
end, seizing control of the fortifications at West Point was critical.

Not quite two weeks before the Battle of Camden, on August 3, 1780,
Peggy's now husband Benedict received a letter from George Washington instructing him to "proceed to West Point and take the command
of the Post, and its dependencies . . ."

Arnold may not have been happy with his position within the Continental Army, but he was more than happy to take on this assignment. In fact, he was banking on it.

The site of West Point remained a crucial point of defense along the Hudson River north of New York City. It stood about five hundred feet above the Hudson and gave its patriot defenders superb views of any ships traveling up- or downriver. There the river narrows considerably. American forces had erected a massive chain across the majestic waterway in April of 1778, like a choke point, designed to physically halt British ships sailing down from points north.

In addition, West Point was now the base for the Invalid Corps, and Margaret Corbin continued to serve the corps as a nurse, among other duties. Corbin's service in the Invalid Corps illustrated that the military now viewed the fighter as a soldier in her own right. She was not "merely" a wife who stepped into her husband's place. She was regarded as a veteran of battle. To that end, in 1779, the Continental Congress proceeded to award Corbin a lifetime military pension for her service to the patriot cause. Additionally, Congress awarded Margaret some new clothes to replace the ones damaged during the battle of Fort Washington.

Though countless women had served unofficially in the military, never before had the government officially acknowledged the military contributions of a single woman or granted her a pension. Of course, Corbin's pension was half what a male soldier would have received. Her sacrifice was no different from that of her fellow man, yet her compensation was a fraction of his.

Washington was aware that in April 1780 the Executive Council of Pennsylvania—and Esther DeBerdt Reed's husband, Joseph—had accused Arnold of "malfeasance" during his brief tenure as military governor of Philadelphia. However, this did not dissuade Washington from placing West Point under control of the hero of Saratoga, whom many considered to be one of the more able leaders in the Continental Army. Yet Arnold deeply resented Reed's accusation. It represented yet another slight in Arnold's eyes at the hands of the country for which he fought.

That Peggy Shippen Arnold's husband was frustrated came as little surprise to some. Lucy Knox well remembered a letter she had received from her husband, Henry, three years earlier describing news of the latest military promotions. Specifically, Henry Knox noted the snub of one particular officer.

"They have skipped over Gen Arnold who was the elder," Henry wrote on March 23, 1777, an act Henry thought might "push [Arnold] out of the service. I hope the affair will be remedied."

It was not, at least not to Arnold's liking.

Peggy's marriage to Benedict had not distanced her from her Philadelphia loyalist-leaning social circle; rather, she welcomed Benedict deeper into it. That circle included the British officer John André. For his part, André missed his time in Philadelphia with the Shippen family and others, and he wrote Peggy's friend Peggy Chew that he was sad he had to "abandon the pleasing Study of what relates to the Ladies." However, he remained in contact with the couple.

Letters passed back and forth between André and Arnold, often via an intermediary, sometimes via a "Lady" whom André indicated "might write to me at the same time with one of her intimates. She will guess who I mean, the latter remaining ignorant of interlining & sending the letter."

Peggy herself also corresponded with André. In a letter written in May of 1779, Benedict sent along the "particular compliments" of his wife, Peggy, whom André had once sought to woo at the ostentatious British Meschianza.

André was the closest thing the British had to a spymaster. He had also been keeping tabs on his new military acquaintance, and on at least one instance that spring he asked British spies to monitor Arnold's movements as he traveled between West Point and New Haven. Letters between André, Arnold, and their various intermediaries focused on Arnold's impending role at the Hudson River post and how that might benefit the British cause—and offer some financial gain to Arnold. For his part, Arnold demanded a fee of £20,000 to provide the British with critical plans of West Point's fortifications. Peggy may have been one of those intermediaries who facilitated the correspondence between the American and British officers. Some of the letters

Peggy exchanged with André included messages written by Arnold to André in invisible ink. It is difficult to imagine Peggy did not know that her husband was communicating with André in this fashion. Though her *precise* role in the ensuing drama remains unclear, those who sought to upend the Continental forces at West Point valued her connection to André.

Shortly after assigning Benedict Arnold to take command of the fortifications at West Point, George Washington and his aide, Alexander Hamilton, were traveling to the stronghold. Along the way, on August 23, they stopped at the home of Oliver Wolcott in Connecticut. Later, Washington was at West Point when, on September 22, Benedict Arnold departed to meet John André in person at Haverstraw, New York. This small Hudson Valley town, roughly eighteen miles south of West Point, may have appeared unassuming, but it was a key lookout for Americans monitoring British troops along the Hudson.

The next day, after meeting with Arnold, André—traveling under the guise of "John Anderson," a New York City merchant—passed through Tarrytown, New York, on his way back to Manhattan. There he encountered a patriot posse. Was he searched by militia? Was he mugged? Did he attempt to bribe the men who detained him? Whatever the circumstances, the men who arrested him were particularly interested in documents tucked in André's boots.

Two days later, on the morning of September 25, George Washington expected to join Benedict Arnold for breakfast at the house where Arnold was living with his family and that he was using as his headquarters. But Arnold had other plans.

Word of André's arrest had reached Arnold, and he knew time was of the essence. The sketches found in André's possession may have been hurried scribblings, but they were damning nonetheless. They described the key defenses at West Point—Fort Arnold among them—and Arnold knew that when their contents were shared with Washington, the general would immediately grasp that Arnold had plotted to reveal those defenses to the British.

After a brief conversation with Peggy upstairs, Arnold made a run for the British lines, his destination the HMS *Vulture*, moored on the

Hudson and destined for New York City. There was no turning back now. He fled his post, his certain punishment, and his wife, Peggy.

Once aboard the *Vulture*, Arnold wrote and dispatched a note to Washington, which carried a request:

"I have no favor to ask for myself," he wrote. "I have too often experienced the Ingratitude of my Country to Attempt it: But from the known humanity of your Excellence I am induced to ask your protection For Mrs. Arnold from every Insult and Injury that the mistaken Vengence of my Country may expose Her to: It ought to fall only on me. She is as good, and as Innocent as an Angel, and is Incapable of doing wrong."

He feared that his beloved Peggy might "suffer from the mistaken fury of Her Country."

Peggy, too, received a letter. Arnold confided that he had requested that Washington "take you under his protection." He urged her to go to friends in Philadelphia, or to eventually come to find him with the British forces. He left that to her but added that he would "be miserable until we meet."

In the aftermath, Peggy was apoplectic. When Washington visited her at the Arnold home roughly two miles south of West Point, she accused the general of attempting to murder her infant son, Edward. She vacillated between raving and sobbing. Alexander Hamilton—who had pursued Arnold but failed to capture him—called it "the most affecting scene I was ever witness to. She for a considerable time entirely lost her senses . . . We have every reason to believe she was entirely unacquainted with the plan . . ."

In the days that followed, Washington offered to trade André for Arnold, but André's superior, Clinton, would not hear of it. If he traded Arnold, he would be sending the message that any American defectors to the British side could expect the same treatment. Also, from the perspective of class, Clinton did not view Arnold to be of the same value as André. Before his military service, Arnold was a commoner, a tradesman. André was a gentleman born to a good British family. Clinton could not have imagined what Washington would do next.

While Arnold eluded punishment, John André was not so lucky.

Hamilton tried to dissuade Washington from condemning André to death, but to no avail. To André, the thought that the Americans were contemplating ending his life came as a shock. Though he was technically responsible for collecting intelligence on behalf of the British, he was not particularly good at this task, and not very organized. He did not regard himself as a spy. Far from it. He was a British officer and a gentleman. By the military code of the time, as a captured soldier, he fully expected to be treated with respect and held until a suitable trade for a high-ranking American officer could be arranged.

It was not to be.

Ever the artist, André sketched a self-portrait the day before his execution. It is a wistful image, handily belying the tragic end he was about to face. In it, he sits, legs crossed, one arm propped over the back of his chair, an inkwell and writing quill on the table before him.

John André was hanged on October 2, 1780, in Tappan, New York. He was thirty years old.

Peggy did decide to go to Philadelphia before hopefully meeting up with her husband, who was now with the British. Along the way she paid a visit to Theodosia Prevost, the wife of a British officer, in Paramus, New Jersey. During that visit, Peggy supposedly confessed to Prevost her "theatrics" in the aftermath of her husband's failed plot. From there, Peggy was off to New York. That would not be her last voyage. And next time, she would not be alone.

Arnold's prediction about the "fury" of his country was not far off the mark. The story of his betrayal spread up and down the coast. Neither he nor Peggy were spared the wrath of the press. By October 3, the day after André met his end, readers of Mary Katharine Goddard's newspaper read the account of Arnold's defection in consummate detail, described as "a scene of the blackest villainy." When the story broke, Peggy was equated with famous women from Roman antiquity. "André, under the mask of friendship and former aequaintance at Meschianzas and Balls, opened a correspondence in August, 1779 with Mrs. Arnold, which has doubtless been improved on his part to the dreadful and horrid issue we have described," the newspaper account opined, "and which but for the over-ruling care of a kind Providence, must have involved this country and our Allies in great distress, and perhaps utter ruin."

A week later, Goddard's readers beheld the traitor's own words: Arnold's letter to Washington was printed in its entirety. One of Goddard's correspondents shared a vivid description of a parade conducted in Philadelphia in which a two-faced effigy of Arnold was carried through the streets on a carriage. Behind the Arnold figure rode the Devil Beelzebub in black robes, shaking a purse of money at the general's left ear and waving a pitchfork, "ready to drive him into hell as the reward due for the many crimes his thirst of gold had made him commit."

At the time, traitors and spies were regarded as the equal of the devil. They practiced deception. They lied about their identities and their social rank. And for what? Money.

The great irony of the Arnold saga was that both sides in the conflict used spies. And of the two, the Americans were far more aggressive practitioners. What would have astonished most citizens of the time was the fact that the creator of the oldest spy ring operating on the East Coast was George Washington himself. In 1778, the general had established the Culper Ring to help him gather intelligence about British operations and movements in New York City. His operatives were based largely on Long Island and in Connecticut. They traveled to New York, spent time chatting up British soldiers and officers, then passed that information on to Washington by a circuitous route that saw them rowing across Long Island Sound to Connecticut in whaleboats to bring letters to their spy chief, Benjamin Tallmadge. In this way the ring uncovered such plots as the British plan to release rounds of counterfeit Continental currency to devastate the American economy. (Tallmadge was also instrumental in identifying Major André as a spy shortly after he was captured.) When the British started checking people's identities as they entered New York City, one male operative of the Culper Ring traveled with a woman to keep up the pretense that they were husband and wife. A surviving letter from this man reveals his plan to travel to the city in the company of "355"—which was the Culper code for a "lady." She was most likely a Setauket, Long Island, woman named Anna Strong, the wife of a patriot leader, Selah Strong.

During the war, other women may very well have served patriot goals by passing information they gleaned from personal experience to the American side. But Anna's is the only name linked specifically to the ring devised by Washington.

The ring was effective throughout the war, transmitting what intel they collected exactly as the general instructed. They used invisible ink and secret codes, practices that would have seemed abominable and highly dishonorable to most Americans at the time had they known of them.

But the public at large never suspected a thing, in part because Washington spoke of such things only to those to whom it mattered. Outsiders and even his soldiers believed he was incapable of lying. He may not have been born a nobleman, but he was regarded as above reproach because he was seen as an officer and a gentleman.

Despite the British having seized control of Charles Town, loyalists there were not as pleased as might have been expected. Their militias reflected this displeasure. In the areas surrounding Charles Town proper, uprisings by patriot fighters continued to thwart the Crown's efforts to control the region. The so-called back country and guerrilla tactics employed by fighting forces proved hazardous for British troops. General Francis Marion and a small militia even managed to rescue a regiment captured during the Battle of Camden.

Then, on October 7, 1780, militia from North and South Carolina, Virginia, and what is now Tennessee attacked British loyalists at the Battle of Kings Mountain. Though they were outnumbered, the patriots killed, wounded, or captured so many troops and loyalist militiamen, the British fighting force was annihilated in a mere sixty-five-minute battle. The patriots walked away as clear victors.

With the attentions of those at the Watauga settlements focused on ongoing skirmishes in the region, some Cherokee saw an opportunity to retake a part of the lands they had sacrificed over the course of the war. In May 1777, representatives from South Carolina and Georgia, along with roughly six hundred Cherokee, had met at DeWitt's Corner, South Carolina, to, in theory, bring an end to ongoing conflicts between settlers and Native Americans in the region and to end what was referred to as the Second Cherokee War. However, the Treaty of DeWitt's Corner—and the Treaty of Long Island of Holston, which followed shortly after—ceded virtually all Cherokee lands in South Carolina to the United States, and huge swaths of their land in North Carolina disappeared as well—more than 5 million acres.

Now, in 1780, the Cherokee sought to recover some of their land and retaliate against those who had decimated their communities. The patriot settlers and militia had other ideas. They also had advance warning—again—of the impending Cherokee attack.

Continental colonel Arthur Campbell, a regimental commander from Washington County, Virginia, was appointed to deal with the situation and keep Thomas Jefferson, then governor of that state, informed about developments.

The warrior Raven and other Cherokee had met with the British in early November 1780 and decided to stage a surprise attack on settlers in Virginia and western North Carolina. However, Campbell wrote Jefferson, several white traders who had been captured by the Cherokee had escaped "by the goodness and address of an Indian woman." That woman was Nanye'hi.

"Our warning is but short . . ." Campbell wrote. "I am, however, endeavouring to raise a force."

Lieutenant Colonel John Sevier and other Americans used this information to their advantage. As Christmas approached, settlers and militia fixed their sights on a key village of the Cherokee.

"We soon were in possession of their beloved Town," Campbell wrote Jefferson of Chota, "in which we found a welcome supply of Provisions."

Many Cherokee in Chota and nearby towns fled. On December 25, Major Joseph Martin set out to determine where the residents and warriors had gone. Most were headed to Tellico and Hiawassee. Martin was not only Virginia's agent to the Cherokee; he was Nanye'hi's son-in-law. Martin had married her daughter, Betsy (though he already had a white wife).

Perhaps this was an added complication for the Beloved Woman. Perhaps it merely cemented her desire for peace with the Americans. Whatever the case, as more American troops set out for the towns of Chilhowee and Tellassee, Nanye'hi went to see Campbell herself to make a plea and even presented him with cattle from her own herd as a gift.

"The famous Indian woman Nancy Ward came to Camp," Campbell wrote Thomas Jefferson, "she gave us various intelligence, and made an overture in behalf of some of the Cheifs for Peace; to which I then evaded giving an explicit answer, as I wished first to visit the vindictive part of the nation, mostly settled at Hiwassee and Chistowee, and to distress the whole, as much as possible, by destroying their habitations and Provisions."

And so they did. This time, Chota was not spared. By December 28, the town was in flames. Nanye'hi and the inhabitants of other Cherokee towns lost everything: their crops, their possessions, their livestock, and more, much of which had been abandoned in anticipation of the onslaught.

"The Towns of Chote, Scittigo, . . . Chilhowee, Toque, Mieliqua, Kai-a-tee, Sattoogo, Telico, Hiwasee and Chistowee all principal Towns, besides some small ones, and several scattering settlements, in which were upwards of One thousand Houses, and not less than fifty thousand Bushels of Corn, and large quantities of other kinds of Provisions, all of which, after taking sufficient subsistance for the army, whilst in the Country and on its return, were committed to [the] flames, or otherwise destroyed," Campbell wrote.

"Never did a people so happily situated, act more foolishly in loosing their livings, and their Country, at a time an advantageous neutrality was held out to them, but such is the consequences of British seduction."

In his communications with Jefferson, Campbell reported that he and his men had killed twenty-nine people and taken seventeen prisoners—"mostly Women and Children"—and left an uncertain number wounded.

"Besides these we brought in the Family of Nancy Ward, who for their good offices, we considered in another light." She and her family were sent to stay with her "son-in-law," Major Martin.

Jefferson wanted the prisoners kept in the event the American forces wanted to make an exchange. Campbell wrote again, this time to the remaining Cherokee chiefs, with a warning:

> *Chiefs and Warriors—We came into your country to fight your young men; we have killed not a few of them, and destroyed your towns. You know you began the war by listening to the bad counsels of the King of England and the falsehoods told to you by his agents. We are now satisfied with what is done, as it may convince your nation that we can distress them much at any time they are so foolish as to engage in a war against us.*

If the Cherokee did not send emissaries within "two moons" to agree to a peace, Campbell warned that more destruction would come.

Nanye'hi remained with the patriots until at least February 1781, which Jefferson noted with some interest.

"Nancy Ward seems rather to have taken refuge with you," Jefferson wrote Campbell. "In this case her inclination ought to be followed as to what is done with her."

Again, Nanye'hi's true intentions—whether stemming from her roles within the Cherokee, or from her own personal relationships with the white settlers—may never be known. But the results after these attacks were devastating for the Cherokee.

This latest assault may have served the American cause well, but the new nation still wanted more.

"We are very desirous of having a fort at the mouth of Ohio," Jefferson wrote to Campbell not long after the fiery campaign. Defending the western frontier and protecting trade with New Orleans were the goals. That desired land still belonged to the Cherokee.

"We would not meddle with it without their leave," Jefferson wrote.

The year 1780 ended on a violent note for the Cherokee. It also ended on a somber note for the Ladies Association of Philadelphia.

Susan Shippen Blair wrote George Washington that she had "the honour to succeed the late Amiable Mrs President Reed as Treasuress of the Ladies Donations in this State . . ."

Esther DeBerdt Reed—the Londoner who had journeyed across an ocean to become a steadfast American patriot—had died of dysentery in September, just three months after her rallying cry to the women of her state. She was thirty-three years old.

Susan Shippen Blair reported that the "the greater part" of 2,005 completed shirts were sewn by the members of the association.

"I am to thank you, in behalf of the Army," Washington responded, "for the trouble you have taken in prosecuting the very benevolent business begun by the late worthy and amiable Mrs Reed . . ."

In December, Benjamin Franklin's daughter, Sarah Franklin Bache, arranged to have the shirts delivered to Washington.

President of Pennsylvania Joseph Reed mourned the loss of his wife. "I never knew how much I loved her," he later wrote his brother-in-law Dennis, "till I lost her for ever. I have sought resignation of philosophy and religion. I have endeavoured to reason myself into a proper submission to the Divine Will, but with little success. I must have the aid of time to feel as I ought to feel."

Esther's "sentiments" would live on. How could they not? In a single essay, she captured what so many women on both sides of the conflict felt: both hope and determination.

"Though the whole country was open to the enemy," the South Carolinian Eliza Wilkinson wrote, "nothing but women and children left unprotected at home; husbands, fathers, brothers, friends, and countrymen far away, where we could not have the least information of them; yet we did not wholly despond, we trusted in more than feeble flesh and blood, and, though our troubles were great, our dependence was not in vain."

CHAPTER 20

Freedom's Wake

Four miles.

Four miles to freedom.

Elizabeth put one foot in front of the other as she marched from the home of her enslaver, Colonel John Ashley, to the town of Sheffield, Massachusetts. She had set out to gain what she had long wanted and might now be able to achieve—if she could enlist the right help.

Her destination was the home of local lawyer Theodore Sedgwick. She had long seen his face in the Ashley parlor and might have recalled a night, years earlier, before open war was upon the colonies, when Sedgwick and others had gathered in the Ashley home to discuss the Sheffield Resolves. But now things were different.

The Articles of Confederation—a document of governance for the United States prior to the U.S. Constitution—went into full effect on March 1, 1781. However, individual states had also begun rewriting their charters to reflect the (hopefully) coming dawn of this new republic, including laws regarding slavery.

On March 1, 1780, the Fifth Pennsylvania General Assembly had passed "An Act for the Gradual Abolition of Slavery." This did not ban slavery outright. If you were enslaved before March 1, 1780, you would remain so. However, the act provided for an incremental approach to abolition.

The Commonwealth of Massachusetts ratified its constitution on June 15, 1780, which had direct bearing on Elizabeth's enslavement.

"Part the First: A Declaration of the Rights of the Inhabitants of the Commonwealth of Massachusetts" consisted of thirty articles. The first of those read:

> *Article I. All men are born free and equal and have certain natural, essential, and unalienable rights; among which may be reckoned the right of enjoying and defending their lives and liberties; that of acquiring, possessing, and protecting property; in fine, that of seeking and obtaining their safety and happiness.*

Elizabeth kept walking, each step nearer, she hoped, to freedom. When she arrived at the Sedgwick home she had a simple message for the lawyer, recalling the documents that preceded—and perhaps inspired—the Massachusetts Constitution: the Declaration of Independence.

"I heard that paper read yesterday that says 'all men are born equal—& that every man has a right to freedom,'" she later told Catharine Sedgwick. "I am not a dumb Critter, won't the law give me my freedom?"

Elizabeth was Black and a woman—two factors of her existence that prevented her *direct* participation in the legal system at the time. But Sedgwick believed she had the law on her side. He agreed to take on not only Elizabeth's case but also that of Brom, an enslaved man who was also working in the Ashley household. Who could say? The case might well test whether this newly adopted Massachusetts Constitution did, in word and in practice, render slavery in that state illegal.

Phillis Wheatley Peters, too, was finding her life embroiled in the judicial system. In 1780, two years into their marriage, Phillis and her husband, John Peters, moved to Middleton, Massachusetts, and the house of Naomi Wilkins. John had once been enslaved to John Wilkins, Naomi's husband, who had died. Naomi needed help running her farm and, seeing an opportunity, John and Phillis moved in. Whatever Wilkins was able to grow, John would bring to market. John was very clear—to both Naomi and her enslaved servant, Dinah—that Phillis was not to do any work whatsoever. Within mere months, disagreements over who was in charge surfaced and tensions grew. After several disagreements and altercations, each alleged they did not feel safe living with the other. Naomi Wilkins sued to have John and Phillis evicted from the property. The legal proceedings would drag on several years, during which time Phillis's health continued to worsen.

Elsewhere on the Eastern Seaboard, the onset of 1781 saw mixed results for the Continental Army: the Pennsylvania and New Jersey lines "mutinied" (primarily over the minuscule pay being offered new recruits), while the South continued to prove problematic for the British.

General Nathanael Greene had taken over command of the Southern Department from General Horatio Gates on October 14, 1780. Shortly thereafter, Greene learned that Benedict Arnold—now a brigadier general with the *British* Army—had departed New York with 1,600 troops and was headed to Virginia.

Both sides knew they would face harsh conditions in the South. Because of this, Greene's wife, Kitty, did not follow her husband on this assignment.

"You have no idea of the distress and misery that prevails in this quarter," Nathanael wrote Kitty.

Greene had been effective at thwarting General Cornwallis's attempt to exert control over the Carolinas beyond British-held Charles Town. On January 17, Continental and militia forces under the command of General Daniel Morgan handed the Crown perhaps its worst loss since Saratoga when they defeated British forces under the formidable Lieutenant Colonel Banastre Tarleton at the Battle of Cowpens in South Carolina. About 1,200 British soldiers went into that battle; only about two hundred escaped to fight another day.

As the military wild-goose chase continued through the Carolinas, Greene, whose forces were outnumbered, divided his troops, eluded Cornwallis, and took full advantage of the militia and women who helped form part of the "back-country" resistance that so vexed the British leader.

Greene outmaneuvered Cornwallis through March. Though the British may have technically "won" the Battle of Guilford Court House in what is now Greensboro, North Carolina, their losses were so intense that continuing their operations in the Carolinas became untenable.

Cornwallis limped to Wilmington, North Carolina, his sights set on returning to Virginia. Greene set out to take control of any remaining loyalist outposts, including the fortified Star Fort at Ninety Six, South Carolina. An established district about sixty miles south of the present-day Greenville-Spartanburg area, Ninety Six was a trading post along the long-established Cherokee trading paths on the western frontier of South Carolina and the site of the first land battle in the southern colonies in 1775. Throughout the South, women and guerrilla warfare continued to play an important part in Continental outcomes. A guide and scout by the name of Kate Barry had helped General Morgan by riding through the countryside, enlisting volunteers, paving the way for the American victory at Cowpens. And in the town of Ninety Six, women were about to take a page from the Prudence Wright playbook.

A widow named Elizabeth Martin had seen seven sons out of her nine children enlist to fight with the Americans. During the ongoing war, Elizabeth and two of her daughters-in-law, Grace and Rachel, supported the patriot cause by nursing Continental soldiers and offering their home as a place for wounded men to recover. The British decided to avail themselves of the food and shelter found at the Martin home as well—whether the Martin women liked it or not. However, the inconvenience of these intruders also brought with it access to information.

In May 1781, the Martin women learned that a British courier would soon be passing through their neighborhood. Grace and Rachel donned their husbands' clothes, grabbed their guns, and staked out a crossroads where they suspected the courier would have to pass. When the courier and his guards approached, Rachel and Grace ambushed them, held them at gunpoint, and stole their documents.

Elizabeth remained home—and thus above suspicion. The ambushed soldiers stopped in, seeking refuge with her after being attacked by "two men." The British soldiers stayed the night, while their confiscated documents made their way to General Nathanael Greene. And from May 22 to June 18, 1781, in part due to the efforts of the Martin women, Ninety Six was the site of a successful siege on the part of the Americans, as Greene continued his back-country blazing. Though Greene was forced to retreat from Ninety Six, two of his officers managed to retake Augusta, Georgia, in the same month.

While the Carolinas saw their fair share of action, the locus of war shifted to Virginia as summer approached. When Cornwallis and the British headed north toward the Chesapeake Bay, the British ship *Savage* moved up the Potomac, attracting more people who sought to escape enslavement by fleeing to the purported protection of the British. In April 1781, Washington's cousin Lund Washington wrote a memo including a "List of General Washington's negroes that went to the British." It included names and descriptions of each individual's perceived value to the plantation at Mount Vernon. Peter, Lewis, Frank, and Frederick were all described as "old man." Two male escapees were about forty-five years of age, one "an Overseer and Valuable Gunner," the other a "man . . . valuable, a Brickmaker Harry." Forty-year-old "Horseler" Tom was also regarded as "valuable," while other younger men, like Sambo and Thomas, were summarized simply as "stout and healthy." The list included farmhands, house servants, coopers, and weavers. Among them was also Deborah, "a Woman about 16 years Old."

"The above Slaves were taken from his Excellency General Washington by Captn Richd Graves in the *Savage* Sloop of War," the document read. Some were eventually "recovered" in different cities. Lund Washington supervised the operations at Mount Vernon while the general was away and took it upon himself to hunt down those who had escaped. This led to some unorthodox transactions that one would not expect from a family member of a commanding general fighting against the British. For example, in exchange for Deborah and the others who had escaped, Lund offered supplies to the British aboard the *Savage*. The British happily accepted the supplies but then refused to surrender the enslaved escapees. Word of Lund's transactions with the enemy became the news of the day, something George Washington would later term "exceedingly ill-judged."

But it was not as if the British were prepared to welcome these newcomers. The threat—or the reality—of starvation, illness, and smallpox outbreaks awaited all enslaved people who escaped and made it through to British lines. Deborah, just sixteen, fought to persevere, hoping to make her way to New York and lasting freedom. "The number of Negroes that attend this Corps," Cornwallis complained, "is a most serious distress to us."

Cornwallis arrived at Petersburg, Virginia, on May 20, joining the troops of Major General William Phillips, who had died of illness seven days earlier. Cornwallis marched north through New Castle and Hanover and west toward Thomas Jefferson's home of Monticello. (During the British raid on Charlottesville, Jefferson narrowly eluded capture.) Cornwallis followed the James River southeast through Richmond, eventually making his way through the former British stronghold of Williamsburg, determined to restore Virginia to Crown rule. But by July 4 he had evacuated Williamsburg and was again on the move.

The Marquis de Lafayette, who had been in Virginia for several months, was tasked with pursuing and harassing Cornwallis until Continental reinforcements could arrive. His dogged pursuit prompted Cornwallis to evacuate the Virginia capital. Cornwallis crossed the James once again, eventually arriving outside Portsmouth on July 12. At General Clinton's behest, Cornwallis soon concentrated his troops farther north, closer to Yorktown. He and his troops encamped at Old Point Comfort, the tip of a peninsula sitting to the south of what is now Hampton, Virginia, directly across from the Willoughby Spit, the site of Mary's former enslavement.

A Virginia man named James was making a careful study of these British movements. James lived in New Kent County, where he was enslaved to a planter and merchant named William Armistead. Between 5,000 and 8,000 Black soldiers served with the Continental forces and militia during the American Revolution; James hoped to join them. Armistead gave his consent but took pains to explain that he was not freeing James. When the war was over, James was to return to his enslavement, where he served as Armistead's manservant. Neither man could have foreseen how this situation would transform James into a valued asset to both the Americans *and* the British.

As a Black man seeking freedom and a Virginian who knew the lay of the local land, James seemed an ideal fit for *British* service. In fact, the Marquis de Lafayette was banking on it. He dispatched James to the British headquarters, where Cornwallis and the turncoat Benedict Arnold quickly perceived James's usefulness as a guide. But they never viewed him as a threat. And so James found himself privy to discussions of British strategies and plans. Benedict Arnold tasked James with guiding British troops through Virginia, which gave him insight into their movements and supplies. Shortly after, the British gave James yet another task: to spy on Lafayette. Lafayette had anticipated this, of course. In addition to receiving the intel that James had gathered during his time in the British encampment, the marquis used James to feed *false* information to Arnold and Cornwallis. In this way James became one of the nation's first double agents.

Intelligence provided by James on July 31, 1781, proved especially invaluable. When Cornwallis and his nearly 10,000 troops decamped from Portsmouth heading north to Yorktown, arriving August 1, the Marquis de Lafayette had a strategically crucial heads-up.

Though the focus of the war had shifted northward, troubles continued to plague those in the Carolinas, especially the Cherokee. On July 26, 1781, the second Treaty of Long Island of Holston saw previous land cessions confirmed and additional Cherokee territory yielded. Nanye'hi pleaded for reconciliation with representatives of the frontier settlements and Virginia.

"Our cry is all for peace; let it continue," Nanye'hi told the settlers gathered at the meeting, John Sevier among them. "This peace must last forever. Let your women's sons be ours; our sons be yours. Let your women hear our words."

"Mother: We have listened well to your talk," Colonel William Christian, member of the Virginia Senate, replied. "No man can hear it without being moved by it . . . Our women shall hear your words . . . We are all descendants of the same woman. We will not quarrel with you, because you are our mothers. We will not meddle with your people if they will be still and quiet at home and let us live in peace."

It made little difference. The Cherokee were now forced to cede their lands north of the Nolichucky River. This was less than the amount of land originally insisted upon by Colonel Christian and other commissioners, but it nevertheless added to the exorbitant losses already felt by the Native Americans at the hands of the settlers. Nanye'hi's cousin Dragging Canoe and the Chickamauga refused to recognize the terms of the treaty.

With advance notice of British movements on their side, Washington's team took little time hammering out a plan. On September 14, Washington and Comte de Rochambeau, who had quietly left New York at the end of August with a small contingent of forces, met Lafayette in Williamsburg. Meanwhile, the French rear admiral Comte de Grasse was arriving from the West Indies with twenty-eight ships and a force of 3,000 troops, tasked with keeping any Royal Navy reinforcements locked in Chesapeake Bay. With his troops blocking the escape route west and inland, the Marquis de Lafayette felt certain that Cornwallis would be trapped. Everything was in place, and on September 28 the Siege of Yorktown began. It would last three weeks.

> *Honor commands great Washington I sing,*
> *The noble feat of Count deGrasse must ring,*
> *Who has Cornwallis now within his power,*
> *With all his Army in an evildoer.*
> *Brave Greene I sing, with all the Patriot Sons,*
> *But most adore Great Godlike Washington;*
> *York-Town once more is freed from British chains,*
> *Rejoice America now Freedom reigns . . .*

This poem, "Spoken Extempore, by a Young Lady, on Hearing the Guns Firing and Bells Chiming on Account of . . . the Surrender of York-Town," was featured on a broadside alongside another bit of verse titled, "His Lordship Humbled: Or, Cornwallis's Lamentation."

The verse was not far off. With de Grasse holding the naval reinforcements at bay, Cornwallis's much-needed help was unable to reach him. Washington, heading a force that included twenty-nine ships and a French and American legion that numbered nearly 20,000, pounced on Cornwallis, who had merely 9,000 troops at his disposal on land and offshore and nowhere to run. On September 19, the British general surrendered roughly 7,000 troops on land alone, with more at sea to follow.

As for "now Freedom reigns," Continental forces gathered up Black men and women who had escaped to British lines and corralled them outside of Yorktown, where they were held under guard along the York River until they could be returned to their enslavers.

Mary Katharine Goddard's *Maryland Journal, and the Baltimore Advertiser* kept up with the news of the day—and then some—admirably, all while Goddard continued her somewhat thankless job of postmaster.

Time constraints and the stream of information—all of which had to be set in type by hand—sometimes led Goddard to include a sort of "to be continued" caveat for her readers at the ends of her articles. But even she could not resist reaching for the large-type letters that proclaimed the greatest news of all: "CORNWALLIS SURRENDERS."

"To give room to the important Dispatches of General Washington, we are obliged to omit, on this occasion, several Articles of Intelligence . . ." Goddard wrote in a late-October issue, which contained the extensive and exceedingly courteous back-and-forth correspondence between Washington and Cornwallis outlining the terms of the latter's surrender.

The news quickly piled up, with long litanies of materials seized from the vanquished army. Goddard ran Henry Knox's report of the "RETURN of Ordnance and Military Stores, Taken at York and Gloucester, in Virginia, by the Surrender of the British Army on the 19th of October 1781," which was a seemingly endless, itemized list that broke down British military possessions into such categories as Brass Ordnance, Iron Ordnance, Cartridge, Shot, Grape, Shells, Firearms, Regimental Standards (drums, fifes, flags, and more), and concluding finally with a list of tools for tradesmen and a quantity of tallow, presumably for candle making.

As news arrived in her Baltimore print shop of celebrations up and down the East Coast, Goddard shared them with her readership, noting, for example, spontaneous and riotous carousing in Philadelphia: "public Demonstrations of Joy . . . and in the evening every Part of the Town was illuminated in the highest taste and elegance."

But "taste and elegance" were clearly in the eye of the beholder, as evidenced by a letter mailed to Goddard by one reader who took issue with some of the reveling. Jubilation was to be expected, the author wrote, "but shall we shew forth this Joy and Gratitude by Excels of Debauchery, by Rioting, Madness and Folly? Shall we pour forth Libations of Wine, as though the Heathen God Bacchus, or Mars, had presided in the Day of Battle!—O my God! thou eternal Arbiter of Nations, can the People think this the proper Way to celebrate thy Praise! to shew their Gratitude to a holy, pure and righteous God!"

The answer in many corners of America, including Philadelphia, was a resounding "*Yes!*"

Taking to her diary, Elizabeth Drinker wrote, "Genl Cornwallace was taken; for which we grievously suffer'd on the 24th. by way of rejoyceing, a mob assembled about 7 o'clock or before, and continued their insults untill near 10." Any house that was not "illuminated" in commemoration of the victory suffered at the hands of revelers.

"Scarcely one Friends House escaped," she wrote, describing "near 70 panes of Glass broken, the sash lights and two panels of the front parlor broke in pieces—the Door crack'd and Violently burst open." The carousers also "threw Stones into the House for some time," and in some cases entered homes and destroyed belongings. "'Tis a mercy no lives were lost."

The new year brought the same old harassment. "Officials" arrived at the Drinker home with an order to search for British goods, "which they accordingly did, examining draws, Trunks and Closets, Presses &c." Henry Drinker, now a free man attempting to rebuild his business, came home and ordered them to leave. When the intruders produced the order giving them the right to search the premises, they realized they in fact had arrived at the home of the wrong Drinker.

"'Tis a bad Gouvernment, under which we are liable to have our

Houses searchd and every thing laid open to ignorant fellows prehaps thieves . . ." Elizabeth noted.

Though Yorktown represented a monumental victory, the British still controlled Charles Town, Savannah, Wilmington, and New York City, where denial lodged in the hearts of the loyalist population.

In mid-November, Goddard printed that in New York City, which was still in the albeit tenuous grasp of the British, the New York newspapers had at last "confessed the surrender of Lord Cornwallis to be real" and "condescended" to reprint the articles of the general's capitulation in their entirety.

"The women are in tears, the soldiery in a panic, the merchants selling off their goods for much less than the . . . cost in Europe, the tories are in the utmost consternation, and Benedict Arnold himself, it is said, trembles like an aspen leaf."

Farther south, South Carolina had borne the brunt of late-stage wartime casualties, with an estimated 20 percent of all Revolutionary War deaths occurring on battlefields in that state between 1780 and 1781 alone. The guerrilla warfare tactics that had proved so advantageous for the Americans in rural areas beyond the southern port city spilled over into the day-to-day conflicts that arose during the ongoing British occupation, resulting in a disregard for any semblance of accepted "wartime decorum."

In and around Charles Town, the British were learning that maintaining control of a large city for an extended period of time, let alone its surroundings, was much more demanding than merely laying siege to one. Tempers and supplies ran short. Destruction and death, ransacking and pillaging—all were daily occurrences afflicting residents, especially women, who were fighting for survival regardless of who had surrendered to whom in Yorktown.

With many men still away, women were heads of their households. They lived in perpetual fear not only of destruction and theft of personal property but also of rape. Both sides of the conflict claimed perpetrators as well as victims. Though Congress had instructed women to report such crimes, very few did.

Women banded together whenever feasible, and independent businesswomen such as Eliza Pinckney, though perhaps possessing more resources, had much to lose personally and found themselves and their properties to be popular targets.

Eliza's sons, Thomas and Charles Cotesworth Pinckney, remained staunch defenders in the fight for independence. Thomas had been badly wounded at the Battle of Camden, nearly losing his leg. Eliza had offered to go to look after him but chose to send two enslaved men in her stead.

Meanwhile, Charles Cotesworth had been taken prisoner shortly after the Siege of Charles Town and was confined at both Haddrell's Point and his cousin Charles Pinckney's Snee Farm. When his infant son took ill while he was in British custody, he asked his science-minded mother, Eliza, who was quite adept at home remedies, to care for him. That she did, but it was not enough: Charles Cotesworth Jr. died in 1781 while under Eliza's care.

That summer, both sons and several hundred other pro-American Charlestonians were freed but exiled to Philadelphia to keep them from taking up arms against the British occupiers. A total of 570 individuals fled by year's end. Eliza's sons took their wives and children with them. Eliza opted to stay behind with her daughter, Harriot, whose husband, Daniel Horry, had denounced his allegiance to the patriot cause and was therefore spared much of the theft and abuse the British could have inflicted upon his property. This also meant that Eliza had a place to stay, and so she joined the couple at Hampton Plantation. The British had ousted her from her home in the city and seized her Belmont plantation, running off with cattle, furniture, jewelry, and more. The countryside was desolate, burnt, and littered with debris and the decomposing bodies of humans and livestock.

Though the Siege of Yorktown was not the end of hostilities, the British fled North Carolina in January 1782 and pulled out of Savannah in July. Replacing thousands of troops surrendered by Cornwallis would have been near impossible, and the dragging on of the war was costing the Crown money—wrenched from an increasingly impatient populace in the form of taxes.

Yet, with no treaty, there was no true peace. As such, in 1782, a woman named Deborah Sampson saw an opportunity to support the American cause. Disguising herself as a man, she enlisted as "Robert Shurtleff" and on May 23 enrolled in the 4th Massachusetts Regiment, joining other women in uniform who had gone before her, and countless camp followers and women of the army who served in their own, very necessary way. Sampson was involved in the skirmishes characteristic of those unpredictable final months of the war that saw the British surrender but still not fully evacuate from the colonies. Sharp and well-read, despite little formal schooling, Sampson served as a member of the Light Infantry, an elite corps whose members acted as scouts and rangers. (As such, they traveled "light.")

Her corps operated on the eastern side of the Hudson River, in the Westchester area of New York. The region was ostensibly divided into three parts: the American (and French) zone, the British zone, and a kind of neutral ground in between. Complicating this mix were Dutch civilians and Tories, whom Continental troops feared might betray their movements to any lurking British guerrillas. During this time, Sampson was reportedly wounded.

That October 1782, General Washington established the Continental Army's winter cantonment near New Windsor, New York. An estimated 7,500 soldiers as well as five hundred camp followers were encamped there for the winter, and Sampson was among them. Six to eight soldiers lived together in huts. However, Sampson managed to secure a post as a "waiter," a personal valet of sorts, to General John Paterson. This helped her to avoid the kind of physical scrutiny that went along with sharing such cramped quarters with other men . . . for a time.

The same month Sampson found herself concealing her gender in camp at New Windsor, another individual found their unconventional appearance in the public eye.

". . . and some days past Jemima Wilkingson left this Town," Elizabeth Drinker wrote in her diary, "a woman lately from New-England who has occasiond much talk in this City—she, and those that accompany'd her (who were call'd her Deciples) resided some short time in Elfriths-Ally . . ."

The Friend and several members of the growing Society of Universal Friends had made their way to Philadelphia, having continued to spread the gospel throughout southern New England. They often preached outdoors or in meetinghouses lent to them by sympathetic groups, among them Free or "Fighting" Quakers. In Philadelphia, the reception was decidedly mixed, and finding a place to stay proved challenging. The Friend and their small group did stay in Elfreth's Alley, lodging with a widow. A crowd tracked the group down and pelted the home with stones and bricks, prompting them to find other accommodations.

But the crowds turned out to hear the Friend speak as well, as Drinker noted: "The crowds went to hear her preach and afterward in the Methodist meeting-House—her Dress and Behavior, remarkable."

But remarkable, too, were the Friend's oratory skills.

François, Marquis de Barbé-Marbois, secretary of the French delegation to the United States, attended and later described the Friend's speaking with "ease and facility" and was awed by their address to the bustling crowd. "She enunciated so clearly, though without elegance," Barbé-Marbois mused, "that I think she was reciting a prepared sermon, and it was difficult for me to believe that she was speaking from inspiration, or as the worldly say, extemporaneously?"

What is considered to be the final battle of the Revolutionary War was fought in November of 1782. Patriots attacked a Shawnee village, clashing with Native American and loyalist fighters in what is now Ohio. Later that month, the United States signed a preliminary peace treaty with the British. The evacuation of Charles Town was imminent.

As a new nation began to take shape, some Black residents opted to place their trust in the courts instead of the British to obtain their freedom. In May of 1781, Theodore Sedgwick and Tapping Reeve had brought Elizabeth and Brom's suit to trial: *Brom & Bett v. J. Ashley Esq.* Court records state that Colonel Ashley considered Brom and Elizabeth to be his "servants for life" and wanted the case dismissed. The jury thought differently. Foreman Jonathan Holcomb and the rest of the jury decided that Elizabeth and Brom "are not and were not . . .

the legal Negro servants of him the said John Ashley during life . . ." The court awarded Elizabeth and Brom "thirty shillings lawful silver Money, Damages, and the Costs of this suit Paned at five pounds fourteen shillings and four pence . . ."

The tide had turned; the case of Elizabeth and Brom was not the only freedom suit being argued in the commonwealth. Ashley appealed the decision but soon caved, offering to keep Elizabeth on as a paid domestic servant. Elizabeth declined. She was ready to move on and chose a surname befitting her new phase of life: Freeman.

She went instead to work for the Sedgwick family. The Sedgwick children called her "Mumbet." Catharine Sedgwick wrote that the name "Elizabeth" had "transmuted to 'Betty,'—& afterwards contracted by lisping lips from Mammy Bet—to Mum-Bet, by which name she was best known." This term of endearment was used by those seven siblings who grew quite close to Elizabeth as their own mother, Pamela, grew increasingly ill both physically and mentally. (Today, she might have been diagnosed as being on the bipolar spectrum.) When Theodore Sedgwick's duties kept him away from home, Elizabeth kept an eye on the children and the property.

Farther east, in Cambridge, the year 1781 saw Tony and Cuba continuing to work the land abandoned in 1775 by their enslavers, the Vassalls, when George Washington took over the home and used it as his headquarters. In light of Cornwallis's surrender and the Massachusetts Constitution, Tony and Cuba petitioned the commonwealth to be permitted to remain in the home they had cared for for eight years now.

In their petition, Tony wrote that the sixty years they had spent enslaved to both the Royall and Vassall families left them "deprived of what makes them now happy beyond expression . . ." Yet they had, he noted, "lived a life of honesty and have been faithful in their master's service."

To that end, he argued, the pair "shall not be denied the sweets of freedom the remainder of their days by being reduced to the painful necessity of begging for bread."

And while the commonwealth denied Tony's request for the Vassall house, it did award him a pension. The pair continued to work the land as they had for years, maintaining at least a little bit of what rendered their lives "happy beyond expression."

These were the success stories, such as they were. The route to freedom remained uncertain for the scores of Black men and women in Charles Town who had gone over to the British lines. Among those awaiting their fate were Harry Washington and Judith Jackson, who had both been working for the Royal Artillery in New York, and traveled with them to the Low Country. Being in South Carolina, they therefore escaped the fate suffered by the formerly enslaved men and women who were collected like property by the Americans after the Siege of Yorktown. However, it remained unclear what would happen to them and others in their situation as Charles Town returned to American control.

Throughout the new American states, loyalist reactions ranged from disbelief to despair.

"Notwithstanding all our Misfortunes, Great Britain can never, must never relinquish America," Charles Town loyalist John Hamilton insisted in a letter to a friend in England. "The last man and shilling must be expended before she gives America her independence . . . [I]f not, and America is given up, Britain must become a Province of France and America."

Hamilton would join thousands fleeing Charles Town at the end of the year. By the time the evacuation of Charles Town ended, on December 14, 1782, roughly 4,200 loyalists and 5,000 Black residents left aboard an estimated 130 Royal Navy ships.

One British officer observed that those who remained in Charles Town after the evacuation were in a terrible state. He described "old grey-headed men and women" roaming the streets alongside large families and the widows of those who had fought for the British, "with a half a dozen half-starved buntings tangling at their skirts . . ."

"The rebels, like so many furies, or rather devils, entered the town and a scene ensued," he wrote, calling the whole ordeal "shocking to the ears of humanity." Loyalists were ejected from their homes, imprisoned, whipped, tarred and feathered, paraded through town, and hanged. The horrors of war did not discriminate.

On Christmas Eve 1782, Mary Katharine Goddard's paper reported that the remaining evacuees—primarily Hessians and loyalists—had arrived at New York and were sent to Queen's County, across the East River, "where they are to linger out a dreary winter of cold and hunger."

The evacuation of Charles Town led inevitably to the much larger one to follow in New York City.

The mood on the island of Manhattan over the roughly six months that had elapsed during the British evacuation of New York was a tense one, no matter whose flag you waved. "The mob now reigns," one loyalist wrote of the situation.

Even before the final ships pulled out of Gadsden's Wharf in Charles Town destined for New York, enslavers were jockeying for the return of what they considered to be their "property."

Still in New York since arriving with Dunmore's fleet, Mary had married a man named Caesar Perth. On August 30, 1782, Virginia governor Benjamin Harrison wrote to the delegates of that state that Mary's former enslaver, John Willoughby, claimed to have knowledge of privateers in New York kidnapping Black loyalists and sending them to the West Indies. Soon, the delegates were told, Willoughby worried "there would be very few left in N. York," and asked, "Can no step be taken to put a Stop to the practice . . ."

Harrison, a signer of the Declaration of Independence and a planter himself, added that Willoughby "had had ninety [enslaved men and women] taken from him and is thereby ruin'd." Willoughby wanted to know what Congress planned to do about it.

Less than two weeks later, on September 10, 1782, James Madison presented the issue to Congress, writing, "Some prisoners return'd from New York have enfused an Opinion into the Heads of our people that their Negros carried away by the Enemy may be obtain'd from Sir Guy Carleton."

Sir Guy Carleton, 1st Baron of Dorchester and commander in chief of the British forces in America, was overseeing the British evacuation of New York, which would be accomplished with a fleet of ships destined for England, Germany, Nova Scotia, Jamaica, and the Bahamas.

The United States and Britain set out the terms of this massive undertaking. One of the key issues to be settled was "the setting at Liberty the Prisoners, the receiving Possession of the Posts occupied by the British Troops and the obtaining [of] the delivery of all Negroes and other Property of the Inhabitants of these States in the Possession of the Forces or Subjects of or adherents to his Britannic Majesty."

George Washington personally requested that Carleton locate any enslaved people who had escaped from Mount Vernon or from any members of his extended family and instructed him to privately imprison them until such time as they could be recovered and transported back to Virginia.

That included the young woman named Deborah. After Deborah had emancipated herself from bondage at Mount Vernon at the age of sixteen, she made her way north to New York City. There she met and married a man named Harry Squash. In addition to the thousands of Black men and women like them already living in New York City, thousands more were arriving from points south.

Mary Perth, Harry Washington, and Judith Jackson now awaited their fates in New York as planters and others from throughout the southern states descended on Manhattan, seeking to reclaim their human property.

"The horrors and devastation of war happily terminated . . . issued universal joy among all parties, except us, who had escaped from slavery, and taken refuge in the English army," the formerly enslaved man Boston King later shared, "for a report prevailed at New-York, that all slaves . . . were to be delivered up to their masters, although some of them had been three or four years among the English. This dreadful rumour filled us all with inexpressible anguish and terror, especially when we saw our masters coming from Virginia, North-Carolina, and other parts, and seizing upon their slaves in the streets of New-York, or even dragging them out of their beds."

Though Congress directed the British to leave and do so without destruction or "carrying away any Negroes," Carleton felt that returning those who had sought freedom behind British lines back to a life of enslavement would represent a serious breach of the Crown's word. He offered a compromise:

Any Black individuals seeking passage aboard ships bound for Nova Scotia or elsewhere had to prove they had been in the service of the British for at least one year. If they had, the Crown would compensate their enslavers. If not, the refugees would be returned to their life of bondage.

Deborah and Harry Squash, Judith Jackson, Harry Washington and his wife, Jenny, Mary Perth, her children, and her husband, Caesar, along with thousands of others would have to submit to an interview process by which the British would determine whether they met the criteria for evacuating along with white loyalists. The resulting record of those permitted to depart and, in some cases, the claims of their former enslavers, came to be known as the "Book of Negroes."

The British and the United States governments each kept their own records. The British version, which contained 3,009 names, was called the "Inspection Roll of Negroes" and listed ships, destinations, and the names of passengers. Passenger descriptions included ages, family members, distinguishing physical traits, and former enslavers.

This is how we know that on April 27, 1783, the ship *Polly*, commanded by John Broome, was bound for Port Roseway in Nova Scotia, carrying aboard "Harry Squash, 22, stout . . . Deborah, his Wife, 20, with thick lips, pock mark'd." Next to Deborah's name, the logbook reads: "Formerly Slave to Gen. Washington, came away about 4 years ago . . ."

On July 31, 1783, the ship *L'abondance* claimed among its passengers Harry Washington, "a stout fellow," also formerly enslaved to George Washington. Also aboard that same ship was the preacher of the Dismal Swamp, "Mary Perth. 43. Stout Wench. Formerly the property of John Willoughby of Norfolk Virginia. Left him seven years ago." At the time she left American shores forever, Mary had her husband, Caesar, and three daughters with her.

As fall arrived, the evacuation continued apace. On September 3, 1783, America and Britain finally signed the Treaty of Paris, which established the United States as bordered by the Atlantic Ocean, the Mississippi River, the Great Lakes, and Florida. Even on a continent as vast as North America, the new nation was surrounded. The British sat to the north, the Spanish to the south and west. On September 26, King

George III issued a proclamation stating that a "Definitive Treaty of Peace and Friendship . . ." would be observed "by sea as land and in all places whatsoever; strictly charging and commanding all Our loving subjects to take notice hereof, and conform themselves thereunto accordingly . . ."

The proclamation reproduced in Goddard's newspaper concluded, "GOD save the KING."

That fall, fifty-three-year-old Judith Jackson and her ten-year-old daughter finally made it aboard a ship bound for Nova Scotia. They waited to depart for their new country and their new life.

And waited.

And waited.

Then officers forced Judith and her child to disembark.

It turned out that a white man named Jonathan Eilbeck had shown up in Manhattan claiming that he had purchased Judith and her ten-year-old from his brother-in-law, John MacLean. Judith disagreed. She defended her right to depart in front of a board of inquiry that had been established to review cases precisely like hers. The board met at the Fraunces Tavern in Manhattan—itself owned and run by a nonwhite entrepreneur. Judith had worked for the British for nearly four years, she argued, and had legitimately received a pass to set sail for Nova Scotia.

As ships continued to depart from Manhattan, Judith's case dragged on. In the month that elapsed, Eilbeck tried to take matters into his own hands and attempted to take her by force. Judith added this abuse to her case, claiming that Eilbeck had taken her child and stolen her clothes and her money. Despite this, Sir Carleton found in Eilbeck's favor.

But that wasn't the end of the story.

Somehow, some way, Judith made it into the Book of Negroes, which reveals that she departed the new United States aboard the ship *Ranger*—one of the last ships leaving for Nova Scotia—on November 30, 1783. Her child, however, did not.

Judith Jackson, Mary Perth, Harry Washington, Deborah and Harry Squash, and many others opened a new chapter of their lives in

Birchtown, a Nova Scotia community created specifically for the incoming population of Black men and women arriving from the United States. Though their circumstances were different in Birchtown compared to the United States, difficulties prevailed.

Some departing loyalists brought their enslaved individuals with them, prolonging the very treatment Black Americans had sought to escape by throwing their lot in with the British. Within ten years, many Black men, women, and children would find themselves on yet another ship, bound across the Atlantic to the African continent, which they or their ancestors once called home.

In early December, Mary Katharine Goddard announced to her readers that on November 25, 1783, troops under General Henry Knox's command "took Possession of the City of New-York; after which their Excellencies General Washington and Governor Clinton, made their public Entry into the City."

"Decency and decorum" were expected of "all ranks of people. They will naturally view him with that pleasing wonder, and heart-felt sincerity, which must expand the human mind on the appearance of a Hero returning crowned with laurels . . ."

Evacuation day had arrived, but challenges for independence remained.

Two years earlier, in 1781, the white merchant Isaac Royall had died of smallpox. He left the enslaved woman Belinda £30 in his will. Belinda's whereabouts between the time Royall fled Medford, Massachusetts, and 1781 are unknown. However, she appeared in Massachusetts to petition the Commonwealth of Massachusetts to receive Royall's bequest. Her first attempt was unsuccessful. In 1783, she renewed her plea.

"Fifty years her faithful hands have been compelled to ignoble servitude for the benefit of an Isaac Royall, untill . . . the present war was Commenced," she remarked in her plea. After "the terror of men armed in the Cause of freedom, compelled her master to fly," her petition explained, "and to breathe away his Life in a Land, where, Lawless domination sits enthroned—pouring bloody outrage and cruelty on all who dare to be free.

"The face of your Petitioner, is now marked with the furrows of time, and her frame feebly bending under the oppression of years, while she, by the Laws of the Land, is denied the enjoyment of one morsel of that immense wealth, apart whereof hath been accumilated by her own industry, and the whole augmented by her servitude."

She was "casting herself at the feet of your honours," she added, "that such allowance may be made her out of the estate of Colonel Royall, as will prevent her and her more infirm daughter from misery in the greatest extreme, and scatter comfort over the short and downward path of their Lives—and she will ever Pray."

Belinda Sutton, as later records would accurately name her, prevailed in the courts. But she and countless others faced the uncertainty of a new era. The war tainted the lives of formerly enslaved men and women who had self-emancipated and gone to the British. It hung over the futures of Indigenous peoples who had sought alliances with both sides in order to preserve possession of lands that, despite their sacrifices or allegiance, were rapidly disappearing. Uncertainty marked the lives of women who had lost spouses, children, businesses, and homes, who had gone to battle themselves or supported the war by nursing, housing, and feeding troops, and had yet to see a dime of financial compensation.

From outside the newly established borders of the United States, and with the distance provided by the passage of time, the world looked quite different. The view of events and those who contributed to them were shrouded by years of recorded or unrecorded history. Everything and nothing had changed, depending on one's lens. Monumental shifts are incremental in their making. The quiet, invaluable contributions of the countless unsung enable the successes of the noted few. British or "American." Indigenous, Black or white, male or female. In words and action and spirit, they brought their best to the day at hand with no thought, for better or for worse, as to how the future would—*if* it would—remember them for it. The next fight always loomed, the battlefield yet to be defined. In a world of uncertainty, the deeds of the unwavering and steadfast emerged, unexpected, like the North Star piercing a clouded night sky, fixed and ever true.

Legacy of Obstinacy

A corpulent, lederhosen-clad, fork-wielding Augustus Gloop stares out from a neon screen of a slot machine, giving the side-eye to whoever passes. "I feel sorry for Wonka," his psychedelic speech bubble proclaims. "It's gonna cost him a fortune in fudge." The occasional shriek of delight punctuates a pervasive din of bells and clangs and chatter. I wander a windowless, clock-free, circuitous route, constantly feeling as though I am right back where I started. That is the goal of the casino floor: keep you here, keep you spinning, keep you spending, wandering, seeking, languishing.

On my first trip to Cherokee, North Carolina, I stay at the Harrah's Cherokee Casino Resort, but I did not come here to gamble. I am here in search of the legacy of one of the more familiar Native American women of the colonial era. I am here looking for Nanye'hi, also known as Nancy Ward.

Despite her playing a pivotal—and controversial—role in the Revolutionary War, mentions of Ward are fewer and further between than I initially anticipated. I keep looking, betting that around the next bend I might see some kind of sign or remembrance. But my road trip slots keep coming up lemons.

Leaving the casino, I head down one of the town's main drags, passing Tribal Pawn and Gun, Tomahawk Mini Mall, Medicine Man Crafts, and a roadside carnival in a parking lot. The Oconaluftee River gurgles alongside this stretch of road, full of visitors and locals seeking respite from the blazing sun. Nearby are the Cherokee Veterans Park, the Bureau of

Indian Affairs, and the Yellow Hill Tribal Council. Sitting beyond and above it all, looming and smoky, are the mountains, fixtures of permanence and a contrasting backdrop to the shapeshifting times far beneath their peaks.

This is the Qualla Boundary, which is not a reservation but rather land owned by, and held in trust for, the Eastern Band of Cherokee Indians (EBCI). This nation remains tied to these mountains despite efforts to remove it. From 1830 until about 1850, when the Trail of Tears forced thousands of Native Americans from their lands in the East to reservations in the West, there were those who chose to resist the U.S. government's forced displacement plan and who sought refuge in the Appalachian Mountains. These survivors were the ancestors of the modern EBCI, which now numbers upward of 13,000 registered members. It is a community committed to preserving and growing its culture, a community discovering ways to thrive and move forward while respecting and celebrating its past. Somewhere between and among the crap tables, the tourist traps, and the historical interpretations lies an authenticity about what it takes for culture to endure.

Street signs and shop names here make countless references to Tsali, the Cherokee leader who led the resistance to Cherokee removal in the early 1800s, and to Sequoyah, who devised the Cherokee syllabary, a written communication system in which symbols represent sounds or syllables. Tsali's story and the story of the Trail of Tears is presented in *Unto These Hills*, a historical outdoor theater performance of story, dance, and song that has run like clockwork for more than seventy-five years. The Cherokee syllabary is present throughout town on everything from diner menus to the welcome signage of the local Ace Hardware.

What I do *not* see as I drive through town are any references to Nancy Ward, until I visit the Museum of the Cherokee People. Located on Tsali Boulevard, the museum sits adjacent to the Qualla Arts and Crafts Mutual co-op, which shares traditional Cherokee arts as practiced today and an opportunity to see (and purchase) art produced by local weavers, woodworkers, metalsmiths, visual artists, and other crafters, many of whom employ techniques that have been used for thousands of years.

The museum presents more than 10,000 years of history through art, lore, historical artifacts, and stories of conflict. It is here, among the panels pertaining to the American Revolution, that I find mention of Nanye'hi.

The "Pocahontas of the West" is a phrase sometimes associated with Nanye'hi, stemming from the choices she made to aid the colonists who settled on Cherokee land, choices that cemented her in history as a friend of the patriot cause. The museum highlights the differences between Nanye'hi and her cousin Tsi yu Gansi ni, or Dragging Canoe, who fought against ongoing incursions onto Cherokee land. Nanye'hi may remain a popular part of the anti-Crown narrative of the American Revolution embraced by Americans, but her approach to seeking a peaceful existence with white settlers is still not embraced by all Cherokee today . . . if they think of her at all.

———

For a look at what life was like in a Cherokee community prior to the people's near eradication, I visit Oconaluftee Village, a "living" exhibit that offers a feel for life in a Cherokee village in the 1750s. Paths lead through and among structures in this wooded area, where docents and volunteers provide a look at how the Cherokee lived, worked, ate, traded, and governed. There are no tepees, as docents are quick to point out, seeking to dispel the popular culture notion that *all* native communities once resided in the manner presented during the golden age of western films in America from roughly 1940 to 1960.

My favorite structure is the medicine hut, partially embedded in the earth, its roof covered with healing plants. Of all medicinal plants grown in the United States, more than two-thirds of them come from Southern Appalachia—the "seed cradle of the continent." Plants such as bloodroot could be made into a tea to treat blood pressure and ulcers, used to create salves for ringworm, and employed as a cauterizing agent. Yellow root was better for sore throats, hemorrhoids, and blood tonics. The roof of the medicine hut is a verdant and inviting reminder of what modern-day, eco-friendly folk might call a green roof.

I pass the better part of a morning in the village, listening as docents present history, relate ceremonial and ritual practices, and describe everything from marriage to the Cherokee preparation for war. The guides stationed at the various interpretive structures are receptive to most questions, though at times they decline to respond to an inquiry, explaining that divulging certain aspects of their cultural practices requires the permission of a tribal elder.

Before leaving, I stop in the small gift shop to buy a book. As I reach into my wallet to pay, I see the face of Andrew Jackson—the American president most closely associated with the Trail of Tears—staring back at me from a $20 bill.

Heading back through town, I drive again past the Oconaluftee River, its shallows now populated with bathers. I am reminded of water as a means of purification for the Indigenous peoples. Water coming toward them, washing over them, continuing on behind them, an eternal flow of spiritual cleansing if one chooses to give oneself over to it.

Driving through town in search of a gas station, I spy a small strip mall alongside the road, backed up against an expanse of hilly green. The sign near the road advertises "Face Painting Here" and "INDIAN SHOWS Free Gift with Moccasin Purchase." A small timber-frame stage extends from the front of the row of stores into the parking lot, anchored by a large stuffed buffalo and flanked by American flags. A man clad in a massive warbonnet with a long train of feathers running down his back stands front and center before a small but rapt crowd. His dress is not traditionally Cherokee, but rather what many tourists have come to Cherokee seeking: Old Hollywood's interpretation of an "Indian."

The presence of these roadside chiefs has declined since postwar America, as economic opportunities for local men in the area have improved. Decades ago, there might have been someone "chiefing" on every other corner, charging tourists for a taste of what white America *expected* to see during their visit, no matter how historically inaccurate it was. One of the best-known roadside chiefs of Cherokee, Carl Standing Deer, was once photographed with President Franklin Delano Roosevelt. I see only two chiefs in town during my stay. I watch as tourists pay a few bucks, sit for a handful of minutes to hear the chief's story, then take their selfies and head on their way.

I stop in at the nearby Shell station and strike up a conversation with the young Cherokee woman working there. We talk about how the town had changed—its economic struggles, the arrival of the casino in 1997, and yes, the weird history of "chiefing." She grew up in Cherokee, and I ask her if she ever learned about Nanye'hi or Nancy Ward in school.

She pauses for a moment, searching for an answer. "A little . . . I guess."

Other opinions of Nanye'hi that I collect are refreshingly cut-and-dried. I chat with three young docents outside the Museum of the Cherokee People, and share with them my reason for coming to town. One turns to his coworkers and asks what they think of Nanye'hi. Without missing a beat, one of the young women replies:

"Traitor."

———

The nineteenth century brought more change and upheaval to the Cherokee. In 1813, Nancy's son, Fivekiller Kingfisher, fought with raiders against the Creek. In May 1817, yet another Cherokee Council met to address further loss of land and lifestyle. Four days before this meeting, a group of thirteen Cherokee women drafted an address, which they planned to present to the assembled chiefs. An aged Nancy Ward was unable to attend the May 6 meeting but sent her walking cane in lieu of her attendance. The Cherokee women's petition read, in part:

> *Our beloved children and head men of the Cherokee Nation, we address you, warriors in council. We have raised all of you on the land which we now have . . . We know that our country has once been extensive, but by repeated sales has become circumscribed to a small tract, and [we] never have thought it our duty to interfere in the disposition of it till now . . . Your mothers, your sisters ask and beg of you not to part with any more of our land.*

The women's council reserved the very bottom of the petition exclusively for Ward's comments alone.

"Warriors," she began, and beseeched them, "to take pity and listen to the talks of your sisters, although I am very old yet cannot but pity the situation in which you will hear of their minds, I have great many grand children which I wish them to do well on our land."

The Hiawassee Purchase of 1819 sold off yet more Cherokee land, including Echota, and Nancy Ward moved, spending the final years of her life near the Ocoee River just northeast of Chattanooga. There she had a parcel of land on Federal Road populated by livestock and tended by enslaved workers, where Ward—known as "Granny Ward"—operated an inn. She died in 1822 and was laid to rest between her son, Fivekiller, and her brother, Longfellow, her grave filled with pots and pans to accompany her to the next life.

Nancy Ward also has a statue.

Sort of.

In the early twentieth century, James Abraham Walker, descended from Nancy Ward's daughter, Catharine, sculpted a small statue of the Cherokee Beloved Woman holding a lamb in her arms, with a circular marker inscribed, "Nancy Ward Watauga 1776." In need of money, he sold it to a Tennessee man who placed the statue on his own wife's grave.

Then it was stolen.

The statue turned up in a private collection and is, as of this writing, in the hands of an antique dealer in New England. Local historical organizations are trying to get it returned to Tennessee.

You can visit Ward's grave site atop a hill in what is now Benton, Tennessee, where the Nancy Ward Chapter of the Daughters of the American Revolution dedicated a bronze tablet commemorating Ward's efforts on behalf of the patriot cause. It reads: "1738-Died 1822 Princess and Prophetess of the Cherokee Nation. The Pocahontas of Tennessee, the Constant Friend of the American Pioneer."

Or "traitor," depending on your point of view.

Certainly, the manner in which we remember individuals varies over time, especially in the age of online memorials and archives. One method that has stood the test of time is the statue. Why we erect statues, and how and when and under what circumstances—sometimes violent—we take them down, is a particularly relevant question today. Washington, D.C., as an example, has numerous statues, many of them depicting women. However, when women are given form in bronze or marble, their bodies often serve as a metaphor for justice or freedom. Robed or sometimes nude, they stand in honor of an ideal rather than a specific woman; not infrequently they stand in honor of a man.

But not always.

The Smithsonian's National Museum of the American Indian in Washington, D.C., displays a bronze sculpture of Polly Cooper, the Oneida woman who traveled to Valley Forge to aid the Continental soldiers living there. Three figures form the 2,200-pound statue: Polly Cooper, the Oneida chief Shenandoah, and George Washington. The Oneida Indian Nation of New York gifted the sculpture to the museum in 2004. It is called *Allies in War, Partners in Peace.*

A likeness of Abigail Adams is one of the three statues forming the Boston Women's Memorial. As first lady of the United States, she was the first to live in the White House. Due to her status, her prolific letters, writings, and thoughts on the issues of the day have been carefully preserved.

A statue dedicated to the memory of her friend Mercy Otis Warren stands in Warren's hometown, Barnstable, Massachusetts. She is perched on a pedestal in front of the Barnstable County Courthouse, a book in one hand and a pen in the other. Warren continued her prolific writings throughout her life and chronicled the events leading up to and surrounding the American Revolution. Warren's three-volume tome, titled *History of the Rise, Progress, and Termination of the American Revolution*, released in 1805, was one of the earliest accounts of the war ever published.

As I mentioned earlier, Sybil Ludington has not one but two statues in her honor despite the ongoing debate about what she did or did not do on that night in April 1777. Ludington married New York assemblyman Edmund Ogden in 1784. He caught yellow fever and died fifteen years later, leaving her with a son, Henry. Since Edmund had served in the war, Sybil in 1838 sought a widow's pension from the government. She was denied because she lacked a certificate of marriage. Nowhere in her application does Ludington refer to her legendary midnight ride, nor did she ever mention her alleged patriotic activities in any of her surviving letters. Similarly, her famous ride was never referenced in her obituary, nor on her gravestone. Despite this lack of evidence, her descendants successfully managed to bring the story of her life to the world, and there are those who celebrate her to this day.

Esther DeBerdt Reed is buried in Laurel Hill Cemetery of the First Presbyterian Church along with other well-known Philadelphians. Joseph died not quite five years after she did, in 1785. He was engaged once after Esther's death but broke it off. His political future stalled as well as his romantic one. Upon his death, the surviving Reed children were parceled out to relatives in England and America.

Lucy Knox's darling "Harry" went on to become the first United States secretary of war, serving under President George Washington. He and Lucy moved to Maine, where the Flucker family had large landholdings. Harry's success as a land baron paled in comparison to his triumphs as a military man. He and Lucy began selling off their vast acreage in order to recoup their losses, and when Henry died in 1806—due to complications suffered after an errant chicken bone got lodged in his throat—the pair had finally dug themselves out of a financial hole. Lucy died in 1824, after spending the last eighteen years of her life as a widow. Of the thirteen children she and Henry had, only three survived until adulthood.

Peggy and Benedict Arnold lived out the rest of their lives in London. The money paid to Benedict by the Crown for his services during the war was far less than the figure he had insisted upon, and the couple didn't quite fit into London society.

After Benedict's death, Peggy apparently fell on hard times. She was eventually awarded a pension by King George III himself, perhaps in thanks for her husband's service to the Crown . . . or perhaps for the services she herself rendered as a liaison—an invisible, once-unacknowledged spy— between her husband and Major John André.

The Arnolds are buried together in a crypt along with their daughter, Sophia, at St. Mary's Church in Battersea, London. If you call ahead, you can visit the crypt in the church's basement.

Before, during, and after the war, publisher Mary Katharine Goddard worked to keep citizens informed and connected, even as she struggled to stay financially solvent.

In 1784, Mary Katharine Goddard's brother, William, decided to take over the Baltimore newspaper. Whether his sister wanted him to or not, he assumed the role of publisher. She was forced to support herself by running a small store, where she sold books and other privately printed items, including her own almanac. Not to be outdone, William published his own to compete with his sister's, which he referred to as "double-faced," deriding its contents as a "mean, vulgar and common-place Selection of Articles."

Adding insult to injury, Postmaster General of the United States Samuel Osgood unceremoniously removed Goddard from her post in 1789 and appointed a gentleman of his inner political circle to take her place. Hundreds of Baltimore citizens sprang to her defense, and Goddard herself personally petitioned George Washington to get her job back.

In her December 23, 1789, letter, Goddard described her fourteen-year tenure, and the public outcry upon her firing, which she calculated amounted to "between two and three hundred of the principal Merchants & Inhabitants of Baltimore" in addition to "sundry private Letters."

She wrote of the financial burdens she had incurred during her tenure, including advancing money to cover the costs of post riders. She wrote (in the third person) of the "heavy losses" which "swallowed up the Fruits of her Industry, without even extricating her from embarrassment to this day..."

Ever the diplomat, Washington declined to intervene on Goddard's behalf. She petitioned the newly formed U.S. Senate in January of 1790, also to no avail. Mary Katharine Goddard died August 12, 1816. Upon her death, Goddard's will freed an enslaved woman, Belinda Starling, who had worked in her home for years, and left her all of Goddard's property. Goddard was buried in the graveyard of St. Paul's Parish, or "Old St. Paul's." The image most commonly associated with her remains the one that was hanging in the Smithsonian's National Postal Museum in Washington, D.C., the last time I visited, the one believed to be that of the aforementioned actress Ann Brunton Merry.

While Goddard's plaque never found a wall to hang upon, a marker in Medford, Massachusetts, remembers the actions of Prudence Wright and her fellow female patriots. And in 1908, the Prudence Wright Chapter of the Daughters of the American Revolution placed a tablet beside her gravestone reading, "In Memory of The Captain of the Bridge Guard, April 1775." In March 1777, the town of Pepperell awarded the women £7, seventeen shillings, and sixpence for their service defending the town from the British.

Another woman who took up arms, Deborah Sampson—aka "Robert Shurtleff"—was eventually found out and discovered to be female. After she fell ill, a doctor discovered Sampson's secret. He arranged for her to be privately cared for in his home. He did report the revelation to her superior officers, but they, too, did not seek disciplinary action. Clearly, Sampson was regarded as a valuable and well-liked soldier.

When her outfit returned to West Point, Sampson received an honorable discharge on October 23, 1783, under orders from Lucy's husband, General Henry Knox. Roughly twenty years after the war ended, Sampson was on the road again—this time on a public speaking tour sharing her remarkable story. At the conclusion of her speeches, Sampson marched and took up arms to perform various maneuvers with her weapon. Sold-out crowds loved it.

The Public Universal Friend continued preaching and building a significant following. They soon began publishing religious texts as well, and eventually established a religious community, the Society of Universal Friends, in Jerusalem, New York. Disputes over property eventually upended the Friend's life, and their resulting declining health made matters worse. The Friend died on July 1, 1819, and was interred in a stone vault in their cellar, though the remains were eventually moved to an unmarked grave.

Americans love to dig up famous people and re-inter them in a fashion more befitting of their memories. But human fallibility practically ensures that things will go awry. As a result, not all the remains of famous individuals are easy to track down.

Margaret Corbin is one such example. In 1780, Corbin's allowance as a Revolutionary War veteran was increased to provide her with additional clothing and rum. Yes, rum. Margaret viewed both as necessities, the latter perhaps too much so. Her personality was reportedly abrasive; one of her superior officers at West Point wrote that he didn't know what to do about the "problem" of "Captain Molly." The final resting place of Margaret Corbin's actual remains has yet to be located, though some dedicated individuals in upstate New York continue to pursue leads.

The final resting place of Eliza Pinckney is one I thought would be straightforward to track down, considering the outsized role the

Pinckneys played in South Carolina and United States history. In 1792, Eliza discovered a tumor in her breast. As the cancer grew and spread, the science-minded woman and her family spent the last years of her life searching for a cure, even ordering a special species of leech from London so that she might bleed herself of the illness. She lived out her final days with her children in Philadelphia, where she had gone to consult with a leading cancer specialist.

On July 4, 1793—ten years after the signing of the Treaty of Paris—*The South-Carolina Gazette* printed news of the death of "Mrs. Pinckney, the mother of gen. Pinckney,—On Saturday last . . ." She would have been seventy years old. Her descendants would later claim that George Washington served as a pallbearer at her funeral, but there appears to be no record of the then president of the United States doing so beyond lore shared by Pinckney's own descendants.

When I went to the cemetery at Saint Peter's Episcopal church in Philadelphia to look for her grave, it took some patience. Luckily, I was not the first person to try to find it. Under a tree in the midst of the peaceful, walled cemetery is a marker reading, "In an unmarked grave lie the remains of Eliza Lucas Pinckney of South Carolina 1723-1793 She Was The Mother Of Charles Cotesworth Pinckney And Thomas Pinckney, Patriots, Soldiers, Diplomats."

Others claim Eliza Pinckney's remains were later moved to Charleston, to rest with members of the Pinckney family in the cemetery of Saint Philip's Episcopal church. No records exist to resolve the matter, so her final resting place continues to be debated.

After departing the Pinckney plantation, John "Quash" Williams, on whom Eliza relied so greatly, ran a successful carpentry business. And today there is an entirely new crop of indigo growers, Black residents and artisans of the Low Country, reclaiming an industry that could not have existed nor thrived without their ancestors.

Few diaries detailing the experiences of Black and Indigenous citizens are available. Records such as payrolls, muster rolls, and pleas to the government for assistance or redress remain some of the best—often the only—resources available to research the lives of nonwhite citizens during the war for American independence.

What we know of Belinda Sutton's life story emerged from petitions written on her behalf and filed (repeatedly) with the Commonwealth of Massachusetts for the money that Isaac Royall Jr. left her in his will. Harvard Law School—and other institutions of higher education—continue to address their connections to wealthy colonial-era families such as the Royalls and the Vassalls. Uncovering the ties that link enslavers to modern university systems is an arduous process. In 2023, Harvard Law School announced a $500,000 gift to the Royall House and Slave Quarters and the Charles Hamilton Houston Institute for Race and Justice. Harvard Law School established the Belinda Sutton Distinguished Lecture and Academic Conference series. This happened after twenty-first-century researchers discovered that an endowment by Isaac Royall Sr. helped establish Harvard Law School.

After the close of the Revolutionary War, the Virginia State Assembly passed an act that freed any enslaved soldiers who fought on behalf of the United States. But not so for the man known as James, who served Lafayette so ably as a double agent at Yorktown. James was not a soldier, the state determined, but actually a spy and therefore excluded from the act.

Upon learning of this, the Marquis de Lafayette was astounded. He petitioned the General Assembly on James's behalf, detailing the crucial role that he had played in the war. "This is to certify that the bearer by the name of James has done essential services to me while I had the honour to command in this state. His intelligences from the enemy's camp were industriously collected and faithfully delivered. He perfectly acquitted himself with some important commissions I gave him and appears to me entitled to every reward his situation can admit of."

James would not receive his freedom until 1787. When he did, he took the surname "Lafayette" (though he may have gone by "Fayette"). His state pension was another matter. After petitioning for twenty-seven years, James finally received an annual payment for his service in 1819. When the Marquis de Lafayette returned to tour the States in 1824, he reunited with James at a public gathering in Yorktown.

For the formerly enslaved people who left with British loyalists to go to Nova Scotia, life in the Canadian settlement of Birchtown left much to be desired, and for many, the familiar abuses continued. In 1792, the Sierra

Leone Company—comprising British citizens who stood against slavery—established Freetown in that West African country, the second British colony on the continent of Africa. Black loyalists who had gone to Nova Scotia were encouraged to resettle there, in a community that followed in the footsteps of earlier British abolitionists.

In 1792, Mary Perth, her husband, Caesar, their family, Harry Washington, his wife, Jenny, and others who had left New York looking for a better life in Canada set sail to start a new life on the continent from which they had been kidnapped and enslaved.

In Freetown, the Sierra Leone Company reneged on its promise of self-government. Harry sought to establish himself as a leader in that community and argued to revise the laws of the colony. For that, the British banned him.

On the land the Perths received, Caesar built a two-story home on Waters Street, which included a farm. They had added a child, Susan, to their family. When Caesar died, Mary sold the farm and turned their home into a successful boardinghouse. After a French attack and raid in 1794 upended her life, Mary took a job with the governor of Freetown as a housekeeper and traveled with him to London. Mary eventually returned to Nova Scotia, where she is believed to have died around 1813.

The Great Dismal Swamp, where Harry dug ditches and Mary ministered, became a stop on the Underground Railroad during the Civil War. Today the swamp is part of a recreational area where ongoing archaeological research strives to piece together the history and traditions associated with *petit marronage* and those who once called the swamp home. You can kayak through the swamp's waters and history, both of which remain murky.

Historians estimate that 5,000 to 8,000 Indigenous and Black men served on the patriot side of the Revolutionary War and as many as 20,000 on the British side. Countless women and children toiled in other ways, whether maintaining farms and businesses or as support for troops. Only a handful have any statues in their honor.

In addition to her statue on Boston Common alongside Abigail Adams and the nineteenth-century suffragist Lucy Stone, poet Phillis Wheatley

Peters is also depicted in a bronze statue that stands in the Smithsonian's National Museum of African American History & Culture in Washington, D.C.

Despite her renown, Phillis's life proved arduous even after her emancipation, and her final years were trying ones. Phillis had been living in Middleton with John for almost three years. Much of that time, John was embroiled in a contentious legal battle with Naomi Wilkins, who finally succeeded in having Phillis and John evicted from the property. Phillis and John returned to Boston and lived in a boardinghouse.

The accruing legal costs of the past several years had taken a financial toll. John cycled in and out of debtor's prison as he looked to start a new venture and get the couple back on their feet. (Repeated trips to debtor's prison were not unusual for any businessman, Black or white, during that unpredictable time. In fact, while in debtor's prison, Robert Morris, a signer of both the Declaration of Independence and the Constitution, received a visit from George Washington during his presidency.) Phillis's health continued to deteriorate.

Early in 1784, she managed to publish two new poems in pamphlet form (one of these, "Liberty and Peace," was inspired by the ratification of the Treaty of Paris). She also saw new light for one of her older verses when it was published in a women's magazine in September. She died just months later, on December 5, 1784, at thirty-one years of age. In 1834, Margaretta Odell—who claimed to be a collateral descendant of Phillis—published *Memoir and Poems of Phillis Wheatley*, in which she included a short biography of Phillis. Odell wrote that Phillis gave birth to three children, all of whom had died and the last of whom was buried with Phillis herself. While certain references point to the existence of at least one child, there is little historical record to confirm this. She may have had children, but if so, none survived to adulthood.

Elizabeth Freeman also has a statue dedicated to her memory in the National Museum of African American History & Culture (NMAAHC). During the years she worked for the Sedgwick family as a free woman, Elizabeth earned enough money to buy her own home in Stockton, Massachusetts, not far from the Sedgwicks. She was a neighbor of Agrippa Hull, a free

Black man and Revolutionary War veteran who also worked for the Sedgwick family. But Elizabeth Freeman's statue in the NMAAHC is not my favorite. My favorite stands in Sheffield, Massachusetts.

———

A few years ago, I found myself at Colonel John Ashley's House, a privately managed historic home in what was once Ashley Falls, Massachusetts, and is now part of the town of Sheffield. Colonel John Ashley was a civic leader and an officer of standing within that colonial community, a man who hosted thought leaders in his home to discuss freedom, and an individual with six people enslaved to him.

But at 9:00 a.m. on this hot, sunny August morning, the crowd I join is not gathered at the Ashley home to honor the colonel. Instead they are there to do their best to walk—in spirit—in the footsteps of Elizabeth Freeman.

The vast majority of what is known about Elizabeth Freeman—or "Mumbet," a name still used to refer to her today—comes to us from the writings of Catharine Sedgwick, daughter of Theodore, the lawyer who took on the case of Freeman and one of the men enslaved along with her, Brom. No matter Catharine's good intentions, we have no idea how Freeman would have, had she been able to, written her story in her own words. Catharine and her siblings were remarkably close with Freeman, who took on a great deal of their caretaking due to their mother's struggles with mental illness and inability to be very present in their lives.

The resulting account of Freeman's life is subject to Catharine's own bias toward her father and family, and rooted in her memories of the woman who helped care for her in the absence of a capable mother. Catharine went on to become a successful author, and her decision to write about Freeman is perhaps the key reason Freeman's story came to light and likely one of the reasons records of Theodore Sedgwick's day in court on Freeman's and Brom's behalf weren't abandoned in a file cabinet. Despite any shortcomings that may exist in Sedgwick's telling of Freeman's story, what is undeniable is that Elizabeth Freeman worked, lived, fought for, and earned her freedom. That is enough for the crowd gathered in the hot August sun to re-create the first four miles Freeman walked in the direction of her emancipation.

A crowd of sixty made the trek that day. Some of us took turns carrying a banner announcing the walk's honoree. Growing along the route were goldenrod, wild grapes, cattails, purple loosestrife, Virginia creeper, poison ivy, and ailanthus tree, aka the "tree of life." Passing cars honked in support of the walk—or because they didn't know why there were so many pedestrians strolling along the highway.

The four-mile journey took us along U.S. 7 and finally to a green space between Sheffield's Old Stone Store and the Old Parish Church. There, later in the day, in front of a packed crowd enduring the stifling midday heat while sitting in the parking lot, the Sheffield Historical Society unveiled a statue of Elizabeth Freeman sculpted by the New Jersey artist Brian Hanlon. The new statue stands across the road from the Sedgwick home where Freeman arrived to ask for help and where she later worked as a free and independent woman.

The crowd gathered at the ceremony was sweaty but enthusiastic, and included senators, Sedgwick descendants, the former governor and first lady of Massachusetts, and a direct descendant of Freeman's coworker and eventual neighbor Agrippa Hull. Though they were unable to attend, Meryl Streep and Barack Obama both sent letters that were read during the ceremony. When the statue was finally revealed, it showed Elizabeth standing tall and defiant, a coal shovel in her hand, depicting the oft-discussed moment when she defended young Lizzie from their violent mistress.

A thousand blessings upon historical societies, the Sheffield Historical Society among them. These groups pick up where larger, better-funded nonprofits leave off. Tireless volunteer archivists, impassioned community-members-cum-genealogists, dig for and preserve the "small" but historically significant aspects of a community's past. Most of these efforts continue without fanfare or appreciation, but the occasional public event brings people together around a common cause, and there is nothing quite like the unveiling of a statue.

After the event, I headed up the road to Stockbridge. Traffic was mad, as it typically is during summer in the Berkshires, clogged with tourists on their way to Tanglewood, to the Norman Rockwell Museum, or to go "antiquing."

I stayed at the Red Lion Inn in the center of Stockbridge, a multilevel hodgepodge of a historic building. The decor ranges from early American tavern to nineteenth-century tearoom kitsch. The floors are uneven, and the wallpaper is so busy it could pass for op art. But the Red Lion possesses an undeniable charm, not to mention an on-site restaurant and a past reaching back to the eighteenth century. Much to my delight, it is also reportedly haunted.

The walk from the Red Lion to the Stockbridge Cemetery is a pleasant one along Main Street, past historic houses, one of which is yet another former home of the Sedgwick family, where Elizabeth Freeman worked while living nearby. It is now privately owned; I know this because I traipsed up the driveway and caught one of the current owners quite by surprise as she unloaded her groceries.

If you enjoy the peace and solemnity of cemeteries as much as I do, the Stockbridge Cemetery does not disappoint. The "Sedgwick Pie" is a circular family plot containing the graves of Theodore Sedgwick and his many descendants. The family plot is also the final resting place of Elizabeth Freeman. As the years wore on, the Sedgwick "children" remained close with Elizabeth. When she died in 1829, she was survived by her daughter, Elizabeth, as well as a granddaughter, Marianne Dean, and a great-grandson and great-granddaughters as well. Elizabeth bequeathed all of them items she had earned over the years, from muslin and muffs to place settings and real estate. What she did not leave behind was debt. Elizabeth appointed Charles Sedgwick executor of her will. Catharine and other members of the Sedgwick family stood witness. Catharine estimated that Elizabeth left an estate valued at around $1,000.

Later in life, as Elizabeth recounted her life story, Catharine wrote that Elizabeth had this to say about her personal road to liberation:

Any time, any time while I was a slave, if one minute's freedom had been offered to me & I had been told I must die at the end of that minute I would have taken it—just to stand one minute on God's earth a free woman—I would.

The inscription on her gravestone reads:

ELIZABETH FREEMAN
known by the name of
MUMBET
died Dec. 28' 1829.

Her supposed age was 85 Years. She was born a slave and remained a slave for nearly thirty years. She could neither read nor write, yet in her own sphere she had no superior nor equal. She neither wasted time nor property. She never violated a trust, nor failed to perform a duty. In every situation of domestic trial, she was the most efficient helper, and the tenderest friend. Good Mother, farewell.

Freeman's resting place is the most visited of all the graves in the Sedgwick family plot, attested to by the numerous rocks left atop her headstone.

Visiting Elizabeth Drinker's grave is more challenging. The diarist is buried *somewhere* in the Arch Street Meeting House Burial Ground. Quaker burial grounds were crowded ones, as they also welcomed non-Quakers, including Black and Indigenous individuals. The Arch Street burial ground was past capacity before the turn of the nineteenth century, and an estimated 20,000 individuals are interred there, some two or three deep.

Quakers discouraged adorning burial sites with ostentatious headstones, which makes locating the remains of various individuals virtually impossible. When Arch Street was widened, workers found bones in unmarked graves. More graves disappeared beneath the roadway.

Drinker is listed among the "notable" persons buried at Arch Street, though the precise location of her final resting place will never be known. A historical marker commemorating Elizabeth Drinker stands near 147 North Second Street at the intersection of Quarry, in the Old City neighborhood of Philadelphia, noting that her home once stood "east of here."

After the war, the next big crisis highlighted in Elizabeth Drinker's diary was the yellow fever epidemic in Philadelphia. The last fourteen years of her diary, from 1794 to 1807, represent about three-fourths of her nearly half century's worth of observations, indicating that she wrote more with an empty nest than when she was a young wife and mother.

The entries give evidence of her thoughts on the political climate: She supported the Federalists over the Democratic Republicans. She was outraged by the French Revolution because it reminded her of the revolution she had just survived. She wrote approvingly after reading *A Vindication of the Rights of Women*, a popular feminist political essay by Mary Wollstonecraft.

Drinker's later years were occupied with the caretaking of extended family members. In 1807, Elizabeth's daughter, Sarah Sandwith Drinker Downing, died of a lymphatic cancer located in her neck. Elizabeth's devastation is evident in her diary. Reeling with pain, she not only wrote about the loss of her adult daughter but also recalled the deaths of children in her past who had died in infancy.

Elizabeth Drinker died on November 24, 1807, from complications related to "lethargy." Writing of her passing in the "73rd year of her age," *Poulson's American Daily Advertiser* mentioned Drinker's diary, assuring readers and mourners alike that "her words flowed from her heart, and that was a source which was ever pure and serene . . ."

Elizabeth Drinker's last diary entry is dated November 18, 1807, not quite a week before she died. On that day she described, in her signature matter-of-fact manner, a "clear and cold all day wind N.W." She described children and visits and a friend suffering from "something of the toothach—it clear'd up last night before 11." After five decades and 2,100 pages, she left five final words for whoever might care to read them: "a clear moon light night."

July 4 . . . REDUX

Charleston, South Carolina, is home to many a spirit, and if you don't believe me, there are many a tour guide in this town who will happily tell you all about it. Some consider this historic city to be one of the most haunted Revolutionary War locales in the nation. I have chosen to visit one such possessed structure, its long history punctuated by blood and battle, its walls permeated with phantasms of the suffering long past.

It is known locally as the "Embassy Suites."

The sprawling, turreted building overlooking Marion Square served as a fortification in the 1750s, and warehoused tobacco shortly after the Revolutionary War. In 1842, it served as the original site of the legendary military college the Citadel—then called the South Carolina Military College. Federal troops occupied it during the Civil War. Now, in the twenty-first century, the building hosts a much more tempered crowd of high school soccer teams, family reunions, and tourists in search of the ultimate shrimp and grits.

This hotel on Meeting Street was once voted the most haunted in the South. (Does one "vote" for a haunting?) Visitors insist that in the halls of this hotel dwells a ghost clad in military attire named "Half-Head" who possesses—you guessed it—half a head. The rest of his cranial anatomy was allegedly blown off by cannon fire during the Civil War. Shortly after checking in, I learn that Half-Head reportedly enjoys hanging out in and around a room on the second floor. My room on the first floor is not haunted—maybe—but it does have its very own cannon port.

The building is, by far, not the oldest in the Holy City, as Charleston is called, with spires of churches reaching skyward from what is otherwise a very modest cityscape, pleasantly devoid of skyscrapers. This is the largest living historic district in the United States (as in not a Williamsburg-esque outdoor museum of sorts but a modern, active city).

To walk the centuries-old cobblestones that line the streets of this four-hundred-year-old city is to traverse time and memory, often getting lost in or misinterpreting both. As I tread down narrow alleys, a single turn often gives way to a view of the harbor, its hazy horizon dotted with blanched sails, its surging waters buttressed by seawalls. The southern sun ricochets off the narrow facades of the historic town's homes, at once brightening and weathering rows of Bermudian limestone in alternating shades of coral, mint, ocher, and lavender. It is a palette that brings to mind rattan ceiling fans, drawls that dance on the tongue like the sweetest of teas, and preppy madras golf trousers.

I visit the Old Exchange and Provost Dungeon. Its cellar—which you can tour—once hid a cache of patriot ammo from the British, then served as a jail during the latter's siege of Charleston, when its brick vaults were populated by women, men, members of Congress, and criminals of all walks.

I am reminded of the imprisoned sisters Mary and Catherine Sarrazin, mentioned in Eliza Wilkinson's diary, during the British siege of Charleston. The pair remind me of all those individuals who do not often get their full stories told, and those whose stories I did not have a chance to share either.

In the course of writing this book, I have come to understand that there are ghosts lurking up and down the East Coast. They dwell throughout the former colonies, they infuse the lands of North America, and they try their best to remind us how many stories remain in the soil and the woods and the water, waiting to be told.

Charleston is a city imbued with such memories—not all of them pleasant, few of them dull. It is a place of contradictions: a city that feels like a town. A region of stifling heat and cool breezes. Those breezes might carry the stench of overworked horses drawing tourist-laden carriages, the scent of sweet magnolias, or the pungently enticing aroma of she-crab soup. The city tourists now adore was once steeped in the pain of oppression, the battle for independence, and the legacy of what was the busiest port of entry in North America for the trans-atlantic slave trade.

More than 40 percent of the individuals abducted from Africa and trafficked in North America arrived at Gadsden's Wharf in Charleston. Sitting in that same spot today, the waters of Charleston Harbor lapping against the nearby docks, is the recently opened International African American Museum. The museum is raised on pillars, and beneath it the outlines of bodies, male and female, big and small, are carved into the stone. Water washes over these silhouettes, a memory of all those brought to Charleston by the sea, alive or dead.

Nearly ten years ago, when I first began thinking about and researching this project, my primary concern was that I would not be able to find enough people to fill its pages. The opposite has turned out to be true. In many ways I have barely scratched the cobblestoned surface.

In January 2013, Congress removed the ban on women serving in combat roles in the military, hundreds of years after they had already done so to support the creation of the nation Congress represents. Women fighters and leaders have been on this planet as long as their male counterparts, from the reign of Egypt's Pharaoh Hatshepsut to the female cavalries and warriors, or *onna-musha*, of thirteenth-century Japan, up through the escapades of the French warrior Joan of Arc.

In 1948, President Truman signed Executive Order 9981, officially desegregating the U.S. military, even though we know that Black and Indigenous troops fought alongside one another as militia during Lexington and Concord and that integrated units such as the 6th Connecticut Regiment were a part of the Continental Army.

During the revolution, the women and girls—Black, white, and Indigenous—who took up arms to protect homes and farms, who risked their lives for what they believed in, did not always easily fall into columns labeled "Patriot" or "Loyalist."

Aside from people, in the course of this work I have seen that the ground itself is sacred. Places worth visiting are far too numerous to list. The Holy Grail of colonial sites, Williamsburg, Virginia, is certainly a must-see for anyone seeking to immerse themselves in revolutionary-era history. Visit their print shop and ponder the responsibilities and accomplishments of Mary Katharine Goddard. Visit Christiana Campbell's tavern, and be reminded of how many women kept the original states up and running during a violent and trying time. Drive over to nearby Yorktown and see the site of perhaps the most crucial battle of the American Revolution.

Other sites along the East Coast pay homage to their history in big ways and small. Edenton, North Carolina, for example, has a historical marker—and bronze teapot—commemorating the tea party held at Elizabeth King's home. Dig far enough beneath the surface of most cities and you'll find some remnant of a time past, often misremembered, but not forgotten.

I suspect my own personal Revolutionary War road trip will be an ongoing one. In my travels over the years, I have witnessed the celebration of the birthday of the United States in many a setting, from backyard barbecues to historical reenactments, from Charleston to Boston. But the most unexpectedly perfect way to spend the Fourth of July is at the Eastern Band of Cherokee's Fourth of July Powwow, one of the largest powwows in America. From Friday evening through Sunday, Native Americans from across the United States and Canada gather to eat, dance, drum, and compete against the backdrop of the nearly five-hundred-million-year-old Appalachian Mountains.

Cherokee, North Carolina, lies about forty miles west of my home in Asheville, a city itself situated on Cherokee land. There are two main routes if traveling by car, offering two very different road trip experiences: The more direct is the highway. The more scenic Blue Ridge Parkway—"America's Favorite Drive"—extends 469 miles from Shenandoah National Park in Virginia to its southern terminus in the Great Smoky Mountains at Cherokee.

The final stretch between Asheville and Cherokee offers a landscape astoundingly devoid of visual reminders of the modern world. Trees and boulders drape the mountainside, a curtain of uninterrupted sky their backdrop. It is a welcome struggle to spot a single structure, electrical line, or cell tower.

The highway provides more eclectic surroundings: Campaign signs reminding drivers to elect a new principal chief of the Cherokee. Santa's Land Fun Park and Zoo—ironically closed during the Christmas season—where you can ride the perennially popular "Rudicoaster" and visit with baby black bears in the petting zoo. Granny's Kitchen and Paw Paw's Peanuts and Pork Skins. A large billboard bearing the painted face of an Indigenous man wielding an axe advertises Cherokee's outdoor theater production of *Unto These Hills*. The tagline: "Boring is Under Direct Attack."

As I arrive at the Acquoni Expo Center, the sounds of Redbone's "Come and Get Your Love" blare from speakers positioned around the large green expanse. The emcees amp up the large and still-gathering crowd with these contagious '70s beats, and this particular hit has enjoyed lasting popularity across generations, having been made famous by the trailblazing, and one of the most notable, Native and Mexican American rock bands ever.

Patrick and Candido "Lolly" Vasquez-Vegas, Native American brothers from California, formed the backbone of Redbone. The term "redbone" has been used in the South and beyond—perhaps most notably southwest Louisiana—to describe someone of multiracial background. The Vegas brothers were of Shoshone, Yaqui, and Sonoran ancestry. As for how they came to use the term as their band's name, one popular origin story purports that it was musician Jimi Hendrix who suggested the brothers use the moniker in a way that honored the pair's Indigenous roots. Whether the legendary guitar virtuoso indeed suggested the name to the group, Hendrix was undoubtedly a fan and early supporter and even jammed with the duo onstage in Los Angeles.

But when the weekend-long festivities begin, that irresistible Redbone groove is replaced by the sound of pounding drums, jingling bells, and voices of all genders and ages crying out in celebratory song. The opening prayer is delivered by Leroy Littlejohn, and welcome speeches given by guests such as Miss Teen Cherokee are spoken in the Cherokee language.

The weekend competitions are in categories including jingle, traditional, fancy shawl, buckskin, grass dance, fancy dance, and tiny tots. I watch as a woman practices traditional dance in a parking lot behind a gaggle of construction trailers while Manitoban elk graze on an adjacent overgrown parcel of land. A mother straightens the headpiece of her young daughter behind the main stage. Tents encircle the area, providing some shade for groups of performers waiting their turn to step into the limelight of the blazing North Carolina sun.

Some contestants in the "tiny tot" group are quite serious for their age; other youngsters intermingle their dancing with running and chasing their fellow participants. A handful seem barely old enough to walk on their own and look as if they might topple from the weight of their traditional ensembles. A few have decided that nothing interferes with nap time, and as they nod off, their smiling parents carry them around the performance ring. When groups of drummers and singers are not competing in their own categories, they provide the soundtrack for the competitive dancers. During, after, and in between contests, vendors sell jewelry, clothes, leather work, and more.

The vast majority of the people in attendance—as either participants or spectators—are Indigenous. However, non–Native Americans, as the emcees make a point of mentioning, are most welcome. The producers of the weekend's spectacle encourage filming but occasionally announce when certain of the days' events are deemed "cameras down"—not to be recorded. One of these is a kind of "dance off," an impromptu freestyle collection of moves with dancers from varying disciplines taking turns in the center of a small circle. The fact that these exuberant eruptions of dance are off-limits to cameras sears the event more permanently and authentically into my memory.

The dress of the competing dancers is elaborately crafted, vivid, and meaningful. Many participants are happy to become a part of someone's cell phone record of the event. Others are not, especially if a stranger snaps a picture of their child without at least first asking permission.

I gravitate toward one of the more gregarious attendees, a tall, sturdily built man bearing a massive crown of feathers. His vibrant regalia is all manner and hue of blues, reds, and oranges, and adorned with beads, bells, and bones. Another bound ring of feathers hangs down his back, while even more extrude regally from his shoulders, like some form of avian epaulettes.

He smiles, poses, and attracts a line of white attendees waiting to snap photos of or with him. He is happy to oblige. He introduces himself as Dave. He lives in the Raleigh, North Carolina, area and is descended of the Lumbee people. He speaks fondly of his grandmother, who taught him about the different types of medicine that the feathers or claws of each animal possess.

I ask about his dress, its origins, and the significance of the various elements, especially those amazing feathers. Dave explains that it took him a long time to amass all of the plumes, as they are genuine eagle feathers. He explains that one must apply for them from the federal government and that there is a lengthy waiting list—like a lottery.

The Fish and Wildlife Service established the National Eagle Repository in the 1970s. Adults who are enrolled members of federally recognized tribes can fill out the "Federal Native American Religious Purposes Permit Application" to obtain body parts or feathers of deceased golden or bald eagles found on federal lands. Options include an entire animal (whole or equivalent parts), a pair of wings, an entire tail, a head, a pair of talons, a bird's trunk, or loose feathers.

The wait time can be substantial, but it is worthwhile. As Dave tells me, "Everything I wear tells a story."

For many of those in attendance, part of that story is one of lifelong military service. An elderly man stands near me wearing, in addition to his traditional Cherokee attire, a sash that bears a large United States Marine Corps patch. Many Native Americans attending as competitors or onlookers are U.S. military veterans. The insignias of various branches—military crests, medals, unit names, and more—emblazon a fair amount of the traditional dress I see this weekend.

To be in Cherokee on the Fourth of July is to embrace diverse notions about what it means to be "American." Countless Native Americans—descendants of the original inhabitants of this land—have fought and continue to fight to defend the very nation whose inception is tied to the abuse and neglect of their people. This has been, and always will be, their land—*and* they continue to protect it. This is one meaning, and a powerful one, of what it means to be an American.

The powwow's organizers take pains throughout the weekend to pay tribute to veterans. This is most apparent during the Grand Entry procession that begins each day's session. Veterans representing all branches of the armed forces march in and present the colors, one of which is a flag bearing the seal of the Eastern Band of the Cherokee Nation. All veterans attending the powwow—Native American or not—are later invited to step into the ring and be recognized. American Legion post No. 143, which is across the street from the fairgrounds, is the oldest Native American post of its kind in the United States.

Down the road from the expo center is Native Brews Tap & Grill, a brewery facing Tsali Boulevard that is 100 percent Native American woman–owned. Behind the bar I spy beer taps offering such brews as Native Girl Pale Ale, The Warrior Blond Ale, and Flaming Arrow IPA. The location used to be a miniature golf course, and a relic of those days—a giant statue of a bare-chested Native American man, arm outstretched, a single feather in his hair—towers over the outdoor seating area on what remains of the course.

As with most cultural gatherings, food and drink play a significant role at the powwow itself, with the sweet or savory snack of choice being fry bread, a staple at festivals and fairs that is also available throughout town. Fry bread—exactly what it sounds like—is an Indigenous food not specific to the Cherokee people alone. The food is universally available, if controversially discussed. The meal, made from simple ingredients, calls to mind the forced relocation and displacement of Indigenous peoples, government food rations, and the abhorrent national Indian boarding schools.

Different nations have different recipes. The bread arrives puffy, hot, and fried and is used as a base for dishes like "Indian tacos" or a crisp, fried, confectioner's sugar–drenched plate with strawberries on top. I see signs advertising the treat everywhere: Reed's Fry Bread. Calhoun's Cherokee Frybread. Nikki's Fry Bread serves up fry bread Indian pizza alongside Rez Dogs and Rez Burgers. The dish is comfort food for many—those selling fry bread have the longest lines of any vendors—providing tasty treats and tasty humor. I see one woman clad in a T-shirt that appears quite serious from the front, emblazoned as it is with the letters "F.B.I." But when she passes by, I read the back: "Fry Bread Inspector." Much of fry bread's history entwines pain with resilience, persecution with the triumph over it. Fry bread recipes are passed down from generation to generation and are as hotly debated as the food's origins.

Fry bread also made an appearance in the work of artist Jakeli Swimmer, an EBCI cartoonist and satirist. Titled "Bob's Frybread," the illustration depicts characters based on the titular family of the popular animated series *Bob's Burgers* dressed in Indigenous attire and hawking Bob's "NDN ['Indian'] Taco of the Day," called "T.G.I.F.: Thank God It's Frybread."

As the weather cools down, the powwow heats up, and the emcees hype the evening activities—"Saturday Night Live"—calling on everyone who is single to "get ready to mingle." I am not in the mood to mingle—regardless of my status—and walk back down the boulevard to my motel. As a merciful breeze sweeps through town, I sit in a plastic chair outside the door to my room at the Great Smokies Inn.

The weekend is the most authentically American celebration of the Fourth of July I have ever experienced, and I think of the Declaration of Independence, a document that vilified the Cherokee nation and others, labeling Indigenous people as "merciless Indian Savages."

During my stay in Cherokee, I see that phrase several times. That infamous and degrading language—which present-day historians refer to as "Grievance 27"—has had some interesting staying power, but has been reclaimed: I see that very term emblazoned on many a T-shirt for sale at the powwow, which has the effect of transforming the phrase into one of strength, defiance, and endurance.

Freedom. Independence. Freedom meant and means different things to different people. For the Public Universal Friend, it meant freeing themselves from the societal and gender roles assigned to them in order to share the gospel more freely. For the Quaker Elizabeth Drinker, it meant freedom from religious persecution. For Elizabeth Freeman and Belinda Sutton, it meant escaping an abusive enslavement. For Mary Perth and countless other enslaved individuals who fled after Dunmore's Proclamation, it meant an alliance with the British. For the Cherokee of the Carolinas, it meant fighting to retain lands that were increasingly and violently encroached upon by European settlers, patriot and loyalist alike. For Nancy Ward, freedom meant forging alliances with those same settlers.

Eerie wisps of clouds drape the Smokies as I sit on this second-floor balcony of sorts, mere feet away from neighboring motel residents similarly seeking a breath of wind. I gaze over the lighted swimming pool below and the darkened mountains beyond. There, in and among the crags and tors, the ghosts of those we have forgotten mingle freely with those we have venerated, equal at last in the shadows of the mountain. As I listen for their stories, my ears catch the distant sounds of "Saturday Night Live" carried on the cooling night air. It is the echoing sound of stories yet to be told, at once airy and thunderous, a chorus of enduring fortitude on joyous display under the Cherokee stars.

ACKNOWLEDGMENTS

During the research and writing of this book, my household experienced everything from medical crises to pandemics to natural disasters. As a result, the creation of a book about the Revolutionary War took almost as long as the actual war itself. Almost.

I am deeply indebted to many people who helped me bring this book into the world.

My agent, Howard Yoon of WME, jumped on board mid-journey and did so enthusiastically. His opinions and guidance have been invaluable.

I am eternally grateful to my editor, Jill Schwartzman, whose keen eye for structure, ear for cadence, and unwavering optimism kept me buoyed. This book wouldn't be the same without her. I also owe a big thank-you to publisher John Parsley, who first brought me and *Obstinate Daughters* to Dutton. I am so glad he did.

Jill was more than ably assisted by the amazing Charlotte Peters, whom I relied upon more than once during this entire process. I am grateful for the rest of the Dutton and Penguin Random House gang: The managing editorial and production team, including production editor Claire Sullivan, production manager Erin Byrne, proofreader Hilary Roberts, and copy editor David Chesanow, asked all the right questions and, more important, cleaned up my mistakes when I could not see them anymore. The publicity and marketing crew—including

Caroline Payne, Amanda Walker, Sarah Thegeby, and Stephanie Cooper—helped this book find its audience. Layout designer Nancy Resnick gave my words a lovely setting on the page; and cover designers Jason Booher and Sarah Oberrender wrapped it all up in a lovely and enticing package.

This book would not have been possible without the countless manuscripts, letters, and other archival materials that routinely transport me and other time-traveling researchers like me into the past. During the COVID-19 pandemic, when libraries were closed to the public, archivists and librarians used that time to scan and otherwise preserve numerous documents that had not been treated to this attention previously. As a result, there are so many more holdings available to anyone with an internet connection. And I always found archivists and librarians just a call or email away and always eager to help. My work can't exist without them, and our culture is a better, richer place with them in it.

The efforts of universities, research libraries, and private foundations to make their holdings available digitally has been a boon, not just to writers but also to teachers, students, and countless citizens, who can now read the thoughts and feelings of people who have long departed this earth, thanks to the words they entrusted to paper, writing by hand using a quill pen. Think on this the next time you beam evanescent electrons to a loved one via text.

I have thanked some archivists and institutions in my Selected Notes and Sources, but there are a few I need to single out, among them Paul O'Brien of the Sheffield Historical Society, who was so very welcoming and helpful, and the incomparable Laura Mina, formerly of the Charleston Library Society, whose historical newspaper holdings from the eighteenth century are a true gift to writers and historians everywhere. The librarians at the Ramsey Library on the campus of the University of North Carolina–Asheville are also wonderful humans who allowed this strange woman who was definitely not a student to commandeer her favorite study pod for days at a time when she needed to consult the library's excellent resources. This is not the first book that has brought me to the Archives and Manuscripts Division at the New

York Public Library, and every time I rely on their remarkable team of archivists and librarians, they exceed my expectations. The staff at the Massachusetts Historical Society were not only helpful in person but were always available from many miles away when I had follow-up inquiries. This was the first time I consulted the William L. Clements Library at the University of Michigan, and I assure you it will not be the last. There are many individuals there who made my research trip to Ann Arbor so worth the time and effort, among them Director of Development Angela Oonk. I truly appreciated the efforts of Jennifer Fauxsmith, research librarian at the Schlesinger Library on the History of Women in America, who went above and beyond, pointing me in directions I would not have considered, including those outside her institution.

I am grateful to the Sharon family—and the comfiest chair on the Eastern Seaboard—where I often parked myself while in Washington, D.C. My thanks to the lovely Kate Andersen Brower for her support, and also to her family, who took me in and endured my gripes about the difficulties of deciphering eighteenth-century handwriting.

On occasion, when I needed help corralling some research in New York City, and when it was not convenient for me to visit, two friends who helped were Deirdre Cossman and Shannon McKenna Schmidt. Their help was more than just boots on the ground. I hope you two know how much I value our friendships and what your support during a very trying time meant, and means, to me. You are truly gems.

I pay tribute to my "home" bookstore, Malaprop's Bookstore/Cafe in downtown Asheville, North Carolina—I could not ask for a better place to offer my books, host my events, or spend my free time.

I want to thank the best cocktail bar in the world, Little Jumbo, where I hosted CRAFT: Authors in Conversation, and all the regulars who showed up month after month to hear from me and my guests.

Elizabeth Kostova's talents as a writer are matched only by her loving, nurturing friendship. To paraphrase M. F. K. Fisher, there is communion of more than our appetites when muffins are broken and coffee drunk. Thank you, Ollie and the whole Sweeten Creek Coffee crew, for being our faithful caffeine enablers. Thank you, Elizabeth, for sitting across from me on good days and bad.

And finally, I thank my husband, Joseph D'Agnese, who is not only an incredible journalist and author but the first set of trusting eyes that ever read any of my words. Your patience and support—in far too many ways to list in a sentence or two—helped keep me on track when times got tough . . . and they did, indeed, get tough.

And like any writer who faces her morning pages alone, I thank Bruno, my dog, who kept me company (and warm) on the couch on ungodly early mornings and who cherishes freedom and independence as much as any wild-eyed patriot, provided these virtues are offered with tasty treats and ear scritchies.

Thank you all for seeing this through with me.

SELECTED NOTES AND SOURCES

Welcome to the notes section! You're about to have a blast. Before you get too carried away, here are some things to keep in mind.

In the interest of economy, and given that many of these individuals are present across multiple chapters, I have grouped selected key sources by topic, and additional materials by chapter. If I have specifically mentioned the origin of a quote in the text—a dated newspaper article, for example—I often do not repeat that information here. Also, if a particular fact is widely known, easily obtained, and extensively documented—dates of, say, the Boston Massacre or the definition of the Mississippian geologic period—I have not included it here. In some cases, sources are grouped by topic or character within a chapter, as opposed to chronologically. Where applicable, I have added a few insights and notes that might not have made it into the final version of the text.

The following sources are substantial but by no means exhaustive.

Global Notes

Conflicting spellings of names are common for the time period. It was not unusual for an individual to spell their *own* name several different ways over the course of their lifetime, and that spelling might contradict what was later inscribed on their tombstone. In the interest of clarity, I have chosen a single spelling for certain individuals. My rationale will be noted in the chapters in which these characters make their first appearance. If contained in a direct quote, I use the spelling—or misspelling—contained within that selection. With regard to locations: I have used place names that correspond to the time period being discussed. These names are taken from historical maps and documents. My methods and choices are presented in greater detail in the Source Notes that follow.

A number of archival resources and institutions have been consulted in person and online throughout this book. For brevity's sake, abbreviations *may* include: William L. Clements Library (CLE); New York Public Library Manuscripts and Archives Division (NYPL); Charleston Library Society (CLS); National Archives (NA); Library of Congress (LOC); The National Archives, official archive of the United Kingdom's government, and for England and Wales (NAUK); National Park Service (NPS), U.S. Department of the Interior; Sheffield Historical Society (SHS); George Washington

Presidential Library at Mount Vernon (MV); Massachusetts Historical Society (MHS); New England Historical Society (NEHS); Gilder Lehrman Institute of American History (GLI); and the Schlesinger Library on the History of Women in America (SCHL).

The National Historical Publications and Records Commission (NHPRC) of the National Archives cooperates with the University of Virginia Press (UVA) to manage "Founders Online" (https://founders.archives.gov), a collection of documents related to the founding of the United States containing transcriptions of thousands of primary documents from the era. Letters accessed via this database will be labeled "Founders Online." Founders is an ongoing project. Additional resources consulted for documentation regarding the operations of the Continental Army: Library of Congress, Manuscript Division, and John Clement Fitzpatrick, *Calendar of the Correspondence of George Washington, Commander in Chief of the Continental Army, with the Officers, in Four Volumes* (U.S. Government Printing Office, 1915).

For *general* timeline information regarding key events in the Revolutionary War, I referred to "The American Revolution, 1763–1783: U.S. History Primary Source Timeline" at the LOC, and to "The American Revolution" and "American Revolution at a Glance 1775–1783," both published by the NPS, U.S. Department of the Interior.

Regarding newspaper archives: It was common for publications to speak in the first person on behalf of the newspaper itself, or the editor, or the editorial board, without identifying an individual author or assigning a formal title to the news item. In these cases, I provide the publication name and date.

All quotes from *The Maryland Journal, and the Baltimore Advertiser* (*MJBA*) published by Mary Katharine Goddard are sourced from the holdings of the special collections of the Maryland State Archives, MSA SC 2830, microfilm reels scm852 (Aug. 20, 1773, to Dec. 1, 1777); scm853 (Dec. 7, 1778, to Nov. 5, 1782); scm854 (Nov. 12, 1782, to Dec. 31, 1784); and scm4255 (Jan. 13, 1778, to Dec. 29, 1778). My thanks to Maria A. Day, senior director of Special Collections, Conservation, & Library Services; Justin Williams; and Dale W. King, Maryland State Archives (MSA).

All quotes from and references to *The South-Carolina Gazette* come from the collection at the Charleston Library Society, Charleston, SC: https://charlestonlibrary society.libguides.com/c.php?g=1111903&p=8781266, and accessed on site in Charleston. CLS possesses one of the most extensive collections of colonial-era newspapers in the nation.

Unless otherwise specified, quotes from the records of the Continental Congress are taken from Paul H. Smith, ed., *Letters of Delegates to Congress, August 1774–August 1775* (Library of Congress, 1976). Nearly eight hundred pages. Wonderful resource. (Congress Letters); and *Journals of the Continental Congress, 1774–1789*, vol. 4, "January 1–June 4, 1776" (*JCC*), edited from the original records in the Library of Congress by Worthington Chauncey Ford, Chief, Division of Manuscripts (Government Printing Office, 1906), https://tile.loc.gov/storage-services/service/ll/llscd /lljc004/lljc004.pdf.

Map Resources

Maps played a crucial role in the writing of this book, for everything from tracking troop movements and analyzing shifting territory boundaries to the evolution of town names and simply to help set a more detailed scene. Digitized versions of the same map are often held at more than one institution. I often used multiple maps to piece together a particular moment in the story.

One remarkable resource that continues to expand is "ARGO: American Revolutionary Geographies Online." A joint project of the Leventhal Map and Education Center at the Boston Public Library (BPL) and the George Washington Presidential Library at Mount Vernon (MV), ARGO brings together maps dating between 1750 and 1800 from numerous institutions and makes them searchable via one portal. Nineteen partner institutions (and more are always being added) whose images I would normally have had to search individually are all collated and presented in one place and include the British Library, MHS, NYPL, CLE, LOC, Boston Athenaeum, Harvard, American Antiquarian Society, and many more.

ADDITIONAL RESOURCES BY CHAPTER

Introduction: Set in Stone

Description and memories of the parade are from my own experience and photographs related to the Bicentennial celebration in 1976, just weeks shy of my eighth birthday. Descriptions of Egypt and information regarding Hatshepsut are drawn from my own experience traveling to Egypt, including the Temple of Hatshepsut. Information regarding Hatshepsut and her rule is widely available and includes Elizabeth B. Wilson, "The Queen Who Would Be King," *Smithsonian Magazine*, September 2006, https://www.smithsonianmag.com/history/the-queen-who-would-be-king-130328511/; "Scarab Inscribed Maatkare (Hatshepsut) Living," The Met, https://www.metmuseum.org/art/collection/search/549725; Joshua J. Mark, "The Temple of Hatshepsut," World History Encyclopedia, July 18, 2017, https://www.worldhistory.org/article/1100/the-temple-of-hatshepsut/; and "Mortuary Temple of Hatshepsut," Explore Luxor, https://exploreluxor.org/temple-of-hatshepsut/.

Chapter 1: How It Begins

Compiling resources for the lives and experiences of the Indigenous individuals in this book often meant relying on the writings and interpretations of the white individuals who left written records and who, in turn, were relating their *own* experiences, observations, and perspectives. Some of these resources conflict with each other. In some cases—during various meetings between agents of the British or Americans and Indigenous groups—a written record (written by the white people present) of the words of various Indigenous leaders were captured.

"Chota" is the spelling I use throughout the book for the principal town of the Overhill Cherokee. Over the centuries, spellings of the Cherokee town that Henry Timberlake described as "the Metropolis" on his 1762 map titled *A Draught of the Cherokee Country, on the West Side of the Twenty Four Mountains, Commonly Called Over the Hills* have included "Chote," "Echota," "Chotte," etc., depending on who was drawing the map.

Three of the more well-known and commonly cited resources on the lives of the Cherokee people during colonial times are Duane H. King, ed., *The Memoirs of Lt. Henry Timberlake: The Story of a Soldier, Adventurer, and Emissary to the Cherokees, 1756–1765* (Museum of the Cherokee Indian Press, 2007); James Mooney, *Cherokee History, Myths and Sacred Formulas* (Cherokee Publications, 2006); and Emmet Starr, *History of the Cherokee Indians and Their Legends and Folk Lore* (Warden Company, 1921).

While Timberlake had lived experience with the Cherokee about whom he wrote, Mooney was relating what he learned essentially second- or thirdhand from the individuals he interviewed about times past. Many of these resources were used together throughout the book. Also consulted (in no particular order): For general information about the Cherokee Nation: https://www.cherokee.org. For an excellent, informed, modern-day assessment of Ward's choices: Michelene E. Pesantubbee, "Nancy Ward: American Patriot or Cherokee Nationalist?," *American Indian Quarterly* 38, no. 2 (Spring 2014): 177–206; Theda Perdue and Michael D. Green, *The Columbia Guide to American Indians of the Southeast* (Columbia University Press, 2001); Charles Adron Farris III, "These Hills, This Trail: Cherokee Outdoor Historical Drama and the Power of Change/Change of Power" (abstract), doctoral thesis, Franklin College of Arts and Sciences, University of Georgia, 2016; Nancy Ward, U.S. Sons of the American Revolution Membership Applications, 1889–1970, National Society of the Sons of the American Revolution, application of Burbon Jones; Ben Harris McClary, "Nancy Ward: The Last Beloved Woman of the Cherokees," *Tennessee Historical Quarterly* 21 (December 1962); Norma Tucker, "Nancy Ward, Ghighau of the Cherokees," *Georgia Historical Quarterly* 53 (June 1969); Natalie Inman, "'A Dark and Bloody Ground': American Indian Responses to Expansion During the American Revolution," *Tennessee Historical Quarterly* 70, no. 4 (Winter 2011); John L. Nichols, "Alexander Cameron, British Agent Among the Cherokee, 1764–1781," *South Carolina Historical Magazine* 97, no. 2 (April 1996); Carolyn Thomas Foreman, *Indian Women Chiefs* (Star Printery, 1954). Overview from GLI on Cherokee, etc., https://www.gilder lehrman.org/history-now/journals/american-indians-leadership. Roberta Estes, "Broken Tennessee Treaties," *Native Heritage Project*, April 15, 2013, https://nativehe ritageproject.com/2013/04/15/broken-tennessee-treaties/. Proclamation Line of 1763, from sources above, maps consulted via ARGO, and: *Indian Congresses and Treaties*, Gage Papers, CLE; Phoenix Archives, "The Cherokee Clan System," February 10, 2006, https://www.cherokeephoenix.org/education/the-cherokee-clan-system/arti cle_a88fcc42-f3f8-5f33-b575-8cff7d3bffd2.html; J. R. McNeill and Jared Dease, "The Columbian Exchange," NCpedia, State Library of North Carolina, January 2024, https://www.ncpedia.org/anchor/columbian-exchange. Cherokee trip(s) to London: Ed Simon, "Indigenous Kings in Londontown," JSTOR Daily, November 8, 2023, https://daily.jstor.org/indigenous-kings-in-londontown/. Print: *The Three Cherokees, came over from the head of the River Savanna to London, 1762*, multiple sources, including the British Museum. Death of interpreter: in print above, and *Maryland Gazette*, December 23, 1762. "Sitting for pictures," etc.: *Leicester and Nottingham Journal*, July 10, 1762. "Curiosities": *South-Carolina Gazette*, October 2, 1762; H. Howard, "A New Humorous Song, on the Cherokee Chiefs, Inscribed to the Ladies of Great Britain," LOC, July 1762, https://lccn.loc.gov/91727495; "Clothed in Scarlet": *Gloucester (UK) Journal*, June 28, 1762. Cherokee chiefs at Vauxhall: *Ipswich (UK) Journal*, July 10, 1762. Cherokee to Tower of London: *Pope's Bath (UK) Chronicle and Weekly Gazette*, July 8, 1762. Theatre in Drury Lane: "Harlequin Cherokee," *Public Advertiser* (London), November 23, 1762. New Theatre in London: *Public Advertiser* (London), July 17, 1762.

"Fort Necessity: The Cherokee and the French and Indian War," NPS, April 2012. Stephanie Pratt, "Reynolds' 'King of the Cherokees' and Other Mistaken Identities in the Portraiture of Native American Delegations, 1710–1762," *Oxford Art Journal* 21, no. 2 (1998): 133–50, http://www.jstor.org/stable/1360618.

Chapter 2: A Bloody Time in Boston

Mercy Otis Warren writings throughout the book: Mercy Otis Warren, *History of the Rise, Progress, and Termination of the American Revolution, from the Stamp Act to the Ratification of the United States Constitution*, vols. 1–3 (Boston: Manning & Loring,

1805). Biographical notes about Warren, her brother, her works, and her relationships with key figures in the revolution from *History* and Nancy Rubin Stuart, *The Muse of the Revolution: The Secret Pen of Mercy Otis Warren and the Founding of a Nation* (Beacon Press, 2008). Crown debt: The currency calculator from UK National Archives may be accessed at https://www.nationalarchives.gov.uk/currency -converter. Details and terms of various Acts of Parliament throughout (identified as Sugar, Stamp, Townsend, etc.): Great Britain, *A Collection of All the Statutes Now in Force: Relating to the Revenue and Officers of the Customs in Great Britain and the Plantations* (London: C. Eyre and W. Strahan, 1780). James Otis, *The Rights of the British Colonies Asserted and Proved* (Boston: Edes & Gill, 1764), https://quod.lib .umich.edu/cgi/t/text/text-idx?c=evans;idno=N07655.0001.001. "Eighteen Daughters of Liberty . . ." and "Our accounts from every Province . . .": "Providence, in Rhode-Island," *Pennsylvania Gazette*, April 3, 1766. "she would purchase nothing where that was . . ." and "homes of Rev. Mr. Abbot . . .": *Virginia Gazette*, December 22, 1768. Ann/ Anne Hulton writings (she is frequently referred to as both): Ann Hulton, *Letters of a Loyalist Lady* (Harvard University Press, 1927). Christopher Seider's death and Boston Massacre: "Christopher Seider: The First Casualty in the American Revolutionary Cause," NEHS, https://newenglandhistoricalsociety.com/christopher-seider-the -first-casualty-in-the-american-revolutionary-cause/; "The Boston Massacre: Setting the Colonies Aflame," *American Battlefield Trust*, updated July 26, 2024, https://www .battlefields.org/learn/articles/boston-massacre; Hulton, *Letters*; *The Bloody Massacre, perpetrated in King-Street, Boston, on March 5th 1770 by a party of the 29th Regiment* (Imprint Society, 1970); "Perspectives on the Boston Massacre," MHS, https:// www.masshist.org/features/massacre; "Today in History—the Boston Massacre," LOC, https://www.loc.gov/item/today-in-history/march-05/; "Women Speaking Softly: Female Voices of the Boston Massacre," Emerging Revolutionary War, March 5, 2017, https://emergingrevolutionarywar.org/2017/03/05/women-speaking-softly -female-voices-of-the-boston-massacre/; "Patrick Carr—One Who Did Not Blame the Soldiers," Boston Massacre Historical Society, http://www.bostonmassacre.net /players/Patrick-Carr.htm; "Crispus Attucks," NPS, https://www.nps.gov/people /crispus-attucks.htm; "Crispus Attucks," American Battlefield Trust, https://www .battlefields.org/learn/biographies/crispus-attucks; J. L. Bell, "King Street on the 5th of March 1770," *Boston 1775* (blog), March 5, 2007, https://boston1775.blogspot.com /2007/03/king-street-on-5th-of-march-1770.html; "The Boston Massacre: John Ad ams Saves a Soldier's Life," NEHS, https://newenglandhistoricalsociety.com/the -boston-massacre-john-adams-saves-a-soldiers-life/; "A Plan of Fort Independence," Collections Online, MHS, https://www.masshist.org/database/418; "Ropewalks and Revolution," adapted from Duane Lucia and Tom Burgess, "Ropewalks of the West End and Beyond," The West End Museum, https://thewestendmuseum.org/history /era/new-fields/bostons-ropewalks/.

Chapter 3: Freedom's Many Trails

All Phillis Wheatley poems quoted throughout the book are taken from Phillis Wheatley, *Poems on Various Subjects, Religious and Moral* (London: A. Bell, 1773); and Phillis Wheatley, *Complete Writings* (Penguin Books, 2001).

Collection of letters from Phillis Wheatley to Obour Tanner from MHS. Accessed on site at MHS, Boston, and via Masshist.org. Additional information on Phillis Wheatley Peters: David Waldstreicher, *The Odyssey of Phillis Wheatley: A Poet's Journey Through Slavery and Independence* (Farrar, Straus and Giroux, 2023). Additional information on the transatlantic slave trade and Boston: "The Transatlantic Slave Trade," Equal Justice Initiative, 2022, https://eji.org/report/transatlantic-slave-trade /boston/#the-port-of-boston. Wheatley in London: "Benjamin Franklin to Jonathan

Williams, Sr., 7 July 1773," Founders Online, NA, https://founders.archives.gov/docu
ments/Franklin/01-20-02-0158; and "Jonathan Williams, Sr. to Benjamin Franklin,
17 October 1773," Founders Online, NA, https://founders.archives.gov/documents
/Franklin/01-20-02-0236. Information regarding Elizabeth Freeman's life in Sheffield,
MA: Catharine Maria Sedgwick, "Mumbett" (manuscript draft), 1853, Catharine Maria Sedgwick papers, MHS. General information on Sheffield and Ashley Falls accessed in person from records of the Sheffield Historical Society, 159 Main St #161,
Sheffield, MA 01257, https://sheffieldhistory.weebly.com. Many thanks to Paul O'Brien
for all his help. Sheffield Resolves or Declaration: *The Massachusetts Spy, Or, Thomas's
Boston Journal*, February 18, 1773, accessed via LOC, https://www.loc.gov/item
/sn83021194/1773-02-18/ed-1/. Alexandra "Mac" Taylor, "Elizabeth Freeman, Her Case
for Freedom, and the Massachusetts Constitution," National Constitution Center,
April 13, 2021, https://constitutioncenter.org/blog/elizabeth-freeman-her-case-for
-freedom-and-the-massachusetts-constitution; Olivia R. Scott, "Glimpses of Their
Lives: Slavery and Emancipation at the Colonel John Ashley House," *Commonplace:
The Journal of Early American Life*, https://commonplace.online/article/glimpses-of
-their-lives/.

    For information on Boston's and other tea parties from this period: Joseph Cum-
mins, *Ten Tea Parties: Patriotic Protests That History Forgot* (Quirk Books, 2012);
Sarah Bradlee Fulton and Nathaniel Bradlee: Helen Tilden Wild, *Medford in the Revolution: Military History of Medford, Massachusetts, 1765–1783: Also List of Soldiers
and Civil Officers, with Genealogical And Biographical Notes* (J. C. Miller Jr., printer,
1903); Harry Clinton Green and Mary Wolcott Green, *The Pioneer Mothers of America: A Record of the More Notable Women of the Early Days of the Country, and Particularly of the Colonial and Revolutionary Periods* (G. P. Putnam's Sons, 1912);
Medford Past and Present: 275th Anniversary of Medford, Massachusetts, June 1905
(*Medford Mercury*, 1905); "The Nathaniel Bradlee Chippendale Mahogany Tall-Case
Clock," Lot 1251, Christie's, auction closed January 2019, https://www.christies.com
/en/lot/lot-6188163; "Ask the Globe," *Boston Globe*, August 18, 1991; "Passing of Bradlee House: Boston Tea Party Assumed Indian Guise in Its Kitchen," *New York Times*,
October 22, 1898; "Sarah Bradlee Fulton," *Dorchester Atheneum*, https://www
.dorchesteratheneum.org/project/sarah-bradlee-fulton/; "Medford Early History—
17th and 18th Centuries," Medford Historical Society & Museum, https://medford
historical.org/mapping-medford/walking-tours/medford-early-history/. J. L. Bell,
who writes extensively about the events of the American Revolution—especially
those taking place in and around Boston—has written more than one blog post on
the Bradlees and Fultons for the Medford Historical Society & Museum's blog and
raised questions about the veracity of the Sarah Bradlee Fulton account. I included
Bradlee Fulton in my book and am including two of Bell's posts here: "A Family Mansion with a History of the Stirring Times," *Boston 1775* (blog), Medford Historical
Society & Museum, November 19, 2019, https://boston1775.blogspot.com/2019/11/a
-family-mansion-with-history-of.html; and "Inspecting the Tea Party House," *Boston
1775* (blog), Medford Historical Society & Museum, November 21, 2019, https://bos
ton1775.blogspot.com/search/label/Sarah%20Bradlee%20Fulton. For makeup techniques: Denise Farmery, "Fashions, Follies & Fatalities: The Regency & Early Victorian
Era," Johnston Collection, https://johnstoncollection.org/FASHIONS-FOLLIES
-FATALITIES-THE-REGENCY-EARLY-VICTORIAN-ERA~68563; and Caroline
Potts, "English Rose: Putting Your Best Face Forward—Cosmetics in 18th Century
Society Portraits," *The Bowes Museum Blog*, Bowes Museum, July 21, 2016, https://the
bowesmuseum.org.uk/english-rose-putting-your-best-face-forward-cosmetics-in-18th
-century-society-portraits/.

Boston Un-Common

Descriptions of historic sites, pubs, parks, monuments, etc., from repeated travels to Boston. Information regarding Mother Goose: Christine Jones, "Mother Goose's French Birth (1697) and British Afterlife (1729)," *Public Domain Review*, May 29, 2013, https://publicdomainreview.org/essay/mother-gooses-french-birth-1697-and-british -afterlife-1729/. Descriptions of Royall House and town from personal travel to Medford, most recently in 2024, at 15 George Street, Medford, MA. Information regarding the Royall family history and involvement with the slave trade is highly documented. Extensive primary source research has been done by the Royall House & Slave Quarters. A collection of primary source documents that they have digitized and made available can be found at https://royallhouse.org/home/education/primary-resources /primary-sources/correspondence/ and includes: "The Royalls," Royall House & Slave Quarters, https://royallhouse.org/the-royalls/. J. L. Bell, "How Isaac Royall Came to Endow a Harvard Law Professorship," *Boston 1775* (blog), Medford Historical Society & Museum, December 6, 2015, https://boston1775.blogspot.com/search?q=royall. "From Africa to Medford: The Untold Story," Medford Historical Society & Museum, https://medfordhistorical.org/medford-history/africa-to-medford/. Frank B. Sarles Jr. and Charles E. Shedd, *Colonials and Patriots, Historic Places Commemorating Our Forebears, 1700–1783* (U.S. Department of the Interior, National Parks Service, 1964), 97–99. *Medford Past and Present: 275th Anniversary of Medford, Massachusetts, June 1905* (Medford Mercury, 1905).

Chapter 4: The Dismal and the Determined

Information on the life of Elizabeth Sandwith Drinker and quotes from her writing here and throughout the book are drawn from Elaine Forman Crane, ed., *The Diary of Elizabeth Drinker: The Life Cycle of an Eighteenth-Century Woman*, abridged ed. (University of Pennsylvania Press, 2010); Elaine Forman Crane, ed., *The Diary of Elizabeth Drinker*, vols. 1–3 (Northeastern University Press, 1991), hereafter "Elizabeth Drinker diaries." Statistics about Philadelphia's population and importance as a colonial port are widely available. The GLI has an excellent overview: https://www .gilderlehrman.org/history-resources/essays/revolutionary-philadelphia. On tea and the revolution: Jane T. Merritt, "Tea Trade, Consumption, and the Republican Paradox in Prerevolutionary Philadelphia," *Pennsylvania Magazine of History and Biography* 128, no. 2 (April 2004); James R. Fichter, *Tea: Consumption, Politics, and Revolution, 1773–1776* (Cornell University Press, 2023). Information regarding various tea parties throughout the colonies is from above sources as well as Joseph Cummins, *Ten Tea Parties: Patriotic Protests That History Forgot* (Quirk Books, 2012). Regarding the saga of Captain Ayres and the ship *Polly*, see above and also J. Jay Smith and John F. Watson, *American Historical and Literary Curiosities; Consisting of Fac-Similes of Original Documents Relating to the Events of the Revolution, &c, &c. with a Variety of Reliques, Antiquities, and Modern Autographs* (Philadelphia: Nat. Pub. Co., 1847). The American Revolution's relationship to and impact on religious thought and freedoms is a topic that comes up repeatedly in a variety of sources and pertains not only to Drinker's experience but also to those of Mary Perth and the Public Universal Friend. Some specific resources on Quaker treatment during the American Revolution can be found at The Revolutionary City, https://therevolutionarycity.org/, a collaborative effort bringing together primary source information and more from a variety of institutions; and Deanna Johnson, "Exiled from Philadelphia: Quakers During the Revolution," American Philosophical Society, October 16, 2022, https://www.amphilsoc.org/blog /revolutionary-phl-exiled-philadelphia-quakers -during-revolution. Regarding Mary Perth and religion: "Singular Piety in a Female

African: Letter from the Rev. Mr. Clark, Chaplain to the Sierra-Leone Establishment, to his Father in Scotland" (July 29, 1796), *Evangelical Magazine for 1796* 4 (November 1796): 460–63; Cassandra Pybus, "'One Militant Saint': The Much Traveled Life of Mary Perth," *Journal of Colonialism and Colonial History* 9, no. 3 (2008), https://dx.doi.org/10.1353/cch.0.0035; John Bedell and Andrew Wilkins, "African American Experience Before Emancipation—Historical Context Narrative," NPS, June 2022, http://npshistory.com/publications/nace/hcn-afam-exp-before-emancipation.pdf; "Mary Perth, 1740–After 1813," Slavery and Remembrance: A Guide to Sites, Museums, and History, https://slaveryandremembrance.org/people/person/?id=PP042; William H. Funk, "The Dismal Swamp: One Road Out of Slavery Took You Straight into the Boggiest Place You've Ever Been," *Humanities* 38, no. 2 (Spring 2017), https://www.neh.gov/humanities/2017/spring/feature/the-dismal-swamp-one-road-out-slavery-took-you-straight-the-boggiest-place-you've-ever-been; Alexa Lawrence, "Great Dismal Swamp an Irreplaceable Hub of Black and Indigenous History," Wilderness Society, February 23, 2021, https://www.wilderness.org/news/blog/great-dismal-swamp-irreplaceable-hub-black-and-indigenous-history#. Also, regarding Galatians, Great Dismal Swamp, etc.: J. Brent Morris, *Dismal Freedom: A History of the Maroons of the Great Dismal Swamp* (University of North Carolina Press, 2022); Janay Draughn, "Elsewheres: Maroons and Fugitivity in the Great Dismal Swamp," MDC, July 12, 2022, https://mdcinc.org/2022/07/12/elsewheres-maroons-and-fugitivity-in-the-great-dismal-swamp/. Willoughby family: George Washington (GW) Papers, Series 4, General Correspondence: John Willoughby, List of Militia Recruits, 1756, https://www.loc.gov/item/mgw442275/; Letter from GW to the Great Dismal Swamp, 15 October, 1763, Founders Online, https://founders.archives.gov/documents/Washington/01-01-02-0009-0001. Nansemond Tribal History: https://nansemond.gov/tribal-history. Ossomocomuck (coastal North Carolina) from "Indian People of Ossomocomuck," First Colony Foundation, https://www.firstcolonyfoundation.org/history/indian-people-of-ossomocomuck/. A note about Mary Katharine Goddard: Goddard's name has been spelled both "Katharine" and "Katherine" by a number of reputable sources. I chose to spell her middle name "Katharine" because that is how she spelled it on the Declaration of Independence. Regarding Mary Katharine Goddard and the history of female printers in the colonies: "Early Women Printers of America," *Boston Public Library Quarterly* 10, nos. 1–3 (1958): 6–26, 78–92, 141–53, https://archive.org/stream/bostonpubliclibr1019bost/bostonpubliclibr1019bost_djvu.txt; "Inside the Vault: Mary Katherine Goddard: Woman Printer, Entrepreneur, and Postmaster in the Founding Era," presentation and online exhibit, GLI, March 3, 2022, https://www.gilderlehrman.org/sites/default/files/2022-05/March%202022%20ITV.pdf; "Women in Printing History Part 2: Women Printers in the American Colonies," The International Printing Museum, https://www.printmuseum.org/blog-3/women-printers-2. Anne Catherine Green sample newspaper with masthead from Maryland State Archives, https://msa.maryland.gov/megafile/msa/speccol/sc4800/sc4872/001282/pdf/m1282-0331.pdf.

"A Woman's Touch: Ann Franklin, Printing Pioneer," Rhode Island Historical Society, March 12, 2018, https://www.rihs.org/a-womans-touch-ann-franklin-printing-pioneer/. Clementina Rind: "A Bold Type: Clementina Rind's Revolutionary Press," Colonial Williamsburg, September 25, 2024, https://www.colonialwilliamsburg.org/discover/18th-century-people/stories-of-women/a-bold-type-clementina-rinds-revolutionary-press/; John A. Harrer, "The Reverend Jose Glover and the Beginnings of the Cambridge Press (Part 1)," History Cambridge (formerly Cambridge Historical Society), 1960, https://historycambridge.org/articles/the-beginnings-of-the-cambridge-press-part-1. Benjamin Franklin regarding Timothy family printing: "Articles of Agreement with Louis Timothée, 26 November 1733," Founders Online, NA, https://

founders.archives.gov/documents/Franklin/01-01-02-0105. Mercy Otis Warren letter to John Adams from the Adams Papers, "Condescended to ask my sentiments," July 14, 1774, MHS, https://www.masshist.org/publications/adams-papers/index.php/vol ume/PJA02/pageid/PJA02p108. Edenton Ladies protest and Penelope, etc.: Edenton Historical Commission, https://ehcnc.org/people/penelope-barker/. Copy of satirical cartoon and petition from "Shaping the Constitution," Resources from the Library of Virginia and the Library of Congress, https://edu.lva.virginia.gov/oc/stc/entries /a-society-of-patriotic-ladies-at-edenton-north-carolina-october-25-1774. March 1775 cartoon satirizing the tea party attributed to Philip Dawe, *A Society of Patriotic Ladies, at Edenton in North Carolina*, mezzotint (London, March 25, 1775), British Cartoon Prints Collection, Prints and Photographs Division, LC-USZC4-4617, LOC, Prints and Photographs Online Catalog, Washington, D.C. Regarding the protest of the "Ladies of Hartford": Samuel Wolcott, *Memorial of Henry Wolcott: One of the First Settlers of Windsor, Connecticut, and of Some of His Descendants* (New York: A. D. F. Randolph, 1881). Letter from Mercy Otis Warren to Hannah Winthrop (letterbook copy, after January 1, 1774), MHS, https://www.masshist.org/database/3373. Mary House and Philadelphia boardinghouses: "Historic Resource Study, Independence Mall, 18th Century Development, Block Chestnut to Market, Fifth to Sixth Streets," Anna Coxe Toogood, Historian, Cultural Resource Management, Independence National Historical Park, August 2001.

Chapter 5: War Comes to All

Quotations from and references to the letters and life of Lucy Flucker Knox and Henry Knox throughout the book: "The Revolutionary War Letters of Henry and Lucy Knox" collection at GLI. Francis S. Drake, *Life and Correspondence of Henry Knox, Major-General in the American Revolutionary Army* (Boston: Samuel G. Drake, 1873); Phillip Hamilton, *The Revolutionary War Lives and Letters of Lucy and Henry Knox* (Johns Hopkins University Press, 2017); Nancy Rubin Stuart, *Defiant Brides: The Untold Story of Two Revolutionary-Era Women and the Radical Men They Married* (Beacon Press, 2013); Henry Knox, *A Catalogue of Books, Imported and to Be Sold by Henry Knox at the London Book Store, a Little Southward of the Town-House, in Cornhill, Boston* (Boston: Henry Knox, 1773). Lucy and Henry wedding announcement: *New England Historical and Genealogical Register* 1882-01: Volume 36, https:// archive.org/details/sim_new-england-historical-and-genealogical-register_1882-01 _36/mode/2up?q=1774; Alexander Hamilton, "The Farmer Refuted," widely available. Letter of Mercy Otis Warren to John Adams, "Dread calamity," April 4, 1775, Founders Online: https://www.masshist.org/publications/adams-papers/index.php/vol ume/PJA02/pageid/PJA02p108. Ann Hulton quotes from Hulton, *Letters.* Paul Revere's ride is thoroughly documented and summed up nicely at https://www.paulrev erehouse.org/the-real-story/, with supporting documentation at Founders Online. On Margaret Gage: "Margaret Kemble Gage: Wife of British General Thomas Gage," Women's History Blog, May 28, 2009, https://www.womenhistoryblog.com/2009/05 /margaret-kemble-gage.html. Quotes from British soldiers: "King Hancock forever" . . . "Even the weamin had firelocks" from Christopher Hibbert, *Redcoats and Rebels: The American Revolution Through British Eyes* (W. W. Norton & Company, 2002). Prudence Wright and poem: Susan H. Wixon, "Prudence Wright," *American Monthly Magazine* 15 (July–December 1899); Mary L. P. Shattuck, "The Story of Jewett's Bridge," in *Prudence Wright and the Women Who Guarded the Bridge* (Prudence Wright Chapter, Daughters of the American Revolution of Pepperell, Massachusetts, April 19, 1964; copyright 1912). Lemuel Haynes: David W. Haynes, *Anglo-American Millennialism from Milton to the Present* (Routledge, 2023). Alex Gerrish, "Lemuel Haynes: America's First Black Ordained Minister," CT History, updated April 17,

2023, https://connecticuthistory.org/lemuel-haynes-americas-first-black-ordained
-minister/. Lemuel Haynes poem: Ruth Bogin, "'The Battle of Lexington': A Patriotic
Ballad by Lemuel Haynes," *William and Mary Quarterly* 42, no. 4 (October 1985).
April 29, 1775, Virginia Committee of Correspondence "the blow . . . is now struck"
accessed via Index of Virginia Printing, Library of Virginia, https://lva.primo.exli
brisgroup.com/discovery/fulldisplay?docid=alma9900034440302057568&vid=01LVA
_INST:01LVA&lang=en&query=any,contains,the%20blow%20now%20struck&offset
=0. Mary Katharine Goddard writings "What Think Ye Now" and "Live as slaves"
from *MJBA* collection at MSA; Erick Trickey, "Mary Katharine Goddard, the Woman
Whose Name Appears on the Declaration of Independence," *Smithsonian Magazine*,
November 14, 2018, https://www.smithsonianmag.com/history/mary-katharine
-goddard-woman-whose-name-appears-declaration-independence-180970816/. Details about Lexington and Concord from "Today in History—April 19: Lexington and
Concord," LOC, https://www.loc.gov/item/today-in-history/april-19/#lexington-and
-concord; "Making the Revolution: America, 1763–1791," "Crisis 8. 1775: The Outbreak
of War," National Humanities Center, https://americainclass.org/sources/makingrev
olution/crisis/text8/text8.htm; "History Resources: The Battles of Lexington and
Concord, 1775," GLI, https://www.gilderlehrman.org/history-resources/spotlight
-primary-source/battles-lexington-and-concord-1775; and "The Coming of the
American Revolution: 1764 to 1776; Lexington and Concord," MHS, https://www
.masshist.org/revolution/lexington.php. Henry Knox as apprentice: "General
Knox," *Niles' Register*, September 7, 1833, 25, https://www.google.com/books/edition
/Niles_Weekly_Register/1uUMAAAAIAAJ?hl=en&gbpv=1&dq=%E2%80%9CGeneral
+Knox,%E2%80%9D+Niles%E2%80%99s+Register,+September+7,+1833&pg=PA25&
printsec=frontcover. Regarding bookstore 1773: H. Knox, *Catalogue*; Allan Korn-
blum, "Henry Knox: Founding Father (and Bookseller)," *Publishers Weekly*, August
23, 2013, https://www.publishersweekly.com/pw/by-topic/columns-and-blogs/soap
box/article/58805-henry-knox-founding-father-and-bookseller.html; "The Diary of
Matthew Patten of Bedford, New Hampshire, April 1775," America in Class, National
Humanities Center, https://americainclass.org/wp-content/uploads/2013/10/Read
ings-Lexington-and-Concord-Tipping-Point.pdf. William Pitt quotes widely available, including "The speech, of the Right Honourable the Earl of Chatham, in the
House of Lords, January 20th, 1775. On a motion for an address to His Majesty, to give
immediate orders for removing his troops from Boston forthwith, in order to quiet
the minds and take away the apprehensions of his good subjects in America,"
accessed via University of Michigan Library Digital Collections, http://name.umdl
.umich.edu/n11389.0001.001. On Breed's Hill, Bunker Hill: Tony Horwitz, "The True
Story of the Battle of Bunker Hill," *Smithsonian Magazine*, May 2013, https://www
.smithsonianmag.com/history/the-true-story-of-the-battle-of-bunker
-hill-36721984/; "John Adams to William Tudor, 23 July 1775," Founders Online,
https://founders.archives.gov/documents/Adams/06-03-02-0050; "In Congress, June
and July 1775; from the Autobiography of John Adams," Founders Online, https://
founders.archives.gov/documents/Adams/01-03-02-0016-0025. The Boston Public
Library's sources regarding the event at Breed's Hill have wonderful details: "American Revolution in Massachusetts," https://guides.bpl.org/marev/breedshill. And as
always, MHS has extensive play-by-play information on this and other battles, including links to maps. I used a variety of maps accessed here and through the Leventhal
Map Collection, both of which are also available via ARGO. Paul Singer, "Behind
a Monument to White Men Lies the History of Soldiers of Color at Bunker
Hill," WGBH Boston, July 19, 2023, https://www.wgbh.org/news/local/2023-07-19
/behind-a-monument-to-white-men-lies-the-history-of-soldiers-of-color-at-bunker

-hill; George Quintal, "Titus Coburn," Patriots of Color, NPS, https://www.nps.gov /people/titus-coburn.htm; Julia Mize, "Samuel Ashbow—a Forgotten Casualty of Bunker Hill," Boston National Historic Park, NPS, https://www.nps.gov/articles/samuel -ashbow-a-forgotten-casualty-of-bunker-hill.htm; George Livermore, "August Meeting: An Historical Research Respecting the Opinions of the Founders of the Republic of Negroes as Slaves, as Citizens, and as Soldiers," *Proceedings of the Massachusetts Historical Society* 6 (1862–1863): 82–248, http://www.jstor.org/stable /25079292. How to make root beer: Susan Verberg, "Root Beer: The Quintessential American Soda," American Homebrewers Association, https://www.homebrewersas sociation.org/beyond-beer/root-beer-the-quintessential-american-soda/. Sites tracing Lexington-Concord militia movements: "A Revolution Begins—a Nation Is Born," Minute Man National Historical Park, NPS, https://www.nps.gov /mima/index.htm. Washington's appointment as commander in chief from "Gen. George Washington, Commander in Chief," America in Class, National Humanities Center, https://americainclass.org/sources/makingrevolution/war/text3/commchief washington.pdf. Broadside: "Wanted for the Continental Army," 1775, from "Early American Imprints, Series I, Doc. 42951," MHS. Lord Dunmore's Proclamation available from NAUK and GLI.

Chapter 6: Of Loss and Loyalty

Boardinghouses, tavern keepers such as Sarah or "Mrs." Yard: Multiple mentions in Adams Papers, including dates of lodging, at Founders Online. Regarding Mary House, Eleanor "Mrs. Nicholas" Trist: Jay Papers, including correspondence between Silas Deane and John Jay, Founders Online. "Miss Jane Port's in Arch Street between Front and Second . . ." in Adams Papers, August 1774, and elsewhere. Both Washington and Jefferson reference Jane Vobe and her tavern on Waller Street in their personal accounts and memoranda as well as Christiana Campbell. Washington, especially, frequented Campbell's tavern on Duke of Gloucester Street: Founders Online. (On more than one occasion I, too, have personally visited the Christiana Campbell Tavern.) Mrs. House's boardinghouse was at the southwest corner of Market and Fifth Streets. Jefferson and Madison were a part of the boardinghouse "family." Ran it with her daughter Eleanor Trist. Anna Coxe Toogood, "Historic Resource Study, Independence Hall, the 18th Century Development, Block One, Chestnut to Market, Fifth to Sixth Streets," Cultural Resource Management, Independence National Historical Park, August 2001, http://npshistory.com/publications /inde/hrs-mall-block-one.pdf. Regarding Mary Miller (GW there on his way out of Philadelphia): "General Orders, 14 September 1777," Founders Online, https://found ers.archives.gov/?q=%22Mary%20Miller%22&s=1111311111&sa=&r=3&sr=. Multiple mentions of the Tun tavern at Founders Online (clearly a popular spot). Its history: The Tun, https://thetun.org. Its relationship to the founding of the Marine Corps: "Tun Tavern: Birthplace of the Marine Corps," MarineParents, https://marinepar ents.com/marinecorps/tuntavern.asp. Esther DeBerdt Reed's name has been, over time and in various publications and archives, written as "de Berdt," "De Berdt," and "DeBerdt." I have chosen the latter, as the most recent scholarly work on her life prefers this spelling. Esther DeBerdt Reed correspondence and life throughout the book taken from Owen S. Ireland, *Sentiments of a British-American Woman: Esther DeBerdt Reed and the American Revolution* (Pennsylvania State University Press, 2017); William B. Reed, *The Life of Esther De Berdt, Afterwards Esther Reed, of Pennsylvania* (Philadelphia: C. Sherman, printer, 1853); William B. Reed, *Life and Correspondence of Joseph Reed*, vols. 1 and 2 (Philadelphia: Lindsay and Blakiston, 1847). Henry Reed, *Life of Joseph Reed* (Boston: Little, Brown, 1848); Silas Deane, regarding

Esther Reed: "Silas Dean Online," Connecticut Historical Society Museum, https://www.silasdeaneonline.org/documents/doc09.htm. "Mrs. Reed," with respect to Joseph Reed, is mentioned repeatedly in Washington's papers at Founders Online. June 12, 1775, Congress declares a day of "humiliation and fasting": *JCC* and Founders Online. Andrew Eliot, April 23, 1775, "What you feared is come upon us": MHS, https://www.masshist.org/database/viewer.php?item_id=1906&img_step=1&mode=dual.

Sarah Winslow Deming, wife of Captain John Deming, quotes from "Sarah Winslow Deming Journal, 1775," MHS, https://www.masshist.org/database/viewer.php?pid=21&ft=Siege%20of%20Boston&item_id=1898. Abigail Adams to John Adams, June 20, 1775, regarding the death of Joseph Warren, and Abigail to JA, "drop in bucket": Founders Online and MHS. Correspondence between Esther, Dennis, and Joseph is from Ireland, *Sentiments*, and Reed, *Life of Joseph Reed*.

Belinda Sutton's life story, including the story of her abduction and life with the Royall family, is taken from petitions filed with the Commonwealth of Massachusetts (listed as Belinda Royall). These and similar documents are part of a growing collection contained in the "Antislavery Petitions Massachusetts Dataverse" at Harvard University: Digital Archive of Massachusetts Anti-Slavery and Anti-Segregation Petitions, Massachusetts Archives, Boston, MA, 2015, "House Unpassed Legislation 1785, Docket 1707, SC1/series 230, Petition of Belinda Royall," https://doi.org/10.7910/DVN/1ZHSM, Harvard Dataverse, V2. Additional primary source documents on Belinda with regard to the Royall family from Royall House, previously cited. Broadside "Wanted for the Continental Army": Issued by Thomas Mifflin, Quarter Master General of the Continental Army under General George Washington, Cambridge, Massachusetts, 21 August 1775, Early American Imprints, Series I, Doc. 42951, MHS. Esther writing from Perth Amboy: Reed sources, previously cited. Mary Katharine Goddard regarding the means of delivering the mail and how it impacted the names of publications: Smithsonian National Postal Museum, 2 Massachusetts Ave. NE, Washington, D.C. 20002. Regarding William Goddard: Ward L. Miner, *William Goddard, Newspaperman* (Duke University Press, 1962). Dunmore's Proclamation available widely, including at GLI: https://www.gilderlehrman.org/history-resources/spotlight-primary-source/lord-dunmores-proclamation-1775. Congress's decision regarding the exclusion of Black soldiers from military: Founders Online. GW regarding those not to be enlisted (boys, old men) and views, "If Virginians are wise . . .": Founders Online. Lund Washington to GW regarding Dunmore's "dreaded proclamation" from Founders Online. Regarding the role of Black soldiers, loyalists, those who escaped enslavement, the Royal Ethiopian Regiment, etc.: extensive historical overview of the opinions of the founders regarding Black individuals in the military and more published by the MHS, including George Livermore, "August Meeting: An Historical Research Respecting the Opinions of the Founders of the Republic of Negroes as Slaves, as Citizens, and as Soldiers," *Proceedings of the Massachusetts Historical Society* 6 (1862–1863): 82–248, http://www.jstor.org/stable/25079292; Sylvia R. Frey, "Between Slavery and Freedom: Virginia Blacks in the American Revolution," *Journal of Southern History* 49, no. 3 (1983); Brian David Palladino, "'From a Determined Resolution to Get Liberty': Slaves and the British in Revolutionary Norfolk County, Virginia, 1775–1781," College of William & Mary, Arts & Sciences, 2000; Charles W. Carey Jr., "Lord Dunmore's Ethiopian Regiment," master's thesis, Virginia Polytechnic Institute and State University, March 1995, https://vtechworks.lib.vt.edu/server/api/core/bitstreams/2cce33bd-d1b2-4109-9877-04e07adfbof5/content. Wheatley letter to GW, and poem: Phillis Wheatley, *Complete Writings* (Penguin Books, 2001), and MHS. GW to Congress, December 31, 1775, regarding Black soldiers in the Continental Army: Founders Online.

Standing in the Circle: Mount Vernon

Details about the grounds, experience, Slave Cemetery wreath-laying taken from personal visits to Mount Vernon as well as participation in wreath-laying ceremony. Additional information about Don Francisco: "Patriotic Piper," George Washington's Mount Vernon, https://www.mountvernon.org/preservation/mount-vernon-ladies -association/behind-the-scenes/patriotic-piper. Individual information about those enslaved at Mount Vernon: "Enslaved People of Mount Vernon" tour. "Saving" of Mount Vernon and history of Mount Vernon Ladies' Association: Denise Kiernan, *We Gather Together* (Dutton, 2020); George Washington's Mount Vernon, https:// www.mountvernon.org/preservation/mount-vernon-ladies-association. Additional information about ongoing research into the lives and remains of the enslaved at Mount Vernon: "African American Burial Ground Survey," George Washington's Mount Vernon, https://www.mountvernon.org/preservation/archaeology/slave -burial-ground-research.

Chapter 7: Prelude to Independence: The Dawn of 1776

Charles W. Carey Jr., *Lord Dunmore's Ethiopian Regiment*, master's thesis, Virginia Polytechnic Institute and State University, March 1995, https://vtechworks.lib.vt.edu /server/api/core/bitstreams/2cce33bd-d1b2-4109-9877-04e07adfb0f5/content; Benjamin Quarles, "Lord Dunmore as Liberator," *William and Mary Quarterly* 15, no. 4 (October 1958): 494–507, https://doi.org/10.2307/2936904. Henry Knox, letter to George Washington, December 17, 1775, "Dragging Cannon from Fort Ticonderoga to Boston, 1775," GLI, https://www.gilderlehrman.org/sites/default/files/inline-pdfs /ready.2437_00222_FPS.pdf; J. L. Bell, "How Many Cannon Did Henry Knox Transport?," *Boston 1775* (blog), January 26, 2017, https://boston1775.blogspot.com/2017/01 /how-many-cannon-did-henry-knox-transport.html; "General Henry Knox Interactive Timeline," Knox Museum, https://www.knoxmuseum.org/henryknox. Fort Ticonderoga: "Fort Ticonderoga: 7 Revolutionary War Site Facts," Fort Ticonderoga, https://fortticonderoga.org/travelerstips/fort-ticonderoga-7-revolutionary-war-site -facts/. "Lake George Watershed," Lake George Association, https://lakegeorgeasso ciation.org/science-protection/citizen-science/lake-george-watershed.

John Adams letter regarding artillery: "1776. Jany. 25. Thursday," Founders Online, NA, https://founders.archives.gov/documents/Adams/01-02-02-0006-0001 -0003. "George Washington's Cambridge Headquarters," NPL, Longfellow House Washington's Headquarters National Historic Site, https://www.nps.gov/long/learn /historyculture/washington-s-cambridge-headquarters.htm. "George Washington," NPL, Longfellow House Washington's Headquarters National Historic Site, https:// www.nps.gov/long/learn/historyculture/george-washington.htm. "Washington, George, 1732–1799, to Henry Knox, February 11, 1776," GLI, https://www.gilderlehr man.org/collection/glc0243700531. "The Burning of Norfolk, 1775–1776," ArcGIS StoryMaps, November 18, 2019, https://storymaps.arcgis.com/stories/792ecb5cb92141 29931f462599714244. Fort Monroe and Old Point Comfort: Joshua Fry et al., *A map of the most inhabited part of Virginia containing the whole province of Maryland: with part of Pensilvania, New Jersey, and North Carolina* (London: Printed for Robt. Sayer, 1775), https://www.loc.gov/item/74693168/; "Fort Monroe," https://fortmonroe .org; "Fort Monroe National Monument," NPS, https://www.nps.gov/fomr/learn /historyculture/index.htm. Burning of Norfolk, movements of the British ships, reports emanating from them, including HMS *Liverpool*, HMS *Fowey*, and correspondence between Dunmore to Germain, Hamond, Snape, and more: *Naval Documents of the American Revolution*, vol. 3, "American Theatre: Dec. 8–Dec. 31, 1775; European Theatre: Nov. 1–Jan. 31, 1776; American Theatre: Jan. 1–Feb. 18, 1776," part 6 of 8 (U.S. Government Printing Office, 1968), electronically published by the American Naval Records Society, 2012; *Naval Documents of the American Revolution*, vol. 4, "American Theatre: Feb. 19–Apr. 17, 1776; European Theatre: Feb. 1–May 25, 1776; American Theatre: Apr. 18–May 8, 1776," part 7 of 8 (U.S. Government Printing Office, 1969), electronically published by the American Naval Records Society, 2012; "Col. John Willoughby, of Norfolk county, and his son, and between 60 and 70 negros, have gone on board lord Dunmore's fleet," *Virginia Gazette*, May 10, 1776, p. 3, https://www.newspapers.com/image-view/40580029/; Matthew Krough, "Lord Dunmore's Navy in Hampton Roads, 1775–1776; Part IV: One Last Grasp for the Old Dominion," Hampton Roads Naval Museum blog, July 3, 2017, https://hamptonroads navalmuseum.blogspot.com/2017/07/lord-dunmores-navy-in-hampton-roads.html; John U. Rees, "'I Offer Freedom to the Blacks of All Rebels That Join Me': Lord Dunmore's Ethiopian Regiment," American Battlefield Trust, October 16, 2020, https:// www.battlefields.org/learn/articles/lord-dunmores-ethiopian-regiment; "Discover Our History," St. Paul's Episcopal Church, Norfolk, VA, https://stpaulsnorfolk.org /about-us/history/. Willoughby Spit versus Willoughby Point: George Holbert Tucker, "Whence Elizabeth River, Willoughby, and Two Points," Norfolk Historical Society, https://www.historicforrest.com/norfolkHistoricalSociety/highlights/03 .html. "Eighteenth Century Virginia Hurricanes," NOAA Climate Prediction Center, https://www.wpc.ncep.noaa.gov/research/roth/va18hur.htm. Willoughby Point mentioned in wills: Jane Griffith Keys, "Virginia Heraldry," *Baltimore Sun*, September 24, 1905, https://www.newspapers.com/image-view/372262537/. Williamsburg resident argues Willoughby did not flee to Dunmore's vessel: Alex Purdie, "It having been incontestably proved to me . . ." (advertisement), *Virginia Gazette*, May 17, 1776, https://www.newspapers.com/image-view/40580035/. Discussion of Willoughby family land, wills, and inheritances: W. G. Stanard, "Abstracts of Virginia Land Patents," *Virginia Magazine of History and Biography* 4, no. 1 (1896): 75–85, http://www.jstor .org/stable/4241940. Regarding enslaved persons who fled Willoughby: Sylvia R. Frey, "Between Slavery and Freedom: Virginia Blacks in the American Revolution," *Journal of Southern History* 49, no. 3 (1983): 375–98, https://doi.org/10.2307/2208101. Location of Mill Point, later Fort Nelson: James Stratton, *A plan of Portsmouth Harbour in the province of Virginia shewing the works erected by the British forces for its defence* (1782), LOC, https://www.loc.gov/item/gm71000689/. "A History of Gwynn's Island," The Gwynn's Island Museum, https://www.gwynnsislandmuseum.org/gwynn-s-island; "Battle of Gwynn's Island," Virginia Places, http://www.virginiaplaces.org/military /gwynnbattle.html#two. Lorenda Holmes and Holland linen: Ann Buermann Wass, "'I Am the Neatest Worker of the Party': Making and Mending the Family's Wardrobe," *Jane Austen Society of America* 36, no. 1 (Winter 2015), https://jasna.org/publi cations-2/persuasions-online/vol36no1/wass/. Dock Street and Burling's Slip: John Montrésor and Georges-Louis Le Rouge, *Plan de New-York et des environs* (Paris: Chez le Rouge, 1775), LOC, https://www.loc.gov/item/gm71000988/. Mortier House: Chris Walters, "Charlton Street & Varick Street," *Corner by Corner* (blog), March 19, 2010, https://cornerbycorner.wordpress.com/tag/abraham-mortier/. "Richmond Hill," HMdb.org: The Historical Marker Database, https://www.hmdb.org/m.asp?m= 163867. George Washington Papers, "General Orders," April 14, 1776, June 10, 1776, July 7, 1776, August 7, 1776, and August 19, 1776, Founders Online, NA, https://found ers.archives.gov/?q=mortier&s=1111211111&sa=&r=1&sr=. Eastchester: Edna Gabler, "Caught Between the Lines: Eastchester, New York, During the American Revolution," *Journal of the American Revolution*, February 14, 2019, https://allthingsliberty .com/2019/02/caught-between-the-lines-eastchester-new-york-during-the-american -revolution/. Wm. Abbatt, "The Battle of Pell's Point or Pelham, October 18, 1776," *Proceedings of the New York State Historical Association* 9 (1910): 267–73, https://www

.jstor.org/stable/42889431. Hickey trial and execution: Anna Diamond, "The Plot to Kill George Washington," *Smithsonian* (online), December 2018, https://www.smith sonianmag.com/history/plot-kill-george-washington-180970729/; George Washington, John Adams, and Thomas Jefferson Papers, "General Orders" et al. pertaining to court-martial and execution of Thomas Hickey, Founders Online, NA, https://founders.archives.gov/?q=%22thomas+hickey%22&s=1111211111&sa=&r=1&sr=; "Warrant for Execution of Thomas Hickey, New York, June 28, 1776," Northern Illinois University Libraries, https://web.archive.org/web/20140911001828/http://lincoln.lib.niu.edu/cgi-bin/philologic/getobject.pl?c.17582:1.amarch; "Court Martial for the Trial of Thomas Hickey and Others," Northern Illinois University Libraries, https://web.archive.org/web/20130929135526/http://lincoln.lib.niu.edu/cgi-bin/amarch/getdoc.pl?%2Fvar%2Flib%2Fphilologic%2Fdatabases%2Famarch%2F.17512; "226 Years Ago: Irishman Thomas Hickey Executed for Plotting Against Washington," *The Irish Echo*, February 16, 2011, https://group.irishecho.com/2011/02/226-years-ago-irishman-thomas-hickey-executed-for-plotting-against-washington-2/; Millard E. Moon, "*The First Conspiracy: The Secret Plot to Kill George Washington*. By Brad Meltzer and Josh Mensch, New York, N.Y.: Flatiron Books, 2019" (book review), *Journal of Strategic Security* 12, no. 3 (2019): 170–74, https://doi.org/10.5038/1944-0472.12.3.1767. Troop Movements, New York, 1776: Vincent J. Esposito and Matthew Forney Steele, *Revolutionary War, New York and Trenton, 1776–1777* (map), Department of Military Art and Engineering, United States Military Academy, 1956, https://www.loc.gov/resource/g3701sm.gcw0096000/?sp=10&st=image&r=0.107,0.203,0.987,0.495,0. Lenape: "History of the Hudson River: The First People of the River," Riverkeeper, https://www.riverkeeper.org/hudson-river/hudson-river-journey/the-first-people-of-the-river/. Mary Smith and Elizabeth Thomson: "George Washington Papers, Series 4, General Correspondence: Mary Smith, June 28, 1776, List of George Washington's Household Goods," https://www.loc.gov/item/mgw445308/; Nancy K. Loane, "General Washington's Housekeeper," Tredyffrin Easttown Historical Society, *History Quarterly* 43, no. 3 (Summer 2006): 84–87, https://www.tehistory.org/hqda/html/v43/v43n3p084.html; Joan Dallas, "Elizabeth Thompson," George Washington's Mount Vernon, https://www.mountvernon.org/library/digitalhistory/digital-encyclopedia/article/elizabeth-thompson/. Records kept by Gibbs in Washington's household: "George Washington Papers, Series 5, Financial Papers: Revolutionary War Receipt Book, May, 1776–November, 1780," LOC, https://www.loc.gov/item/mgw500027/; "Richmond Hill House, Varick Street, Between Charlton and Vandam Streets," New York Public Library Digital Collections, The Miriam and Ira D. Wallach Division of Art, Prints and Photographs, https://digitalcollections.nypl.org/items/04a1db30-c55e-012f-e0d3-58d385a7bc34; "George Washington Papers, Series 4, General Correspondence: Mary Smith, June 28, 1776, List of George Washington's Household Goods"; Kennedy House: "The Campaign of 1776 Around New York and Brooklyn, Including a New and Circumstantial Account of the Battle of Long Island and the Loss of New York," Project Gutenberg, https://www.gutenberg.org/files/21990/21990-h/21990-h.htm#Page_86; Tom Miller, "Lost 1745 Kennedy House—No. 1 Broadway," *Daytonian in Manhattan* (blog), July 9, 2012, http://daytoninmanhattan.blogspot.com/2012/07/lost-1745-kennedy-house-no-1-broadway.html; "Residence of Governor George Clinton, in Pearl Street Opposite Cedar Street—Washington's Quarters on Assuming Command of the Army in New York," NYPL Digital Collections, https://digitalcollections.nypl.org/items/03eafcb0-c55e-012f-d5d6-58d385a7bc34; Francis W. Maerschalck and G. Duyckinck, *A Plan of the City of New York from an Actual Survey, Anno Domini, M[D]CC,LV* [New York? Printed, ingraved for, and sold by G. Duyckinck? 1755], LOC, https://www.loc.gov/item/73691802/. Fraunces Tavern: "Long Room Party and Social Life" and "History of Fraunces Tavern," Fraunces Tavern Museum,

https://www.frauncestavernmuseum.org/the-long-room-exhibition, https://www
.frauncestavernmuseum.org/history; Henry Russell Drowne, *A Sketch of Fraunces
Tavern and Those Connected with Its History* (Fraunces Tavern, 1919), https://www
.google.com/books/edition/A_Sketch_of_Fraunces_Tavern_and_Those_Co
/I5dQD4S4-ZEC?hl=en&gbpv=0; "Fraunces Tavern Block Historic Designation Report," City of New York, Landmarks Preservation Commission, 1978, http://s-media
.nyc.gov/agencies/lpc/lp/0994.pdf; "The Bombing of Fraunces Tavern [1975]," in
"Fraunces Tavern, New York, NY," CityDays, 2025, https://citydays.com/places/fraun
ces-tavern/; Jonildo Bacelar, "Fraunces Tavern Architecture," Geographic Guide, Old
New York, Historic Hotels, May 2023, https://www.geographicguide.com/united
-states/nyc/antique/hotels/taverns/fraunces-tavern/architecture.htm. Jacob Walton
Estate, Belview: Tom Miller, "The 1799 Gracie Mansion," *Daytonian in Manhattan*
(blog), January 24, 2011, http://daytoninmanhattan.blogspot.com/2011/01/1799
-gracie-mansion.html; David W. Dunlap, "Drawing Reveals What Stood on Site of
Gracie Mansion," *City Room* (blog), *New York Times*, October 22, 2007, https://ar
chive.nytimes.com/cityroom.blogs.nytimes.com/2007/10/22/drawing-reveals-what
-stood-on-site-of-gracie-mansion/. Bedloe's Island, oyster beds, Lenape: "Liberty Island Cultural Landscape," NPS, https://www.nps.gov/articles/000/stli-liberty-island
-650003.htm. Harry Washington: Cassandra Pybus, "Washington's Revolution
(Harry That Is, Not George)," *Atlantic Studies* 3, no. 2 (2006): 183–99, https://doi.org
/10.1080/14788810600875414. New York campaign: Ziyad Rahaman Azeez, "New York
Campaign [1776]," George Washington's Mount Vernon, https://www.mountvernon
.org/library/digitalhistory/digital-encyclopedia/article/new-york-campaign/; "Intelligence extraordinary; Itinerant governor; Generalissimo," *Virginia Gazette* (Williamsburg), June 1, 1775, 3; image reproduced in the Colonial Williamsburg Digital
Library, "Virginia Gazette, 1775, Image 0098hi," https://research.colonialwilliams
burg.org/CWDLImages/VA_GAZET/Images/PI/1775/0098hi.jpg, and at https://
www.newspapers.com/image-view/1144064241/?match=1&terms=%22intelligence
%20extraordinary; Gerald Holland, "The Seizure of the *Virginia Gazette, or Norfolk
Intelligencer,*" *Journal of the American Revolution*, January 20, 2016, https://allthings
liberty.com/2016/01/the-seizure-of-the-virginia-gazette-or-norfolk-intelligencer/.

"What Was the Battle of Great Bridge?," in "How Did Virginians Secure
Their Freedom from British Occupation?," Jamestown-Yorktown Foundation, https://
www.jyfmuseums.org/learn/research-and-collections/essays/what-was-the-battle-of
-great-bridge; Patrick H. Hannum, "The Battle of Great Bridge," Encyclopedia Virginia, November 27, 2023, https://encyclopediavirginia.org/entries/the-battle
-of-great-bridge/. Thomas Elliott, "Ships in Norfolk and Hampton Roads, Dec. 30,
1775," *Naval Documents of the American Revolution*, vol. 3, "American Theatre: Dec.
8–Dec. 31, 1775; European Theatre: Nov. 1–Jan. 31, 1776; American Theatre: Jan. 1–Feb.
18, 1776," part 2 of 8, p. 309 (U.S. Government Printing Office, 1968), electronically
published by the American Naval Records Society, 2012. "Public Prints . . . Dirty Little Borough": Lord Dunmore to Lord Dartmouth, *Naval Documents of the American
Revolution*, vol. 2, "American Theatre: Sept. 3–Oct. 31, 1775; European Theatre: Aug.
11, 1775–Oct. 31, 1775; American Theatre: Nov. 1, 1775–Dec. 7, 1776," p. 316 (U.S. Government Printing Office, 1966). Washington Papers Editors, *The Papers of Martha
Washington* (University of Virginia Press, 2022). Robert Howe (Continental Colonel),
"Report on the Losses of Civilians in Norfolk, 1775," *Papers of the Continental Congress* 3, no. 12 (1776): 212–13; "The Revolutionary War Letters of Henry and Lucy Knox"
collection at GLI, previously cited. Arnaud Balvay, "Colonies and Empires: French
Colonial Expansion and Franco-Amerindian Alliances," Canadian Museum of History, selected articles, https://www.historymuseum.ca/virtual-museum-of-new
-france/colonies-and-empires/colonial-expansion-and-alliances/. "Spy Letters of the

American Revolution: John André," William L. Clements Library, University of Michigan, https://clements.umich.edu/exhibit/spy-letters-of-the-american-revolution/people/. "Early History of 105 Brattle Street," Longfellow House Washington Headquarters, NPS, https://www.nps.gov/long/learn/historyculture/early-history-of-105-brattle-street.htm. Caitlin De Angelis et al., "Black History at the Vassall Estate," NPS, September 15, 2025. "George Washington to Phillis Wheatley, 28 February, 1776," Founders Online, NA, https://founders.archives.gov/documents/Washington/03-03-02-0281. George Washington, "Letter to Lieutenant Colonel Joseph Reed (regarding Wheatley)," February 10, 1776, Founders Online, NA, https://founders.archives.gov/documents/Washington/03-03-02-0209. "John Adams, Letter to Mercy Otis Warren, April 16, 1776," Founders Online, NA, https://founders.archives.gov/documents/Adams/06-04-02-0044. Mercy Otis Warren, "Letter to John Adams, 11 October, 1773," Founders Online, NA, https://founders.archives.gov/documents/Adams/06-01-02-0106. Isaac Royall selling his enslaved people: Royall House primary sources, previously cited; "The Revolutionary War Letters of Henry and Lucy Knox" collection at GLI.

Chapter 8: Manahatta

Additional resources for Lenni-Lenape, Hudson, Dutch, etc., in "Hidden City" sources. Lenape: "Native American Indian Resources: Lenape/Delaware People," College of Staten Island, The City University of New York, https://library.csi.cuny.edu/c.php?g=1429930&p=10684392#:~:text=Lenape%2FDelaware%20People&text=In%20the%2017th%20cent.%2C%20they,vicinity%20of%20the%20Delaware%20River. Lenni-Lenape, young women, Staten Island: "Women and the American Story," The New York Historical, https://wams.nyhistory.org/tag/lenni-lenape/. Wampum from time of Dutch settlers, Dutch-Lenape interaction, more early Manhattan history: Russell Shorto, *The Island at the Center of the World: The Epic Story of Dutch Manhattan and the Forgotten Colony That Shaped America* (Doubleday, 2004). Maritime importance: "Exhibition Text—New York at Its Core: Port City," Museum of the City of New York, https://www.mcny.org/nyaic-portcity-online; Ives Goddard, "Origin and Meaning of the Name 'Manhattan,'" Smithsonian Libraries and Archives, https://repository.si.edu/bitstream/handle/10088/16790/anth_Manhattan.pdf. "New York Slave Market About 1730," NYPL Digital Collections, https://digitalcollections.nypl.org/items/510d47e1-4097-a3d9-e040-e00a18064a99. "Mannahatta Park, New York's Municipal Slave Market," New York City Department of Parks & Recreation, https://www.nycgovparks.org/parks/mannahatta-park/highlights/19696. All information regarding Lorenda Holmes's personal experiences and observations from the following collection: Lorenda Holmes, "North America: Compensation: Memorial and petition of Lorenda Holmes for compensation for loss of property in New York city, and Sufferings experienced when acting as a courier for the Loyalist cause, 1789," The National Archives, Kew, UK, https://discovery.nationalarchives.gov.uk/details/r/C7666871. (Much appreciation to the NAUK for getting the documents scanned and over to me so quickly.) Queens Head tavern, architecture, ads, "all sorts of pickles," etc.: Jonildo Bacelar, "Fraunces Tavern," Geographic Guide, Old New York, Historic Hotels, May 2023, https://www.geographicguide.com/united-states/nyc/antique/hotels/taverns/fraunces-tavern/fraunces-tavern.htm#google_vignette; Fraunces Tavern Museum, "Long Room Archive," "Sign of the Queen's Head" advertisement, Fraunces Tavern Museum, https://www.frauncestavernmuseum.org/long-room-archive; Bacelar, "Fraunces Tavern." Kennedy House: Harry Schenawolf, "Washington's New York City Headquarters—No. 1 Broadway," *Revolutionary War Journal*, July 9, 2013, https://revolutionarywarjournal.com/washingtons-headquarters/; "Kennedy House: Washington's headquarters, No. 1 Broadway," NYPL Digital Collections, https://digitalcol

lections.nypl.org/items/510d47e0-d45b-a3d9-e040-e00a18064a99; Tom Miller, "The Lost 1745 Kennedy House—No. 1 Broadway," *Daytonian in Manhattan* (blog), July 9, 2012, http://daytoninmanhattan.blogspot.com/2012/07/lost-1745-kennedy-house-no-1-broadway.html. Lucy shows up in New York, Lucy, Henry correspondence: previously cited. Willoughby departs: *Virginia Gazette*, May 10, 1776, https://www.newspapers.com/image/405800291; "Portsmouth Naval Hospital, 'Hospital Point,' Fort Nelson Park," HMdb.org: The Historical Marker Database, https://www.hmdb.org/m.asp?m=83941; Naval Shipyard (miscellaneous files); Bernie Kirsch, "A Shipyard in Portsmouth, Virginia to the American Revolution," RootsWeb genealogy, https://freepages.rootsweb.com/~vancgenealogyrecords/genealogy/Misc%20Files/our_naval_shipyard.htm; "Thomas Jefferson, June–July 1776, Map of Action at Gwyn's Island, Chesapeake Bay," LOC, https://www.loc.gov/resource/mtj1.001_0555_0555/; W. Hugh Moomaw, "The British Leave Colonial Virginia," *Journal of the Early Republic* 5, no. 2 (1985): 231–54, https://www.jstor.org/stable/4246423. For Perth: Cassandra Pybus, "'One Militant Saint': The Much Traveled Life of Mary Perth," *Journal of Colonialism and Colonial History* 9, no. 3 (2008), https://dx.doi.org/10.1353/cch.0.0035; Perth, others, to Gwynn: *Virginia Gazette*, August 31, 1776, 3, https://www.newspapers.com/image/40483539/; Black Pioneers: "A History of the Black Pioneers," The On-Line Institute for Advanced Loyalist Studies, https://www.royalprovincial.com/military/rhist/blkpion/blkhist.htm; "Revolution: The Black Pioneers," Black Loyalists: Our History, Our People, https://blackloyalist.com/cdc/story/revolution/pioneers.htm; Kemisa Kassa, "The Black Pioneers Loyalist Company," NCpedia, State Library of North Carolina, 2024, https://www.ncpedia.org/anchor/black-pioneers-loyalist. Perth among those who left with Dunmore to go to Gwynn and Mill Point: Pybus, "One Militant Saint," previously cited. Hannah Thomas, lighthouse keeper: Mary Louise Clifford and J. Candace Clifford, *Women Who Kept the Lights: An Illustrated History of Female Lighthouse Keepers* (Cypress Communications, 1993).

Chapter 9: A Plot Is Afoot

All references and information regarding Lorenda Holmes's experience from Holmes, "North America," NAUK. "Life Guards," George Washington's Mount Vernon, https://www.mountvernon.org/library/digitalhistory/digital-encyclopedia/article/life-guards. Mary Smith "taken up," needs housekeeper: "George Washington to Colonel James Clinton, 28 June 1776," Founders Online, NA, https://www.founders.archives.gov/documents/Washington/03-05-02-0088. Hudson and British activity: Charles Stark, "The Twin Mysteries of Henry Hudson—His 1609 Voyage," Hudson River Valley Institute, https://www.hudsonrivervalley.org/the-twin-mysteries. Peas as sustenance for troops, price of peas: "George Washington to John Hancock, 4–5 August 1775," https://founders.archives.gov/?q=%20Author%3A%22Washington%2C%20George%22%20peas&s=1111311111&r=20; "General Orders, 24 December 1775," Founders Online, NA, https://www.founders.archives.gov/documents/Washington/03-02-02-0555. Regarding Fraunces Tavern: Henry Russell Drowne, *A Sketch of Fraunces Tavern and Those Connected with Its History* (Fraunces Tavern, 1919). "Fraunces Tavern Block Historic Designation Report," City of New York, Landmarks Preservation Commission, 1978, http://s-media.nyc.gov/agencies/lpc/lp/0994.pdf.

Shades of Indigo: South Carolina Low Country

Personal experience at Middleton Place. Middleton Place offers indigo programming throughout the year. Events calendar: https://www.middletonplace.org. Barbara Doyle et al., *Beyond the Fields: Slavery at Middleton Place* (University of South Carolina Press, 2009). Historical Marker Indigo: HMdb.org, Historical Marker Database,

https://www.hmdb.org/map.asp?markers=224198,30544,224196,30804,224191,67735,2
24189,224187,67734. Original Site of Wappoo: CLS and SCHS collections.

Chapter 10: Planter. Mother. Patriot.

Eliza Pinckney background, writings, letters throughout chapter and book taken from the Papers of Eliza Lucas Pinckney (collection), South Carolina Historical Society, Charleston; Harriott Horry Ravenel, *Eliza Pinckney* (Charles Scribner's Sons, 1896); Lori Glover, *Eliza Lucas Pinckney: An Independent Woman in the Age of Revolution* (Yale University Press, 2020); Margaret F. Pickett, *Eliza Lucas Pinckney: Colonial Plantation Manager and Mother of American Patriots, 1722–1793* (McFarland, 2016); and Elise Pinckney, ed., *The Letterbook of Eliza Lucas Pinckney* (University of South Carolina Press, 1972). All citations from *South-Carolina Gazette*, including references to "Agricola" and "500,000 pounds of indigo," from collection at CLS. Nic Butler, "Quarantine in Charleston Harbor, 1698–1949," April 10, 2020, https://www.ccpl.org /charleston-time-machine/quarantine-charleston-harbor-1698-1949. Charleston Time Machine, Charleston County Public Library, https://www.ccpl.org/charleston -time-machine/nearly-1000-cargos-legacy-importing-africans-charleston. Charleston, Lowcountry, and its role in the slave trade widely documented and also from Nic Butler, "Nearly 1,000 Cargos: The Legacy of Importing Africans into Charleston," October 15, 2018, Charleston Time Machine, Charleston County Public Library, https://www.ccpl.org/charleston-time-machine/nearly-1000-cargos-legacy-importing -africans-charleston; and "African Passages, Lowcountry Adaptations," Lowcountry Digital History Initiative, College of Charleston, https://ldhi.library.cofc.edu/exhibits /show/africanpassageslowcountryadapt/sectionii_introduction/africans_in_carolina.

About indigo production in general, from my personal experience/instruction at Middleton Place Plantation, SC, and articles in *South-Carolina Gazette*, already referenced. Quash/John Williams at Pinckney plantations and after, from Glover and Pickett. Nic Butler, "Florence O'Sullivan: South Carolina's Irish Enigma," Charleston Time Machine, Charleston County Public Library, March 10, 2023, https://www.ccpl .org/charleston-time-machine/florence-osullivan-south-carolinas-irish-enigma. Leigh Jones Handal, "Florence O'Sullivan Faded into History, yet His Name Has Survived with Sullivan's Island," *Post and Courier*, July 14, 2025, https://www.postandcourier .com/news/sc-history-sullivans-island-florence-osullivan/article_60c11316-9be0-4c 09-a4e4-52bdd3ce973c.html. Patrick Melvin, "Captain Florence O'Sullivan and the Origins of Carolina," *South Carolina Historical Magazine* 76, no. 4 (1975): 235–49, http://www.jstor.org/stable/27567338. Pesthouses, what sea captains must do when approaching SC: Thomas Cooper, ed., *The Statutes at Large of South Carolina*, vol. 2 (Columbia, SC: A. S. Johnson, 1837). Matthew Darly and Mary Darly, print/etching, *Miss Carolina Sulivan—one of the obstinate daughters of America, 1776*, British Cartoon Prints collection, LOC.

Chapter 11: Shades of Freedom: July 4, 1776

Weather in Philadelphia on July 4, 1776: Thomas Jefferson, Weather Observation, July 4, 1776, Memorandum Books, 1776, Founders Online, NA, https://founders.archives .gov/documents/Jefferson/02-01-02-0010; "Weather Observations," Thomas Jefferson Encyclopedia, Monticello.org, https://www.monticello.org/research-education /thomas-jefferson-encyclopedia/weather-observations; discussion of the thermometer Thomas Jefferson bought on July 4, 1776, in Philadelphia, in "Thermometers," Thomas Jefferson Encyclopedia, Monticello.org, https://www.monticello.org/research -education/thomas-jefferson-encyclopedia/thermometer. News from Lisbon: *Maryland Gazette*, July 4, 1776, https://www.newspapers.com/image-view/590965895/;

Pennsylvania Evening Post, Saturday, July 6, 1776, NYPL Digital Collections, https:// digitalcollections.nypl.org/items/36fcc270-c606-012f-0aa5-58d385a7bc34. Abigail Adams to JA regarding "Manly sentiments" being expunged from the Declaration: "Abigail to John Adams, 13 July 1776," Founders Online, NA, https://founders.archives .gov/documents/Adams/04-02-02-0026. "Jefferson's Original 'Rough Draught' of the Declaration of Independence, 11 June–4 July 1776," Founders Online, NA, https:// founders.archives.gov/documents/Jefferson/01-01-02-0176-0004. Jefferson's stay at Declaration House in Philadelphia: "Declaration House," Independence National Historic Park, https://www.nps.gov/inde/learn/historyculture/places-declaration house.htm; "Robert Hemmings," Thomas Jefferson Encyclopedia, Monticello.org, https://www.monticello.org/research-education/thomas-jefferson-encyclopedia/robert -hemmings. Committee of Five: "Declaration of Independence (1776)," Milestone Documents, "Declaration of Independence (1776)," NA, https://www.archives.gov /milestone-documents/declaration-of-independence. Children born into slavery at Monticello: "Monticello Enslaved Community Database," search engine results from https://www.monticello.org/enslaveddb. Removal of anti-slavery clause of Declaration of Independence: "Extract from Thomas Jefferson's Notes of Proceedings in the Continental Congress," Jefferson Quotes & Family Letters, Monticello: https://tjrs .monticello.org/letter/54#X3184736; Abigail Adams's letter with "Remember all Men would be tyrants if they could": "Abigail Adams to John Adams, 31 March 1776," Founders Online, NA, https://founders.archives.gov/documents/Adams /04-01-02-0241. "Dunlap Broadside (First Printing of the Declaration of Independence)," National Archives, https://www.archives.gov/dc/highlights/dunlap -broadside; Michael North, "Printing the Declaration of Independence," *Bibliomania*, Library of Congress Blogs, July 4, 2023, https://blogs.loc.gov/bibliomania/2023/07/04 /printing-the-declaration-of-independence. Henry Knox letter to brother William announcing Lucy had arrived safely at Fairfield: "Knox, Henry, 1750–1806, to William Knox [July 4, 1776]," GLI, https://www.gilderlehrman.org/collection/glc0243700360. Henry Knox letter to brother William informing him that Lucy was ill: "Knox, Henry, 1750–1806, to William Knox," GLI, June 13, 1776," https://www.gilderlehrman.org /collection/glc0243700341.

Chapter 12: Two Weeks (or So) in July

See notes in chapter 1 for an overview of Nanye'hi/Nancy Ward sources. Proclamation Line of 1763, Oconostota, and comments from congresses and treaty talks of 1760s, including role of wampum: *Indian Congresses and Treaties*, Gage Papers, vol. 137, *Journal of the Superintendent's Proceedings of Congress held at Hard Labour, South Carolina, 28 Sept.–17 Oct. 1768*, 14 pp.; Augusta, Georgia, 12–14 Nov. 1768, pp. 1525, copy by William Ogilvy, CLE document. Henry Hamilton, British lieutenant governor of Detroit, induced Indigenous allies to raid frontier settlements: "Henry Hamilton," George Rogers Clark National Historical Park, National Park Service, https:// www.nps.gov/people/henry-hamilton.htm. Scholarly discussion of Hamilton's coordination with the Cherokee and the broader Cherokee-American war: Jordan Baker, "The Cherokee-American War from the Cherokee Perspective," *Journal of the American Revolution*, July 29, 2021, https://allthingsliberty.com/2021/07/the-cherokee -american-war-from-the-cherokee-perspective. Ward and choices: Michelene E. Pesantubbee, "Nancy Ward: American Patriot or Cherokee Nationalist?," *American Indian Quarterly* 38, no. 2 (Spring 2014): 177–206. White (or sometimes "black") drink: King, *Memoirs . . . Timberlake*, previously cited. Cherokee clans and Aniwahya ("wolf") clan specifically from author visit to Oconaluftee Indian Village and the Museum of the Cherokee People, Cherokee, NC; and Bonnie Ramsey, "The Seven Clans of the Cherokee," Owlcation, October 25, 2023, https://owlcation.com

/humanities/The-Seven-Clans-of-the-Cherokee. Wampum war belts presented at 1768 meeting: *Indian Congresses and Treaties*, CLE document, previously cited. Further discussion of wampum, war belts: NAIS (School of Arts & Sciences, University of Pennsylvania), "Wampum Belts in American Museums," NAIS Events, University of Pennsylvania, March 16, 2023, https://nais.sas.upenn.edu/events/wampum-belts -american-museums; Kerr Houston, "Rereading Wampum: The Penn Treaty Belt and Indeterminate Iconographies," *Panorama: Journal of the Association of Historians of American Art* 9, no. 1 (Spring 2023), https://journalpanorama.org/article/re-reading -wampum/; *Haudenosaunee Guide for Educators*, Smithsonian National Museum of the American Indian, George Gustav Heye Center (NMAI, Smithsonian Institution, 2009); Anthony Brown, "Wampum and the Cherokee People," The Cherokee One Feather, November 18, 2013, https://theonefeather.com/2013/11/18/wampum-and-the -cherokee-people/. Gwynn's Island: Michael Cecere, "Battle of Gwynn's Island: Lord Dunmore's Last Stand in Virginia," *Journal of the American Revolution*, May 26, 2016, https://allthingsliberty.com/2016/05/battle-of-gwynns-island-lord-dunmores -last-stand-in-virginia/. Dunmore's injury: "Battle of Gwynn's Island," Virginia Places, http://www.virginiaplaces.org/military/gwynnbattle.html. Washington's order to gather troops for a reading of the Declaration: George Washington, "General Orders, 9 July 1776," Founders Online, NA, https://founders.archives.gov/documents /Washington/03-05-02-0176. Samuel Blatchley Webb's recollections of the riot: George Washington, "General Orders, 10 July 1776," Founders Online, NA, https:// founders.archives.gov/documents/Washington/03-05-02-0185; and Worthington Chauncey Ford, ed., *Correspondence and Journals of Samuel Blachley Webb*, vol. 1 (New York: publisher unknown, 1893–94). Maps as cited in Global Notes. Progeny of Oliver Wolcott the signer: Descendants of the Signers of the Declaration of Independence, "Oliver Wolcott, 1726–1797," Descendants of the Signers of the Declaration of Independence 1776, https://www.dsdi1776.com/signer/oliver-wolcott/. Wolcott family and story: Ellen G. Miles, "'Memorials of Great & Good Men Who Were My Friends': Portraits in the Life of Oliver Wolcott, Jr.," American Antiquarian Society, 1998; Roger Wolcott, *Family Jottings* (privately printed, 1939). Elizabeth C. Barney Buel, "A Mother of the American Revolution," *Daughters of the American Revolution Magazine*, January 1924, https.//www.google.com/books/edition/Daughters_of_the _American_Revolution_Mag/1vwKAAAAIAAJ?hl=en&gbpv=1&dq=Elizabeth+C.+ Barney+Buel,+%E2%80%9CA+Mother+of+the+American+Revolution,%E2%80%9D& pg=PA561&printsec=frontcover.

The Hidden City

Descriptions, observations from numerous personal travels to New York. Former location of Richmond Hill house from overlaying maps, present-day and historical (ARGO). (Bowling Green) PMH Staff, "Frederick Philipse and the Bowling Green," Philipse Manor Hall State Historic Site, May 4, 2023, https://www.philipsemanorhall .com/blog/frederick-philipse-and-the-bowling-green; New York City Shoreline marker from repeated visits to site; "Ear Inn in the James Brown House," CityLore, October 2011, https://citylore.org/places/ear-inn-in-the-james-brown-house/; Sam Moskowitz, "I Feel Good About the James Brown House Landmarking," Village Preservation, November 19, 2020, https://www.villagepreservation.org/2020/11/19/i-feel -good-about-the-james-brown-house-landmarking/; "Ear Inn (James Brown House)," HMdb.org, Historical Marker Database, https://www.hmdb.org/m.asp?m= 23058; Walker Schulte Schneider, "Five Hidden Secrets of NYC's Iconic Bar the Ear Inn," *TimeOut New York*, March 20, 2024, https://www.timeout.com/newyork/news /five-hidden-secrets-of-nycs-iconic-bar-the-ear-inn-032024; "1700–1775 NYC: Metropolitan Progress: Setting the Stage for American Independence," History101.NYC, https://www.history101.nyc/new-york-city-in-the-1700s; "A Tour of Native New York," Barnard College, November 1, 2019, https://barnard.edu/news/tour-native-new-york; Jenna Kunze, "Native New York: Dispelling the Myth of the Sale of Manhattan & More," *Native News Online*, December 8, 2021, https://nativenewsonline.net/arts-entertainment/native-new-york-no-manhattan-wasn-t-sold-to-the-dutch-for-24-worth-of-trinkets-and-beads; "Selling Staten Island," Women and the American Story, The New York Historical, https://wams.nyhistory.org/early-encounters/dutch-colonies/selling-staten-island/; SoHo Broadway Initiative, "Looking Back at Broadway's Origins as a Lenape Trail," SOHO Broadway, September 29, 2023, https://sohobroadway.org/looking-back-at-broadways-origins/; "Lenape/Delaware People," College of Staten Island, The City University of New York, https://library.csi.cuny.edu/c.php?g=1429930&p=10684392. Colleen Connolly, "True Native New Yorkers Can Never Truly Reclaim Their Homeland," *Smithsonian Magazine*, October 5, 2018, https://www.smithsonianmag.com/history/true-native-new-yorkers-can-never-truly-reclaim-their-homeland-180970472/; Walter Licht et al., "The Original People and Their Land: Lenape Pre-History to the 18th Century," West Philadelphia Collaborative History, University of Pennsylvania, https://collaborativehistory.gse.upenn.edu/stories/original-people-and-their-land-lenape-pre-history-18th-century; "Manahatta to Manhattan: Native Americans in Lower Manhattan," Smithsonian Museum of the American Indian, 2010, https://ospi.k12.wa.us/sites/default/files/2023-10/manahatta_to_manhattan.pdf; Brian, "Kintekoying," *Off the Grid: Village Preservation Blog*, March 4, 2011, https://www.villagepreservation.org/2011/03/04/the-native-american-origins-of-astor-place/; "Common Myths About Native Americans," Muwekma Ohlone Tribe, August 2021, https://muwekma.org/blog/2021/august/common-myths-about-native-americans.html; Ann Vettikkal, "The Lenape of Manahatta: A Struggle for Acknowledgement," The Eye, *Columbia Spectator*, September 6, 2022, https://www.columbiaspectator.com/the-eye/2022/09/06/the-lenape-of-manahatta-a-struggle-for-acknowledgement/; "Entity Description: Tribe—Wappinger," Mapping Early New York/Encyclopedia, New Amsterdam History Center, 2020, https://encyclopedia.nahc-mapping.org/node/8161; "Early Encounters in Native New York: Did Native People Really Sell Manhattan?," National Museum of the American Indian, https://americanindian.si.edu/nk360/manhattan/pdf/manhattan-rr-timeline.pdf; Jason Graziadei, "Nantucket's 'Quentin the Quahog' Predicts an Early Spring," *Nantucket Current*, February 2, 2025, https://nantucketcurrent.com/news/quentin-the-quahog-predicts-an-early-spring; "Land of the Lenape: A Violent Tale of Conquest and Betrayal," *The Bowery Boys* (podcast), July 23, 2020, https://www.boweryboyshistory.com/2020/07/sad-tale-lenape-original-native-new-yorkers.html; Nora Thompson Dean, "Some of the Ways of the Delaware Indian Women," Official Web Site of the Delaware Tribe, https://delawaretribe.org/blog/2016/08/07/some-of-the-ways-of-the-delaware-indian-women/; "Wappinger—Easterner," Hudson River Valley Institute, https://www.hudsonrivervalley.org/wappinger. "The Siwanoy Nation—a History," Tribal Council of the Siwanoy Nation, https://www.siwanoynation.org/tribal-history. Taylor Smith, "Lenni-Lenape: The Original Residents of New Jersey," *Princeton Magazine*, September 15, 2021, https://www.princetonmagazine.com/lenni-lenape/; "Wampum and Colonial Currency," Philipse Manor Hall State Historic Site, https://www.philipsemanorhall.com/explore3/wampum-and-money; "Wampum," Ganondagan Seneca Art and Culture Center, https://www.ganondagan.org/wampum; Denise Neil-Binion et al., "Lenape Beadwork," Delaware Tribe, https://delawaretribe.org/wp-content/uploads/Lenape-Beadwork.pdf; Ann C. Tweedy, "From Beads to Bounty: How Wampum Became America's First Currency—and Lost Its Power," *Indian Country Today*, January 14, 2023, https://ictnews.org/archive/from-beads-to-bounty-how-wampum-became-americas-first-currencyand-lost-its-power/;

Wynne Dough, "Verrazano Expedition," NCpedia, 2006, https://www.ncpedia.org /verrazano-expedition; "South Street Seaport," Historic Districts Council, https:// hdc.org/borough/south-street-seaport/.

Chapter 13: Choices, Consequences, and an Island Lost

Goddard printing Declaration of Independence: *MJBA* at MSA, previously cited. Information regarding Nanye'hi/Nancy Ward sending warnings, Dragging Canoe party and injury, Lydia Bean encounter, the importance of mounds to Indigenous culture, from previously cited Nanye'hi/Nancy Ward sources, including James Mooney, *Cherokee History, Myths and Sacred Formulas* (Cherokee Publications, 2006); and King, *Memoirs . . . Timberlake*, previously cited. Also: Philip M. Hamer, "Watauga and the Cherokee Indians in 1776," reprinted from East Tennessee Historical Society, *Publications, Number Three*, 1931. Christopher B. Rodning, "Mounds, Myths, and Cherokee Townhouses in Southwestern North Carolina," *American Antiquity* 74, no. 4 (2009), https://www2.tulane.edu/~crodning/rodning2009A.pdf; Josie J. Tunnell, "Cherokee Architectural Traditions: A Southeastern Environmental Design Precedent," Chancellor' s Honors Program Projects, University of Tennessee, 2022, https://trace.tennessee.edu/utk_chanhonoproj/2470; Lydia Bean: John P. Brown, *Old Frontiers: The Story of the Cherokee Indians from Earliest Times to the Date of Their Removal to the West, 1838* (Southern Publishers, 1938). For Cherokee attacks and aftermath, see "Williamsburg, August 10," *Virginia Gazette*, August 10, 1776, https:// www.newspapers.com/image/40483522/?match=1; "Williamsburg, August 17," *Pennsylvania Evening Post*, August 27, 1776, https://www.newspapers.com/image /1033732372/?match=1&terms=watauga; "Cherokee War": Nadia Dean, "A Demand of Blood: The Cherokee War of 1776," *American Indian Magazine* 14, no. 4 (Winter 2013), https://www.americanindianmagazine.org/story/demand-blood-cherokee-war-1776; Buncome County Register of Deeds, "As Long as the Grass Shall Grow: A History of Cherokee Land Cessions and the Formation of Buncombe County," September 17, 2021, https://storymaps.arcgis.com/stories/e9913eb717dc4e68aebe7a7c7d3f42c3; Jordan Baker, "The Cherokee-American War from the Cherokee Perspective," *Journal of the American Revolution*, July 29, 2021, https://allthingsliberty.com/2021/07/the -cherokee-american-war-from-the-cherokee-perspective/. "New York City (NYC) The Great Fire of 1776," NYC Data: Disasters, Baruch College, https://baruch.cuny .edu/nycdata/disasters/fires-1776.html; Richard Howe, "Notes on the Great Fires of 1776 and 1778," The Gotham Center for New York City History, December 31, 2014, https://www.gothamcenter.org/blog/notes-on-the-great-fires-of-1776-and-1778. R. P. Stephen Davis Jr. and I. Randolph Daniel Jr., *The Projectile Point Classification Project: The Classification of Projectile Points in Existing Archaeological Collections from North Carolina*, Technical Report No. 19, UNC Research Laboratories of Archaeology, March 1990, https://archaeology.sites.unc.edu/wp-content/uploads/sites/187 /2015/03/RLA-Technical-Report-19-1990.pdf. Overhill Towns, Virginia militia, Chota spared, and myth of the burning belt: "The Legend of the Burning Belt," The Teaching and Sharing Center, https://wsharing.com/WSphotosCherokeeNCtxt-lbb.htm, as well as personal visits to the Museum of the Cherokee People, Cherokee, NC, where the legend is also presented. Lucy Knox, William Knox correspondence, deriding mercenaries, describing Hessians: *Letters*, previously cited. Battles in and around Manhattan: Henry P. Johnston, *The Campaign of 1776 Around New York and Brooklyn, Including a New and Circumstantial Account of the Battle of Long Island and the Loss of New York, with a Review of Events to the Close of the Year* (The Long Island Historical Society, 1878). Dunmore to Germain, Hamond, Snape: *Naval Documents of the American Revolution*, vol. 5, "American Theatre: May 9, 1776–July 31, 1776, part 7 of 8 (U.S. Government Printing Office, 1969), electronically published by the American

Naval Records Society, 2012, https://ibiblio.org/anrs/docs/E/E3/ndar_v05p07.pdf. Harry Washington, Black Pioneers: "Harry Washington: Loyalist," *The American Revolution Experience*, https://american-revolution-experience.battlefields.org/people/harry-washington#washington-charlestonl; Cassandra Pybus, "Washington's Revolution (Harry That Is, Not George)," *Atlantic Studies* 3, no. 2 (2006): 183–99, https://doi.org/10.1080/14788810600875414; Museum of the American Revolution, "Harry Washington Discovery Cart," Museum of the American Revolution, https://www.amrevmuseum.org/learn-and-explore/revolution-at-home/blog-posts-and-recent-content/harry-washington-discovery-cart; William J. Harris, "Harry Washington," Enslaved.org, https://projects.kora.matrix.msu.edu/files/16-23-126804/Harry_Washington_AANB.pdf; Francine Uenuma, "Enslaved by George Washington, This Man Escaped to Freedom—and Joined the British Army," *Smithsonian Magazine*, June 14, 2023, https://www.smithsonianmag.com/history/enslaved-by-george-washington-this-man-escaped-to-freedomand-joined-the-british-army-180982362/; Tabitha de Bruin, "Black Pioneers of the American Revolution," *The Canadian Encyclopedia*, March 25, 2024, https://www.thecanadianencyclopedia.ca/en/article/black-pioneers-of-the-american-revolution. Congress and the engrossed copy of the Declaration of Independence: Denise Kiernan and Joseph D'Agnese, *Signing Their Lives Away* (Quirk Books, 2009). Letter from Bartlett to Langdon regarding Dunmore: *JCC*, previously cited; Elizabeth Drinker diaries. Rutherford campaign: Jonathan Martin, "Rutherford's Campaign," NorthCarolinaHistory.org: An Online Encyclopedia, North Carolina History Project, https://northcarolinahistory.org/encyclopedia/rutherfords-campaign/; "Map of Rutherford's Expedition, 1776," https://www.ncpedia.org/media/map/map-section-rutherfords; Roy S. Dickens Jr., "The Route of Rutherford's Expedition Against the North Carolina Cherokees," *Southern Indian Studies* 19 (October 1967): 3–24.

Chapter 14: Three Women, One Friend, Shifting Tides

Cornell University Library is the home for the Jemima Wilkinson papers, 1772–1849, Collection Number 357, cited by Paul B. Moyer, *The Public Universal Friend: Jemima Wilkinson and Religious Enthusiasm in Revolutionary America* (Cornell University Press, 2015). Information regarding Margaret Corbin taken from Edward Hagaman Hall, *Margaret Corbin: Heroine of the Battle of Fort Washington* (The American Scenic and Historic Preservation Society, 1932); and William Henry Egle, *The Private Soldier of the Army of the Declaration: An Address Delivered at the Unveiling of the Monument Erected by the State of Pennsylvania to William Denning, the Soldier Blacksmith of the Revolution, at Newville, October 6, 1890* (Harrisburg Publishing Company, 1890). (Also mentions Mary Macauley.) Corbin as matross: Thomas Lynch Montgomery, ed., *Pennsylvania Archives, Fifth Series*, vol. 3, "Continental Line. Fifth Pennsylvania, Jan. 1, 1777–Jan. 1, 1783" (Harrisburg Publishing Company, State Printer, 1906). Froggs Neck/Throggs Neck/Pell's Point: Orientation from maps at Leventhal Map Collection, accessed via ARGO. Troop reports and movements: "Extract of a letter from a gentleman in the army . . . ," *Pennsylvania Evening Post*, November 14, 1776. All Lorenda Holmes information from Holmes, "North America," NAUK. Fort Washington information regarding battles from multiple sources, including https://www.battlefields.org/learn/revolutionary-war/battles/pells-point. About Philip Pell: "Philip Pell: Revolutionary War Leader, Last member of the Continental Congress," https://www.nps.gov/articles/000/philip-pell-revolutionary-war-leader-last-member-of-the-continental-congress.htm. Excellent map of the Fort Washington redoubts is available at ARGO (Leventhal Map Collection). Margaret Morris sources: "The Revolutionary Journal of Margaret Morris, of Burlington, NJ, December 6, 1776, to June 11, 1778," *Bulletin of Friends' Historical Society of Philadelphia* 9, no. 1 (1919): 2–14, http://www.jstor.org/stable/41945131; "Revolutionary Journal of Margaret Morris of Burlington, New Jersey, II," *Bulletin of Friends' Historical Society of Philadelphia* 9, no. 2 (1919): 65–75, http://www.jstor.org/stable/41945472; "The Revolutionary Journal of Margaret Morris, of Burlington, N.J., December 6, 1776, to June 11, 1778," *Bulletin of Friends' Historical Society of Philadelphia* 9, no. 1 (1919): 2–14, http://www.jstor.org/stable/41945131. Esther Reed: Ireland, *Sentiments*; Reed, *Correspondence*; Reed, *Life*. Information regarding crossing the Delaware (both times) widely available. Good, concise detail for reference: "Myths and Legends About the Crossing," Washington Crossing Historic Park, https://www.washingtoncrossingpark.org/cross-with-us/myths/; "How Did the Continental Army Get Artillery and Horses Across the Delaware?," Washington Crossing Historic Park, https://www.washingtoncrossingpark.org/artillery-horses-cross-delaware/; "The Durham Boat," Durham Historical Society, https://durhamhistoricalsociety.org/durham-history/the-durham-boat/; Treaty of Watertown, 1776, Historical Society of Watertown, MA, http://historicalsocietyofwatertownma.org/HSW/HSWdocs/treatyofwatertown.pdf. West Point and the formation of the Invalid Corps: *The Centennial of the United States Military Academy at West Point, New York, 1802–1902*, vol. 1 (U.S. Government Printing Office, 1904). Keith House: Private residence in Newtown, PA. Multiple references to "HQrs at Keiths" in GW papers at Founders Online; Benedict Arnold Photo Archive, https://benedictarnold.smugmug.com/Retreat-from-the-Champlain-Val/GW-HQ-1215-1224-Keith-House. Congress movements, including to Baltimore, from *JCC* and John Adams correspondence at Founders Online. Specifics on items Goddard sold through her newspaper: *MJBA* at the MSA; "George Washington to the Chiefs of the Passamaquoddy Indians, 24 December 1776," Founders Online, NA, https://founders.archives.gov/?q=passamaquoddy&s=1111311111&sa=&r=7&sr=.

About the Passamaquoddy: "Passamaquoddy: Culture and History," Passamaquoddy Tribe @ Indian Township, https://www.passamaquoddy.com/?page_id=24. GW details on the crossing of the Delaware: George Washington to John Hancock, December 27, 1776, Founders Online. Knox writes Lucy about crossing: "The Revolutionary War Letters of Henry and Lucy Knox" collection at GLI, previously cited. Goddard printing details regarding Delaware crossing: "This Morning Congress received the following Letter from General WASHINGTON," *MJBA*, December 31, 1776; Travels of Declaration: Kiernan and D'Agnese, *Signers*; "The Declaration of Independence: A History," NA, https://www.archives.gov/founding-docs/declaration-history.

Chapter 15: In Ink. In Stone. In Metal.

Congress's request to create an authenticated copy of the Declaration of Independence: *JCC*. "In Congress, July 4, 1776. The unanimous declaration of the thirteen United States of America" (Baltimore: printed by Mary Katharine Goddard, 1777), https://www.loc.gov/item/90898037/. Fite House details from diary of John Adams at Founders Online, https://founders.archives.gov/documents/Adams/01-02-02-0007-0002. "The Continental Congress in Baltimore, Dec. 20, 1776 to Feb. 27, 1777," *Maryland Historical Magazine* 42 (March 1947): 21–28, https://archive.org/stream/marylandhistoric42brow/marylandhistoric42brow_djvu.txt. A. P. Folie, cartographer, James Poupard, engraver, *Plan of the town of Baltimore and it's environs: dedicated to the citizens of Baltimore: taken upon the spot*, Philadelphia, 1792, LOC, https://www.loc.gov/resource/g3844b.ct000792/. General Baltimore history: The City of Baltimore Comprehensive Master Plan, https://planning.baltimorecity.gov/sites/default/files/History%20of%20Baltimore_1.pdf; Lee H. Burke and Richard Sharpe Patterson, *Homes of the Department of State, 1774–1976: The Buildings Occupied by the Department of State and Its Predecessors* (Historical Office, Bureau of Public Affairs,

Dept. of State, 1977). Paul H. Smith, *Letters of Delegates to Congress, 1774–1789* (Library of Congress, 1976). About Colonel Henry Ludington: "Brigadier General Alexander McDougall to George Washington, 29 March 1777," Founders Online, NA, https://founders.archives.gov/documents/Washington/03-09-02-0018; "Orders to Nathaniel Sackett, 4 February 1777," Founders Online, NA, https://founders.archives .gov/documents/Washington/03-08-02-0259 (mentions Ludington home). "George Washington to Brigadier General Samuel Holden Parsons, 10 July 1779," Founders Online, NA, https://founders.archives.gov/?q=ludington&s=1111311111&sa=&r=5& sr=. Ludington and conspiracies in New York: New-York Historical Society, *Collections of the New York Historical Society for the Year . . .* (New York: Printed for the Society, 1868). William S. Pelletreau (William Smith), *History of Putnam County, New York: With Biographical Sketches of Its Prominent Men* (Philadelphia: W. W. Preston, 1886). Regarding troops quartered at Drinker house, additional persecution of Quakers, mention of Quakers being asked to "take the test": Elizabeth Drinker diaries. Information regarding Tryon's invasion of Connecticut is widely available. Ed Hynes, "The 1777 Danbury Raid and the Battle of Ridgefield," Ridgefield Historical Society, May 4, 2021, https://ridgefieldhistoricalsociety.org/the-1777-danbury-raid -and-the-battle-of-ridgefield-ed-hynes/. "Oneidas Played Vital Role in the Battle of Oriskany," Oneida Indian Nation, https://www.oneidaindiannation.com/oneidas -played-vital-role-in-the-battle-of-oriskany/. Han Yerry Doxatader/Tweahangarahken, "He Who Takes Up the Snow Shoe," and Tyonajanegen, "Two Kettles Together": Visits to the Museum of the American Revolution and museum's "Official Guidebook," https://www.amrevmuseum.org/virtualexhibits/meet-the-figures-oneida -nation-theater/pages/han-yerry?queryID=847076671be51e4eee2f596a49da4ffb&index =global; "Hanyery: Beyond Oriskany," Oneida Indian Nation, https://www .oneidaindiannation.com/hanyery-beyond-oriskany/; William Sawyer, compiler, "The Oneida Nation in the American Revolution," NPS, https://www.nps.gov/arti cles/the-oneida-nation-in-the-american-revolution.htm. "Sir William Johnson," Fort Stanwix National Monument," NPS, October 15, 2024, https://www.nps.gov/people /sir-william-johnson.htm; James Taylor Carson, "Inventing a Past: Molly Brant's Life in Leadership," *History Now*, no. 59 (Winter 2021), GLI, https://www.gilderlehrman .org/history-resources/essays/inventing-past-molly-brant's-life-leadership; "Life Story: Molly Brant aka Konwatsi'tsiaienni (Mohawk) (1736–1796), Mohawk Loyalist: The Story of a Mohawk Leader During the American Revolution," Women & the American Story Project, The New York Historical, https://wams.nyhistory.org/colonies -and-revolution/the-american-revolution/life-story-molly-brant/. "Miss Molly Brant's influence" quote from "Molly Brant: An Exceptional Woman," April 13, 2022, *Kingston Museums Blog*, https://museumskingston.ca/molly-brant-an-exceptional -woman/, and originally from Alexander Fraser to Frederick Haldimand, 21 March 1780, Unpublished Papers, 58:21787, as cited in Carson, GLI article, above. Information about Laura Wolcott and the Wolcott family, including letters from Oliver Wolcott, from Miles, *Memorials*, and Wolcott, *Jottings*. Litchfield, Connecticut, and Revolutionary War, including Wolcott and bullets: *The History of the Town of Litchfield, Connecticut, 1720–1920*, compiled for the Litchfield Historical Society by Alain C. White (Enquirer Print, 1920). One-year anniversary of Declaration of Independence in Philadelphia: https://declaration.fas.harvard.edu/blog/july-1777. Drinker experiences, including windows broken and Henry being taken with other Quakers, Battle of Brandywine: Elizabeth Drinker diaries.

Of Those Both Missed and Mystical

Descriptions of Baltimore and Washington, D.C., based on personal visits to those cities; Dan Rodricks, "Looking to Mark History at the Local Rite Aid," *Baltimore Sun*,

January 15, 2015, https://www.baltimoresun.com/2015/01/15/looking-to-mark-history-at-the-local-rite-aid/; Smithsonian National Postal Museum: https://postalmuseum.si.edu; Alison M. Gavin, "In the King's Service: Hugh Finlay and the Postal System in Colonial America," *Prologue* 41, no. 2 (Summer 2009); National Archives and Records Administration, https://www.archives.gov/publications/prologue/2009/summer/finlay.html; "Buildings of the Department of State: Henry Fite's House, Baltimore, Dec. 20, 1776–Feb. 27, 1777," Office of the Historian, United States Department of State: https://history.state.gov/departmenthistory/buildings/section4. Sybil Ludington: In her lifetime and afterward, from her gravestone to her pension application to statues in her honor, a wide variety of first-name spellings have been used to identify the woman I call Sybil Ludington. If I am quoting a written source, I retain the spelling used in that source; otherwise, her name is "Sybil." Signage at the Old Baptist Burial Ground, 91 Gleneida Avenue, Carmel, New York, directed me to a route that approximates the one Ludington may have taken.

"Remarks of Hon. Robert R. Barry, of New York, at Garden Party, National Woman's Party Extension of Remarks in the House of Representatives, Monday, May 20, 1963," *Congressional Record*, p. A1368, United States Congress (U.S. Government Printing Office, 1963); George W. Hotchkiss, *Industrial Chicago: The Lumber Interest* (Chicago: Goodspeed Publishing Company, 1894), https://babel.hathitrust.org/cgi/pt?id=uiuo.ark:/13960/t5h99273r&seq=294&q1=sibyl&view=1up; Berton Braley, "Sybil Ludington's Ride," *This Week* magazine, Washington, D.C., April 4, 1940; Paula D. Hunt, "Sybil Ludington, the Female Paul Revere: The Making of a Revolutionary War Heroine," *New England Quarterly* 88, no. 2 (June 2015);

Willis Fletcher Johnson, *Col. Henry Ludington: A Memoir* (Lavinia Elizabeth Ludington and Charles Henry Ludington, 1907); Vincent T. Dacquino, *Sybil Ludington: The Call to Arms* (Purple Mountain Press, 2000); George S. Turner, "Putnam County's Feminine Paul Revere," *Putnam County Courier*, July 19, 1929; previously published in slightly different form by the author as "A Feminine Paul Revere," *Minute Man*, July 1929; R. F. O'Connor, *Map of Putnam County, New-York* (Philadelphia: M. H. Traubel & Co., 1854), LOC, https://www.loc.gov/item/2013593260/; James C. Sidney et al., *Map of Dutchess County, New-York: from actual surveys* (Philadelphia: John E. Gillet, 1850), LOC, https://www.loc.gov/item/2012593656/; The Workers of the Dutchess County Unit, Federal Writers' Project, of the Works Progress Administration in the State of New York, Dutchess County edition (William Penn Association, 1937), https://babel.hathitrust.org/cgi/pt?id=uc1.$b728017&seq=152&q1=ludington; Erick Berry, *Sybil Ludington's Ride* (Viking Press, 1952). Threat to burn Colonel Ludington's house: *Minutes of the Committee and of the First Commission for Detecting and Defeating Conspiracies in the State of New York, December 11, 1776–September 23, 1778*, vol. 1 (New-York Historical Society, 1924), 151, https://babel.hathitrust.org/cgi/pt?id=wu.89067950105&seq=175&q1=ludington. Sibyl Luddington–Joel Dawson marriage, 1787: Lucy Ann (Morris) Carhart, *Genealogy of the Morris Family, Descendants of Thomas Morris of Connecticut*, 107 (A. S. Barnes Company, 1911), https://babel.hathitrust.org/cgi/pt?id=wu.89069681062&seq=125&q1=%22sibyl+luddington%22; Sarah E. Hughes, *History of East Haven* (Tuttle, Morehouse & Taylor Press, 1908), 17, https://babel.hathitrust.org/cgi/pt?id=nyp.33433081884870&seq=407&q1=%22sibyl+Luddington%22.

"Saratoga, Freeman's Farm/Bemis Heights," American Battlefield Trust, https://www.battlefields.org/learn/revolutionary-war/battles/saratoga. Descriptions of Wolcott house, Reeve house, Union Savings Bank, Litchfield Historical Society, James Calvert Smith painting, from personal visit to Litchfield, CT. Tapping Reeve House & Litchfield Law School: "About the Museum," Litchfield Historical Society, https://www.litchfieldhistoricalsociety.org/museums/tapping-reeve-house-and-law-school/; Litchfield Historical Society, https://www.litchfieldhistoricalsociety.org; *Litchfield*

Patriots Revolutionary War Living History Day, September 7, 2019, Souvenir Booklet (The Greater Litchfield Preservation Trust, 2019). Margaret Corbin: description of Corbin sarcophagus at the Cloisters from personal visit and interview on site with artist Zaq Landsberg; Jennifer Minus, "Margaret Corbin's Legacy Lives On," Daughters of the American Revolution, December 5, 2017, https://blog.dar.org/2017/12/05/margaret-corbins-legacy-lives. Margaret Corbin at West Point and in Manhattan: "Still Revolutionary: The West Point Corbin Forum," Daughters of the American Revolution, https://www.dar.org/sites/default/files/MargaretCorbinForum.pdf; Kathy Eastwood, "West Point Hosts Monument Rededication and 92nd Anniversary Ceremony for Margaret Cochran Corbin," U.S. Army, May 2013, https://www.army.mil/article/204658/west_point_hosts_monument_rededication_and_92nd_anniversary_ceremony_for_margaret_cochran_corbin; Shane Cashman, "The Missing Grave of Margaret Corbin, Revolutionary War Veteran," Atlas Obscura, January 14, 2020; Ted Spiegel, *West Point Guide Book* (Involvement Media, 2017); Emma Auburn, "West Point," Mount Vernon, Digital Encyclopedia, https://www.mountvernon.org/library/digitalhistory/digital-encyclopedia/article/west-point.

Chapter 16: Melted Majesty

Marvin L. Brown Jr., *Baroness von Riedesel and the American Revolution: Journal and Correspondence of a Tour of Duty, 1776–1783* (University of North Carolina Press, 1965). "Revolutionary War Turning Point, 1776–1777," United States History Primary Source Timeline, LOC, https://www.loc.gov/classroom-materials/united-states-history-primary-source-timeline/american-revolution-1763–1783/revolutionary-war-turning-point-1776-1777/. Elizabeth Drinker diaries. Congress in Lancaster and York, Pennsylvania: "Meeting Places for the Continental Congresses and the Confederation Congress, 1774–1789," *History, Art & Archives of the U.S. House of Representatives,* United States House of Representatives, Office of the Historian, https://history.house.gov/People/Continental-Congress/Meeting-Places/; Robert Fortenbaugh, *The Nine Capitals of the United States* (The Maple Press Company, 1973). "Saratoga/Bemis Heights, Oct. 7, 1777, 3:30–4:00 p.m.," American Battlefield Trust, https://www.battlefields.org/learn/maps/saratoga-bemis-heights-oct-7-1777-330-400-pm; "Saratoga: Freeman's Farm, September 19, 1777, 1:00–1:30 PM," American Battlefield Trust, https://www.battlefields.org/learn/maps/saratoga-freemans-farm-sep-19-1777-100-130-pm; "Freeman's Farm - 6 - John Freeman Farm (Balcarres Redoubt) (Continued . . .)," Saratoga National Historical Park, NPS, https://www.nps.gov/places/freeman-s-farm-6-john-freeman-farm-balcarres-redoubt-continued.htm.

Chapter 17: Forged in the Valley

Information on the history, layout, historic structures, population, daily life, number of cabins to be built, and lack of supplies at Valley Forge are drawn from extensive visits to Valley Forge National Historical Park (VHNHP), Pennsylvania, National Park Service, Visitor Center and Museum, as well as its official map. Extensive information and collection of primary source documents available through the George Washington Presidential Library at Mount Vernon, https://www.mountvernon.org/library/digitalhistory/digital-encyclopedia/article/valley-forge. An excellent resource on the day-to-day activities, orders, and more of the Continental Army, not only at Valley Forge but on other campaigns in the years of 1777 and 1778: George Weedon and the American Philosophical Society, *Valley Forge Orderly Book of General George Weedon of the Continental Army Under Command of Genl. George Washington: In the Campaign of 1777–8, Describing the Events of the Battles of Brandywine, Warren Tavern, Germantown, and Whitemarsh, and of the Camps at Neshaminy,*

Wilmington, Pennypacker's Mills, Skippack, Whitemarsh, & Valley Forge (Dodd, Mead, 1902). Harry Clinton Green and Mary Wolcott Green, *The Pioneer Mothers of America: A Record of the More Notable Women of the Early Days of the Country, and Particularly of the Colonial and Revolutionary Periods* (G. P. Putnam's Sons, 1912). An excellent resource on life at Valley Forge in general, as well as the lives of women in particular: Nancy K. Loane, *Following the Drum: Women at the Valley Forge Encampment* (Potomac Books, University of Nebraska Press, 2009). GW quotes describing ordeal at Valley Forge, "unless some great and . . . Starve, dissolve, or disperse": "George Washington to Henry Laurens, 23 December 1777," Founders Online, NA, https://founders.archives.gov/documents/Washington/03-12-02-0628. GW quotes describing "see[ing] men without clothes to cover their nakedness": "George Washington to John Banister, 21 April 1778," Founders Online, NA, https://founders .archives.gov/documents/Washington/03-14-02-0525. Regarding the Stephens family quartering soldiers and General Varnum, Isaac Potts and the Potts house, and serving as Washington's headquarters: "Varnum's Quarters," Valley Forge National Historical Park, NPS, https://www.nps.gov/places/varnums-quarters.htm. Valley Forge life and day-to-day, including entertainments and games, shifting currencies, families hiding foods and more, "firecake," and rations ("24 oz protein . . . 1 lb. bread"): VFNHP; Weedon, *Valley Forge*; Loane, *Following the Drum*. About Friedrich von Steuben: "General von Steuben," VFNHP, https://www.nps.gov/vafo/learn/historyc ulture/vonsteuben.htm; Friedrich von Steuben, *Regulations for the Order and Discipline of the Troops of the United States, 1786*, facsimile edition (Applewood Books, 2019). Medical details, Camp Follower poem, etc., "boast of every fair shaped vice," Christmas Day tent/hut comment, powders and pills observations from Albigence Waldo, "Valley Forge, 1777–1778: Diary of Surgeon Albigence Waldo, of the Connecticut Line," *Pennsylvania Magazine of History and Biography* 21, no. 3 (1897): 299–323, http://www.jstor.org/stable/20085750. GW women are a "clog . . .": GW, "General Orders, 4 August 1777," Founders Online, NA, https://founders.archives.gov/docu ments/Washington/03-10-02-050. Quakers headed to Valley Forge: Elizabeth Drinker diaries; Norman E. Donoghue, *Prisoners of Congress: Philadelphia's Quakers in Exile, 1777–1778* (Penn State University Press, 2023), https://doi.org/10.5325 /jj.5736152. Onesimus and Cotton Mather: "Smallpox, Inoculation, and the Revolutionary War," Boston National Historic Park, NPS, https://www.nps.gov/articles/000 /smallpox-inoculation-revolutionary-war.htm#ftnref19; Kara Norton, "How African Indigenous Knowledge Helped Shape Modern Medicine," *Nova*, PBS Online, March 30, 2022, https://www.pbs.org/wgbh/nova/article/smallpox-epidemic-boston -onesimus-african-indigenous/.

GW re smallpox: "George Washington to William Shippen, Jr., 6 February 1777," Founders Online, NA, https://founders.archives.gov/documents/Washington/03 -08-02-0281; "History of the Smallpox Vaccine," World Health Organization, https:// www.who.int/news-room/spotlight/history-of-vaccination/history-of-smallpox -vaccination.

"William Shippen, Jr., 1736–1808," University Archives & Records Center, Penn Libraries, University of Pennsylvania, https://archives.upenn.edu/exhibits/penn -people/biography/william-shippen-jr/. Regarding nurses, "camp whores," the arrival of Catharine Greene, Martha Washington, Alice Lee Shippen, Lord and Lady Stirling, Rebecca Biddle: Loane, *Following the Drum*. Highest-ranking Native American in Continental Army: "Atayataghlonghta—Colonel Louis Joseph Cook," Fort Stanwix National Monument, Saratoga National Historical Park, Valley Forge National Historical Park, NPS, https://www.nps.gov/people/atayataghlonghta-lewis-cook.htm. Hannah Till: (Interview with) John F. Watson (John Fanning), *Annals of Philadelphia: Being a Collection of Memoirs, Anecdotes, & Incidents of the City and Its Inhabitants from the Days of the Pilgrim Founders. Intended to Preserve the Recollections of Olden Time, and to Exhibit Society in Its Changes of Manners and Customs, and the City in Its Local Changes and Improvements: To Which Is Added an Appendix, Containing Olden Time Researches and Reminiscences of New York City* [five lines of verse] (Philadelphia: E. L. Carey & A. Hart, 1830); "General Orders, 23 June 1780"; "Hannah Till," VFNHP, https://www.nps.gov/people/hannah-till.htm. Washington "loaning" Hannah Till to Marquis de Lafayette: Diane M. Spivey, "Sustenance for Sustaining American Liberty," in *At the Table of Power: Food and Cuisine in the African American Struggle for Freedom, Justice, and Equality* (University of Pittsburgh Press, 2022), 34–47, https://doi.org/10.2307/j.ctv2z862gr.6. Marquis de Lafayette at Valley Forge, general timeline, and recruitment of Indigenous allies: Mary Thompson (originally compiled by), "The 'Adopted Son' of George Washington: Marquis de Lafayette: A Timeline of the Life of the Marquis de Lafayette," George Washington Presidential Library, Mount Vernon, 2005–2006, https://catalog.mountvernon.org/digital/collection/p16829coll4/id/3484/. Oneida arrival at Valley Forge, Han Yerry (previously cited), Polly Cooper, shawl: William Sawyer, compiler, "The Oneida Nation in the American Revolution," NPS, https://www.nps.gov/articles/the-oneida-nation-in-the-american-revolution.htm; literature and displays of Smithsonian National Museum of the American Indian, Washington, D.C.; "The Polly Cooper Shawl: Testimony to a Pact of the Revolutionary War," Oneida Indian Nation, https://www.oneidaindiannation.com/the-polly-cooper-shawl-testimony-to-a-pact-of-the-revolutionary-war/; "Polly Cooper: From Humble Cook to Oneida Icon," Oneida Indian Nation, https://www.oneidaindiannation.com/polly-cooper-from-cook-to-oneida-icon/; "Oneida," Center for Digital History, The George Washington Presidential Library at Mount Vernon, https://www.mountvernon.org/library/digitalhistory/digital-encyclopedia/article/oneida; George Washington, *George Washington's Accounts of Expenses While Commander-in-chief of the Continental Army, 1775–1783* (Houghton Mifflin, 1917). Lucy Knox arrival: Henry writing Lucy, from "The Revolutionary War Letters of Henry and Lucy Knox" collection at GLI, previously cited, including: https://www.gilderlehrman.org/collection/glc0243700670. Chastellux regarding Lucy Knox and "scarves," "gauzes," "unable to describe" taken from Loane, *Following the Drum*. Information regarding Howe resigning is available widely, including "Richard and William Howe Collection, 1758–1812," CLE, https://findingaids.lib.umich.edu/catalog/umich-wcl-M-510how. The Mischianza (spelled as such based on John André's own writings): John André, "Particulars of the Mischianza." Information on John André in Philadelphia, Benedict Arnold taking over in Philadelphia after the British evacuation, etc., is widely documented, including details regarding Monmouth Courthouse from Henry Knox to Lucy, from sources previously cited.

Chapter 18: Colonial Dames

Letter of Arnold to Shippen, flirtations of John André: Rubin Stuart, *Defiant Brides*; Clements Library, Henry Clinton papers, previously cited; "Arnold and André" issue, *The Quarto* 43 (Spring–Summer 2023), https://clements.umich.edu/wp-content/uploads/2019/09/quarto43-arnold-andre.pdf. John André, "Particulars of the Mischianza Exhibited in America at the Departure of General Howe," May 23, 1778, The Clements Library, Clinton Papers, University of Michigan. Drinker on Reed: *Diaries*, previously cited; Molly Gutridge, *A new touch on the times: Well adapted to the distressing situation of every sea-port town, By a Daughter of Liberty living in Marblehead*, broadside (Ezekiel Russell, 1779), Patricia D. Klingenstein Library, New-York Historical Society. "Reflections on the Homefront," Women and the American Story (teaching resource), The New York Historical, https://wams.nyhistory.org/settler-colonialism-and-revolution/the-american-revolution/reflections-from-home

-front/; *Sarah Fayerweather Cookbook*, 1764, A/F283, Schlesinger Library, Radcliffe Institute, Harvard University, Cambridge, MA, https://fromthepage.com/harvardli brary/colonial-north-america-schlesinger-library/sarah-fayerweather-cookbook-1764 -a-f283-schlesinger-library-radcliffe-institute-harvard-university-cambridge-mass; [Hannah Glasse,] *The Art of Cookery, Made Plain and Easy: Which far exceeds anything of the Kind yet published* (Printed for W. Strahan, J. and F. Rivington, J. Hinton [et al.], 1774), https://archive.org/details/artcookerymadepo2glasgoog/page/n8/mode /2up. Elizabeth Graeme Fergusson: Simon Gratz, "Some Material for a Biography of Mrs. Elizabeth Fergusson, née Græme," *Pennsylvania Magazine of History and Biography* 39, no. 3 (1915): 257–321, http://www.jstor.org/stable/20086221; Anne Hollingsworth Wharton, *Salons Colonial and Republican, with numerous reproductions of portraits and miniatures of men and women prominent in colonial life and in the early days of the republic* (J. B. Lippincott, 1900); Anna Young Smith, "An Elegy to the Memory of the American Volunteers Who Fell in the Engagement Between the Massachusetts-Bay Militia, and the British Troops, April 19, 1775," *Schager Anthology of the American Revolution*, https://www.schlagergroup.com/document-spotlight -anna-young-smiths-an-elegy-to-the-memory-of-the-american-volunteers/. For the work of Milcah Martha Moore, Hannah Griffitts, Susanna Wright, and Elizabeth Graeme Fergusson, see Catherine La Courreye Blecki and Karin A. Wulf, eds., *Milcah Martha Moore's Book: A Commonplace Book from Revolutionary America* (The Pennsylvania State University Press, 1997); and also [Milcah Martha Moore,] *Miscellanies, Moral and Instructive, in Prose and Verse: Collected from Various Authors, for the Use of Schools, and Improvement of Young Persons of Both Sexes* (Philadelphia: J. Phillips, 1787), https://archive.org/details/miscellaniesmoroounkngoog/page/n25 /mode/2up. Goddard's almanac: "Inside the Vault: Mary Katherine Goddard: Woman Printer, Entrepreneur, and Postmaster in the Founding Era," March 3, 2022, notes of online talk, GLI, https://www.gilderlehrman.org/sites/default/files/2022-05/March %202022%20ITV.pdf; "Mary Katharine Goddard, 1738–1816, MSA SC 3520-2809," Archives of Maryland, https://msa.maryland.gov/megafile/msa/speccol/sc3500 /sc3520/002800/002809/html/2809bio.html. Black troops to fight in South Carolina and Georgia: Henry Laurens, "To George Washington," March 16, 1779, Founders Online, NA, https://founders.archives.gov/documents/Washington/03-19-02-0499; George Washington, "To Henry Laurens," March 20, 1779, Founders Online, NA, https://founders.archives.gov/documents/Washington/03-19-02-0533. Philipsburg Proclamation: Sir Henry Clinton, "By His Excellency Sir Henry Clinton, K. B. General and Commander in Chief of all this Majesty's Forces, within the Colonies laying on the Atlantic Ocean, from Nova Scotia to West-Florida, inclusive, &c., PROCLAMATION," Philipsburg Proclamation, *Royal Gazette*, July 4, 1779 (New York: James Rivington, 1779); PMH Staff, "The Phillipsburg Proclamation," Philipse Manor Hall State Historic Site, June 30, 2023, https://www.philipsemanorhall.com/blog/the -philipsburg-proclamation. Slave Enlistment Act, Rhode Island: "Act creating the 1st Rhode Island Regiment, also known as the 'Black Regiment,' 1778," transcript of original document, *Acts & Resolves of the General Assembly* 17, no. 14 (February 14, 1778), Rhode Island State Archives, C#0210, https://docs.sos.ri.gov/documents/civicsande ducation/teacherresources/BlackRegiment.pdf; scan of original document at https:// www.sos.ri.gov/divisions/civics-and-education/for-educators/themed-collections /american-revolution#:~:text=In%201778%2C%20the%20General%20Assembly,free% 20at%20the%20war's%20end.

Lenape treaty: "Treaty with the Delawares, 1778," *Indian-Affairs. Laws and Treaties. Vol. II. (Treaties.) Compiled and Edited by Charles J. Kappler, Clerk to The Senate Committee On Indian Affairs* (U.S. Government Office, 1904), https://americanin dian.si.edu/nationtonation/pdf/Treaty-with-the-Delawares-1778.pdf. Daniel Niham,

son Abraham, Stockbridge losses Battle of Kingsbridge, https://www.americanin
dianmagazine.org/story/road-kingsbridge-daniel-nimham-and-stockbridge-indian
-company-american-revolution. Losses, August 31, 1778: "The Stockbridge Indian
Company had taken heavy casualties. Its leaders, the sachem Daniel Nimham and
his son Abraham, were dead." Philis Wheatley Peters moves to Queens Street,
and after marriage: David Waldstreicher, *The Odyssey of Phillis Wheatley: A Poet's
Journey Through Slavery and Independence* (Farrar, Straus and Giroux, 2023); MHS;
Cornelia H. Dayton, "Lost Years Recovered: John Peters and Phillis Wheatley Peters
in Middleton," *New England Quarterly* 94, no. 3 (2021): 309–51, https://www.jstor.org
/stable/27066316; Jupiter Hammon, "An Address to Miss Phillis Wheatley," *Empire
State Historical Publications Series*, no. 82 (Kennikat Press, 1970). Information
regarding Judith Jackson: Adam McNeil, "Norfolk to Nova Scotia: Judith Jackson's
Crooked Road to Freedom," Colonial Williamsburg, September 23, 2024, https://
www.colonialwilliamsburg.org/discover/18th-century-people/stories-of-black-life
/judith-jacksons/. Tryon attacks New Haven and Norwalk: "Connecticut Raids," George
Washington Presidential Library at Mount Vernon, https://www.mountvernon.org
/library/digitalhistory/digital-encyclopedia/article/connecticut-raids. British
agents supplying Chickamauga, Shelby's warning, later mission: Zella Armstrong, "Chickamauga Fight of 1779; Isaac Shelby," *New York Times*, April 28, 1929,
https://www.nytimes.com/1929/04/28/archives/chickamauga-fight-of-1779-isaac-shelby
.html; George Washington, "Orders to Major General John Sullivan, May 31, 1779,"
Founders Online, NA, https://founders.archives.gov/documents/Washington/03
-20-02-0661. About Madam Sacho and Clinton–Sullivan campaign: "The Clinton–
Sullivan Campaign of 1779," The Military History of Fort Schuyler, NPS, https://www
.nps.gov/articles/000/the-clinton-sullivan-campaign-of-1779.htm; Sarah M. S. Pear-
sall, "Madam Sacho: How One Iroquois Woman Survived the American Revolution,"
Humanities 36, no. 3 (May/June 2015), https://www.neh.gov/humanities/2015
/mayjune/feature/madam-sacho-how-one-iroquois-woman-survived-the-american
-revolution; Brian Barrett, "Colonial Canandaigua in War and Peace," *New York Al-
manack*, January 14, 2021, https://www.newyorkalmanack.com/2021/01/colonial
-canandaigua-in-war-and-peace/. Shelby on the Great Warrior of Chota: Evan Shelby,
"Letter to Patrick Henry," June 4, 1779, Founders Online, NA, https://founders.ar
chives.gov/documents/Jefferson/01-02-02-0116; Evan Shelby, "Washington, June 4,
1779," *Poulson's American Daily Advertiser*, July 3, 1779, 2 (on same page: summary of
destruction achieved; letter of Thomas Jefferson), https://www.newspapers.com/im
age-view/1034016037/. Haudenosaunee during Revolutionary War: "The Six Nations
Confederacy During the American Revolution," Fort Stanwix National Monument,
NPS, https://www.nps.gov/articles/000/the-six-nations-confederacy-during-the
-american-revolution.htm; "Haudenosaunee (Iroquois) Lands and the American
Revolution," teacher resource, National Museum of the American Indian, https://
americanindian.si.edu/nk360/haudenosaunee-lands/the-american-revolution/pdf
/Haudenosaunee-Classroom-Connections.pdf.

Chasing Molly, Finding Betsy

Observations, historic sites, etc., from personal travel to Valley Forge National Historic Park, Valley Forge, PA; Philadelphia; and, yes, the Molly Pitcher Service Area,
New Jersey Turnpike; as well as "Waysides Honoring Patriots of African Descent
Unveiled at Valley Forge National Historical Park," news release, Valley Forge National Historical Park, June 19, 2022, https://www.nps.gov/vafo/learn/news/patriots
-of-african-descent-waysides-unveiled.htm; and *Museum of the American Revolution
Official Guide Book* (Beckon Books, 2019). The Museum of the American Revolution
offers an interactive site with multiple articles, videos, and scans of primary sources

detailing the history and provenance of Washington's War Tent: https://www.amrev museum.org/collection/washington-s-war-tent. See also Marla R. Miller, *Betsy Ross and the Making of America* (Henry Holt, 2010); Arnold Tubis and Crystal E. Mills, "Two Conundrums Concerning the Betsy Ross Five-Pointed Star: The Provenance of the Pattern-for-Stars Artifact and the Surprising Incompleteness of Fold and One-Cut Descriptions for Making the Star," *The Fold*, no. 4 (May–June 2011), available at https://origamiusa.org/thefold/article/betsy-ross-five-pointed-star (paywall), https://www.ushistory.org/betsy/more/two-conundrums.htm; Emily J. Teipe, "Will the Real Molly Pitcher Please Stand Up?," *Prologue* 31, no. 2 (Summer 1999); Ray Raphael, "Molly Pitcher and Captain Molly," *Journal of the American Revolution*, May 8, 2013, https://allthingsliberty.com/2013/05/molly-pitcher-and-captain-molly; Jennifer Eaton, "Two Faces of Molly Pitcher," *Pennsylvania Heritage Magazine* 48, no. 2 (Spring 2022); other Corbin sources previously cited; and Kathy Eastwood, "West Point Hosts Monument Rededication and 92nd Anniversary Ceremony for Margaret Cochran Corbin," U.S. Army, May 8, 2018, https://www.army.mil/article/204658/west_point _hosts_monument_rededication_and_92nd_anniversary_ceremony_for_margaret _cochran_corbin.

Chapter 19: Tides Turn South

Esther DeBerdt Reed sources previously cited. A scan of Esther DeBerdt Reed's original broadside and a transcript of it may be found at the website of the New-York Historical Society: https://wams.nyhistory.org/settler-colonialism-and-revolution/the -american-revolution/sentiments-of-an-american-woman. The correspondence of George Washington, Joseph Reed, Esther DeBerdt Reed, and Abigail Adams on the women's fundraising crusade may be found at Founders Online. Eliza Yonge Wilkinson and Caroline Howard Gilman, eds., *Letters of Eliza Wilkinson: During the Invasion and Possession of Charleston, S.C., by the British in the Revolutionary War* (New York: S. Colman, 1839). Information about the Siege of Charleston from Carl Borick, *A Gallant Defense: The Siege of Charleston, 1780* (University of South Carolina Press, 2003); Andrew Jackson O'Shaughnessy, *The Men Who Lost America: British Leadership, the American Revolution and the Fate of the Empire* (Yale University Press, 2013); and Bernhard A. Uhlendorf, *The Siege of Charleston: With an Account of the Province of South Carolina, Diaries and Letters of Hessian Officers* (University of Michigan Press, 1938). The account of Robert Sheffield, prison ship survivor, is from Henry Onderdonk, *Revolutionary Incidents of Suffolk and Kings Counties: With an Account of the Battle of Long Island and the British Prisons and Prison-Ships at New-York* (New York: Leavitt & Co., 1849). Eliza Pinckney sources previously cited. Boston King's experiences: Boston King, "Memoirs of the Life of Boston King, A Black Preacher," *Methodist Magazine* 21 (March and April 1798); Gary Sellick, "'Undistinguished Destruction': The Effects of Smallpox on British Emancipation Policy in the Revolutionary War," *Journal of American Studies* 51, no. 3 (2017): 865–85, https://www.jstor.org /stable/26803453. Arnold, André, and Shippen sources previously cited. Arnold's treason plot, Washington's creation of the Culper Ring, the elusive 355 code, and Anna Strong are discussed in Alexander Rose, *Washington's Spies: The Story of America's First Spy Ring* (Bantam Dell, 2006). Corbin sources previously cited. Additional details of the Invalid Corps at West Point from *The Centennial of the United States Military Academy at West Point, New York, 1802–1902*, vol. 1 (U.S. Government Printing Office, 1904); and Joan Brown Wettingfeld, "Our History: 'Invalid Corps' Created in Wake of the Battle of Long Island," QNS.com, August 25, 2010, https://qns.com/story /2010/08/25/our-history-invalid-corps-created-in-wake-of-the-battle-of-long-island/. Knox sources previously cited. Hamilton's perspective on the Washington–Shippen meeting summarized in a letter to his fiancée, Elizabeth Schuyler, Founders Online, https://founders.archives.gov/?q=%20Author%3A%22Hamilton%2C%20Alexander%22%20mrs.%20arnold&s=1111311111&r=1. Shippen's "confession" is detailed in several books, among them Carl Van Doren, *Secret History of the American Revolution* (Viking Press, 1941). Contemporary coverage of Arnold's treason and Philadelphia effigy parade, *MJBA* newspapers at MSA, previously cited. Nanye'hi/Nancy Ward's advance warnings of a Cherokee attack, subsequent discussion of her contributions and movements, correspondence of Thomas Jefferson with Arthur Campbell: Founders Online.

Chapter 20: Freedom's Wake

Elizabeth Freeman's walk to Sheffield: Sedgwick, "Mumbett," previously cited; papers of the Sheffield Historical Society, Sheffield, MA. Cornelia H. Dayton, "Lost Years Recovered: John Peters and Phillis Wheatley Peters in Middleton," *New England Quarterly* 94, no. 3 (2021): 309–51, https://www.jstor.org/stable/27066316. Nathanael Greene to Kitty regarding conditions of the southern campaign: NPS. "Distress and Misery Prevails: General Nathanael Greene About Civilians, 1781," American Battlefield Trust, https://www.battlefields.org/learn/primary-sources/distress-and-misery-prevails-general-nathanael-greene-about-civilians-1781; Margaret Catherine Moore, aka "Kate Barry," from the South Carolina Encyclopedia, https://www.scencyclopedia.org/sce/entries/barry-margaret-catherine-moore/. The story of the Martins: Gladys Buckner, "The Martintown Road," *Daughters of the American Revolution Magazine* 108, no. 1 (January 1974): 25, 56, https://services.dar.org/members/magazine_archive/download/?file=DARMAG_1974_01.pdf; "Daring Exploits of Elizabeth, Grace and Rachel Martin," American Battlefield Trust, January 18, 2022, https://www.battlefields.org/learn/articles/daring-exploits-elizabeth-grace-and-rachel-martin.

This map clarifies Cornwallis's movements May to July 1781: "MARCH of the ARMY under Lieut. General EARL CORNWALLIS in VIRGINIA, from the JUNCTION at Petersburg on the 20th of May, til their arrival at Portsmouth on the 12th of July 1781," hand-drawn map, Norman B. Leventhal Map & Education Center, https://collections.leventhalmap.org/search/commonwealth:hx11z253w. Lund Washington, "List of General Washington's negroes that went to the British," April 1781, primary source at the George Washington Presidential Library at Mount Vernon, https://catalog.mountvernon.org/digital/collection/p16829coll22/id/1015, and from the Mount Vernon Slavery Database, https://www.mountvernon.org/kiosk/slavery-database. George Washington's reaction to Lund's recovery attempts aboard the HMS *Savage* from Mount Vernon article, archived: https://www.mountvernon.org/library/digitalhistory/digital-encyclopedia/article/h-m-s-savage. Cornwallis's response to smallpox: Gary Sellick, "'Undistinguished Destruction': The Effects of Smallpox on British Emancipation Policy in the Revolutionary War," *Journal of American Studies* 51, no. 3 (2017): 865–85, https://www.jstor.org/stable/26803453. Contributions of American double agent James Armistead Lafayette (aka Fayette): "Good Intelligence Led to Victory at Yorktown," Defense Intelligence Agency, https://www.dia.mil/News-Features/Articles/Article-View/Article/566988/good-intelligence-led-to-victory-at-yorktown/; "James Armistead Lafayette," The National Museum of the United States Army, https://www.thenmusa.org/biographies/james-armistead-lafayette/; George Washington's Mount Vernon, "Lafayette," Mount Vernon—American Spies & Espionage, https://www.mountvernon.org/george-washington/revolutionary-war/spying-and-espionage/american-spies-revolution/lafayettes; "James Fayette: Revolutionary Spy," Virginia History, https://virginiahistory.org/learn/james-fayette-revolutionary-spy; Ruth Quinn, "James Armistead Lafayette (1760–1832)," U.S. Army, February 21, 2014, https://www.army.mil/article/119280/james_armistead_lafayette_1760_1832. Nancy Ward and Colonel William Christian's peace talk discussions are from Samuel

Cole Williams, *Tennessee During the Revolutionary War* (University of Tennessee Press, 1974); and Emmet Starr, *History of the Cherokee Indians and Their Legends and Folk Lore* (The Warden Company, 1921). The poems "Spoken Extempore, by a Young Lady, on hearing the Guns firing and Bells Chiming on account of . . . the Surrender of York-Town" and "His Lordship Humbled: Or, Cornwallis's Lamentation" are from a Philadelphia broadside, collection of the American Antiquarian Society, https://collections.americanantiquarian.org/earlyamericannewsmedia/exhibits/show /age-of-revolution/item/36. Contemporary coverage of Cornwallis's surrender, jubilation in various cities, and criticism of those events: *MJBA* newspapers at MSA; Drinker diary, previously cited. Twenty percent fatalities occurring in the South, Pinckney family circumstances, response: Glover, previously cited. Sampson's exploits in the Continental Army and subsequent national tour: Alfred F. Young, *Masquerade: The Life and Times of Deborah Sampson, Continental Soldier* (Vintage Books, 2004). Public Universal Friend's travels, talks, and reactions to them in Pennsylvania: Moyer and Elizabeth Drinker diaries, previously cited. Disposition of Elizabeth Freeman and Brom court case: *Brom & Bett v. J. Ashley Esq.*, Inferior Court of Common Pleas, Berkshire County Courthouse (Great Barrington, MA), vol. 4A, no. 1 (May 28, 1781): 55, https://elizabethfreeman.mumbet.com; additional scans of the *Brom & Bett* case available via Massachusetts Constitution and the Abolition of Slavery, https://www.mass.gov/guides/massachusetts-constitution-and-the -abolition-of-slavery. The resolution of petitions on behalf of Tony and Cuba, formerly enslaved to the Vassall and Royall families, and the modern-day Harvard University response, are in "The Early History of 105 Brattle Street" and "Though Dwelling in a Land of Freedom," Longfellow House Washington's Headquarters National Historic Site, Boston, via https://www.nps.gov/long/index.htm; Caitlin DeAngelis et al., "Black History at the Vassall Estate," NPS, September 15, 2025; and Michela Moscufo, "Harvard Hired a Researcher to Uncover Its Ties to Slavery. He Says the Results Cost Him His Job: 'We Found Too Many Slaves,'" *Guardian* (London), June 21, 2025, https://www.theguardian.com/news/2025/jun/21/harvard-slavery decendants-of-the-enslaved. Further details on the postwar life of Harry Washington via Francine Uenuma, "Enslaved by George Washington, This Man Escaped to Freedom—and Joined the British Army," *Smithsonian Magazine*, June 14, 2023, https://www.smithsonianmag.com/history/enslaved-by-george-washington-this -man-escaped-to-freedomand-joined-the-british-army-180982362/. Reaction of loyalist John Hamilton and others: Catherine S. Crary, ed., *The Price of Loyalty: Tory Writings from the Revolutionary Era* (McGraw-Hill, 1973). Street scenes from Charleston and New York City around the time of the British evacuation: Joseph W. Barnwell, "The Evacuation of Charleston by the British in 1782," *South Carolina Historical and Genealogical Magazine* 11, no. 1 (1910): 1–26, http://www.jstor.org/stable/27575255; "British Evacuation of Charleston," NPS, https://www.nps.gov/articles/000/british -evacuation-of-charleston.htm. "A New York Loyalist to Lord Hardwicke," 1783, from John Rhodehamel, ed., *The American Revolution: Writings from the War of Independence, 1775–1783* (Library of America, 2001). Governor Benjamin Harrison's letter to Virginia delegates re: Willoughby: Founders Online. Sir Guy Carleton's role in the evacuation of New York and demands for the return of enslaved persons: "Account of a Conference Between Washington and Sir Guy Carleton," May 6, 1783, Founders Online, NA, https://founders.archives.gov/documents/Washington/99-01-02-11217; *JCC*, previously cited; James Madison's notes on congressional debates on the evacuation (1782–1783; 1787), https://founders.archives.gov/documents/Madison/01-05-02-0102; December 11, 1782, https://founders.archives.gov/documents/Madison/01-05-02-0167; April 16, 1783, https://founders.archives.gov/documents/Madison/01-06-02-0168; Thomas Walke to Virginia Delegates, May 3, 1783, https://founders.archives.gov

/documents/Madison/01-07-02-0003; *Fourth Report on the Royal Commission on Historical Manuscripts* (London: George Edward Eyre and William Spottiswoode, 1874), https://www.google.com/books/edition/Fourth_Report_of_the_Royal_Commission_on/MFg-AAAAYAAJ?hl=en&gbpv=1.

Deborah Squash information: Lund Washington's list, previously cited; and "Book of Negroes," Nova Scotia Archives, https://archives.novascotia.ca/africanns/book-of-negroes/ and https://archives.novascotia.ca/africanns/book-of-negroes/page/?ID=20&Name=Harry%20Squash. Further information on the "Book of Negroes": Lawrence Hill, "Behind the Book of Negroes," *Canada's History*, February 10, 2015, https://www.canadashistory.ca/explore/books/behind-the-book-of-negroes. Judith Jackson's fate: Adam McNeil, "Norfolk to Nova Scotia: Judith Jackson's Crooked Road to Freedom," Stories of Black Life, Colonial Williamsburg, September 23, 2024, https://www.colonialwilliamsburg.org/discover/18th-century-people/stories-of-black-life/judith-jacksons. Mary Perth's fate: "Book of Negroes," https://archives.novascotia.ca/africanns/book-of-negroes/page/?ID=45&Name=Mary%20Perth. Harry Washington's involvement in Black Pioneers: *Fourth Report on the Royal Commission on Historical Manuscripts*, previously cited; American Revolution Experience, "Harry Washington," Battlefield Trust, NPS, https://american-revolution-experience.battlefields.org/people/harry-washington#washington-journey. Proclamation of King George III, New York City evacuation procession: *MJBA* newspapers at MSA, previously cited. Petition of Belinda Sutton, previously cited.

Legacy of Obstinancy

Descriptions of Cherokee, North Carolina, and its attractions; Philadelphia; and Sheffield and Stockbridge, Massachusetts, are from personal visits to these cities and their regions. Museum of the Cherokee People official website, https://motcp.org; *Unto These Hills* outdoor drama official website, Cherokee Historical, https://cherokeehistorical.org/attractions/unto-these-hills/; Qualla Arts and Crafts Mutual Co-Op official website, https://quallaartsandcrafts.org; Oconaluftee Village official website, Cherokee Historical, https://cherokeehistorical.org/attractions/oconaluftee-indian-village/. Carl Standingdeer (1881–1954) and the history of "chiefing" are from visits to the Museum of the Cherokee People and sources such as North Carolina Digital Collections (historic images), https://digital.ncdcr.gov; Museum of the Cherokee People Online Catalog (and Digital Libraries), https://cherokeemuseum.pastperfectonline.com; Family Search, https://ancestors.familysearch.org/en/MY5H-Z9K/gar-lie-ka-is-kie-ar-wee-gar-da-ya-%22carl-wesley-standingdeer%22-1881-1954; and "Culgaluski Standingdeer Student File," Carlisle Indian School Digital Resource Center, National Archives and Records Administration, RG 75, series 1327, box 6, folder 278, https://carlisleindian.dickinson.edu/student_files/culgaluski-standingdeer-student-file and https://carlisleindian.dickinson.edu/sites/default/files/docs-ephemera/NARA_1327_b006_f0278.pdf. Nancy Ward sources, previously cited. D. Ray Smith, "Nancy Ward Statue: Update on Recent Events and Status of Historic Art Sculpture," *Oak Ridger*, December 22, 2008, https://www.oakridger.com/story/news/local/2008/12/23/nancy-ward-statue-update-on/63342616007/. "Nancy Ward Gravesite," National Register of Historic Places, Digital Archive on National Register of Historic Places (gallery), https://npgallery.nps.gov/NRHP/AssetDetail/89701d71-0c73-4328-b994-35b9a70dc636. The 1817 Council meetings attended by Nancy Ward and other Cherokee women: Theda Perdue, "Cherokee Women and the Trail of Tears," in *Native Women's History in Eastern North America Before 1900: A Guide to Research and Writing*, ed. Rebecca Kugel and Lucy Eldersveld Murphy (University of Nebraska Press, 2007), 277–302, http://www.jstor.org/stable/jj.32942797.21; Carolyn Thomas Foreman, *Indian Women Chiefs* (The Star Printery Press, 1954), pp.

79–80. "Allies in War, Partners in Peace," George Washington, Polly Cooper, Shenendoah, 20-foot bronze sculpture at Smithsonian Museum of the American Indian, Oneida Indian Nation, https://www.oneidaindiannation.com/allies-in-war-partners-in-peace-smithsonian-museum-of-the-american-indian/. Mercy Otis Warren, *History*, previously cited. Sybil Ludington materials: Dacquino, previously cited. Prudence Wright Memorial Marker, Pepperell, Massachusetts, https://monuments.freedomsway.org/monuments/prudence-wright-memorial-stone/. Deborah Sampson: Young, previously cited. Public Universal Friend: Moyer, previously cited. Margaret Corbin sources, previously cited. Eliza Pinckney sources, previously cited. Modern indigo growers: Repeated travels to Low Country, South Carolina, and International Center for Indigo Culture, https://www.internationalcenterforindigoculture.org. Belinda Sutton sources, previously cited, including Sutton's petition, Massachusetts Anti-Slavery and Anti-Segregation Petitions; Passed Resolves; Resolves 1787, c.142, SC1/series 228, Massachusetts Archives, Boston, MA, Collection Development Department, Widener Library, HCL, Harvard University, https://iiif.lib.harvard.edu/manifests/view/drs:48612852$2i. Moscufo, previously cited, https://www.theguardian.com/news/2025/jun/21/harvard-slavery-decendants-of-the-enslaved. Armistead sources, previously cited. Harry Washington sources, previously cited. Mary Perth sources, previously cited. "Mary Perth, 1740–after 1813," Slavery and Remembrance: A Guide to Sites, Museums, and Memory, The Colonial Williamsburg Foundation, 2025, https://slaveryandremembrance.org/people/person/?id=PP042. Great Dismal Swamp National Wildlife Refuge, Virginia Department of Wildlife Resources, https://dwr.virginia.gov/vbwt/sites/great-dismal-swamp-national-wildlife-refuge/. Esther DeBerdt Reed sources, previously cited. Knox sources, previously cited. Arnold sources, previously cited. Goddard sources, previously cited. Mary Katharine Goddard, "Letter to George Washington, December 23, 1789," Founders Online, NA, https://founders.archives.gov/documents/Washington/05-04-02-0302. Goddard freed Belinda Starling in her will: Mary Katharine Goddard, MSA SC 3520 -2809, Archives of Maryland, https://msa.maryland.gov/megafile/msa/speccol/sc3500/sc3520/002800/002809/html/2809bio.html. The Smithsonian National Museum of African American History and Culture (NMAAHC) holds two statues of Phillis Wheatley in its collection, along with a selection of her works in manuscript and published form. Interactive online exhibit: https://www.searchablemuseum.com/ocean-by-phillis-wheatley-peters/. Phillis Wheatley Peters's last years, poems: David Waldstreicher, *The Odyssey of Phillis Wheatley: A Poet's Journey Through Slavery and Independence* (Farrar, Straus and Giroux, 2023); Dayton, previously cited. NMAAHC holds a statue of Elizabeth Freeman, along with her beaded bracelet: https://www.searchablemuseum.com/black-voices-of-freedom/#elizabeth-freeman-demanding-justice. Associated Press, "A Statue Honors a Once-Enslaved Woman Who Won Her Freedom in Court," National Public Radio, August 22, 2022, https://www.npr.org/2022/08/22/1118733517/a-statue-honors-a-once-enslaved-woman-who-won-her-freedom-in-court. The annual Elizabeth Freeman walk and the recent statue creation and unveiling are the work of the Sheffield Historical Society, https://sheffieldhistory.weebly.com. Elizabeth Freeman's last years, estate, and will accessed from collections at Sheffield Historical Society. Elizabeth Drinker diaries, previously cited.

Epilogue: July 4 . . . REDUX

Descriptions of Charleston and environs; Colonial Williamsburg, Virginia; and Cherokee, North Carolina, from personal visits. Robin Jarvis, "The Historic Embassy Suites in South Carolina Is Notoriously Haunted and We Dare You to Spend the Night," Only in South Carolina, September 1, 2022, https://www.onlyinyourstate.com/stays/south-carolina/haunted-hotel-charleston-sc; "Haunted Charleston,"

Charleston Magazine, October 2013, https://charlestonmag.com/features/haunted _charleston. Old Exchange and Provost Dungeon official website, https://www.old exchange.org. Nic Butler, "The Story of Gadsden's Wharf," Charleston County Public Library, February 2, 2018, https://www.ccpl.org/charleston-time-machine/story -gadsdens-wharf; Adam Parker, "What Really Happened at Gadsden's Wharf, Importation Site of Enslaved Africans?," *Charleston Post and Courier*, June 27, 2023, https://www.postandcourier.com/news/what-really-happened-at-gadsdens -wharf-importation-site-of-enslaved-africans/article_a9ef24ae-11e7-11ee-800e-ab772 ee218e3.html (paywall). International African American Museum, Charleston, official website: https://iaamuseum.org. Elisabeth Bumiller and Thom Shanker, "Pentagon Is Set to Lift Combat Ban for Women," *New York Times*, January 23, 2013, https://www .nytimes.com/2013/01/24/us/pentagon-says-it-is-lifting-ban-on-women-in-combat .html. Executive Order 9981: Desegregation of the Armed Forces (1948), Truman's Executive Order with Transcript, NA, https://www.archives.gov/milestone -documents/executive-order-9981. "The Edenton Teapot, Commemorative Sculpture, 1905," Museum Trail, Edenton Historical Commission, https://ehcnc.org/historic -places/museum-trail/museum-trail-1905-edenton-teapot/. Fourth of July Cherokee Powwow, https://visitcherokeenc.com/culture/cherokee-annual-powwow/; Jim Beviglia, "The Story and Meaning Behind 'Come and Get Your Love': Redbone's Trailblazing Smash," American Songwriter, February 16, 2025, https://american songwriter.com/the-story-and-meaning-behind-come-and-get-your-love-redbones -trailblazing-smash/; Don C. Marler, "The Louisiana Redbones," The Multiracial Activist, Multiracial.com, June 1, 2001, https://multiracial.com/index.php/2001/06/01 /the-louisiana-redbones; Cary Darling, "Beyond 'Come and Get Your Love': Why Redbone Matters," *Houston Chronicle*, October 24, 2020, https://www.houstonchronicle .com/entertainment/music/article/Beyond-Come-and-Get-Your-Love-Why-Redbone -15672998.php; Robert Jumper, "Fair Food Vendors Selected, Menus Approved," The Cherokee One Feather, June 23, 2017, https://theonefeather.com/2017/06/23/fair-food -vendors-selected-menus-approved/; Kate Nelson, "For Many Native Americans, Fry Bread Is Complicated," *Condé Nast Traveler*, August 23, 2023, https://www.cntraveler .com/story/for-many-native-americans-fry-bread-is-complicated; Kinfolk Farms, "Fry Bread: History, Controversy, and Cultural Significance," Visit Four Corners, https://visitfourcorners.com/the-controversial-tradition-of-frybread/; Kevin Noble Maillard, "Fry Bread Is Beloved, but Also Divisive," *New York Times*, November 1, 2021, https://www.nytimes.com/2021/11/01/dining/indigenous-people-fry-bread .html; Twyla Baker et al., "How to Talk About Native Nations: A Guide," Native Governance Center, NativeGov.org, May 27, 2021, https://nativegov.org/news/how-to -talk-about-native-nations-a-guide/; Jakeli Swimmer official website, Around the Boundary Ink, https://www.aroundthebound828.com; National Eagle Repository, U.S. Fish & Wildlife Service, https://www.fws.gov/program/national-eagle -repository; Steve Youngdeer American Legion Post No. 143, https://cherokeeameri canlegion.com; James M. Deitch, "The 27th Grievance of the Declaration of Independence," *Journal of the American Revolution*, April 26, 2022, https://allthingsliberty .com/2022/04/the-27th-grievance-of-the-declaration-of-independence/; Steven Paul Judd, The NTVS, "Merciless Indian Savages Tee," circa 2020, accession number EL2024.039, Spencer Museum of Art, University of Kansas, Lawrence, https://spen cerart.ku.edu/art/collections-online/object/104559.

ABOUT THE AUTHOR

Denise Kiernan is an award-winning author and journalist with three decades of storytelling experience whose books have been translated into numerous languages. Her previous titles—*The Last Castle* and *The Girls of Atomic City*—were instant *New York Times* bestsellers in both hardcover and paperback. She is also the author of a family read on the true story behind American Thanksgiving, whose titles include *We Gather Together*, *We Gather Together* (Young Readers Edition), and the children's picture book *Giving Thanks*. Kiernan has also coauthored several popular history titles, including *Signing Their Lives Away, Signing Their Rights Away*, and *Stuff Every American Should Know*. She has been published in *The Washington Post*, *The New York Times*, *The Wall Street Journal*, *The Village Voice*, *Rolling Stone*, *Time*, *Ms.* magazine, and many more publications. Throughout her career, Kiernan's engaging personality and expertise has made her a featured guest on many radio and television shows, including NPR's *Weekend Edition*, PBS *NewsHour*, MSNBC's *Morning Joe*, and *The Daily Show with Jon Stewart*.